ISBN 978-1-331-58782-8
PIBN 10209487

This book is a reproduction of an important historical work. Forgotten Books uses state-of-the-art technology to digitally reconstruct the work, preserving the original format whilst repairing imperfections present in the aged copy. In rare cases, an imperfection in the original, such as a blemish or missing page, may be replicated in our edition. We do, however, repair the vast majority of imperfections successfully; any imperfections that remain are intentionally left to preserve the state of such historical works.

English
Français
Deutsche
Italiano
Español
Português

www.forgottenbooks.com

Mythology Photography **Fiction**
Fishing Christianity **Art** Cooking
Essays Buddhism Freemasonry
Medicine **Biology** Music **Ancient**
Egypt Evolution Carpentry Physics
Dance Geology **Mathematics** Fitness
Shakespeare **Folklore** Yoga Marketing
Confidence Immortality Biographies
Poetry **Psychology** Witchcraft
Electronics Chemistry History **Law**
Accounting **Philosophy** Anthropology
Alchemy Drama Quantum Mechanics
Atheism Sexual Health **Ancient History**
Entrepreneurship Languages Sport
Paleontology Needlework Islam
Metaphysics Investment Archaeology
Parenting Statistics Criminology
Motivational

OFFICERS 1912

NEW YORK STATE HISTORICAL ASSOCIATION

President

HON. JAMES A. ROBERTS, New York.

First Vice President

HON. GRENVILLE M. INGALSBE, Hudson Falls.

Second Vice President

SHERMAN WILLIAMS, Pd. D., Glens Falls.

Third Vice-President

DR. WILLIAM O. STILLMAN, Albany.

Treasurer

HON. JAMES A. HOLDEN, Glens Falls.

Secretary

FREDERICK B. RICHARDS, Glens Falls.

Assistant Secretary

DR. W. A. E. CUMMINGS, Ticonderoga.

TABLE OF CONTENTS

LIST OF ILLUSTRATIONS

NOTE.—The views of old Saratoga Springs are reproductions of a few of the most interesting pictures shown by Mr. Frank J. Wilder in connection with his informal talk on "A Century and a Half of Saratoga History," and they are distributed through the book without regard to the adjacent subject matter.

TRUSTEES
1913

STANDING COMMITTEES

Program

Sherman Williams   George K. Hawkins   James G. Riggs

The President ex-officio.

LEGISLATION.

James A. Roberts   James A. Holden   William O. Stillman

Thomas E. Finegan   William T. Bennet

MARKING HISTORIC SPOTS.

Sherman Williams Frederick B. Richards Gilbert D. B. Hasbrouck James A. Holden Charles L. Davis

ESTABLISHMENT OF CLOSER RELATIONS BETWEEN HISTORICAL SOCIETIES OF THE STATE.

Frank H. Severance   William Wait   Henry M. MacCracken

NECROLOGY.

Frederick B. Richards   John H. Brandow   Walter C. Anthony

LAKE GEORGE BATTLEGROUND PARK.

James A. Holden   Elwyn Seelye   Everett R. Sawyer

The President, ex-officio.

CROWN POINT RESERVATION.

Ex-Officio President of Association, State Architect of New York, State Historian of New York.

Berne A. Pyrke   Frank H. Severance   Richard L. Hand

Howland Pell   W. A. E. Cummings

PUBLICATION.

The Secretary, with power to add to the committee

SPECIAL COMMITTEES.

Isle du St. Sacrement.

Mrs. Harry W. Watrous David Williams Rev. Thomas J. Campbell George O. Knapp John D. Crimmins

On High Schools and Libraries of State, and Prizes for Historical Essays.

Thomas E. Finegan   George K. Hawkins   Sherman Williams

HON. JAMES A. ROBERTS, A. M., LL. D.
President of the Association from 1899 to 1912.

HON. JAMES A. ROBERTS, A. M., L. L. D.

AN APPRECIATION

By James A. Holden, Treasurer, New York State Historical Association.

It has been deemed just and fitting at this time that some word of appreciation of our retiring President, Hon. James A. Roberts, shall be placed upon the records of this Association. For years interested in historical matters, a member of various patriotic societies and historical organizations, it was not surprising that, at the time of the formation of the New York State Historical Association in 1899, Colonel Roberts was the unanimous choice of his associates for its presidency. In this connection, a brief résumé of his career may be not without interest.

He was born at Waterboro, York county, Maine, March 8, 1847. At the age of seventeen he enlisted in the 7th Maine Battery as a private, being present at the closing scenes of the War of the Rebellion at Petersburg and Appomattox. Returning to Maine, he entered Bowdoin College, graduating there with the degree of A. B. in 1870. The degree of A. M. was conferred upon him in 1873, and that of LL. D. in 1897. Removing to Buffalo, he studied law and was admitted to the bar; his firm eventually becoming one of the leading law establishments in that city. He served as one of the Republican Assemblymen from Erie county in 1878-79. He practised law in Buffalo from 1875 to 1893. He was one of the founders of the Depew Improvement company. He was Park Commissioner of the city of Buffalo from 1891 to 1893. In the fall of 1893, Colonel Roberts was nominated as Comptroller on the Republican State ticket and elected by a satisfactory plurality over the nominees of other parties. He served most acceptably in charge of this important fiscal and financial department of the State, being renominated at the next State convention, and re-elected to serve until 1898.

During his term of service, Comptroller Roberts discovered and brought to light records in his office showing the services of New York men in the Revolution. Up to that time it had generally been supposed that New York had been lax and derelict in furnishing men and money for the support of the cause of liberty. Colonel Roberts discovered, on the contrary, that by the records of his office, New York took second place only to Massachusetts "in number of troops furnished, and under the circumstances surrounding her," was "second to none in lofty patriotism." These records, under the title of "New York in the Revolution as Colony and State," were published by the State in 1897. Owing to the great demand for this valuable and monumental work, a second edition was arranged for and published with additions in 1898. The work begun by Colonel Roberts was continued by Comptroller Erastus C. Knight, who in 1901 brought out a supplement to "New York in the Revolution." Had he done nothing else for the cause of New York's history than to publish this wonderful series of records, Colonel Roberts would have won and deserved the eternal thanks of every patriotic and faithful citizen of New York State.

But he has done even more during the thirteen years he has served us so faithfully and well as President of our Association. Probably no one, aside from the writer and a few of those intimately connected with the Association's history, will ever know the many timely donations made by Colonel Roberts, at times when the Association was financially embarrassed, or will ever realize the tower of strength he has been to us during the formative years of this Association in the way of able counsel, sagacious advice and quiet but effective work at Albany, where his worth as a financial expert was fully realized by those in authority, when it came to the securing of necessary funds for the matters in which this Association has been interested. One of the last evidences of President Roberts' generosity and beneficence was his supplying a great part of the funds for the work done upon the Kingston Records, this work having been undertaken by his suggestion and paid for mostly by his personal contributions.

The time having come when Colonel Roberts feels it necessary to lay down the gavel and to retire from the position which he has held so ably, efficiently and satisfactorily since the beginning of the organization, we, who have been his co-workers, feel it only proper that this permanent record of our appreciation and thankfulness to him shall be placed in our proceedings.

We trust that, in President Roberts' retirement, we shall not lose his able counsel and great interest in our undertaking, and that his scholarly ability, his cultured pen and studious mind may, as time goes on, still be employed on **our** programs in promoting our historical work. That all success, prosperity and good fortune may be his from now on, and that he will accept this appreciation as the earnest and heartfelt expression of everyone of us who have known and regarded him so highly, is the hope and wish of each member of this Association.

PROCEEDINGS

OF THE

Fourteenth Annual Meeting of the New York State Historical Association, held at Saratoga Springs, Bennington and Schuylerville, September 17, 18, 19, 20, 1912.

The Fourteenth Annual Meeting was planned to embrace every feature of Burgoyne's Saratoga Campaign, and while the headquarters were at Saratoga Springs, side trips were taken and meetings were held at Bennington and Schuylerville.

The meeting place at Saratoga was the Casino which proved the most magnificent place of entertainment which the Association has yet enjoyed. The public receptions were held in the large drawing room once the most famous gambling place in America, and the literary exercises were held in the well known dining room built by Canfield at such great expense. The surroundings therefore were luxurious and the welcome from the good people of Saratoga most cordial.

The first session of the meeting was held in the Casino, Tuesday evening at eight o'clock, at which the Hon. Edgar Truman Brackett of Saratoga Springs gave the address of welcome, and the Hon. James A. Roberts, LL. D., New York City, delivered the annual President's address. The exercises were followed by a reception to the members of the Association and their friends given by the Saratoga Chapter of the Daughters of the American Revolution.

Wednesday morning a special train was taken for Bennington. The Saratoga meeting was rather unfortunate in regard to weather and as the indications were that it would be a rainy day, this undoubtedly discouraged many who would otherwise have gone, but those who did go were well rewarded as aside from a mist which obscured a good view from the monument, the weather was fairly good and the trip was most enjoyable.

The party was met at Hoosick Junction by E. T. Griswold, an antiquarian and dealer in souvenirs of Bennington, Vt., and James A. Beckett, superintendent of the Walter A. Wood Co., of Hoosick Falls. The train moved along slowly after leaving Walloomsac and Mr. Beckett gave a talk on the Bennington battlefield and the historical points of interest along the route. The visitors were met at the local station by a number of automobiles and carriages and were conveyed directly to the battle monument at Old Bennington, where they also visited other places of historical interest including the Old First church and the site of the first house built in the village. They also made a brief visit to the Walloomsac Inn.

Main street put on a gala appearance in honor of the occasion, many of the stores along the street displaying the national colors and being draped in bunting.

Following the trip to the historical points of interest, the visitors were taken to the parlors of the Second Congregational church, where they were received by a committee, of which Mrs. Henry S. Bingham was chairman and which was composed of Mrs. Henry G. Root, Mrs. Arthur J. Holden, Mrs. William A. Root, and Mrs. Charles A. Tibbals, all of whom are members of the National Society Colonial Dames of America and of the D. A. R.

The decorations in the parlors were the colors and pennants from the gunboat Bennington, which are in the possession of the local chapter of the D. A. R. There was an artistic arrangement of flags and the floral decorations were carried out to harmonize with the national colors, large vases of salvia, white asters and Queen Anne's lace being used.

At one o'clock, luncheon was served in the chapel by the members of the Ladies' Aid Society of the Second Congregational church, of which Mrs. Laura B. Cole is president, and who was chairman of the committee in charge of the arrangements. The committee was made up of the following members of the society: Mrs. James E. Burke, Miss Maude Belden, Mrs. Maurice Rudd,

Mrs. Sherman Thompson, Mrs. Harry J. Cole, Mrs. Calvin Endress, Mrs. Charles Mathers, Mrs. Henry Fonda, Mrs. E. B. Patterson, Mrs. C. A. Perry and Mrs. R. S. Buss.

The committee had prepared for 150 guests and about that number sat down to the tables, which were decorated with the red and white flowers.

A vote of thanks was given to the ladies of the church by the members of the Association and it was unanimously agreed that a better luncheon was never eaten.

The program carried out in the auditorium of the church was as follows:

Address of Welcome, Rev. G. S. Mills.

Response, Thomas R. Kneil.

Singing by the audience, The Star Spangled Banner.

Paper—Relation of the Battle of Bennington to the Battle of Saratoga, Rev. Isaac Jennings, D. D., Bennington, Vt.

Address—A Plea for the Closer Relationship of Historic Societies, Eugene W. Lyttle, Ph. D., Albany.

Address—What America owes the Vermonters, Hon. William S. Bennet, LL. B., M. C., New York City.

Singing by the audience—America.

The committee who had charge of the local arrangements were Col. Olin Scott, Rev. Isaac Jennings, D. D., and Hon. Edward L. Bates, members of the Bennington Battle Monument and Historical Association.

The return trip was made to Saratoga Springs late in the afternoon and the third session of the meeting was held at 8:30 that evening at the Casino, the whole session being devoted to a most excellent paper on Burgoyne by Rev. Henry Belcher, M. A., LL. D., rector of St. Michael in Lewes, Sussex, England, who had honored the Association by making a special trip from England to attend this meeting.

The business meeting of the Association was held Thursday morning at nine o'clock, followed by a meeting of the Board of Trustees.

One of the most attractive features of the meeting was to have been an automobile trip planned by the citizens of Saratoga to the Saratoga Battlefield, and Frank A. Gallup, A. M., Principal of the Albany High School, was to have given an address on the battlefield descriptive of the different historical points. The weather, however, again interfered and on account of rain the automobile trip had to be abandoned and the meeting was held in the Casino. Mr. Gallup drew so vivid a word picture that the members were almost able to see the different points of interest as he described them. The annual address, "The Place of the Battle of Saratoga in the Struggle for Independence," by Hon. Andrew S. Draper, LL. B., LL. D., Commissioner of Education of the State of New York, was to have been given at 11 A. M., but was postponed until afternoon on account of the rain.   Dr. Draper was unable to be present because of illness and the paper was most ably read by Dr. Sherman Williams of Glens Falls.

After the meeting in the Casino, the members of the Association were honored by an invitation to a reception given by Mrs. Ellen Hardin Walworth at her home on North Broadway.

The historic old Walworth mansion was thronged with a crowd of visitors from three o'clock, when the reception commenced, until seven, when it was brought to a close.   For the occasion Mrs. Walworth threw the entire house, with its priceless collection of historical relics, and memories of colonial days, open to the inspection of the guests, and it was with the greatest pleasure that they roamed through the rooms enjoying the treasures.   In each chamber a cheery fire was burning in the open fireplace and in some the illumination was supplied entirely by candles, creating a genuinely colonial atmosphere.

Mrs. Walworth received, assisted by officers and members of the local chapter of the D. A. R., Mrs. Louise E. Kelley, the regent; Mrs. George F. Comstock, Mrs. C. H. Bosworth and Mrs. H. P. Pendrick.

Mrs. Frederick Menges and Mrs. Corinne Walworth poured tea and coffee, and Miss Bosworth presided at the punch bowl.

At the evening meeting, September 19th, a paper was read by Hon. James A. Holden, A. B., State Historian, on "The Influence of the Murder of Jane McCrea on the Burgoyne Campaign."   At the conclusion of the program, the women of the Saratoga County Society tendered a reception to the members of the Association and their friends.   Mrs. George F. Comstock and Mrs. Charles T. Fish served punch. Mrs. Fred Menges and Mrs. James Mingay poured coffee. The reception committee consisted of Mrs. William H. Bockes, Mrs. James M. Andrews, and Mrs. Stephen Vail.

One of the features of this meeting which attracted a great deal of attention was the exhibit of several old engravings illustrating historical scenes connected with this region, loaned by Senator Brackett. One engraving depicted the death of Jane McCrea, the event which has aroused so much discussion in historical circles, and which was of particular interest because of the paper on the subject read by State Historian Holden. The engraving, which is a very old and valuable one, shows the girl being murdered by two Indians. A line at the bottom of the picture says that it is "an accurate view of the place where it occurred."

Another engraving dated 1804, and dedicated to the "Rt. Hon. Earl of Barrington," depicts the burial of General Fraser.

A third shows the famous incident of Lady Harriett Ackland surrendering herself to the Americans in order that she might care for her wounded husband who had been captured by them. She is shown in a boat, accompanied by a clergyman bearing the flag of truce, extending to the sentry on the bank the letter from General Burgoyne to General Gates.

The collection also contained autograph letters of President Lincoln and Daniel Webster. One of Abraham Lincoln's is a legal document in the great martyr's own hand.

The second is the passport issued by Daniel Webster, to Washington Irving when the latter was embarking as minister plenipotentiary to Spain.

Friday morning the members left at 8:30 on a special train for Schuylerville. The first meeting place was at the monument where Rev. John H. Brandow of Albany gave a brief address descriptive of the points of interest connected with the battle of Saratoga, pointing out the different places which could be seen from the monument. Some of the party visited the old Schuyler house and other points of interest, and then all assembled at the parlors of the Methodist church where luncheon was served, after which we adjourned to the auditorium where an address of welcome was given by William S. Ostrander of Schuylerville, to which a response was made by Dr. William O. Stillman of Albany, who presided at the meeting.

Papers were then read by Francis Whiting Halsey, New York City, on General Schuyler's Part in the Burgoyne Campaign; Rev. John H. Brandow, A. M., Albany, on General Morgan's Part in the Burgoyne Campaign; and Edgar W. Ames, A. M., Troy, on Benedict Arnold—Patriot.

After the literary exercises the members visited the Màrshall house and the latter part of the afternoon boarded the special train for Saratoga Springs where the eighth and last session of the meeting was held at the Casino at 8 P. M. A paper was read by Freeman H. Allen, Ph. D., Colgate University, "St. Leger's Invasion and the Battle of Oriskany," followed by an illustrated lecture by Frank J. Wilder, Saratoga Springs, "A Century and a Half of Saratoga History."

At the conclusion of this meeting the following resolution was adopted:

"As all things finite have an ending, so this particular meeting with its pleasant features, its charming sociability, its delightful gatherings, is now drawing to a close.

"It is only fitting then, that the members of this Association should express their feelings of appreciation at this time to those who have so cordially ministered to their comfort and aided so greatly in their entertainment.

"To the citizens of Saratoga who have done so much to make the meetings of the Association the success they have been; to the local committee in charge who have so ably and thoroughly carried out the plans and program; to the ladies of the various patriotic and historical societies of Saratoga, as well as to Mrs. Walworth, historian and exponent of patriotism, for their most pleasant receptions; to the director of music and the students of the public schools; to the owners of automobiles who offered them for Thursday's ride to Saratoga Battlefield; to the Thursday night soloists; to one and all who have contributed in any way to our local comfort and pleasure; to the good people of Bennington and Schuylerville who so lavishly and cordially bestowed upon us their generous hospitality, to all of these we extend our heartiest and most sincere thanks, assuring them of our appreciation and delight for all that we have received at their hands. Therefore, be it

"RESOLVED, That this appreciative tribute be recorded on our minutes and furnished to the press."

MINUTES.

Business meeting, 9 A. M. , September 19th, 1912. President Roberts in the chair.

Upon motion resolved to dispense with the reading of the minutes of the previous meeting.

Treasurer Holden reported as follows:

ANNUAL STATEMENT OF J. A. HOLDEN,

TREASURER NEW YORK STATE HISTORICAL ASSOCIATION,
For Year Ending September 16, 1912.

RECEIPTS.

Cash on hand Sept. 11, 1911	$193.03	
Receipts from dues, books, etc	1279.14	
State Checks—Lake George Park	786.86	
State Checks—Crown Point	721.39	
		$2980.42

DISBURSEMENTS.

Postage, stamped envelopes, etc., for Secretary's and Treasurer's offices	$85.24
Expense—Secretary and Treasurer at Kingston	22.20
Bullard Press	94.30
Sandy Hill Herald	25.50
Post Star	26.35
G. F. Publishing Co. (balance on printing Vol. X.)	824.62
E. C. Sisson—Dowling matter	3.75
Samuel Oppenheim—Kingston Records	10.00
Rev. E. T. Corwin—Kingston Records	39.75
Insurance (Library)	45.00

Essay Prizes 60.00
Sending out statements and stenographic
    work, etc 24.00
Sundries 11.95
Crown Point 721.39
Lake George Park 786.86
Expenses 69.18
                            $2850.09

     Balance cash on hand................. $130.33

ASSETS.

Cash on hand........................... $130.33
Unpaid dues 544.00
                            $674.33

LIABILITIES.

Postage, express, etc..................... $6.21
Stenographic work in Secretary's office..... 24.00
Sending out statements, stenographic work,
    etc., Treasurer's office.................. 27.00
Printing, etc., Vol. XI, (?)................
                            $57.21

     Assets Over and Above Liabilities. $617.12

Amount in Endowment Fund.............. $609.54

     Upon motion resolved that the Treasurer's report be accepted and placed on file and that the bills presented by the Treasurer be approved and ordered paid.

     Mr. Holden made the following report for the Committee on Legislation:

REPORT OF COMMITTEE ON LAKE GEORGE BATTLE-GROUND PARK, CROWN POINT RESERVATION AND LEGISLATION.

Glens Falls, N. Y., September 17, 1912.

To the President and Trustees of the New York State Historical
    Association:

Gentlemen:

As chairman of the committee on the "Lake George Battleground Park," and a member of the "Crown Point Reservation Committee," and that of "Legislation," I desire to make the following report covering the work done by those committees during the past year:

The progress made by the committees on the two State parks, under the custodianship of this Association, was quite fully covered in the report made at the semi-annual meeting of the Association, which report is printed in the eleventh annual volume, to which reference is made for further information.

The question of water supply for the Lake George Park has been agitated by the committee for some time, but on account of the seemingly high price charged by the Lake George Water Supply Company, either for rental or installing a water supply on the premises, your committee would recommend that an additional appropriation of $360 be asked for from the State to pay for the rental of such supply. The only other method of securing water would be to sink an artesian well, (which in that rocky locality would be an expensive proposition) or to install a pumping plant and bring the water from the lake, which again would present some unhygienic features not to be desired. An appropriation for this measure is therefore deemed a most sensible thing under the circumstances.

I take pleasure in presenting herewith the annual report of the caretaker showing the work done up to the present time:

Lake George, N. Y., September 10, 1912.

Hon. James A. Holden, Glens Falls.

Dear Mr. Holden:

As requested I submit the following report, respecting the Lake George Battle Park:

The completion of the iron pipe fence begun last year, extending the entire south line, beginning at the D. & H. R. R. tracks on the east and running westerly to the Dowling road, thence westerly to the southwest corner of the Dowling property; thence along the westerly line running north to the highway on the south side of property owned by the D. & H. R. R. This above mentioned fence has been painted and is now complete. The survey for the erection of the fence was made by the State Engineer, corners were properly designated with stone and cement, and care was taken to place the fence exactly according to the lines designated.

We have also repaired the dwelling house, on the so-called Dowling property, the east wing has new tin roofing properly painted, the piazzas have been re-sheeted where needed and covered with galvanized iron roofing. A new sill has been placed under the east wing; also some new flooring in the piazza. The work has been well done and will no doubt last a long time. The dead timber lying about the park property has been cleaned up. The logs, though badly decayed, had some market value and I am pleased to report the sale of them amounted to $77.50 and the money was paid to the State Comptroller. The cleaning and removing brush has been partly done, but is not yet completed.

Sign boards marking places of interest about the park property are being made and will be ready for placing soon.

ELWYN SEELYE, Caretaker.

On July 5, 1912, Governor John A. Dix was present at Crown Point to take part in the dedicatory exercises at the unveiling of the Tercentenary Champlain Memorial Light House at Crown Point. At the same time he dedicated and turned over to your Treasurer as the representative of the Association, the memorial tablet erected by the Society of Colonial Wars; this in turn was presented to the Secretary by your Treasurer and delivered by the Secretary into the keeping of our local representative ,Hon. Berne A. Pyrke. At this time your Treasurer had an opportunity to talk with Governor Dix about the repairs to the ruins, for which an appropriation of $10,000 was granted and approved by him at the legislative session of 1912. The Governor agreed to send, and did send, the State Architect to inspect the ruins and in accordance with his recommendations a contract will be signed with some concern to so repair the ruins as to prevent further disintegration and falling down. No attempt at present will be made in the way of restoration, but it is hoped to put these historic walls in such condition that they will be safe and protected from further decay.

The State Architect and State Historian being ex-officio members of the Crown Point Committee, have had several interviews and considerable correspondence regarding the erection on the property of a public comfort station, which is to be built after plans appropriate for the place and its history. It was also deemed necessary to build a cottage for the caretaker which should also contain the custodian's office and a room for relics and curiosities found in and about the ruins.

Last year $2,000 was appropriated for a public comfort station, but unfortunately this was not sufficient for the construction of the building, so that it was considered best by the State Architect and the State Historian ,and Judge Pyrke, the chairman of the committee, to ask the State for an appropriation of $2,500 additional for the public comfort station and for $4,300 for the erection of a caretaker's cottage.

The report of Judge Pyrke has not yet been received but will be added to this report when printed. [It follows herewith] :

To the New York State Historical Association:

The undersigned, the Chairman of the Committee on the custody of the Crown Point Reservation begs to submit the following report:

In the fall of 1911 the Park received an official call from the then State Architect, Mr. Franklin B. Ware. He subsequently made a report of what he found and certain recommendations for the care and improvement of the property. He recommended that protective work be done at once upon the Barracks of Fort Amherst to carry out the State's obligation to safeguard the ruins from further decay, that a public comfort station be erected, that the underground passage be explored, the old Amherst well be pumped out, and the property substantially fenced. A requisition was made by your Committee for funds to carry out these several objects, and as a result the Legislature appropriated $10,000.00 for the protective work and $2,000.00 for a public comfort station. The other requests were not favorably acted upon. In view of the demands upon the State treasury, we cannot feel otherwise than that the Legislature was liberal with us.

As will be recalled the legislative session was a prolonged one, and the money for this work was not available as early in the season as could be wished for. Some little time ago the present State Architect, Mr. Herman W. Hoefer, at the request of Governor Dix visited the property, and he is now actively engaged in planning for the protective work and the erection of a public comfort station. Owing to the lateness of the season, it will probably not be possible to erect this fall the public comfort sta-

tion or entirely complete the protective work. Sufficient work upon the Barracks, however, will undoubtedly be done to put them
in condition to resist the destructive action of the frosts of the
coming winter. Mr. Hoefer has prepared plans for the public
comfort station, and acting under suggestions of the State Historian, Mr. Holden, it is expected that this building will closely con-
form to the architecture of the period of the forts. Mr. Hoefer
has also drawn plans for a modest cottage for the caretaker. The
money for its erection is not exactly in sight, but there is a possibility that the protective work upon the walls will not exceed the
appropriation, and that something may be available from that
appropriation for the cottage.

In connection with the dedicatory services at the Crown Point
Memorial Light House nearby there was unveiled on July 5, 1912,
a handsome and appropriate tablet erected at the Barracks of
Fort Amherst by the Society of Colonial Wars in the State of New
York.

During the past year some modest improvements have been
made upon the property,which have added to its usefulness. The
driveway leading from the highway to the parade ground within
the ramparts of Fort Amherst has been rebuilt so as to be suitable
for automobile traffic. About one hundred rods of fencing has
been built so as to prevent cattle from adjoining farms straying
upon the property. Though, as above stated, the Legislature failed to make any direct appropriation for fencing, the straying of
the cattle was found so objectionable that it was thought wise to
erect this temporary fence out of the funds provided for general
maintenance.

Visitors are coming to the property in ever increasing numbers. So far this present season there have been 5,600 visitors to
the property, not counting the throng of about 2,000 that were
there at the time of the unveiling of the tablet above referred to.

During the present summer at the express request of Gov-
cruor Dix your Committee extended to Mrs. W. C. Witherbee permission to make excavations upon the property. While up to date
nothing of especial historical value has been discovered, her operations have uncovered a glacial mill or "pot hole," which from a
geological standpoint has proved full of interest. It is located
upon the parade ground within the ramparts of Fort Amherst,

and is about fourteen feet deep and seven feet in diameter, and is said to be a most characteristic specimen of glacial mill.

Dated, Port Henry, N. Y., September 18, 1912.

BERNE A. PYRKE, Chairman.

COMMITTEE ON LEGISLATION.

The committee on legislation is pleased to report that all the appropriations asked for by the Committee on the Lake George Battleground Park, i.e. $250.00 for custodian's salary; $433.05 re-appropriation of balance left from 1910; $100.00 for the painting and erecting of sign boards; $750.00 repairs to Dowling house, and $1,200 for proposed iron fence around the Colonial Wars Monument, were granted by the Governor.

He also signed the appropriations for the Crown Point Reservation, i. e. $1,500 for maintenance; $10,000 for preservation of barracks, and $2,000 for a public comfort station.

The committee also approved, and through State Historian Holden, presented briefs in favor of the acquirement by the State of several battlegrounds and historic spots and places within the State. These items were most of them passed by the Legislature but were finally vetoed by the Governor in the last analysis of the Appropriation and Supply Bills, on purely economic grounds, it having been found necessary to radically cut these bills to keep the expenses of the State within its income.

In this connection your committee would recommend that this Association urge upon all persons introducing bills for the acquirement of historic battlegrounds or memorable spots, the absolute necessity of combining on one proposition and working to secure that particular piece of property, rather than to make an open field of the matter, which unfortunately has so far led to disastrous results in the end.

The Legislature is apparently willing to allow about so much money for historical purposes, but when the items come before the Executive it has usually been found necessary to reduce, very materially, the percentage of those passed upon favorably.

If the action of the committee in these matters is satisfactory, its work can be continued along the same lines as heretofore.

All of which is respectfully submitted.

J. A. HOLDEN,
For the Committees Named.

Upon motion it was resolved that the matter of water for the Lake George Battleground Park be referred to the Committee on that Park with power.

Upon motion, it was resolved that the matter of future appropriations referred to in the report of the Committee on Legislation be left to the discretion of that Committee.

The question raised by Mr. Holden, "Shall we endorse the Bennington and Saratoga bills, etc." precipitated an animated discussion in which the following took part: Judge Atkins was of the opinion that it was a local matter and should be taken care of by the people of Saratoga County and cited Yonkers in its purchase and restoration of its old manor house as an example. Dr Williams was of the opinion that the question was national and not local. Rev. Mr. Chorley, who formerly lived in Saratoga, stated that the place had already assumed a heavy burden in paying $100,000 for the Canfield Casino. Messrs. Wilder and Brandow raised the point that there was a great deal of difference between the Philips' manor house and the wilderness of the Saratoga Battlefield. Dr. Ingraham objected to having the Saratoga Battlefield set so far back in the wilderness and stated that there was good connection from Schuylerville by trolley. Colonel Vrooman was of the opinion that the purchase of the battlefield of Saratoga was of both national and local importance. Mr. Holden was of the opinion that if it became in any way a public park, the New York State Historical Association should be alive to whatever interest it should have in the matter.

At the conclusion of the debate the following resolution was adopted: "Resolved, That the matter of the purchase of the battlefields of Saratoga and Bennington by legislative appropriation be referred to the Committee on Legislation with power to use the name and influence of this Association in procuring such appropriation as they decide to be wise, the Committee to have power to appoint local sub-committees.

Dr. Sherman Williams of Glens Falls then reported orally for the Committee on Marking Historic Spots. Upon motion his report was accepted.

Hon. Frank H. Severance of Buffalo made the following report for the Committee on the Establishment of Closer Relations Between Historical Societies of the State:

REPORT OF THE COMMITTEE ON CLOSER RELATIONS BETWEEN THE SOCIETIES OF THE STATE.

By Hon. Frank H. Severance, Buffalo.

At the Kingston meeting of this Association, Dr. William O. Stillman, of Albany, Mr. Walter C. Anthony, of Newburgh, and myself, as Chairman, were constituted a Committee on Closer Relations between the Historical Societies of New York State. Early in August, after some correspondence with my associates, I sent to every Historical Society that I knew of in the State, the following letter:

Buffalo, N. Y., August 6th, 1912.

Dear Sir:

The New York State Historical Association desires to bring about closer relations between the local societies of the State and has made the undersigned a committee to that end. At a meeting of the Association in Saratoga, September 17-20, this committee will make its report.

We interpret "closer relations" to mean any form of co-operation which shall aid or strengthen the local societies or the State Association, and promote the objects for which they exist.

It is suggested that the local societies make a brief annual report to the State Association, stating what they are doing, what they plan to do, and what they would undertake if they were able. These reports might be printed by the State Association and given suitable distribution.

Students are constantly seeking manuscript material. A list of what your society has, or, if you have much, a brief report on it, similarly published through the State Association as a clearing-house, would tend to make your collections better known and more widely useful.

Have you a museum? If so, do you wish, by reporting on it to the State Association, to increase your opportunities for strengthening and building it up?

Do you mark historic sites? Do you have lecture courses, entertainments of any sort, for your members or the general public? Do you publish anything?

Would it help you in your work to know what other societies are doing on these lines? or to confer with them?

Have you a membership in the State Association? You would find it both pleasant and profitable, and we assure you of a welcome. The meetings are stimulative and the publications, which all members receive free, are valuable additions to any library devoted to New York State history.

Our committee respectfully asks:

Does your society desire closer relations with other historical societies?

Can you give us any suggestions for co-operative work which will be in any way helpful?

Your prompt response (addressed to the chairman of the committee) will be greatly appreciated by the New York State Historical Association.

FRANK H. SEVERANCE, Chairman,
Historical Building, Buffalo.

DR. WILLIAM O. STILLMAN, Albany.

WALTER C. ANTHONY, Newburgh.

The foregoing letter was sent to 60 organizations. I have had replies from 28, including the Buffalo society. I consider this a gratifying percentage. It is fair to assume that some of the societies which have not replied are active and doing good work. The persons to whom our circular was addressed may be abroad, or for other reasons may have failed to receive it. This suggests one first and obvious duty to the State Association—to perfect its directory of historical organizations in the State and to keep it up to date with names of officers.

The societies which have replied represent in answers the whole scale from moribund inertness to scholarly achievement and usefulness. The Broome County Historical Society reports that it has not held a meeting in two years—this in so large and cultured a city as Binghamton, in the heart of one of the richest regions, historically, in our State! Rev. William Elliot Griffis, the one live wire of the DeWitt Historical Society at Ithaca, writes: ''The DeWitt Historical Society is entirely inactive and has been for years.'' Yet in one activity, the marking of sites, it has made an excellent record.

The Oswego Society reports: "Our Society here is not a very active association. We are not what you could call an aggressive society." Secretary Elisha B. Powell adds: "I am of opinion that closer relations with other historical societies would help us and if you can give me some suggestions as to how best to interest some good men who should take part in it, I would be obliged to you." That is the note struck by many replies: Show us what to do and we will gladly join in.

President Charles F. Milliken of the Ontario County Historical Society, Canandaigua, writes: "Our Society would welcome any movement designed to bring about closer relations with similar organizations and I am sure would co-operate in such a movement. I will present the matter for consideration at its next meeting." This society, by the way, has a building project in hand, has some resources, and an interested membership, and I predict will take its place soon in the front rank of such organizations.

Without multiplying these extracts at tedious length, it is well to note in this connection the local societies in the State which are best established and are most active. Such a list must include the City History Club, The New York Historical Society and the Holland Society, all of New York City; the Kings County Historical Society of Brooklyn; the Oneida Historical Society, Utica; the Onondaga Historical Society, Syracuse; the Albany Institute; and, I may be permitted to add, the Buffalo Historical Society. No historical organization in the State is more active or doing more good in its field than the City History Club of New York. I have a most cordial letter from Frank Bergen Kelley, superintendent of the City History Club, expressing interest in the work of the State Association and pledging any possible co-operation. The other societies just named are well known to you as being possessed of buildings and collections and of admirably doing the work expected of them in their local fields. Still others in smaller communities from which I have had responses are wideawake and doing things, and for that very reason ready to work with us. Among these are the Chappaqua Historical Society, which is to erect this autumn a magnificent monument to Horace Greeley and proposes to unveil a tablet commemorating the retreat of Washington after the battle of White Plains. The Warwick Historical

Society, of Warwick, and the Minnisink Valley Historical Society, of Port Jervis, are working together in marking sites in their home region. They are already represented in the State Association.

The Rochester Historical Society, which I believe has not heretofore shared in the work of our Association, has just taken a new lease of life, moved into fine new quarters and is ready for work.

The Onondaga Historical Association in Syracuse owns its building, has comfortable resources, and will soon publish a substantial volume "Onondaga Soldiers of the Revolution," by Rev. Wm. M. Beauchamp.

The Cayuga Historical Society, at Auburn, publishes excellent reports, holds a few meetings each season, and is ripe for larger things. "I realize," writes President Frank W. Richardson, "in the future we must broaden our sphere of interest." Such an organization, with splendid traditions, could accomplish much through associated work.

Not many suggestions for co-operative work have been received. The Oneida Historical Society suggests "A yearly meeting of all historical societies in the State." This could be accomplished practically by all societies sharing in the work of the State Association. Mr. Anthony, of our committee, offers the following: "If each local society could be induced to have a careful index made of every article owned and book published by it, and deposit with the State Association a duplicate of such index, the latter body could then prepare an index of all these local indexes —perhaps publish it—and thus serve as a 'clearing-house' as it were for the local bodies. This might be made to be of great assistance to students and probably would save much duplication of work."

Dr. Stillman, of our committee, suggests that an annual subscription dinner for members of the Association, with distinguished speakers, would arouse interest. Every local society in the State should be represented at the dinner, following which matters of common interest could be discussed.

From Huntington and from Sag Harbor, the most eastern societies in the State, have come cordial responses, indicating a desire to be associated in any work set on foot among the State societies.

The status of many a local society is probably well expressed by President C. E. Holden, of the Historical Society at Whitehall. Mr. Holden writes:

"We hold a public meeting about twice a year, have papers of local interest, and we delay the next meeting until people begin to stop us on the street and ask when there will be another. It is here, as I suppose it is everywhere; while a great many people are "interested," yet half a dozen of us have to keep the society alive. Most people we approach are perfectly willing to help us the next time, but this time there is some good and sufficient reason why someone else should do it. I think the idea of making a report to the State society is good."

There are in my judgment several useful things which the historical societies throughout our State might accomplish by co-operation. There are few, however, that would appeal to any but the student and the specialist. Your committee recommends as a practicable and useful work which will interest many, that we call on all of the societies to report on the historic sites that have been marked, and those that have not been but should be, in that part of the State which shall be assigned to them. In most cases, this territory would naturally be the home county. The northern part of the State could fairly be divided among the nearest societies. Each society would be able to make a thorough and accurate survey of that part of the State which it knows best and is most interested in. These reports should be sent in to this Association in time to be edited and printed in our next annual volume. Such a work would be sought for and prized by each contributing society. Its publication would be a credit to this Association. Some general sale of it to libraries, colleges, etc., could be expected. It could be illustrated, more or less, according to available funds.

This is one specific suggestion for setting all of the societies at work on a task for the common good.

Furthermore, it is in line with the efforts which the State Historian is making through the schools to gather historical data. The cause of history could be equally well served if all the data on this subject were gathered by the State and published by the State. We do not understand that this is at present contemplated.

Numerous other fields of work offer opportunity for co-operation. Reports on manuscripts is one. The trouble with that is
that while it appeals very strongly to a few workers, it means little or nothing to many. Probably most of the local societies have
few if any manuscripts of general value. It is best not to attempt
too much. Let us interest as many societies as possible in one
piece of work which will be of use to each institution. Follow
this up with determined efforts to bring all the societies into membership in this Association. If delegates from any local society
attend these annual meetings, they will not fail to carry home new
enthusiasm and get new results.

Respectfully submitted,

FRANK H. SEVERANCE, Chairman.

This report was followed by a discussion in which the following took part: Messrs. Bigelow, Roberts, Vrooman, Williams,
MacCracken; and Mrs. Pitcher, Mrs. Tuttle and Miss Haldane.
Mr. Holden congratulated Mr. Severance and stated that the
State Historian had been working along the same lines for the
past year. Upon motion it was resolved that the report be accepted and the Committee be instructed to carry out the suggestions made and report at the next meeting.

Mr. Richards of Glens Falls made an oral report for the Publication Committee.

Judge Ingalsbe made the following report for the Committee
to Amend the Charter:

Saratoga, September 19, 1912.

To the New York State Historical Association:

Your Committee appointed to take such steps as might be
necessary to have the proposed amendments to the Charter of the
Association, which were authorized at a special meeting of its
members called for that purpose, duly incorporated in the Charter,
would respectfully report as follows:

A Certificate was prepared and duly executed by Trustees
Everett R. Sawyer, Joseph E. King, Frederick B. Richards, Sher-
man Williams, James A. Holden, James A. Roberts, William Wait,
Francis W. Halsey, Howland Pell, Jacques W. Redway, T. Astley
Atkins, W. O. Stillman, Victor H. Paltsits, W. A. E. Cummings
and Grenville M. Ingalsbe, setting forth the action taken at the

Special Meeting of the Association, and such other facts as were necessary upon an application for an extension of corporate purposes.

This Certificate, after its approval by a Supreme Court Judge, was forwarded to the Board of Regents of the University of the State of New York, by which the original Charter of the Association was granted.

The Chairman of the Standing Committee of the Regents on Charters, the Honorable Pliny T. Sexton, has approved this Certificate as to its form. It is now ready to be acted upon formally by the Regents at their next meeting, which will be held in October, and the corporate purposes of the Association will then be extended in accordance with the desire of its membership, as expressed at the special meeting, to which reference has already been made.

The effect of this proceeding will be to amend the Articles of Incorporation of the Association, so that the principal objects for which the Corporation is formed will be as follows:

FIRST: To promote and encourage original historical research.

SECOND: To disseminate a greater knowledge of the early history of the State, by means of lectures, and the publication and distribution of literature on historical subjects.

THIRD: To gather books, manuscripts, pictures and relies relating to the early history of the State, and to establish a museum therein.

FOURTH: To suitably mark places of historic interest.

FIFTH: To acquire by purchase, gift, devise, or otherwise, the title to, or custody and control of, historic spots and places.

The territory in which the operations of this Corporation are to be principally conducted is the State of New York.

The principal office of said Corporation is to be located at the City of Albany, New York.

As the work assigned to your Committee is now performed, we would ask that this Report be accepted and the Committee discharged.

All of which is respectfully submitted.

Dated, September 17th, 1912.

GRENVILLE M. INGALSBE,
THOMAS E. FINEGAN,
Of the Committee.

Upon motion it was resolved that the report be accepted and that the thanks of the Association be extended to the committee and the committee discharged.

The Wiltwyck Committee reported that Mr. Samuel Oppenheim of New York City had been engaged to correct the translation of the old Dutch records of Kingston and that between one and two hundred pages were then in press and would appear in Vol. XI of the Proceedings of the Association.

Under the head of the election of Trustees, the following were unanimously elected:—

> Dr. W. A. E. Cummings, Ticonderoga.
> Hon. D. S. Alexander, Buffalo.
> Rev. John H. Brandow, Albany.
> Hon. Grenville M. Ingalsbe, Hudson Falls.
> Gen. Charles L. Davis, Schenectady.
> Rev. Henry M. MacCracken, D. D., New York City.
> Hon. Gilbert D. B. Hasbrouck, Kingston.
> Frank J. Wilder, Saratoga Springs.
> Hon. William S. Bennet, New York City.

Under the head of new business, it was resolved that this Association make special request that every historical society in the State appoint a member to represent their society at the annual meeting of the Association and send as an annual offering $2.00 to meet the expenses of the State Association and receive in return the annual publication.

The following list of new members was read:

Allen, Freeman H., Ph. D.	Hamilton
Atkins, Miss Kate	Yonkers
Bailey, Dr. Theodorus	New York
Bassette, Alfred S.	Red Creek
Betts, Hon. James A.	Kingston
Bigelow, Rev. Dana W.	Utica
Bosworth, Mrs. C. H.	Saratoga Springs
Brockway, Miss Mary L.	Saratoga Springs
Bullard, Charles E.	Glens Falls
Cayuga County Historical Society	Auburn
Callanan, James H.	Schenectady
Chalmers, Arthur A.	Amsterdam
Chalmers, Mrs. Arthur A.	Amsterdam

Cheesman, Mrs. T. M.	Garrison-on-Hudson
Colonial Dames of America	New York
Corbin, Harold H.	Saratoga Springs
Corbin, Miss Sarah E.	Rome
Curtis, Miss May Belle	Glens Falls
Curtis Memorial Library	Meriden, Conn.
de Laporte, Mrs. Theo.	Rhinebeck
DeMott, John J.	Metuchen, N. J.
Don, John	Saratoga Springs
Duffey, Edwin	Cortland
Farnham, Mrs. George A.	Yonkers
Ferriss, Mrs. Cornelia Wing	Glens Falls
Fielding, Dr. Fred G.	Glens Falls
Foulds, Dr. Thomas H.	Glens Falls
Goodridge, Edwin Alonso, M. D.	Saratoga Springs
Graul, John C.	Saratoga Springs
Griswold, E. S.	Bennington, Vt.
Hempstead High School	Hempstead
Heermance, Van Ness	Brooklyn
Herkimer County Historical Society	Herkimer
Hill, Richmond C.	Schenectady
Historical Society of Newburgh Bay and the Highlands	Newburgh
Howland, Miss Emily	Sherwood
Hunt, William J., M. D.	Glens Falls
Irish, Edward F.	Glens Falls
Jones, Sebastian C.	Cornwall-on-Hudson
Kelly, J. M.	Saratoga Springs
Lansing, J. Townsend	Albany
LeFevre, Dr. Sherwood	Glens Falls
Ludlow, Henry S.	Saratoga Springs
MacCracken, Rev. Henry M.	New York
MacDonald, Benjamin J.	Newburgh
Martin, Rev. Daniel H., D. D.	Glens Falls
McCabe, John H.	Glens Falls
McVicker, Mrs. Robert	Mount Vernon
Menges, Mrs. Frederick	Saratoga Springs
Mills, Miss Phebe	Glens Falls
Mingay, Mrs. James	Saratoga Springs

Mingay, James	Saratoga Springs
Morehouse, Frank D.	Glens Falls
Newark High School	Newark
Oppenheim, Samuel	New York
Powellson, Miss Louise	Middletown
Public Library, High School	Saratoga Springs
Potter, Hon. J. Sanford	Whitehall
Queen of the Rosary Academy	Amityville
Robertson, D. L.	Glens Falls
Rowe, Franklin A.	Glens Falls
Schuyler, Ackley C.	New York
Singleton, J. Edward	Glens Falls
Sister M. Margaret	Highland Falls
Sister M. Ignatia	Buffalo
Sister Mary Dolores	Cohoes
Sister Mary Patricia	Rouses Point
Slade, John A.	Saratoga Springs
Tefft, Miss Frances A.	Hudson Falls
Tewey, Miss Margaret M.	Irvington
Thompson, Charles B.	Glens Falls
Tibbits, Miss Mary Edla	New Rochelle
Tuxedo High School	Tuxedo Park
Van Buren, Miss Catherine G.	Spring Lake, N. J.
Van Cortlandt, Anne S.	Croton-on-Hudson
Vermilyea, Miss Helen F.	Cohoes
Wait, Mrs. J. W.	Hudson Falls
Waddell, Miss Helen	Hoosick Falls
Waterbury, W. H.	Saratoga Springs
West, Charles F.	Glens Falls
Wheat, Benj. P.	Saratoga Springs
Wheeler, Charles B.	Buffalo
Williams, Mrs. Helen	Saratoga Springs
Wilmarth, Miss Bertha C.	Glens Falls
Wilson, Mrs. Georgianna Richards	Glens Falls
Wilson, Mrs. J. S.	New York

LIFE MEMBER

Tracy, Dr. Ira Otis	Brooklyn

Upon motion it was resolved that the persons on the above list be formally elected members of the Association.

Upon motion it was resolved that Rev. Henry Belcher, M. A., LL. D., Lewes, Sussex, England, be elected an honorary member of the Association.

Upon motion it was resolved that Chaplain Roswell Randall Hoes, U. S. N.,Washington, D. C., be elected an honorary member of the Association.

Upon motion the meeting adjourned.

MEETING OF TRUSTEES.

At the conclusion of the meeting of the Association, the meeting of the Trustees was called to order.

There were present Hon. James A. Roberts, Rev. Henry M. MacCracken, Rev. John H. Brandow, Dr. Sherman Williams, Hon. Frank H. Severance, Miss Mary H. Haldane, Hon. James A. Holden, Hon. T. Astley Atkins, General Charles L. Davis, Mr. Frank J. Wilder, Hon. Grenville M. Ingalsbe, and Mr. Frederick B. Richards.

Upon motion by President Roberts, seconded by Mr. Atkins, the Secretary was instructed to cast one ballot for Hon. Grenville M. Ingalsbe as President of the Association.

Moved by Dr. MacCracken, seconded by Mr. Brandow, that Mr. Holden write an article reviewing Mr. Roberts' good work as president of this Association, for publication in the next volume of the Proceedings.

.The following officers were then duly elected:

First Vice President—Sherman Williams, Pd. D.

Second Vice President—Dr. William O. Stillman.

Third Vice President—Rev. Henry M. McCracken, D. D.

Treasurer—Hon. James A. Holden.

Secretary—Mr. Frederick B. Richards.

Assistant Secretary—Dr. W. A. E. Cummings.

The following invitations were then received for the next annual meeting: Gen. Charles L. Davis, for Schenectady; Rev. Mr. Bigelow, for Utica; letters from James G. Riggs for Oswego; and one read by Dr. Williams for Syracuse.

Upon motion it was resolved that the special and regular committees be appointed by the incoming President at his leisure.

Upon motion it was resolved that the place of the next annual meeting be referred to the President and the Program Committee.

Upon motion it was resolved that Mr. Holden be appointed a committee to prepare resolutions to be presented at the last session expressing the thanks of the Association for the many courtesies extended by Saratoga Springs and the other places visited at this meeting.

Upon motion the meeting was adjourned subject to the call of the President.

At the last session of the meeting, Friday evening, September 20th, the following resolutions were adopted:

Resolved, That a committee of three, consisting of President Ingalsbe, Treasurer Holden and Secretary Richards, be appointed to co-operate with the New York State Commission on the dedication of the Schuylerville monument.

Resolved, That in order to carry out the suggestions of Mr. Wilder and Miss Haldane that this Association co-operate with the historical and patriotic societies of the State in their endeavor to stir up or awaken greater interest in the historical matters in their locality; that the President appoint a special committee to select speakers or lecturers and that a circular letter be prepared to send to the different historical and patriotic societies of the State advising them that they may secure such aid as the Association can give in the way of lectures on application to the Secretary of the Association, it being understood that such local society pay the traveling expenses of the speaker but that there will be no other fee.

FREDERICK B. RICHARDS,

Secretary.

MID-WINTER MEETING.

The semi-annual meeting of the Trustees of the New York State Historical Association was held at the State Historian's office in the Education Building, Albany, at 2 P. M., January 18, 1913.

There were present Grenville M. Ingalsbe, Gen. Charles L. Davis, T. Astley Atkins, Frank J. Wilder, James A. Holden, Thomas E. Finegan, Rev. Joseph E. King, Sherman Williams and Frederick B. Richards.

As the minutes of the last meeting were in print in Vol. XI it was upon motion resolved to dispense with the reading of the same.

The Treasurer reported as follows:

SEMI-ANNUAL STATEMENT OF J. A. HOLDEN, TREASURER NEW YORK STATE HISTORICAL ASSOCIATION.

January 15, 1913.

RECEIPTS.

Cash on hand Sept. 16, 1912..............	$130.33
Receipts from dues......................	549.52
Crown Point Reservation................	414.00
Lake George Battleground Park..........	325.12
	$1418.97

DISBURSEMENTS.

Postage, stenographic work, sending out statements, etc., as listed on annual statement	$57.21	
Buffalo Historical Society................	5.40	
Rev. Mr. Belcher........................	50.00	
F. J. Wilder............................	27.40	
F. B. Richards. Annual Meeting..........	16.95	
Bullard Press	54.25	
Stationery, postage, etc., for Secretary's office	11.36	
Express	1.90	
Express	.55	
Lake George Battleground Park..........	250.00	
Lake George Battleground Park..........	75.12	
Crown Point Reservation................	414.00	
		964.14
Essay prizes		60.00
		$1024.14
Balance cash on hand..............		$394.83

ASSETS.

Cash on hand $394.83

Unpaid dues 954.00
(Including only those owing for one and
two years).

In addition there is $366.00 owing for
3, 4, and 5 years......................   ————   **$1348.83**

LIABILITIES.

Bullard Press $45.81

Samuel Oppenheim (?)..................

G. F. Publishing Co. (?)...............

LIFE MEMBERSHIP.

Endowment Fund $634.54

Upon motion it was Resolved that the Treasurer's report be accepted.

Hon. James A. Holden made the following reports for the Committees on Lake George Battleground Park, Crown Point Reservation and Legislation:

Albany, N. Y., January 18, 1913.

To the Trustees of the New York State Historical Association.

Gentlemen:

I take the liberty at this time of combining in this report those of the Committees on Legislation, Lake George Battleground Park and Crown Point Reservation.

So far, the Committee on Legislation has had little or nothing to do and no matters have as yet appeared requiring its attention or co-operation in the Legislature.

The following report has been received from Mr. Seelye, the caretaker of the Lake George Battleground Park, with items showing the work performed there since the annual meeting:

To the Trustees of the New York State Historical Association.

Gentlemen:

In addition to the report presented at the annual meeting I would state that the following items represent the work done since that time:

For labor performed on Lake George Battle Ground Park
from October 9, 1912, to November 2, cutting and
burning brush $52.12

For horse hire to draw the brush where it was safe to
burn it 6.00

For putting up signs and guides about the grounds, including cost of bolts, etc........................... 3.00

_____
$61.12

The work has been carefully and economically performed.
We have on hand about ten cords of pine wood which we offer at
Three Dollars per cord.

ELWYN SEELYE,
Caretaker.

I also present herewith the report of Judge Pyrke, the chairman of the Crown Point Reservation Committee:

Port Henry, N. Y., January 18, 1913.

Below I give you a brief outline of the work done the past
fall toward the preservation of the stone barracks on the State
Park at Crown Point.

Owing to the prolonged session of the Legislature last year
the appropriations for this work were not available until a date
much later than usual, and this fact in conjunction with the
change in the incumbency of the office of State Architect made it
impossible to start the work as early as should have been done
for the best results. In fact, the work was so long delayed that
it was impossible last fall to do very much more than to do
emergency work to carry the barracks safely through the winter
and spring. An embarrassment was also found in the fact that
the law required that the work should be done by contract, and
this work was of such a character as not to render itself readily
subject to that manner of performance.

Preliminary to the starting of the work the State Architect,
Mr. Herman W. Hoefer, made a personal visit to the property,
and recommended the filling of all of the interstices in the walls
with cement placed under pressure by means of a cement gun.
The contract was made between the State and a cement gun company, by which the necessary paraphernalia was placed upon the

ground in charge of an operator furnished by the company. Some work was done by this gun, but it was not entirely of a satisfactory nature. Its operations were somewhat handicapped by the lack of a dependable water supply. A power pump was installed above the old well upon the property, and it was believed that this would furnish a satisfactory supply of water, but it was found after a short operation that the well was so filled up with a century's accumulation of debris that the supply was very inadequate. The gun and its equipment has been placed in storage upon the property, and it is believed that this year with a water supply direct from the lake more satisfactory results will be reached. A good deal of very satisfactory hand labor by masons was done upon the principal barracks, largely in the way of making solid the foundations. The work so far as it was carried along was done in a sympathetic spirit, and while calculated to permanently preserve the walls, has been done in such a manner as not to give the impression of any attempt at restoration.

It is believed that with the experience of last fall's work and with the necessary paraphernalia assembled upon the ground, the work will go forward this spring with greater efficiency and economy.

We have received no statistical report from the State Architect's office as to quality of work done or as to the cost thereof.

BERNE A. PYRKE,

Chairman.

In addition to Mr. Pyrke's report I would state that the State Architect's records show that in the reconstruction of the barracks, the work executed to date calls for the expenditure of $2072.51 of which $1386.92 has already been paid, leaving a balance of $685.59 still due on this work. The State Architect's office will, as I understand it, begin the work of reconstruction again at as early a date as possible in the spring.

The following suggestions for appropriations have been prepared and forwarded to the State Comptroller:

APPROPRIATION BILL
LAKE GEORGE BATTLEGROUND PARK

CUSTODIAN'S SALARY.

For salary of custodian, two hundred and fifty dollars.   **$250.00**

FENCE.

For additional appropriation for construction of proposed iron fence around the monument erected by the Society of Colonial Wars on the Lake George Battleground Park, owned by the State of New York, five hundred dollars...................... 500.00

SURVEY OF PARK.

For finishing survey of park and properly mapping park, five hundred dollars...................... 500.00

CROWN POINT RESERVATION.

MAINTENANCE.

For general maintenance including employment of a caretaker, one thousand five hundred dollars.... 1,500.00

FENCING FOR RESERVATION.

For fencing reservation as planned by State Architect, two thousand dollars......................... 2,000.00

SUPPLY BILL

LAKE GEORGE BATTLEGROUND PARK.

WATER SUPPLY.

For the purpose of renting from the Lake George Water Company a supply of water for domestic and fire protection purposes, one hundred eighty dollars... $180.00

IMPROVEMENTS.

For the purpose of cleaning up the paths and roads around said park, the cutting down of brush and dead trees, and for the proper disposal of same, three hundred fifty dollars...................... 350.00

GUIDE POSTS.

For the erection of markers and guide posts within said park, one hundred dollars...................... 100.00

DOCK.

For the erection on the lake front of a suitable dock for the landing of steam or motor boats, or other small craft, five hundred dollars...................... 500.00

CROWN POINT RESERVATION.

PUBLIC COMFORT STATION.

For deficiency in appropriation made by chapter five hundred forty-seven of the laws of nineteen hundred twelve for a public comfort station in accordance with the plans and designs of the State Architect, two thousand five hundred dollars.......... $2,500.00

CARETAKER'S COTTAGE.

For the erection of a suitable cottage for the use of the caretaker, custodian's office and relic room in accordance with the plans and recommendations of the State Architect, four thousand three hundred dollars 4,300.00

ROADWAY.

For the construction of a proper, suitable and necessary road to and through the park, between such places as may be designated by the committee in charge, two thousand dollars......................... 2,000.00
How much of this will meet the approval of the Legislature this year is necessarily problematical.
this year is necessarily problematical.

JAMES A. HOLDEN,

For Committees Named.

Upon motion it was resolved that the reports submitted by Mr. Holden be accepted and made a part of the minutes of this meeting.

The following list of new members was read by the Secretary:

Sept., 1912, to Jan. 18, 1913.

Hon. Miles R. Frisby	Schenectady
Walter R. Selth	Mt. Vernon
Mrs. Jennie E. Wright	Saratoga Springs
Louis Fiske Hyde	Glens Falls
Miss Louise Fletcher	Norwood
Col. John W. Vrooman	Herkimer
William H. Manning	Saratoga Springs
Charles C. Allen	Schuylerville

Mrs. Charles C. Allen	Schuylerville
Dept. of Education	Oswego
Fortnightly Club	Oswego
James G. Riggs	Oswego
George Noyes Burt	Oswego
Robert A. Downing	Oswego
F. A. Emerick	Oswego
John S. Parsons	Oswego
F. B. Shepherd	Oswego
Carrington Macfarlane	Oswego
John D. Higgins	Oswego
Saranac Chapter, D. A. R.	Plattsburgh
C. F. Powers	Schuylerville
Elliott B. Mott	Oswego
Luther W. Mott	Oswego
Mrs. Wm. T. Scully	Schuylerville
Thos. P. Kingsford	Oswego
Henry A. Dows	New York
F. A. Gallup	Albany
Neil Gray, Jr.	Oswego
Wm. Pierrepont White	Utica
Thos. Bailey Lovell	Niagara Falls
Tawasentha Chapter, D. A. R.	Slingerlands
F. Robert Swart	Peekskill
Clarence Willis	Bath

LIFE MEMBER.

Stuyvesant Fish	New York City

Upon motion it was Resolved that the above list of members be formally elected.

Sherman Williams made an oral report for the Program Committee stating that Oswego had been chosen for the next annual meeting, to be held there Sept. 29, 30, October 1 and 2. Arrangements for the meeting were already well under way and it was expected that the plans would include a trip to Kingston, Ontario, and that a meeting would be held there which would be addressed by some prominent Canadian historians.

Sherman Williams reported as follows for the Committee on Essays:

To the Trustees of the New York State Historical Association.

Gentlemen:

Your committee is glad to report a very great increase in interest in the contest for prize essays on historical subjects. This year there were fifty-nine competitors representing twenty-three counties, more than four times as many contestants as last year. The prizes were awarded as follows:

First prize of $30 in gold to Walter B. Stevens, North Tonawanda.

Second prize of $20 in gold to Pearl D. Thurber, Buffalo

Third prize of $10 in gold to Alvan LeRoy Barach, New York.

Your committee would recommend the continuance of the plan of offering prizes for essays on matters pertaining to some phase of New York history and would suggest for next year the following topic: "The Naval Warfare of 1812 on Lakes Erie and Ontario."

There has arisen in the minds of the committee whether it might not be well to increase somewhat the number of prizes offered in view of the large number of competitors. It is also thought that when a student has once won a prize he or she ought not to be allowed to compete in any future contest.

Respectfully submitted,
THOMAS E. FINEGAN,
SHERMAN WILLIAMS,
GEORGE K. HAWKINS,
Committee.

Upon motion it was resolved that the report be accepted.

Upon motion it was resolved that the sum of $60 be appropriated for essay prizes for the coming year, the said amount to be divided into five prizes instead of three as at present, and that the Committee may grant honorable mention in their discretion.

Upon motion it was resolved that only the essay receiving first prize should be published in the Proceedings of the Association.

The Committee on Publication reported for Vol. XI by handing a copy just received from the printers to each of the Trustees. As to Vol. XII it was promised that this volume would be gotten out before the next annual meeting.

Upon motion is was Resolved that Frank J. Wilder and the Secretary be a committee to draw up a form for bequests to be published in the annual Proceedings of the Association.

Upon motion it was Resolved that a Committee of three be appointed, of which the President of the Association should be chairman, to revise the Constitution and By-Laws of the Associa-, tion in accordance with the changes in the Charter.

Upon motion it was Resolved that the Treasurer be author- ized to pay Mr. Samuel Oppenheim the balance due for work on the translation of the old Dutch Records of Kingston.

Upon motion it was Resolved that the thanks of the Associa- tion be extended to Mr. Henry E. Nichols for his courtesy in the matter of obtaining a photograph for the Association of Isle du St. Sacrement.

Upon motion Resolved that Mr. Holden be instructed to thank Colonel Roberts for his generosity and interest in the matter of the publication of the translation of the old Dutch Records of Kingston.

Upon motion the meeting adjourned.

FREDERICK B. RICHARDS,
Secretary.

MEETING OF EXECUTIVE COMMITTEE.

Glens Falls, N. Y., October 5, 1912.

At a meeting of the Executive Committee of the New York State Historical Association, held pursuant to call at the Crandall Free Library, Glens Falls, on this date, there were present Messrs. Ingalsbe, Williams, Holden and Richards, constituting a majority of the committee.

President Ingalsbe in the chair.

The question of meeting place and some other matters con- cerning the affairs of the Association were informally discussed.

The Treasurer having advised the committee that it would be necessary to appoint a representative to sign legal instruments in connection with reservations or state parks over which this Asso- ciation had been or might be designated as custodian, the following resolution was upon motion duly carried and unanimously adopted:

RESOLVED, That James A. Holden, the Treasurer of the New York Historical Association, be and he is hereby authorized and empowered to act for and in behalf of the Association in all matters connected with the affairs of the Lake George Battleground Park, the Crown Point Reservation or any other State park or reservation whose custody shall be imposed upon this Association by law or appointment, whensoever and wherever those affairs have to do with any of the State Departments, in any way or form. And be it further

RESOLVED, That the said Treasurer of this Association be and he is hereby authorized to sign, execute and deliver and attach the seal of this Association to any legal papers, documents or instruments which may be necessary to be signed and executed in behalf of the Association or which may be demanded by any State Department or officer in connection with the transac-- tions of this Association with such officers or such departments of the State.

On motion adjourned.

FREDERICK B. RICHARDS,

Secretary.

I hereby certify that the above is a true transcript of the minutes of the Executive Committee, at a meeting held on above date.

FREDERICK B. RICHARDS.

Sworn to before me this 7th
    day of October, 1912.
        Annabel Beaudoin,
          Notary Public,
            Warren County.

ADDRESS OF WELCOME

Hon. Edgar Truman Brackett, Saratoga Springs.

Mr. President and Members of the State Historical Association:

It is with especial satisfaction that, on behalf of the county of Saratoga and the village of Saratoga Springs, I welcome you here at this time. This community is acquainted with the purposes of your organization and it prides itself that there is no spot on which the sun shines in its course that can more claim the right to be interested in matters historical, than that chosen by you for your present meeting,—that can, with surer right, insist on the privilege of hospitality to an association, the aim of which is to rescue, and correctly establish, matters of historical interest.

Situated along the highway of the nations, on the trail where, for centuries, savage travelled to meet his equally savage foe; upon which, in civilized war, every column of invasion, or army of defense, has marched to victory, or defeat; the route by which Howe, the idol of the English army, advanced to his death at Ticonderoga; along which Ephraim Williams gave up his life; traveling upon which Jane McCrea met her fate; on the line of which Ethan Allen made his fame immortal; upon which, in final close of its military history, were fought Ticonderoga and Hubbardton, and Bennington, and Stillwater, and Bemis Heights; and, crowning all, upon which was surrendered the army of invasion under Burgoyne—the principal county situated along the historic route, extending from Albany to Montreal, gives you cordial and hearty welcome to her borders, and wishes you a pleasant and a useful meeting. Whatever of pride comes to a host entertaining an honored guest, is ours; whatever of satisfaction comes to a guest of a willing host, shall be yours.

But that genial gentleman who, as a member of your body, armed with a proper authority, asked me to greet you here,—I mean him known in the flesh as Sherman Williams—whispered to me, as he was leaving, after extending your invitation, and after I had truly said that it would delight my soul to express the satisfaction of my neighbors and myself at your coming, that the occasion demanded something more than a mere formal welcome; that such a distinguished body must have the genuine article; that the eminent men and women who compose its membership were to be received in a little different way than would be provided for a local fireman's association, and that it would be expected that, in addition, I should treat some matter of historic interest. I knew in a minute that I had made a mistake, so far as my comfort was concerned, but he had gone, and I have never set eyes on him since.

I have so long stood in awe of some of the individual members of your society that to attempt anything serious before you, appalls me. When I sit down and talk with Ingalsbe on matters historical, I always feel as if I were a fly buzzing around an historical encyclopedia. When I approach Holden I am like a Chinese coming into the presence of his Joss. When, the rare times, I see your President, I feel like an untutored savage in the presence of a philosopher. When I recall the learning and the interest in your work of that dear friend of the years, Robert O. Bascom, who has passed on, I know that any little historical knowledge of mine is very poor indeed, and, paraded before this body, will seem very poor indeed. And, so, this admonition of Professor Williams, added to an already overload of scare when I thought of addressing you, put me in a condition of funk, from which I do not hope to escape until I go down the steps from this platform.

I, therefore, shall not venture upon any attempt to develop any point of history. Several have suggested themselves. One time I had it in mind to speak a word for Benedict Arnold—not in full defense, but by way of mitigating circumstances. No one who has read the account of his services can fail to want to speak for him as kindly as he may. Arnold, who more than any one save only Schuyler, and perhaps almost equally with him, rendered really heroic service in the Saratoga campaign; Arnold, that strange combination of infamous plotting and heroic doing; Arnold, who was compelled to stand and see men of inferior abilities preferred to, and promoted over, himself. Arnold, who saw the solemn, mediocre Gates, who, if he ever had an original idea, failed to put it where we now can learn of it, crowned as a victorious commander, when, as I read, about all he did was to receive Burgoyne's sword. Arnold, whose name for an hundred and thirty years has been anathema by those he sought to betray and by those with whom he negotiated, alike—I would have loved to develop the facts and see if, somewhere, some way, a word could not be said to help him a little to kindlier thoughts in the future —to see if, really and truly, there was not, in Congress, or out, somewhere, a ring, the bosses of which, to use a present day term, acted together to keep him down and whether they did not use very practical, present day, methods to accomplish it—here is a taking field, but, on your program, it will be treated by some one much abler to do justice to the subject than I, and so I do not enter upon it.

Then, too, there came the attractive idea of a little analyzing the causes of Burgoyne's failure and surrender. Why was it that this very flower of the British forces, an army, for its purposes, magnificent in numbers; commanded by a general at once the favorite of his comrades and of his Sovereign and who had demonstrated ability in former campaigns; officered by men the most skilled in the service; trained in all the military science of the time—why was it that this army went to inglorious failure, to a collection of militia? Was the plan of three columns converging on Albany fundamentally wrong, as some experts have argued, exposing each column to assault separately and without possibility of help from the others? Should Burgoyne have gone from Montreal to New York by sea, and, there joining Howe, have made a united force that would have been irresistible in its march to Albany and the north? In his haste to get to the country for the week end, did the failure of Germain to sign the despatch taking away from Howe any discretion, and giving the same positive instructions for him to proceed up the Hudson, that Burgoyne had to proceed down—did the failure to send these instructions, for the lack of which Howe, in his discretion and, as we know now influenced by the plan of that arch traitor, Charles Lee, then a prisoner, sent the most of his force to the south, instead of the north,—did this cause or contribute to the final catastrophe? Or was it simply a succession of little circumstances, one after the other, that demonstrated that there was lacking that capacity for infinite detail which constitutes genius? It may not be profitable to speculate on these questions, but, at least, it would be mighty interesting.

A distinguished author has recently published a series of lectures designed to illustrate the part that chance has played in matters military and diplomatic—the omnipotence of luck in matters of war. His conclusion is that, by every rule, the patriot forces were placed in a position at the battle of Bunker Hill where all that the British had to do was to seize the neck of land between the mainland and the American trenches and wait a few hours, when surrender by Prescott would have been inevitable. But, with singular fatuousness, Howe chose the only method he could have taken, that would not have resulted in complete victory—a frontal attack.

At Long Island, Washington made practically the same error as had been made at Bunker Hill—threw his army into a position where the English had but to wait and annihilation of the Revolutionary forces was inevitable. But, again, Howe would not accept the help of time and circumstance, but risked a direct attack.

An English contemporary writing in 1778 of these operations of 1777 said, "In short, I am of the opinion * * * * that any other General in the world than Howe would have beaten General Washington; and any other General in the world than General Washington would have beaten General Howe."

However, Washington's subsequent retreat from Long Island was masterly, and atoned largely for any fault of the earlier dispositions.

But a chain of current circumstances patent to you all, turns me from a consideration of any of these things here, to what politeness would perhaps call some very brief philosophic reflections on the uses of history.

We have, apparently, come to a time when there is a tremendous disposition to ignore the standards and the experience of the past; to turn out the lights of history; to travel by the shifting present notions, unillumined, and unguided, by the experience of the past. I deplore this tendency.

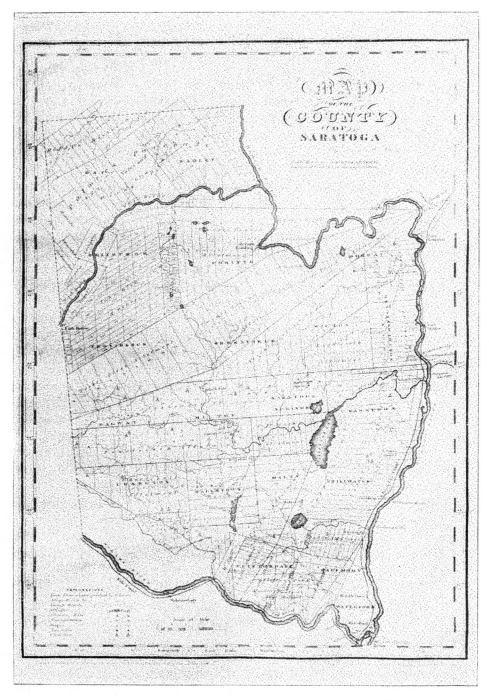

FIRST MAP OF SARATOGA COUNTY, 1829.

Do not misunderstand me, I am more than a thousand miles from any politics in this statement. I stand by the front cover motto of the North American Review, *"Tros, Tyriusque"* &c., which, liberally translated, means, Troy and Tyre do not make a damned bit of difference to me. Republicans, Democrats, Socialists, the horned crew—and, too, any other, even if it have the cloven hoof—look alike to me in my view of the situation, and all are alike, culpable for it.

"History," says Bolingbroke, "is philosophy teaching by examples." Whoever truly records the history, the doings, of his time; who puts down in correct chronology the succession of events that have passed under his observation; who impartially deduces from such events, enlightened by his recollection, or his research, the reasons actuating the persons who have taken part in the events so chronicled; who, reasoning truly, draws from such events the resultant effects and the lessons they teach; whoever, in orderly fashion, does this, whether great, or small, renowned or obscure, is truly an historian, serves truly his time and is truly a benefactor of the future. No one who studies such a record can fail to increase his own learning. The flux of what the wisest and best have done in the past, under given conditions, is the surest evidence of what the wisest and best of any present time should do, under like conditions. To deny this is to deliberately deny ourselves the value of precedent. To ignore it is to shut our eyes to all the past and, foolishly, trust our own impressions, untaught by the wisdom of all the ages.

I take it that, in this position, I shall invite no attack, encounter no opposition. Certainly the members of the society organized to rescue and preserve the illumining events of the past, will not deny the wisdom of studying the events thus rescued, of being guided by the lessons of history thus preserved. In vain is the harvest gathered if it is allowed to moulder and rot in the barns. Worse than useless is the work of your society, and kindred societies the country over, if, having exploited the examples of the past, they are derided, or ignored, in the teachings of the present.

It is my privilege to be a member of a profession, a great part of the work of which is to study precedents; to see how great minds, impartial and true, approached, and reasoned upon questions presented to them—with a view of drawing from these intellectual wells of the past, a wisdom to treat questions of the present and to view them from every angle. Perhaps that fact and the habits formed of forty years of work in that profession, have warped and twisted my viewpoint out of all semblance of true observation. But in this year of grace 1912, in spite of false lights on the shore, in spite of the attempts to silence the bells that mark danger spots along our beach, in spite of the tumult and confusion of the time, I want to plead for the wisdom of the past; to pray for respect for the landmarks; to urge that the lessons of our history shall neither be ignored, nor forgotten.

The fathers, in constructing our system, had before their eyes, very recent and very concrete examples of executive tyranny and oppression and they had, too, very exact notions of what was necessary to prevent that tyranny in the future. They had learned from the lives of Pym, and Hampden and Old Noll Cromwell, and not one of the lessons was forgotten when they came to draft the basis of their government in the Constitution they adopted and every reason existing then for its adoption exists now for its preservation.

If we are to continue a government of laws, and not of men, we will preserve every one of its features and hand them to the future unweakened and in full force. The spirit I would have upon you is that of Daniel Webster, when he wrote these words, deposited on the 4th day of July, 1859, in the corner stone of the national capitol at Washington:

"If it shall be hereafter, the will of God, that this structure shall fall from its base, that its foundation be upturned and this deposit brought to the eyes of men, be it then known that on this day the Union of the United States of America stands firm, that their Constitution still exists unimpaired, with all its original usefulness and glory, growing every day stronger and stronger in the affections of the great body of the American people, and attracting more and more the attention of the world. And all here assembled, whether belonging to public life or to private life, with hearts devoutly thankful to Almighty God for the preservation of the liberty and happiness of the country, unite in sincere and fervent prayers that this deposit, and the walls and arches, the domes and towers, the columns and entablatures now to be erected over it, may endure forever.''

So my plea to you this evening is to make practical, the work in which you are engaged as a society. Having rescued the past from oblivion, having spread on your pages the things done by the fathers in their wisdom, let your work, thus done, be the precedent for the future. Wisdom was not born with the present generation—she will not depart with its going. It still stands true that the experience of the past is the safest guide for the future; that an intelligent study of history is the surest road to wisdom in statecraft, in philosophy, in economics. As the engineer places the stakes behind him, that, sighting backward over them, he may correctly determine his course in front, it behooves us, not only, ourselves to take counsel of the records of the past, but to resist, as the height of unwisdom, their disregard by others. Laying on ourselves this burden, let us see to it that your work, and the work of kindred spirits the country over, reaches its fullest fruition in its practical application to the affairs of the present day—in establishing the wisdom that shall safely keep us a Nation, a thousand years.

PRESIDENT'S ADDRESS

Hon. James A. Roberts, LL. D., New York City.

With a presumption worthy of far higher achievement, I attempted a few years ago to give this Association some reasons why in the present limitations of human knowledge, no philosophy of history, that is to say, no rule by which the course of a nation may be foreseen, as the course of the stars, the planets, recurring seasons are foreknown, was possible. Some who doubt the cognizable existence of a philosophy of national history, believe that there does exist a progress or movement in world history which may be reduced to fairly definite rule. Others ably argue that from the nature of things both national and world progress is impossible; that it may reach a certain height but it then subsides, like the waves of the storm-beaten ocean. These claim that the study of the rise and fall of the older nations and civilizations supports their contention. It was the theory of the philosophers, whom we denominate ancient, that, as Vico puts it, "Progress was like the swing of pendulum, perpetually backwards and forwards," or as Aristotle expressed it "Everything is a cycle." It was Plato's belief that human progress in the nature of things is impossible. Machiavelli, whom we are not much accustomed to follow as our guide, philosopher and friend, believed that the world had always contained and would always "contain the same quantity of virtue and vice." Schopenhauer, with an incomprehensible logic, decalred "since the world is eternal, the theory of progress is necessarily false." It is the contention of such writers, that while there may be a more general diffusion of knowledge, more comforts and enjoyments in life now than in the past, we have acquired these at an expense of physical strength, courage and the manly virtues; that briefly expressed, the amount of vitality and capacity stored in a human being is practically uniform from age to age, and if these be expended in mental improvement, just so much has been taken from physical development. As Goethe has summarized it, "Man becomes cleverer and more intelligent, but not better, happier or more effective in action." This theory, so contrary to our conceit and belief in ourselves, that we are heirs of the intelligence and virtues of all the ages, has interested me so far that I would like to consider in the briefest way the foundation upon which it rests and whether such foundation be upon solid ground. To prove the theory historically a comparison is instituted between the mental attainments of today and the accomplishments of the great nations of antiquity, particularly those of the Greeks, both of Greece and Alexandria. The comparison is in a way disquieting, and we must acknowledge that in philosophy, science and art and in the comforts and enjoyments of life, the human race at the beginning of the XIX Century had attained no higher level than that attained by the Greeks more than 2000 years before. One may consistently go farther and assert that the mental attainments and attitude of men and the salient features of their lives one hundred years ago differed less from those presented, for instance, by the Sumerian, Babylonian, Egyptian and Greek nations, than they do from those of today. It will not be inapposite to recall some few of the attainments of these older nations that we may better judge if progress has really been made in the intervening centuries. These older nations, each one, had large libraries inscribed upon clay tablets or on papyrus; their architecture, as shown in their temples and mausoleums, surpassed in grandeur any modern work; they were sculptors, workers in precious metals and even in their plumbing they were not far behind the present time. Heraclitus two thousand years ago promulgated the doctrine of evolution. No significant principle has been discovered in geometry since Euclid; Archimedes knew algebra and he taught that the earth is a ball, that the sun is the centre of the system and that it was the revolution of the earth on its axis that produced the alternations of day and night. Pythagoras had taught the motions of the earth 500 years before Christ. These truths lay as dead for 2000 years. A convex lens was found in the excavated palace of Nimrod, dis-

closing that in that time the microscope was in use. It has been
shown by recent excavations in Accad that Sargon nearly 3000
years before Christ had a system of mail delivery throughout his
kingdom. Who does not acknowledge his debt to that old Pha-
raoh, the father of the novel, whose inventive ingenuity was so
great that, it is said, every story told since his time differs from
his only in circumstances and details but not in its elements. It
was Hero of Alexandria who discovered the principle of the tur-
bine engine, which lay dormant for 2100 years and was only practically applied in our own day. In speculative philosophy and in
art how little progress has been made since the time of Pericles.
Somewhere among the old Greek writers will be found a forecast of almost every great modern scientific discovery, a discussion of almost every great moral problem. Prof. Robinson of Columbia University has recently written, "So abounding is the
intellectual vitality of Plato and Aristotle, so inexhaustible the
range of their speculations, so profound their philosophical pene-
tration, that one who dedicates himself to a study of their works
is apt to feel that all intellectual history since their day is the
record of a degeneration." Of the five great philosophies of life,
evolved by our western civilization, which have been the moral
light and the great support of men down thro' the centuries, four
are of Greek origin, the Epicurean, the Stoic, the Platonic, and
the Aristotelian, and it was only "He that spake as never man
spake" who has offered a better. It is safe to say that no modern
has attempted to lay down a philosophy of life, be it John Stuart
Mill, Herbert Spencer or Mother Eddy, who has not copied or
combined some of these great Greek philosophies. Even Greek
religion, with its deifications of the powers of nature, was truly a
reaching out after God if haply they might find him. It taught
the sweet humanities, the loving kindness of the Supreme Being,
as the false interpretation and perversion of the teachings of
Christ, continued almost to our own times, did not teach them.
Their religion taught the brotherhood of man, the efficacy of
prayer, the value of friendship. It taught that God is a spirit,
that even in this life man can attain to divine communion, and
that the purified soul can enter into full fellowship with the Deity
forever; that the gods were cognizant of every sin, even sinful
thought; that the spirit of piety made the sacrifice acceptable,

however small. The goddess of justice was not a poet's dream. but an actual cult; and who can forget that sublime passage from Oedipus, "Pity sits by the throne of Zeus, his peer in power over all the deeds of men." Pythagoras held that we could not be injured by the anger of the gods, because anger was alien to their nature, and that God has no fairer temple on earth than the pure soul.

It is not strange when one studies the attainments in philosophy, art, morals and religions of these older people, particularly the Greeks, he should feel doubt whether the world has progressed since their day. It may humble our pride to find how profoundly wise those people were, how high their ideals, and how little has been the progress during the 2000 or 3000 years concerning which we have record; nevertheless, it seems to be true that the scholar of today has all the knowledge of these older people with much in addition.

But such a comparison, even if it should be determined that no advance had been made in the last 2000 years, would be far from deciding that man is not progressing. Modern Science has completely upset Archbishop Usher's laborious calculation, that man and all terrestrial animals were created Friday, October 28th, 4004 years before Christ. The evidence is, that man has been an inhabitant of this earth for at least 250,000 years, and, speaking comparatively, Socrates and Plato, and the Pharaohs are not ancients, but almost our contemporaries. There can be no doubt that the man of today is a far higher type than his progenitor of the preglacial period. We do not need to go back with Darwin to the ape to determine that man has progressed. The evidence seems to be fairly certain that for the first 200,000 years of man's existence on this earth, his progress was exceedingly slow. Then some Tubal Cain discovered bronze and progress was given an impetus. At last came the discovery of iron and man may be said to be fairly on his road to higher achievement. So down through the ages progress has not been regular and along lines which could be predetermined, but spasmodic and stimulated to rapid advance from time to time by some great useful discovery.

But it is by no means necessary to admit that the world of today has not progressed far beyond the Greek period. There can be no doubt that the lights of civilization are much more widely diffused than ever before. They have penetrated the dark continents and the farthest islands of the sea and have there introduced the comforts, pleasures, and moralities of civilized life. Not only is the world more generally enlightened than ever before in its history, but there is more of the spirit of human kindness. No better evidence of progress can be found than the widening triumph of justice in humanity. There is a sympathetic fellowship among men of every degree all over the world such as has never existed before; a strong general feeling that none shall be oppressed; that equal and exact justice must be meted out to all. It may be that the deeds of the blackhand and gunmen in our large cities, the atrocities of peonage in Peru, the reported barbarities of the Turkish war, make us doubt for a moment that man has yet emerged from savagery. The prompt and vigorous protest against and denunciation of such acts by the whole civilized world, however, is an evidence of the fact that mankind generally are governed by sentiments of justice and mercy. Contrast with this the fact that it was a rule of war scarcely 300 years ago, that if a city withstood siege but was of its condition. World progress has not been steady, but by fits put to the sword. It is significant that no nation on earth would dare to commit or countenance such a horror today. Again, it is only in modern times that real progress has been made in accumulating and applying knowledge to the relief and betterment of man's condition as a man. Formerly it was the King and nobles, including perhaps what John Adams unfortunately for himself called the well born, for whose special support and delectation the earth and the fullness thereof were supposed to have been created, and the poor unfortunate outside of these higher castes must get along as his own strenuous efforts and fate might decree. I quote again from Professor Robinson,—"The most original and far reaching discovery of modern times is the growing realization of the fundamental importance of common men and common things." We are not without hope that the time is not far distant when arbitration will take the place of war. These seem to me to be the highest possible manifestations of progress.

I have said that there had been more changes in mental ideals and manner of living in the past two centuries than had taken place in the 2500 previous years, and it is undoubtedly so. During those twenty-five centuries if man did not retrograde, he simply marked time. So great is our debt to Grecian philosophy, that it is almost a pleasure to find something in it to kick about. It was Greek philosophy and its adoption by the Fathers of the Christian Church that cast a spell of stagnation over the occidental world. The idea that the contemplative life was the only worthy life to live, and that the common material things of life should be set aside as unworthy of attention, dominated nearly all Greek Philosophy. It was much as Lord Bacon, the great magician who more than any other waved the magic wand which released mankind from its long slumber, says, "They tumbled up and down in their own reason and conceits." Both Plato and Aristotle were firm in the expression of their belief that the common things of life and even the earth itself was unworthy of serious consideration and study. Aristotle in his metaphysics speaks as though all possible practical inventions had long before his time been made. It was the turning of thought and study from the mental and the spiritual to the tangible and material, to causes of natural phenomena, and their effects, that has produced the startling changes of the past two centuries. The great advance in intelligence and in the comfort of living and the rapid spread of civilization over the world must be attributed to that greatest sister of the sisterhood of knowledge, Science; to men like Gutenberg, Watts, Morse, Bell and the hundreds who have aided in the discovery of the wonderful potencies of electricity, from Benjamin Franklin down; to men like Pasteur, the discoverer of the microbe, who without reward except in the gratitude of a world, gave his life to the finding of the means of exterminating disease in men, in animals, in plants;—to men like Berthelot, the intellectual Colossus of our time, who in an equally disinterested spirit, turned aside from his chosen work in organic and synthetic chemistry in which his success had been marvelous, and applied his vast ability and knowledge to the development of scientific agriculture;—to men like Roentgen who has enabled the doctor and the surgeon to look through the human system and locate and diagnose the trouble;—to men like Marconi, who, while not the inventor, has been the practical demonstrator of wireless telegraphy;—to the thousands of scholars all over the world who "scorn delights and live laborious days," in their search after causes and cures, reasons and effects. It is as Berthelot has well said, "Science yields a deeper knowledge of the universe, a new conception of human destiny; today it claims direction at once material, intellectual and moral of society." It is science that has applied knowledge to human needs and comforts, as it never had been before.

The world moves, mankind progresses, but no rule can be formulated which will enable us to forecast its speed or results. It is the human element which prevents our foreseeing world progress as it does national progress. No one can possibly divine what new and far reaching discoveries science will yet bring forth for the further advancement of mankind and the betterment of its condition. World progress has not been steady, but by its and starts. The invention of the art of printing, the harnessing of steam, the taming of that most wonderful servant of man, electricity, have enormously stimulated progress. By these discoveries intelligence and knowledge take the wings of the morning and fly to the uttermost parts of the earth. Buckle says, "The discoveries of genius alone remain; it is to them we owe all that we now have; they are for all ages and all times; they are cumulative, * * * * and they influence the most distant posterity." These discoveries themselves are progressive. They did not spring into existence full grown, but are the ripened product of slow, laborious progress. Unless one can foresee to what greater heights existing discoveries and inventions may be carried, or what new inventions and discoveries may yet be made, how is it possible to foresee what progress may be made in the world?

Some on has said, "It displeases us to be the sport of chance," and that is true. In a way man is the architect of his own fortune, the determiner of his own destiny. It is because we cannot look into the mind of the architect and see what he may plan or build, that we cannot with any degree of assurance foresee along what lines progress will travel. While some basis for calculating the future may be found in the persistency of motive and the permanence of habit in man through succeeding generations, no one can know what changes in motives and habit will be compelled by man's ambition, his constant struggle to know and control his environment, and by some glimpse vouchsafed to him through the eye of genius into nature's secrets. Pascal said that the history of the world would have been different had Cleopatra's nose been of different shape. It is because we cannot control the shape of the nose of genius nor the direction it will take that we cannot foresee the world's progress. We must still be satisfied to let prophecy wait on knowledge.

RELATION OF THE BATTLE OF BENNINGTON TO THE BATTLE OF SARATOGA

Rev. Isaac Jennings, D. D., Bennington, Vt.

That the subject which has been assigned for this paper was chosen by the Committee will absolve the speaker from any charge of local prejudice in its selection, and also from any presumption in presenting to you a theme so well worn; as though he had something new to say on the subject. He wasn't there, nor has he ever seen any body that was.

The evact wording of the subject as given is:—The Relation of the Battle of Bennington to the Battle of Saratoga. By this I understand our subject to be really the Relation of the Battle of Bennington to Burgoyne's Surrender—which occurred on the heights of Saratoga two months after. It shall be my object then to show the effect of this engagement, both upon the mind and plans of the British General, and upon the spirits of our own forces.

To do this I shall ask you to traverse with me some events leading up to this date, that we may better appreciate the frame of mind of the participants when the fatal day came.

On the 25th of May, 1775, the then Brigadier-General Burgoyne first entered Boston harbor, in company with Generals Howe and Clinton, bringing a large reinforcement for the Royal troops, beleaguered in that city. As they approached, the rebel camp was pointed out, in which under the command, each of its own chosen officers, a somewhat motley crowd of militia from the several New England provinces, presented to these tried veterans of Europe anything but a threatening aspect.

SCENES AT BENNINGTON, VT.

Burgoyne could not restrain his well bred contempt for the Americans, as he burst forth, "What! Ten thousand peasants keep five thousand King's troops shut up! Well, let us get in and we will soon find elbow room!" They got in. On the 17th of June following they wished they hadn't. Though they drove those despised rebels back to Cambridge that day, it was a costly job.

On the 3rd of June, two weeks before this battle of Bunker Hill, Captain John Stark, an Indian fighter of some local note, received from New Hampshire a commission as Colonel of the first regiment of foot soldiers raised in his native province, by order of the Congress, for the defence of the American Colonies. That regiment was soon on the way to Boston. They constituted the left wing of the American line at Bunker Hill and protected only by a rail fence stuffed with hay withstood the Welsh fusileers, the finest light infantry regiment in the Boston Army, who, although seven hundred strong in the battle, mustered but eighty-three at the next roll call. If General Burgoyne had any time to make observations and noted the breastwork behind which Stark gave such a good account of himself and his doughty New Hampshire farmers, he may have soon forgotten it, but I suspect he recalled it that sultry 17th of August, 1777, when he first heard from the field of Bennington.

These two men soon went, each his own way, the Colonel to the defences about New York and the General to Canada, where with three men, at least, who were later to become factors in our story—Phillips, Riedesel and Fraser—we find him, far from idle, serving his King.

The intrepid Stark too, who, as a young man, had run the gauntlet of his savage captors, with approval from their aged chief, who had refused to hoe corn, because it was squaw's work, and who had finally bought himself with the price of an Indian pony, with the same disregard of danger to himself, and the same keen eye for defences, soon followed, and we find him at Mount Independence, on the opposite side of Lake Champlain from Ticonderoga, then a forest of ancient trees, marking out and building a fort, which was later to figure in this campaign.

General Burgoyne having spent the summers of '75 and '76 in Canada, and about our lake, conceived the idea of a sally from

Canada, which should put an end to the long drawn out war, and put into active force the project which had been a dream in the King's mind for many days. Soliciting permission to return to England, he set sail in the Apollo frigate, November 5, 1776, amid the prayers of a well wishing army, and we soon hear of him as closeted with the King, in developing the matter. A paper remains to us which he laid before the ministry, doubtless at the King's suggestion, which embodies his plan for this proposed expedition. This plan involved placing in his hands a tried force of about ten thousand men, including some provincials, Indians, and a fine park of artillery, with necessary transports, wagons and horses, and foresters as well as fighters from Canada. His proposition was to proceed by the Lakes Champlain and George, form depots of supplies as he went along, capture Fort Ticonderoga, and, soon penetrating to the Hudson, there to meet a supporting force under St. Leger, which was to be previously despatched by the way of the St. Lawrence, Lake Ontario, Oswego, and the Mohawk, and both soon to form a junction with Lord Howe at Albany. The object of all this, to so separate the northern colonies from their neighbors on the west and south that the country might be conquered piecemeal and the rebellion crushed.

The General's "Thoughts for Conducting the War from the Side of Canada," also included the suggestion of a diversion through "The Grants," now Vermont, and crossing the Green Mountains, to descend the Connecticut River, and by its threatening aspect to terrify the inhabitants win great numbers of hesitating sympathizers, and, perhaps, ultimately carry out his threat of the year before, of showing the Bostonese what the King's troops could really do, if they were led by a General who knew something about it. It is true this last thought was not put into words. The ministry, however, took a different view of it, and cut from this enticing program all this side issue, confining him to the direct path, and they, not the Generals, planned the war and its details, from London.

So much of the plan adopted, the office of Lieutenant General bestowed upon the Brigadier, and troops hired for him from German relatives, which "Cousin Kittie," Russia's Queen, although approached, indignantly refused to supply, he set sail in the early spring of 1777, bearing in his hands a warrant of knighthood for

General Carleton, to salve his wounded feelings if there should be any resentment at being thus superseded in a plan he too had been revolving for some time, as the result of his experiences of the preceding year in this neighborhood,—and landed in Quebec, in May of the eventful year.

General, now Sir Guy Carleton, had everything so advanced and preparations so well made, that a few trifling matters, such as weather and bad roads, unwillingness of the Canadians to respond, and the non-arrival of the ammunition and provision ships, did not delay Burgoyne, for he writes to Lord Germain, that he has enough ammunition to make an effective showing before Ticonderoga, which he understands is "intending to make a stout resistance."

General Burgoyne seems to me to have been a favorite of fortune, up to this ill-starred campaign. His had been many of her choicest and most partial gifts; well born and trained, and favorably married, though somewhat head-strong, and traduced by later enemies, he had won renown on the fields of war, parliament and literature. He wore on his finger a diamond ring, the gift of the King of Spain for gallantry, as he had received the commendation of the Count de Lippe for his bravery at D'Alcantara; his written plays had won attention in the drawing rooms of London and as a carpet knight he had also proved a success. Above all he was the recipient of complimentary recognition from King George the 3rd, who had promised him a red ribbon, perhaps a garter, in case of success in this venture. He was in the prime of his vigor and he naturally felt that this campaign was to blazon his name on the scroll of history.

Ready for his conquering march, or sail and march, he set forth with an army some nine thousand strong, about seven thousand regulars, and as fine a body of men as ever mustered, upon the beautiful lake which separates New York from Vermont at our northern border, and I suppose of all the pageants which had disturbed her pristine quiet, Indian, French or English, none had ever equalled this. The old forests looked down upon a beautiful sight, that lovely June day, as they answered to the notes of his bugles and the waters reflected the scarlet of the coats of his soldiers and the brass of their helmets and armor as well as their banners, which, by the way, were most of them secreted and kept from us at the final surrender.

Thomas Anburey, a Lieutenant in the British service has left us a vivid and careful description of their order of march. "In front the Indians, in their birch canoes, containing twenty to thirty each. The advance corps in regular line came next with the gunboats. Then the Royal George and Inflexible, towing large booms to be thrown across from one point of land to another adjacent to Fort Ticonderoga. With these were the other brigs and sloops following. After these the first brigade in regular line. Then Generals Burgoyne, Phillips, and Riedesel in their pinnaces. Next to them came the Second Brigade, followed by the German Brigade. And the rear was brought up by the sutlers and usual camp followers." They made Cumberland head, their first point. Then to the inflow of the River Bouquet, where they encamped. Here quite a body of Indians joined the expedition, and observing the custom indispensable, Burgoyne made them a bombastic speech, in which he proved a proficient before the campaign was ended, gave them a feast and witnessed the wild antics of their war dance. To this speech, in which he warned them against excesses of scalping, and the indignities of savage attacks upon women and children, they responded expressing their approbation and willing obedience, through their affection for their father over the seas, on which, they said, they had sharpened their hatchets.

Nor was this all; in his over-weening conceit of the terror he was to spread among those peasant pioneers in the wilderness, he issued broadcast in the vicinity an invitation to return to loyalty, to conserve their cattle and corn for the King's forces, for which they should receive pay in coin, and not to burn down the bridges, for should they dare to disobey, he would let loose his savages upon them.

He has left on paper his thought at the time of what lay before him—"A short, sharp resistance at Ticonderoga, I shall beat them; I shall give them no time to rally. We shall soon hear from St. Leger. The panic will be complete. In an eight days walkover, we shall be in Albany. Our task done."

Just before reaching Ticonderoga he made another stirring, if high flown, address to his soldiers, in which he pronounced those fateful words, "This army must not retreat."

From the River Bouquet they came to Crown Point, where they made their first depot, and whence they marched up the lake, the British on the west side, the Germans on the east side and the artillery still on the lake with the commanding officers. Cautiously they approached the famous old French fort, where Ethan Allen, two years before, had as he was wont to do, mixed his patriotism and such religion as he had, when he demanded De-la-Place's sword.

This caution, however, was unnecessary. Somebody had blundered. St. Clair, the commander, did not feel himself sufficiently strong to maintain it, though it was well provided with stores and ammunition, and when he looked out and saw the red coats and some mounted brass pieces looking right down into the fort from Mount Defiance on the south, he planned a night retreat into Vermont. This would have been successful, but somebody blundered again, and a burning house on Mount Independence, on the Vermont side of the lake, lit up the scene and told the enemy of the hasty flight of our troops.

The light infantry of Fraser was soon set in motion, in pursuit, with the Germans, who had come down on the Vermont side of the lake, following close after. Two days later in the morning the battle was joined, at breakfast time, in Hubbardton. It was a sad though brave affair. St. Clair had already made good his escape to Castleton, by way of Hubbardton, sending the sick and wounded and so much of his baggage and provisions by water to Skenesboro as he was able to get away in his hurry. When he passed through Hubbardton, he left behind him three regiments to collect the stragglers and those delayed for any cause, saying he would keep within a mile and a half of them. Francis, Warner and Hale were in charge of these men.

For three hours eight hundred men maintained a gallant and stubborn resistance against the picked soldiers of Burgoyne's army in superior numbers led by the intrepid Fraser, and the victory was almost theirs, when the sound of psalm singing voices, in a language they knew not, rose above the din of battle. It was the Germans under General Riedesel. The day was by these soon decided. Our brave Francis had fallen in the battle—Hale had disappeared with his whole regiment,—later all were taken prisoners,—Warner bore the brunt of the fight so long as he could and then is said to have issued the unusual order—"Take to the woods and meet me at Manchester." Thus met face to face for the first time troops that in a few weeks should meet again under reversed conditions, but they little dreamed of such a thing then. And thus the name of Warner, the pride of his neighbors and the dread of his foes, first became known to the Baron.

But we must go back to the lake. The defenders of the fort had thrown a boom across the lake to prevent the enemy's ships from going above Ticonderoga. Like similar devices employed on the Hudson and elsewhere, the force of the enemy's vessels soon broke down this impediment and in the exultation of the moment were in full pursuit of the ships and batteaux of the flying Continentals.

Overtaken soon, near Skenesboro, these were necessarily destroyed by the Americans, to save them, and they made as good a retreat as possible to the block house, called Fort Ann. Thither Burgoyne pursued them without delay. Our men sallied forth to meet him at once upon his arrival and were almost in possession of the victory, when a surprise from the woods, a flank attack from the Indians with their horrid yells, sent panic amongst the spartan band, and burning the block house they made good their escape to Fort Edward, while Burgoyne with his British troops, who "never retreat," went back to Skenesboro, now Whitehall.

It was rather a tame ending of his scheme of annihilation. But, I fancy he thought the rebels so well scattered and so well scared, it was just as well, for even when the glorious news of the fall of Ticonderoga reached King George, he is said to have burst into his wife's apartments, in his enthusiasm, with the exclamation, "I have beaten all the Americans." Henry B. Dawson says that was where Burgoyne began to be beaten, was indeed morally undone.

Thus we have seen Burgoyne brought up to the point, step by step, where a hardier man than he might be excused if he lost his head. "The fool of fortune," as another has said, "Whose favors he neither knew how to deserve when offered him—nor how to compel when withheld."

Let the conditions to which his planning and successes had brought him speak for themselves. The deserters and stragglers from Hubbardton and Fort Ann had carried exaggerated accounts to every quarter of the sparsely settled lands adjoining the lake and beyond. Settlers were fleeing their cabins and little pitches in the woods, for places farther south. Burgoyne's agents were tampering with and in some cases overthrowing their loyalty. Some put themselves under British protection, and the red flag or cap or mark of a Tory was in evidence. Scores more fled across the mountains spreading consternation as they went. Burgoyne and his Indians were expected guests at almost every fireside within reach. And the memory of those days remained a terror inspirer for years, mothers using it as a threat to quiet rebellious or unwilling children. Many of those who were with the patriot army felt it their first duty to return to their families for their protection.

By a message from Warner to the Convention sitting in Windsor, on the great question of the formation of the State of Vermont, the news of the danger and the demand for help was conveyed,—shortly succeeded by the news of the fall of Ticonderoga,—and the panic seized them,—they were only held in leash by the elements. A thunder storm was presiding at the accouchement of baby Vermont.

But the young state and all to the eastward were practically without military defense. General Schuyler, in charge of operations in the north, did not believe the enemy would come this way, and when apprised of our defenseless condition had replied, "He had forgotten about that."

Warner, however, had not forgotten and he writes again to the Convention that "He should be glad if a few hills of corn unhoed should not be a motive sufficient to detain men at home." This prior to the fall of Ticonderoga. He never got there himself—though he did get to Hubbardton, as we have seen.

Following Hubbardton and the retreat of the remnant of our troops to Fort Edward, and later further south, was the time for Burgoyne to have struck a decisive blow. General Riedesel, who was on this side of the lake and the river, saw this, and suggested it to Burgoyne. But he had troubles of his own then. The retreating army had not left the way behind them in good condition for automobile travel, at all events.

From Skenesboro to Fort Edward was a hard road at best, but especially hard, when every rod of the way must be cleared of heavy trees felled to fill the waters, or block the way. There was a route by Lake George, but the General had said, "The British Army never retreats." So the army had to go over the road their enemies had made all but impassable, while the provisions and baggage and stores of other kinds were carried around by Lake George, and thus transformed to the needs of the workers in forest and morass and by the way. Now was discovered the great need of those wagons and horses promised from Canada, and of those men fitted for such tasks as were just now in exigency, which had never materialized. Do the best they could they could hardly get more than four days' provisions ahead for those who were toiling to make their way to Fort Edward. It was lucky for them that they had the people so badly scared. They sent General Riedesel to Castleton to keep this sense of terror alive. He had with him many unmounted dragoons. It is said he coveted the horses he saw among our thrifty settlers as he looked about.

The Indians (and at this point a new increment of them joined Burgoyne's army from the still more savage Ottawas), who were employed in this region to intimidate and capture where they could, needed to be handled with care, for they were headstrong and irrepressible as well as irresponsible. They exacted full toll from the British, for all they contributed. At length they went the limit, and in the wanton murder of beautiful Miss McCrea, drew down on their heads the censure of the General, though he dared not punish them. But they did more, they awakened all the resistance that could express itself on the part of the natives. Their hostility for the Tories was boundless, for the Indians almost frenzy. Men came to the rescue whom no other call could reach. The appeal of the Council of Safety, sitting in the Catamount Tavern on the hill yonder,* reached into Massachusetts and over beyond the Connecticut. "If we are driven back, the invader will soon be at your doors; we are your buckler and shield. Our humble cabins are the bul-

*Old Bennington.

wiark of your happy firesides. But we can't do it alone; you must help us or we and you later perish.''

To this pitiful appeal the presiding officer of the New Hampshire Assembly, John Langdon, addressing that body, made answer: ''I have three thousand dollars in hard money, my plate I will pledge for as much more, I have seventy hogsheads of Tobago Rum which shall be sold for the most they will bring. They are at the service of the state. If we succeed I shall be remunerated, if not they will be of no use to me. We can raise a brigade and our friend Stark, who so nobly sustained the honor of our arms at Bunker Hill, may safely be entrusted with the command and we will check Burgoyne.'' This was like an electric thrill to that assembly, almost in despair, not knowing which way to turn for means.

Colonel Stark who, stung with the injustice of the Congress in promoting junior officers over him, had retired to his saw-mill and farm, heard their appeal and replied he would undertake the job. He had, wisely or unwisely, no confidence in the commander of the Northern Army, but he would enter young Vermont and hang upon the rear and flanks of the enemy, provided they gave him full authority to direct his own motions and he be accountable to no one but New Hampshire. They accepted his terms. Men flocked to his standard, as they had always done, and he was soon on the way to Manchester, and in a few days was rendezvoused about four miles west of this village,* while he counselled with Warner and the Council of Safety sitting in the Catamount Tavern.

Meanwhile, on the enemy's side, General Riedesel had rejoined the main army at Fort Edward, and all had moved forward to the point where the Battenkill flows into the Hudson. At this point Burgoyne bethought himself of the advice of General Reidesel and requested him to make out a plan of his suggestion, that a diversion be made toward the Connecticut river. This was not exactly General Riedesel's intent, nor was it now in his mind as feasible a thing as it had been before, but he obeyed as he was in duty bound, insisting, so far as he might, that, if such diversion be made, it be simply for the purpose of checking the uprising apparent to the eastward, for financing which astute Ira Allen,

---

*Bennington.

Ethan's younger brother, had worked out a scheme of sequestration.

Burgoyne had not forgotten his long ago plan of a sally toward the Connecticut and Boston. He knew Riedesel's dragoons wanted horses; he had promised them. He also wanted wagons and horses and provisions and Provincials, for the weakening of his main body by the giving up of a few regulars here and there for guards at the points made up to the present, the slowness of the enfeebled provision trains in catching up with him, from the base of supplies now farther and farther behind him, the watchfulness of his enemy in preventing forage and provisions falling into his hands, all made it important that something be done. He was persuaded that the inhabitants this way would not be hostile to him in the main, but if some of them were, he was tempted by the fallacious reasoning that if he could keep the New England troops at home, it would leave St. Leger freer to make his proposed march down the Mohawk. He reflected that he could throw General Fraser across the Hudson to keep Schuyler's attention busy and prevent Arnold's carrying succor either to right or left. He could please the Germans by mounting their dragoons, always a desirable thing. He could provide himself with stores and beef cattle, supposed to be in this vicinity, though on the 13th deputy commissioner Tichenor drove a large body of these cattle to Albany. Of this he knew nothing, however. This move successful would enable him, if he should so decide, to cut loose from his supplies at the rear and to push Fraser forward for a rapid run to Albany. So expecting nothing else but an easy victory if fight they must, and a profitable excursion in any case, and with General Riedesel's suggestion as a basis, he planned an excursion on paper to Arlington, Manchester, over the mountain to Rockingham, down the Connecticut, and back again by the main road to Albany, perhaps covering his real design.

This would in some sense enable him to do what he had always wanted to do and not offend against his positive orders from London. It was to go into a reputed Tory stronghold; it promised everything desirable and offered very little that was undesirable. On paper it was a brilliant coup. Had it worked out as planned it would have passed for the stroke of the campaign.

These orders were given in detail and great completeness to Lieutenant Colonel Baum of General Riedesel's command, to execute, and he was set on his way with a corps of Riedesel's unmounted dragoons as a nucleus, a company of sharpshooters, a corps of Provincials, a body of Canadian rangers, one hundred and fifty Indians and two cannon, with Hanau artillerists. He had not gone far when he was overhauled and ordered to get to Arlington by the way of Bennington, where it was reported there was a storehouse of provision and cattle and wheel carriages. There was also a Council of Safety sitting there and only a few raw militia to defend the place. The outcome might be more than he dared to hope. He hadn't much respect for our peasant soldiers.

Baum too had imbibed the contempt of his master for these same soldiers, in their hunting shirts and armed only with their fowling pieces. His first advance met with nothing more difficult than poor roads and ignorance of the way.

Burgoyne, however, for some reason, possibly the lack of enthusiasm of his advisers in this move, or, it may be native caution, made expected success doubly sure by providing a support in the nature of Colonel Breyman's regiment of German troops to follow at a moment's notice, and retired to ponder on the glory which this stroke would add to his expedition, and count up the horses and provisions he expected as a result. So confident was he of a successful outcome that on the very day of the battle a bridge had been thrown across the Hudson and the army received orders to proceed on their march to Albany the following morning.

It was too bad to waken him so early, but he had to be told, despite the encouraging despatches Baum had sent him thus far on the way, that there were many more men at Bennington than he supposed and his eight hundred could not cope with them. Word was sent to Breyman to march at once. He was slow about getting off. Slower about his advance, lost his way and finally reached his destination only to find Baum and all his men in the hands of the rebels, those despised farmers. They had not thought of meeting both Stark and Warner here. One were enough, but when we add to both of these some thousand more, every one of whom Stark's own words called, "the equal of an Alexander or a Charles the 12th," they had nothing to do, after fighting brave-

ly, but lay down their arms, and fly as well and as fast and as
many of them as could. That about one thousand of them never
returned to Burgoyne's army, had an effect upon the effectiveness
of that army at Saratoga.

There is not time to go into the details of this battle, so familiar. Stark said, "In this action I think we have returned the
enemy a proper compliment for their Hubbardton engagement."
But what Burgoyne thought about it is more to our point.

Following Breyman's departure from the camp, upon his orders to succor Baum, Burgoyne had crossed the Battenkill and advanced along the way to give aid, if necessary. He had not heard
from St. Leger at Fort Stanwix, as yet. But he heard from him
soon. It was too late. He too was on the run, defeated and out-
done. Arnold had sent succor there despite Burgoyne's reasoning. Two such reverses rarely fall out of a clear sky on one man
within so short a time of each other. He felt that, right and left,
he was beset, and behind too, and he was right, for he soon found
Vermont troops were harrassing him on flank and in rear. His
base of supplies was in danger. The forts he had taken and magazines he had planted were either retaken or threatened. He
heard nothing from the succor he was to receive from the front,
and on which all this movement so greatly depended. He was
learning that no dependence could be placed on the Indians and
little on the Provincials. Indeed, the misleading encouragement
he had received from their leaders had cost him dear on this
Bennington diversion.

But even all this was not the worst of it, bad as it was. The
affair at Bennington had been like the harbinger of a glorious
sunrise to the country. Washington had written to Schuyler in
the dark days just before. "Though our affairs for some days past
have worn a dark and gloomy aspect, I yet look forward to a fortunate and happy change. I trust General Burgoyne's army will
meet, sooner or later, an effectual check and that the success he
has had will precipitate his ruin. From your accounts he appears to be pursuing that line of conduct, which, of all others, is
most favorable to us. I mean acting in detachment. Could we
be so happy as to cut off one of these, supposing it should not exceed four, five or six hundred men, it would inspirit the people
and do away with much of their present anxiety." This was July

CHALYBEATE SPRINGS, 1787, (NOW HIGH ROCK SPRING)
From Columbian Magazine, March, 1787
Courtesy of Frank J. Wilder

UNION HALL, LATER GRAND UNION HOTEL, (Circa 1840)
Courtesy of Frank J. Wilder

22nd. He did not designate any dates, but, Bennington responded by cutting off double that number on the 16th of August, and
on the 22nd St. Leger started back for Oswego, leaving everything behind him, even the tents standing and the artillery in the
trenches. When Washington heard of Bennington, he regarded it as deciding the fate of Burgoyne and dismissed from his
mind all further anxiety about this invasion. Madam Riedesel,
in her account of the affair,—you know she accompanied her husband in this campaign and so did several others of the officers'
wives.—"Why! They thought this expedition only a kind of pleasure excursion, when they began it, hence brought their families
along, but by this time, she was inferring differently, and says:—
"By Baum's failure the army was prevented from advancing.
This unfortunate affair caused a sudden cessation of all our operations. Our boats, provisions, in fact nothing was received from
Fort George. The army therefore could not advance further and
the despondent spirits of the enemy became so elated that its army
grew daily stronger. Its numbers, which at the beginning of August did not exceed four or five thousand strong,—meaning by
that Schuyler's entire force—now increased to between fourteen
and twenty thousand." While her husband in a letter to Charles
of Brunswick, his ruler, explaining the affair, denied that he advised it, but pathetically includes in his report, the fact that, "of
the dragoons who left here one hundred and fifty men strong, only
seven returned." And a German correspondent from Riedesel's
army writes to friends at home: "This affair was to us a severe
blow. It caused us to halt in the midst of a successful march. The
magazine at Bennington escaped our outstretched hands; and we
were obliged to fall back upon our stores of flour and salt meat,
stored at Fort George. It was August. The hottest time of the
year. The dysentery was also causing fearful havoc among us.
And nothwithstanding it all, we were obliged to work like beavers, since the very life of our army depended upon it. Enough
time was gained by the enemy, by their lucky coup at Bennington,
to allow three brigades to join them. The farmers left their
plows, the blacksmiths their anvils, the shoemakers, tailors, etc.,
their several vocations and came as volunteers. Meanwhile General Arnold was sent against Colonel St. Leger, who was on the
point of capturing Fort Stanwix. While the report that our entire

army had been defeated at B— caused him to raise the siege and return to Oswego.''

But to Burgoyne it was the saddest blow. In his defence he says:—''The circumstances of the action at Bennington established a yet more melancholy conviction of the fallacy of any dependence upon supposed friends. The noble Lord Germain has said that I never despaired of the campaign before the affair at Bennington—that I had no doubt of gaining Albany in as short a time as the army, in due condition of supply, could accomplish the march. I acknowledge the truth of the assertion in their fullest extent, all my letters at the time show it. I will go further and in one sense apply with the noble Lord the epithet 'fatal' to the affair at Bennington. The knowledge I acquired of the professors of loyalty was 'fatal' and put an end to every expectation from enterprise, unsustained by dint of force. It would have been excess of frenzy to have trusted for sustenance to the plentiful region of Albany. Had the march thither been unopposed, the enemy finding the British army unsupplied would only have had to compel the Tories to drive off the cattle and destroy the corn and the capitulation of Albany instead of Saratoga must have followed.''

In these last words we have a frank admission of the workings of the brave General's mind. At Bennington he was convinced of that which he had refused to believe before that, not only were the Indians no use, but a detriment to him, but that his hitherto cherished hope, that he might expect something from those we call Tories was an ignis fatuus—a pipe dream. To find that out was, under the conditions, to find out that his days were numbered, no matter where the end came. He was reduced in numbers, not over thirty-five hundred or four thousand effective men crossing the Hudson with him. He was deserted, as we have seen, by his Indians and most of his Canadians and Provincials. He heard nothing from the south and report from St. Leger only heightened the gloom. There were only three days' provisions, short allowance, on hand. He was beset on his flanks, his depots behind him were also beset by men released from guarding stores here*. The army ahead was daily growing in numbers; you say, he delayed nearly a month! He had to, failing in the supply

*Bennington.

he expected from Bennington and vicinity. He must bring it up from the rear as best he could, lacking both horses, wagons and men. Do you ask why didn't he make another attempt in this region, as might have been expected? He tells us himself in words that mean even more than they say: "The great bulk of the country is undoubtedly with the Congress," and adds, "The Hampshire Grants in particular, a country unpeopled and almost unknown in the last war, now abounds in the most active and rebellious race on the continent, and hangs like a gathering storm on my left."

Burgoyne had now fair proof that hunting shirts and shot guns might have heart enough back of them to storm entrenched foes, and drive from their breastworks the tried warriors of countries that made a trade of war and trafficked in such murderers; that they who have been stung to the quick by insult haeped upon insult, and threat added to threat, could and would defend their wives and little ones, their homes and firesides against all the minions of the King.

But he was in a sore dilemma, there was the order, perhaps the garter, awaiting him if he went on, probably the royal displeasure if he went back. He had said, "This army never retreats," and good reason for it now. Lincoln, with Warner and his men, was, with others, between him and his Canadian embarking place. General Riedesel advised him to try it. Fraser was far advancing—he did not know that he was going to his death. Phillips was non-committal. They crossed the Hudson. They hoped for an attack from Gates, who now had superseded Schuyler in command. Gates knew as well as Burgoyne that he, Burgoyne, was on his last legs, that he had only to bide his time, when he should receive his sword. Burgoyne, defeated already, delayed, hesitating to hear the doomful word. He put up a bold front at Freeman's Farms and then delayed some more. Then backed up a little, then engaged the foe again, or had to, albeit with the desperation of despair, and then trying a ruse was out-witted, and fled in the night, only to run up against Stark once more, in possession of the ford that he must cross to reach Fort Edward. Then changing his plan he proposed to continue on the west side of the river, and, reaching another ford above, return, but learned that some of these same Hampshire Grants men he so much dreaded

had possession, and there was nothing to do but capitulate, which he did, and the glorious army which nine thousand strong had sailed up the lake in all the glory of June, now that the autumn frosts had touched the leaves, with bared heads laid down their arms at Saratoga, some distance from Albany, and took up their enforced march for Boston, as Burgoyne had all along wanted to do, under other conditions.

Now what did it all mean? The results of this victory can scarcely be overestimated. It was due to this, that the numbers of the British forces which could fight on the west side of the Hudson were less by at least a thousand, probably fifteen or eighteen hundred, than they would have been, and of a body of men, of many of whom Burgoyne said to Baum, "Always bear in mind that your corps is too valuable to let any considerable loss be hazarded." It was due to this that they had to fight hungry, when they did fight, and surrender at discretion. While the knowledge was gradually percolating their intelligence that even New England peasants with their fowling pieces and scarcely a bayonet could and would storm intrenchments, against chosen men from all the British regiments, a thing not known before, and, moreover win the victory, a defeated army, over a body of veterans flushed with a series of successes. It was inspiration indeed for the anxious Continentals. Men of all classes flocked to the standard of the Congress. The Provincials in Burgoyne's army, the Canadians and the Indians slunk away. "The latter scalped no more after Bennington."

"Mount your dragoons and send me thirteen hundred horses, seize Bennington, Council of Safety and all. Cross the mountains, try the affections of the country, take hostages, meet me a fortnight hence at Albany," ordered Burgoyne—"Aye, Aye, Sir," responded Baum. He writes on the head of a barrel that it is being done. He sends back for more help in a few hours. A few more hours and he is dying in the humble cottage of a Vermont peasant, his troops on the way to Massachusetts and his Provincials led two by two with rope attachments, to the meeting house on the Green in Old Bennington, prisoners. "Thus," says the Connecticut Courant of the day, "was the seed sown of all the laurels Gates reaped during the campaign." This achievement of Stark emboldened the Green Mountain rangers to infest and break up Burgoyne's communications with his depots of provisions, and threw them into a month of practically enforced idleness, so far as active operations were concerned, from August 16th to September 19th, and in the end prevented as we have seen, his escape to Canada.

False rumors flew thick and fast at the time, as at all such times, but they added to the conditions which compelled Burgoyne's surrender. They were the outcome of this battle. Butler says:—"A handbill was published in Boston within a week, with an exaggerated account of Stark's victory. The criers announced it on the streets and the church bells pealed it from their belfries." By skillful use of the same, Fort Stanwix saw its besiegers no more and the announcement that Burgoyne had been taken at Stillwater was only by a short time premature. Bennington was indeed "fatal"!

Nor is this all, if the colonies thought they saw Burgoyne's finish in this defeat, yes, even the King's ultimate defeat, no less so did our friends abroad, for we had them in England and on the continent. At least, it was plain if England was to crush the rebellion over here they must fight a continent which would rob its cradles and its graves before it would give in. "Lord North," as another man said, "owned it and grieved in his blind old age, that he had not followed his convictions." Edmund Burke was for making terms at any price when Saratoga had shaken hands with Bennington. Charles Fox said, "The ministers know as little how to make peace as war." The Duke of Richmond and the historian Gibbon, both of whom had cast their votes hitherto against us, now agreed that America was lost. While the King of France told Franklin, who had long been suing at his doors for aid, that a fleet should soon sail for our shores to stay with us until the war was done.

It was four years, it is true, before Cornwallis, on the plain of Yorktown, followed Burgoyne's example at Saratoga, but the handwriting on the wall was put there at this time. Outsiders saw it, we saw it ourselves, and today as we, the descendants and heirs of those heroes, recount our numberless blessings, comforts and luxuries they never dreamed of, we may not neglect the thought that we whom only an imaginary line divides, in these facts of our history have an indissoluble bond, which ought to draw us closer together for the profits of the present and the promises of the future.

A PLEA FOR THE CLOSER RELATIONSHIP
OF HISTORICAL SOCIETIES

Eugene W. Lyttle, Ph. D., Albany.

Historical societies have not been brought up. Like Topsy in Uncle Tom's Cabin they have "just growed." In some cases, their origin has been largely social; in others, scholastic; in all cases they have been fostered by local pride and local patriotism. The very impulses that have created historical societies have for the most part kept them from hearty co-operation. The native of Vermont claims the Bennington memories for Vermont. He dislikes to share these revolutionary glories with New York. And we have heard historians of New York State claim Bennington both geographically and historically with more pertinacity than their forefathers of revolutionary days displayed in claiming Vermont State.

Is there any hope then that closer relationships between historical associations may be fostered when the very mainsprings of their being are local and often antagonistic? Can the "clan" spirit in historical societies be overcome? If the "clan" spirit can be subdued, will not the most powerful incentives supporting local associations be dangerously weakened? Essentially this is the same question in miniature, that confronted the fathers assembled in convention to draw up our national constitution. May the answer be as fortunate. To establish a closer relationship between historical societies two things are needed: intelligent leadership; some common purpose. Now intelligent leadership may be had through state associations, such as ours, possibly also through the American Historical Association; it may be supplemented greatly by official recognition from the State, such as the State of New

York inaugurated when it established the office of State Historian. A common purpose also must be clearly discerned, and happily it may be found in the very structure of our local associations. Without doubt that purpose should be to create in the young people of the land an historic sense.

It is not enough that our local societies cherish and maintain the social pride of a community, valuable though that be; it is not enough that they look carefully after local records and local landmarks, valuable and essential as that work is. The fostering of local pride and the preservation of local records should be only a means to the dominating purpose, the establishment of an historic sense in the youth of the land.

To be explicit, for over fifty years, ever since public free schools were established, we have been studying history in our schools, the history of the United States; but we have not been learning history. We have been learning text books of history, we have been storing our minds with historic facts that were so much useless lumber in the mind. The characters of history have been vague and unreal to the children, they have been as shadowy and unreal, yes even more shadowy and unreal than such mythical heroes as Hercules and Ulysses. The events of history have had little meaning. Often they have not been associated with any given locality nor with any period of time. Often children have gone through the schools without developing much true historic sense. Roughly speaking the children and youth classify events as occurring before they were born or since. So far as they are concerned Abraham the father of Isaac was contemporary with Abraham Lincoln. Some times they get the two characters mixed. Not even the small aid that might be gained from geography and map study is not used by teachers in making history concrete and real; so we need not be surprised when the boy writes in examination that "Jacques Cartier sailed up the St. Lawrence River, entered Chesapeake Bay and landed where New York City now stands."

It is a well accepted maxim of teaching that the teacher should proceed from the concrete to the abstract; from the known to the related unknown. Teachers of history and text books of history in practice have done otherwise. They have proceeded from the abstract and the general to the particular and concrete, from

the absolutely unknown to something that is to the pupil the unrelated unknowable. Beginning with some unknown past, these
teachers of history and these books of history have started down
the ages to the present, but generally they have never arrived.
In the opening chapter of Knickerbocker's History of New
York this practice of the ordinary teacher of history has been
well satirized. Now it is absolutely impossible to really teach history by this method. The child may learn some history in spite of
our teaching; usually what he does learn is the words of the book
without much real sense of their meaning. Hearing of the cotton
gin, which he has never seen, he associates it closely with the gin
mill which he has seen. He must interpret the past by what he
sees in the present, if he takes the trouble to interpret at all. We
laugh at the Dutch artist who painted in his picture of the cruci-
fixion Roman soldiers with pipes in their mouths; yet he was only
making one of the many similar mistakes that every one makes in
learning history. The Dutch artist possibly had never seen soldiers who did not smoke.

In brief, the point is this. History to be learned must be
learned by the imagination. We all in our early years and many
of us in our later years imagine the past from what appears in
the present. But the imagination of the child cannot be cultivated or strengthened by the study of words and sentences. It
needs concrete things. The child learns from a book that his
forebears ate out of trenchers, and may recite the words glibly
enough without in the least understanding their meaning. But
show him the trencher in a museum, show him the rough table on
which it sat and the rough hewn benches beside it, show him
some of the garments that the early settlers wore, some of the
tools they used, the guns with which they fought, the rude pestle
with which they crushed their corn, and his imagination will proceed by leaps and bounds to reconstruct past life and people it
with real men, women and children.

Now it is a most proper function and purpose of an historical
society to bring those concrete materials of history to the notice of
school children and school teachers, to make this material available by arranging it in some sort of historic sequence and order,

A VIEW OF THE CONGRESS SPRING IN THE VILLAGE OF SARATOGA

a thing seldom done by any historical society. Relics are jumbled together in such fashion, mixed with such collections of bric a brac, old laces, old china, geological specimens, natural history collections, etc., that looking for a lesson in an historical museum is to the teacher with a class of youngsters about as dismaying as the proverbial search for a needle in a haystack.

Again it is or should be the function of historical societies to cultivate interest in local history by pageants, by competitive contests among pupils on historical topics of local interest, by rewards for finding things of historic significance, by making collections of pictures to supplement collections already possessed. The Fourth of July, now that we have abolished the noisy firecracker and the noisome pistol, belongs to historical societies. The birthdays of Washington and Lincoln are also theirs to use for the public good.

But why all this trouble? Because we teachers need your help in teaching history; because in a large way and in a true way history cannot be learned at all unless like charity it begins at home; because an historical sense and an historical understanding needs to be developed among our people in a degree to which it never has been developed. It is not too much to say that our national safety depends in no small measure on the success of the history teacher; for as a people we are terribly lacking in historic sense and historic understanding. We know very little history in spite of our much teaching and many books, and what little history we do know, we do not know how to use.

This statement sounds unpatriotic and derogatory, but isn't it true that the American people lack historic understanding? Historic feeling we may have in abundance, in an overabundance sometimes; but how about historic understanding and historic appreciation? We look at the statue of Gen. Stark and admire the courage and faith in the right that characterized the man. But do we feel that General Starks are needed now just as much as then as district attorneys, as health officers, as judges on the bench. We admire the courage of those patriots who struck down the tyranny of George III., and in almost every city of the land we have allowed some corporate tyranny or tyrannies to lay taxes upon us which we never vote.

We despise the treachery of an Arnold, but we do not see an Arnold in every man who sells his vote or an arch enemy in every man who buys a vote.

We know that the great empire of Rome, the greatest historic creation of ancient times, fell before the attacks of ignorant barbarians who came down upon her with irresistible hordes faster than they could be assimilated. In a somewhat different way, but inspired by a common greed, we are inviting hordes of the half civilized to occupy our fair land and seize the birthrights of our children.

Do we not lack historic sense and application? History, our own history, twice tells the tale of what happens when a people debases its currency. After the Revolution, and again after the Civil War we did this. Yet it is not twenty years since we engaged in a political campaign to determine whether it were not better to deliberately commit the same folly again, and it is even rumored that the people had to be persuaded not to be foolish a third time by "ways that were dark and tricks that were vain."

Today we have nearly completed the greatest work of engineering the world has ever seen. The eyes of greedy nations are turning toward Panama, yet as a people we haggle over the price of an extra war vessel or two and over the cost of an adequate navy.

There lies on our western coast the fairest unoccupied or partly occupied portion of the globe. The eyes of starving Asiatic millions are on this land and only an ocean Broadway lies between; all history tells us what happens or what always has happened under similar circumstances; yet we refuse to avoid danger by vigorous preparations to meet it. Forsooth the Congressional Pork Barrel is of more importance than adequate military preparation.

The fact is that the youth of Sparta had a better historic sense than the American boy. He learned his history not from books but in the barracks and from the voices of his elders. Today the greatest nation of Europe teaches its boys history in much the same practical way. The greatness of Germany today in every line of endeavor is in one degree the result of this practical historical training.

Now this is not the time nor is this the place to argue for military training in our public schools. Possibly few of us would agree that such a step is desirable; but putting this aside, we may learn from the Germans to make history concrete and real by giving much attention as Germans do, to historic excursions, and to the obvious concrete historic material that lies at our very doors.

WHAT AMERICA OWES THE VERMONTERS

Hon. William S. Bennet, LL. D., New York City.

In assessing the debt due from our common country to any one of its members, or any particular portion of it, we inevitably meet with difficulty. Each member of the nation is for so many things indebted to the nation as a whole, that when one speaks of the debt of the country due a particular State, he ought rather to speak of it as a contribution of the State toward the notion's highest good. In discussing Vermont, its past, its present and its future in relation to the country at large, I prefer indeed to refer to it as a large contributor rather than as in any sense an exacting creditor.

It is impossible to discuss Vermont at all without alluding to the respects in which her early history differs from that of all the other colonial States. In these days when the right of the people to rule is being brought before the public rather prominently it is interesting to recall that while the other States relied upon royal charters as the basis of their power, the State of Vermont defied the asserted rights of two and at times three colonies basing their claims upon royal charters, and that the sturdy citizens of Vermont based their claim to rule upon the solidarity of the people and their willingness to fight for the rights, which in the end, through struggle, they did obtain. I have come to believe that those long years of struggle against New York, New Hampshire, Massachusetts, the Continental Congress, Great Britain, the French and the Indians gave to the earlier population of Vermont the cohesiveness of interest and purpose and a like shaping of desire, which created in the State the real distinctiveness of existence which usually pertains only to a nation. Of the old stock, at least, it could be said, once a Vermonter always a Vermonter, and that wherever one went, as many did go, he carried with him toward all that was susceptible to influence and power an extra-territorial portion of Vermont.

The large contribution of Vermont to the progress of the nation has been good citizens. Other States point, and justly, in far greater measure to contributions of the mine, the field, the factory and the forest, but no State can claim a larger contribution of men and women of the best sort to the citizenship of the whole country. Vermont has furnished not only men but leaders in religion, in finance, in statesmanship and in business; Vermont has furnished the men who have been successful. I do not regard this as at all accidental. The healthfulness of your mountains and the necessity for toil gave them strong bodies. The contests of their ancestors for the maintenance of their personal and property rights gave them self-reliance, and the negotiations with the Colonies, the Congress and the English carried on by practically the whole people gave them unrivalled training and diplomacy and the arts both of persuasion and assertion. Religion too was widespread in the State and took its proper place as the foundation of character upon which the sturdy citizens built. Today out of every one hundred born in Vermont, forty are bearing their share of the world's burdens and winning more than their share of the world's successes in places other than Vermont. This is but a portion of your past and but the beginning of your present. These royal Vermonters take with them, not only the strong body and the fine mind, but they have dared to take with them and to maintain the ideals of all that is best in America's past. Materialistic as our age is said to be, the genuine Vermonter leads us all because he is not ashamed to remember the things of the spirit. You have never forgotten the band of daring patriots who secured the surrender of a British fort upon the warrant of their belief that righteousness and justice were with their cause and that they needed no other authority. To my thinking the value of the knowledge of that high spirit handed down as it has been from father to son outweighs by far even the material value of Allen's bold and successful exploit. It was this same spirit that led the Council of Safety to organize the riflemen of Vermont into that little army, which in conjunction with General Stark's New Hampshire brigade fought the decisive battle of Bennington on August 16, 1777. It was given to Vermont then to contribute probably more substantially, though less conspicuously, to the advance of the American cause than even at Ticonderoga. Competent historians maintain that the blow he received at Bennington was the beginning of the defeat of Burgoyne which culminated at Saratoga.

Not only through the men that have gone out from Vermont to make their homes in other States have you been a contributor to the progress of the nation, but in those who have remained behind. No other State has ever been as careful as Vermont in the selection of those who represented her in high office, and no other State has been as intelligently and steadfastly faithful to her representatives. Elsewhere the public servant on occasions found his constituency fickle, uncertain, at times ungrateful and lacking in discernment; but Vermont, following the wise custom that it established in the long service of its first Governor, has recognized that those who serve the public are, after all, but human, and that the knowledge that good service will be rewarded by continued service will in itself from the first bring out the best that is in a representative. By its policy of staunchly standing by its representatives it has not only secured for the State a place of continued importance and power in the councils of the nation, but has given to the nation the invaluable service of men who knew that so long as they stood for the right as they saw it, their constituents though they might not fully agree with them would yet remember that a representative is not a mere echo but owes a duty to the country he serves to give it the best that his independent and uninfluenced judgment dictates.

In no one single particular has Vermont been a larger contributor to us all than through the service which we have had from the men whom she has so staunchly continued in the councils of the nation.

Upon every point which I have so far touched except mere historical recitals, the past and the present of Vermont have merged. The future of a State, as of an individual, is a matter of absolute speculation. I have always disputed the right of any other to put himself in the place of omniscience in predicting the future of an individual. There is somewhat less of assurance in predicting the future of a community which for a long term of years has maintained its traditions. It would be idle, however, to say that the Vermont of the present is precisely the Vermont of the past. No State can for a long series of years lose from its citizenship 40 per cent., and this from the young and the vigorous, and remain the same. As Americans we must face facts. We must face the fact that among the Vermonters of today there are fewer of the young and more of the old. That because of the increase in manufacturing industries while the percentage of foreign born populations is not greatly changing, the stock is, and that the hills and valleys once peopled almost exclusively by the Anglo-Saxon are now the birthplace of Americans of Italian ancestry. Will these citizens of a sunnier blood maintain the traditions and respect the ideals of the days that are gone? The answer to that question is for Vermont to make and not the Italian. If you will teach him by precept and example the value of your traditions and of your ideals, he will respect, cherish and maintain them. If you yourselves become ashamed of them, he will not even learn them, but there are no ideals or traditions spiritually too high to be taught to a race which followed Garibaldi through blood and bitterness to a united Italy.

There is need also for those ideals. A purely materialistic age perishes. It is only the things of the spirit which continue from generation to generation. In the scheme of national conservation it has been the function of Vermont to produce the man to mold the material more than the material to mold the man. There is no reason why this high function exercised now by Vermont for nearly a century and a half should not continue to be her chief function. You have everything which your fathers had, and in addition, the knowledge of their success. You have their traditions for your inspiration, their health-giving mountains, their spiritual surroundings and the knowledge that upon Vermont lies the responsibility of continuing that intellectual and spiritual leadership which has distinguished her in the sisterhood of States.

THE PLACE OF SARATOGA IN THE REVOLUTIONARY WAR

Hon. Andrew S. Draper, LL. B., LL. D., Commissioner of Education of the State of New York.

The foreplanning which arranged that this meeting of the New York State Historical Society should be held at Saratoga, and provided for the discussion of all phases of that New York campaign in the Revolution which culminated at this place with such decisive triumph for the patriot arms, was patriotically and thoughtfully done. In thus illustrating the doings of our fathers and portraying to some extent the cost of our institutions, we are doing quite as much as we can do in any other way to help on popular education. It is really a very great pleasure, a sort of patriotic holiday, to turn from the routine and details of the Education Department, and revel in that unparalleled and inspiring inheritance which we of the State of New York have in both the civic and military history of the American Revolution.

The preliminary situations, the strategy, the fighting, the heroisms, the chivalry, and the tremendous results of the battle of Saratoga, are fascinating to all students of history, and enticingly so to all lovers of America. My pencil would skip across the pages if it were to trace Britain's comprehensive plan of campaign and the vehement opposition of the patriots; if it were to follow the deliberate, haughty, grim advance of Burgoyne from the North; if it were to chuckle over the failure of Sir Henry Clinton to come up from the lower Hudson; if it were to glory over the scattering of St. Leger and his Indians by those gallant old Dutchmen, Nicholas Herkimer and Peter Gansevoort, with a handful of regulars, supported by the doughty farmers of the Mohawk valley; and if it were to celebrate the fast gathering of more farmers, the gallant earnestness of other regular troops, the untiring sagacity and the sure-shooting of Daniel Morgan and his riflemen, the voluntary and perhaps the frenzied soldiership of Benedict Arnold, and the overgenerous moral support and magnanimous chivalry of Philip Schuyler, which, taken together, and in spite of the meanness and cowardly stupidity of Gates, forced, for the first time, a British army to ground its arms to Continental troops.

But the affair to which I am invited to make a contribution is no such hilarious revel. My task here is to measure the importance of Saratoga in the American Revolution and therefore in the revolutionary history of the world. No one will doubt the difficulties of doing that in a brief paper, for it can not be done without a serious study of all the leading men and the large events associated with the Revolution, in the fields of politics, of diplomacy, and of battle, or without a good understanding of the subsequent influence of American independence upon the progress of constitutional freedom in America and throughout the world. But happily we may avoid details and we may ignore the common disputes over minor facts. We are to discern the main events upon a widespread field and see which looms the largest in forcing culminations and in creating law and security and opportunity in the world.

A moment or two for a foreword will not be misspent. Doubtless it was settled when the stars were hung in the heavens that a new and independent nation would be compounded in America, but it had to come about through thinking and doing, by occurrenees and events. And it is hard to realize the differences and dissensions among men and women and the minor happenings that give trend to vital history, when it is set forth so glibly on a few pages in a book.

The English masses knew little and cared little about men and events in America. The colonists were not at all united in wishing independence. The common people of England and America were homogeneous enough. It is quite true that there had been much contention and not a little fighting among the nations of the Old World about their possessions in the New World, and there had been more or less maneuvering about governmental relations and the royal prerogatives, and there had been abuses which had stirred protests, but nothing occurred to make an armed resistance inevitable until the King put away the judicial and patriarchal attitude of the crown, became an unscrupulous partisan, manipulated Parliament, and toyed with the rights and freedoms of English subjects without the actual knowledge of the English people.

Only a half dozen years before the accession of George the Third the northern colonies had held a convention at Albany to form a union to fight the Indians without any thought of revolutionary issues with the mother country; and only a year or two before his accession Yankee continentals and English grenadiers and Scotch highlanders had marched and died together to make sure that the British power and the great things that it stood for should long be dominant in the government of America. In a half dozen years after he became king, this unscrupulous, half-educated politician had stirred a revolt in America which compelled his complete recession, and in fifteen years, learning nothing by experience, he had forced a revolution which recession could not placate and arms could not suppress.

In his long reign of sixty years this head of the English Church and boss in English politics had plenty of time to go stark mad, and the subtle processes which brought the noble Empire nearer to overthrow than she ever was before or ever has been since were amply sufficient to make him so. But until long after his throne had lost its noblest possessions, his mind was as keen and methodical as his purposes were groveling and insatiable. Determined that the saying of his father that ''Ministers are the real kings'' should no longer be true, and intent upon ruling as well as reigning, he drove the strong men, including the great Chatham, from his cabinet and assumed the personal direction of the affairs of his kingdom. Ignorant of the mighty undercurrents of English history and the stubborn virtues of his people, his conception of government could go no further than the dominance of a clique, and his methods for assuring that could not rise above bribing the vices which create the only vital needs for exercising the forces of government at all. He bought boroughs; was up at daybreak to scan the tally sheets of the votes in Parliament on the night before; and carried his ends by favor, patronage, and money. And the ends he carried forced the dismemberment of his kingdom. Lecky has said that the course of George the Third, during the latter part of the American war, "was as criminal as the acts which brought Charles the First to the scaffold."

His ends were certainly idle and his methods ran amuck in America. The English colonies in New England were peopled by as true Englishmen as England ever had. They had come from the northeastern counties where faith was refined by persecutions and martyrs grew in the natural order. The Dutch of New York had inherited somewhat less severe views of life, rather more aptness at commercial progress, and just as hardy character, with quite as strong a love for liberty and for learning, from a people who, through valorous experiences, had developed these qualities in pre-eminent degree. Hardly less may be said of all the other people in the thirteen colonies of Great Britain in America. Of course there were good and bad, learned and unlearned, industrious and shiftless, among these people, but, all in all, they were the most homogeneous, unselfish, and aspiring believers in God and lovers of liberty in the world. Life in the remote wilderness, encompassed by dangerous beasts and savage men, had given edge and point to the great attributes they brought across the sea. The great body of them met all the demands of the new manner of life with unsurpassed acuteness, and their exceptional men responded to the highest demands of intellectual, civic, and military leadership with genuineness, adroitness and forcefulness that have surprised the great men of the world. There was hardly a man among them who could not manage a boat, test all the qualities of a horse, or get the utmost out of the possibilities of a rifle and when it came to statecraft and diplomacy, their leaders showed that there was nothing wanting. And not I alone but the leading English writers of English history say that these people saved English freedom against this English king.

When he and his clique pushed their demands and asserted their control across the lines that had been established in the great charters of English liberty, it was natural that the Englishmen in New England at the north should be the quickest to resent and the first to resist. They did it with remarkable unanimity of sentiment and surprising energy of action. Of course the King had his adherents in America as well as in England, and more of them than we now commonly think, but there was no such division

into parties, no such fooling or debauching of so many people as in
England. Of course the middle and the southern colonies had
their own peculiarities and their own interests to influence their
courses. Of course this and that people were quickened most by
the special considerations that appealed very directly to them; of
course the people of a region responded most completely to a danger that came directly to their doors; of course in their
weariness, and their poverty, and their exhaustion, they re-
laxed when the menace recoiled or the immediate campaign
was over; and of course the doings and even the honor of an
inexperienced Confederation fell into confusion; but above it all
looms the great fact that they played both a waiting and a
fighting game so adroitly and so valorously that British armies
had to withdraw, independence had to be admitted, and the
English government itself had to be radically recast. And the
great turning point of it all was right here at Saratoga.

From a strictly military point of view nothing so important
happened in the long and slow course of the Revolution as the
surrender of Burgoyne's army. The significance which it had in
the British mind is clear enough when one remembers that the
head and front of the American revolt seemed to be in New England and New York; that if this great northern revolution could
be quelled the rest would appear easy; that the old warpath of
the Indians and of the English and French, along the Hudson
river, and Lake Champlain, was the natural, short, level, and easy
channel of communication between the British army and navy at
New York city and the loyal English colonies in Canada. It is
particularly significant when one sees the careful and comprehensive preliminary arrangements for the campaign by which three
armies were to converge at Albany, scattering death and destruction along the roads, and leaving no doubt of ending all resistance
by the time their forces came together and crushed their enemy in
the vortex. It was a great plan and it was to be executed by vet-
ran troops with plenty of Hessian and Indian allies led by the best
officers sent to America in the course of the war. Burgoyne himself was a braggart, but he was no mere braggart. On his way he
took Fort Ticonderoga and then Fort Edward, and came on
boasting that "Britons never retreat." He found that when he
wanted to retreat he couldn't, but that does not overthrow the

fact that that army was the most important one sent upon the most vital mission of any English army in the Revolution, and he was in command of it because he was the most pompous, dogged, vigorous and ambitious soldier in the English service. That army was overwhelmed because it **had to be**. The Yankees were not always successful, but they could be when they had to be. Saratoga proved it. Individual or incidental details like Bennington, Oriskany, the dastardly flunk of Clinton, were fine contributions to the splendid end, but notwithstanding them the end might have been otherwise. The great issue had to be made here and the great result had to be gained right here. Saratoga itself was as vital to the Union in the Revolution as Gettysburg was in the Civil War. If the Confederacy could force a battle in Pennsylvania and triumph, there was no hope. If the English could make such plans in New York and succeed, there was no hope. Saratoga and Gettysburg both **had to be**.

One will never understand the progress of the Revolution unless he realizes the attitudes and theories of the colonial statesmen and military leaders. The loyalists had more men and greater resources and technically the more experienced soldiers. The patriots had the whole country, were more accustomed to warfare in the woods, and were able and willing to wait for battles on their own grounds and at their own times. The British were three thousand miles from home, across a rough sea, without steam, disappointed in their American support, cooped up in the cities and camps, and having on their shoulders the burden of offensive operations. The Yankees were a singularly aggravating people to professional soldiers. They were at home, could and did go about their store-keeping, their milling, and their farming, between the British interruptions, and if necessary could play the game a thousand years. They could evacuate a town and, in every instance except the deplorable mistake of General Lincoln at Charleston, they did unless it was clearly worth while not to do so; they could retreat and maneuver with equanimity until the time and the place for retribution came to them. Old Sam Adams had it in mind when, after Bunker Hill, he said they had more hills to sell to the British at the same price, and General Greene was thinking of it when he said that while the Yankees had the sovereignty of the country, the British sovereignty never extended beyond their own out-sentinels. But the New York campaign, and particularly the capitulation at Saratoga, proved that the Colonials could do a thing when they had to, and the twenty thousand men they gathered here gave notice, writ large, that in the end their triumph would be complete.

The loss of men and munitions of war was of itself a serious British loss. The campaign had certainly annulled the efficiency of no less than ten thousand men. And British grenadiers had money value so far from home; the Hessians and Brunswickers had cost them a vast deal of good money; and they had paid dearly, too, for the Indians, who, keener than the whites and not caring whether it was to be a "capitulation" or a "convention," had not stayed to see it out. Before the capitulation the patriots had killed, wounded or captured eighteen hundred men. The Canadians and local Tories followed the example of the Indians in skulking off through the woods. Fifty-eight hundred were included in the terms of the convention. The Yankee farmers did not care for uniforms and they disliked drill, but they were very expert at killing in their everyday clothes. Men who could shoot a deer running in the woods or over the hills had no trouble in slaughtering the draft horses of the artillery or the mounts of the general officers. The loss of British officers of distinction at Saratoga is surprising. It is said that six members of Parliament were among the slain. Of twenty English officers hit by bullets at Freeman's farm, ten were shot dead. The stores captured amounted to five thousand muskets, seventy thousand rounds of ball cartridges, four hundred sets of harness, and the finest train of brass artillery that had then been made. And their cannon and small arms and stores were precisely what the Yankees needed. But the real point of the British loss was in the loss of prestige. At other times the issue had been indecisive or might be clouded, but there was no chance for that here. In strategy, in maneuvering, in flanking, in straight fighting center to center and man to man, upon the most vital field and thoroughfare that had been or could be in the course of the war, they had had to lay down their arms and ask for terms. It overthrew any reasonable expectation that it would be different at any other time. And in fact it did save New York and New England from further fighting north and east of the mouth of the Hudson through all the after days in the slow and aggravating war. Of course there was plenty of fight-, ing and no end of suffering in the patriot cause for five long years thereafter, but neither before nor after was there any such strategic campaign, with so many men, so much dependent, such testing of soldiership, and ending in such complete disaster to British arms, and such utter humiliation to the British spirit, as in the New York campaign which had its far-reaching culmination at Saratoga. It was enough to signify to as honest a people as the English were, if they had been permitted to know the facts, that the war should have ended then and there.

But the Revolution grew out of English politics, and although it had to go on because the necessities of English politics refused to accept a disaster to the army which would be an equivalent disaster to the Tory party, to the King's cabinet, and to the King himself, yet Saratoga was immediately reflected in the parliamentary debates, and encompassed the Empire with the gravest perils that staunch structure has ever been called upon to withstand.

The news of Saratoga reached the English government about the first of December, being six weeks on the way. The parliamentary discussion of the American question had all along been behind closed doors and studiously kept from the public, and it was attempted to keep even the hard news of the disaster to Burgoyne from Parliament itself. But there were giants in the opposition who were entirely equal to larger tasks than making the House of Commons open its doors to the people or compelling cabinet ministers to admit a truth so momentous. The slowly rising tide of popular discontent helped to force the doors, and the apprehension which had been aroused by Burke's foretelling of the worst, doubled the opposition which supported his little party in compelling the disclosure of the facts. When Colonel Barre demanded that the Secretary for American Affairs inform the House what had become of General Burgoyne and his army, it was admitted that they had all been made prisoners, but is was coolly urged that the House should suspend judgment. But such news as that was not conducive to a suspension of the judgment of the English Commons, and amid much disorder an acrimonious debate ensued.

Barre, who had a soldierly record that was brilliant and a soldierly opinion that was of weight, charged the disaster upon the minister, Germain, rather than upon Burgoyne, and asserted that the whole plan for the invasion of New York had been condemned in advance by every soldier in the kingdom as "unworthy of a British war minister and too absurd for an Indian chief." The situation was so tense and the talk so hot that Burke called Lord Wedderburne, the Solicitor General, out to a fist fight or something worse, and Fox demanded that members of the cabinet should not only vacate their places but also be tried for criminal neglect. The government was arraigned for worse than the stupid planning of a British campaign and the heartless neglect of a British army that had been sent upon a vital mission into untold perils. Old soldiers and sailors who had led the forces of the kingdom to victories on land and sea minced no words in laying bare the unfit condition to which incapable and corrupt administration had brought the army and navy, and foretold early wars with more powerful enemies nearer home, which might repeat, upon British soil, the story of Saratoga, unless the bootless quarrel with the colonies was speedily ended and peace with America should be immediately concluded. With the finest irony and with withering scorn the government was pilloried for hiring mercenaries to help England make war upon English citizens in opposition to the law of the Empire and to the law of nations, and for holding out all that was opposed to English freedom to savage Indians who would burn the homes and scalp the wives and children of British subjects.

So Saratoga appealed to the pride and indignation, even to the conscience and apprehension, of the British nation, by the tongues of the ablest men in a Parliament that Cowper has said embraced the largest number of the ablest men of any Parliament that ever sat. The appeal was not without effect upon the government itself, and the doors were open enough to make the appeal exceedingly effective upon the public opinion of the realm. The ministers met the assault for the moment, as weak or corrupt men commonly do, with flippancy and boasting, and then adjourned for a six weeks' holiday vacation; but the masses thought it more fitting to meet it with a day of fasting, humiliation and prayer. Soon after the return from the roast beef and

SARATOGA

SARATOGA, SHOWING CONGRESS HALL ON THE RIGHT, AND UNION HALL ON THE LEFT.

Courtesy of Frank J. Wilder

plum pudding of the holiday recess, the prime minister brought in
a proposition to send a commission to America to promise the
colonists all that they had ever asked, together with representa-
tion in Parliament, upon the only condition that they would return to their allegiance. With the approval of Parliament he
sent it by a commissioner who, Horace Walpole said, was a fit
commissioner to make a treaty that would   never   be   made.
Whether Horace was altogether correct or not, he certainly was
so in part, for the Continental Congress unanimously resolved not
to confer with any commissioners from Great Britain until independence was recognized in express terms by the cabinet ministers themselves. Saratoga had turned the corner of the struggle
which was writing "American Independence" across the skies.

But the news of Saratoga set new forces in motion that were
even more compelling in the direction of independence than was
pride, or fear, or conscience. Apprehension of those new forces
on the other side of the sea doubtless compelled the overtures for
peace; and the hope and expectation of them, joined with the
great confidence which Saratoga had inspired, may explain the
unanimity with which those far-reaching overtures were rejected
on this side of the sea.

There was hardly a court in Europe from Madrid to Moscow
that had not for years been disposed to throw stones at the Court
of London, or to hold the coats of those who would. They had
hitherto preferred to do it in the dark, and had done a good deal
of diplomatic lying about it, but they were about ready to do it in
daylight. The King of England had been sending royal messengers with autograph notes to the sovereigns of Europe praying
them to supply soldiers to reduce his rebellious colonies in America, with assurances that he would not regard the cost. Brave little Holland recalled her own revolutionary history, remembered
her children upon the Hudson and Mohawk, and sharply refused.
Even the giddy dame and subtle sovereign on Russia's throne
resented the bald proposition that she might plunge her hand
as deeply as she pleased into Britain's treasury if she would send
twenty thousand troops to help her royal brother in distress. She
held it to be an offense to her honor, and she does not seem to have
been overfastidious about honor either. She asked the King's
emissary if it would not disgust the people of England, and

assured him that it was "not consistent with the dignity of England to employ foreign troops against her own subjects." It was left to the petty princes of Hesse-Cassel and Brunswick in Germany to sell their subjects upon abhorrent terms and for vast sums upon which one of the best of the English historians says England is paying interest to this very day. But the bluff and great Frederick, King of Prussia, characterized the performance as driving men to the shambles like cattle, for nothing but money.

But of all the enemies that England had in Europe, France and Spain were the nearest, the strongest, the bitterest, and the most superficially polite. They were both hereditary rivals of England for the possession of America, and it was not two score years since Wolfe and Montcalm had fought their doubly tragic duel upon the Plains of Abraham, as a result of which England had taken Canada from France and would drive her out of America for good, and was pushing Spain beyond the Mississippi with rather serious intimations, which we have seen realized, that she too might be obliged to get off the American continent altogether. These two powerful nations, united by heredity, religion, military efficiency, and discomfitures, were not the kind to lose sight of the opportunity for crippling their arch enemy by encouraging the American revolt.

They acted together not only in giving encouragement but in supplying money, clothing, cannon, small arms, shot and powder to the colonists. This began in May, 1776, two months before the Declaration of Independence. Of course it had to be disguised, for any public knowledge of it would have been tantamount to the declaration of another war across the English channel. They were no strangers to war, but they knew their old antagonist very well and they realized the danger of clashing with her again unless at a time when she was handicapped or crippled. Under such tense circumstances the French and Spanish supplies flowed rather freely when the patriots were successful, but the stream was more sluggish whenever the Revolution seemed to face the possibility of failure. It almost dried up in the summer and fall of 1777, when the colonial outlook was so discouraging that the secret agent of France told Franklin that there was danger of France "cutting my throat as if I was a sheep." But in October the conquest at Saratoga opened the flood-gates and threw off all disguise.

Early in December an evening dinner party at Doctor Franklin's house at Passy, a suburb of Paris, was very properly interrupted by a courier with news of the disaster to Burgoyne, and that agent, who was enjoying the doctor's hospitality, rushed off to carry the news to the court at Versailles with so much elation over the increased safety to his throat that in his haste and in the darkness he upset his coach and dislocated his shoulder. But the news led the King to move almost as precipitously as his agent, for on December 6th the American representatives in Paris received the direct assurances of Louis the Fourteenth written on the gilt edged stationery which he reserved exclusively for his correspondence, that France was now ready to give to the United States every proof of his interest and affection. Six days later Vergennes granted the American delegates a formal audience and with such favorable results that in another six days, in replying to the dispatch from Congress announcing the capture of Burgoyne, the delegates assured Congress that the "surrender of Burgoyne had created as much joy in France as if it had been a victory of their own troops over their own enemies." The preliminary articles of alliance with France were signed on January 17th, and the formal ones on February 6th. The alliance was tantamount to a declaration of war against England, and the brief delay in the public proclamation of the treaty was for military reasons.

There were in fact two of these treaties. One was for amity and trade. The other established a complete military and civic alliance. The latter contravened the instructions of the Continental Congress, for that body had expressed views that were greatly to its honor and far in advance of the accepted tenets of international diplomacy of that day. Foreshadowing a course which the United States, with the exception of this single instance, has always consistently adhered to, the Congress had instructed its representatives to avoid a treaty which might "entangle us in any future wars in Europe" and it exemplified its statesmanship as well as its love of Old England by directing its ambassadors to refuse "to unite with France in the destruction of England." This was the first treaty that our country ever made, and it is the only offensive and defensive alliance that it has ever entered into. And the time came when even this had to be renounced rather ruthlessly and without reparation. But all good and patriotic Americans have weighed the motives of the parties and witnessed the historical results, and have been glad that such a spotless character and able jurist as John Jay could say, when it came to renouncing this treaty so vital to the life of the Union, that he would break the instructions of the Congress as readily as he would the pipe that he then threw upon the hearth.

The course of the United States in this great matter is easily enough understood, for it seems to have been dictated by absolute necessity, but it is difficult to justify the diplomacy of France. The French King with his Queen perished upon the scaffold of a revolution which was the logical descendant of the one he was now aiding and abetting. The cost to France of aid given to the colonies was over 1,280,000,000 francs or $256,000,000. That was enough of itself to bring on the French Revolution. This aid was given to Anglo-Saxon liberty in America in order to menace England and thus help despotism in France. But it had the contrary effect. It promoted liberty in America, in England, in France, and in all the world. So God makes His own use of human agencies to promote His own ends.

The dispatches announcing the execution of the French treaties were received by Congress on Saturday, May 2, 1778. It was after adjournment for the week when they were delivered, but Congress reconvened at once in order that the good news need not be concealed over Sunday. On the ensuing Monday the treaties were ratified by Congress. Robert Morris wrote Washington, "Our independence is undoubtedly secured: our country must be free." The army at Valley Forge had a holiday; the commander in chief gave a dinner; Lafayette was given the command of a division; and the whole was solemnized by thanksgiving to God in acknowledgment of the divine goodness which had vouchsafed to the colonies the alliance with France.

France followed the treaties very soon with a formal declaration of war against England, and with earnest appeals to Spain to act in concert with her. Indeed, she had already notified Spain that the months of January and February, 1778, would be the outside limit of time when Spain must unite with France in an alliance with the colonies and a declaration of war against England in order to make the assistance effective enough to deserve American gratitude in case of success. The moment the French ministry received the news of Saratoga, Vergennes sent a courier to Madrid urging combined and immediate action. Fortunately France took the important step from which she could not draw back without waiting for the return of the courier. Spain refused an immediate declaration of war on the ground that she was not prepared for it, and urged that the building up of an independent republic in America was of questionable expediency.

In the light of subsequent events the attitude of the leading Spanish statesmen is singularly interesting. France, with whom their country was allied by blood, religion, system of government, ideals, dangers, and disappointments, was urging her to aid the colonies, and they were urging upon her far greater rewards than they could afford to give her, and yet she stood firm in her opposition to a republic in America for the reason, as one of her statesmen advised her king, that "this federal republic is born a pigmy; a day will come when it will be a giant; even a Colossus formidable to these countries," and as another put it, "if the union of the American provinces shall continue, they will become by force of time and of the arts, the most formidable power in the world."

In the following year Spain declared war upon England, but happily for us avoided the American alliance which the colonists urged and for which we now know they were ready to pay too heavy a price. The year after that England was at war with Holland too because she gave the colonies her sympathy and some financial assistance. And with it all there was a recognition of the new-born republic and a declaration of neutrality by Russia, Denmark, and Sweden.

Britain with a formidable revolution on her hands was now menaced by the great military forces of Europe. No real lover of English freedom can be devoid of sorrow and pity that a people with such qualities, such a history, such constitutional power and such capacity for exercising it, could let an over-ambitious and unscrupulous monarch carry them to such an extremity of danger and humiliation. For it was no more a question as to whether the colonies should go free than it was whether the British Empire should survive. Happily the colonies did go free, and, happily, the Empire did survive.

Condensed into few words, the immediate military results of the destruction of Burgoyne's army may be stated as follows: it took from Britain in the field ten thousand of the best officers and soldiers in the British army; it transferred from the British to the Colonists vast stores of war of which the little Confederacy stood sorely in need; it destroyed all confidence in the Indians as allies of value in systematic warfare, and opened the way for punishing the Iroquois so severely that they feared and respected white civilization ever after; it cut off for all time all communication between the English loyalists in Canada and their army and navy at the mouth of the Hudson; and it completely ended all resistance to the Revolution in New York and New England, where there was the most in America that could give strength and substance to the British crown. It opened the doors of the House of Commons, appealed to English sense, pride and conscience, and led to immediate overtures for peace from Britain on any terms but separation, and to the unanimous and unhesitating rejection of these overtures. It produced the French alliance and the consequent war by France upon England, the war of Spain upon England, the Dutch loan to the Colonists and then the warfare of the Netherlands upon England, and the early recognition of American independence by all the leading powers of Europe.

No one suggests that the Revolution ended at Saratoga. Completely foiled in the northern colonies, the Mother Country turned to the southern colonies. She probably reasoned that there were more loyalists and perhaps not so many hardy fighters there. If so, she had occasion to realize that in part at least she was mistaken. As horrid war receded from their cabins the exhausted settlers, north or south, became indifferent. They were without men to send long distances; there was lack of roads and of means of transportation; and they could not go far from their own firesides without grave danger to their wives and children. They were not only without money, but they were without government or the experience which could make government effective. Worse still, perhaps, the states were jealous of each other and of all central power. Each knew that with the help of its neighbors at least it could defend itself against invasion, and reasoned that far away states must do the same. So the war dragged its slow course through months and years of suffering and death, until the men of the South proved at Cowpens, and King's Mountain, and Yorktown, what the men of the North had proved at Oriskany, and Bennington, and Saratoga. But the time never was before the surrender at Saratoga when the separation from Great Britain was altogether certain, and the time never was after Saratoga when there was any reasonable doubt about it.

But if Saratoga was a turning point in the Revolutionary War, it was also very much more than that, for the success of the American Revolution brought new lights into the world and opened wholly unprecedented opportunities for the unhampered advance of the noblest qualities of men and women. The separation from Britain must have been in the divine plan. The Colonists were not seeking independence except as independence, in view of the unscrupulous conduct of the English king and the hot-headed course of the English Parliament, was the last refuge of English liberty in America. They did not want war; they went to great pains to prove that they did not begin it. But their inherent qualities—self-reliance, self-confidence, love of fair play, gifts for establishing social order, the matter-of-course assumption that the fundamental rights of English freemen could not be impaired, and the purpose to manage their own business in their own way, made the Colonists invincible. They were invincible not because they loved war or were in rebellion against English institutions. Neither was true. They abhorred war and were in love with English institutions. Indeed, they were not dissatisfied with the form of the English government. They were invincible because the soul of a new and a free nation was ripe for its birth.

Independence had to be, not only because of what compelled it, but because the world was ready and waiting for what was to flow out of it. There are no bonds strong enough to confine the mind and soul of a human being, and surely there are none strong enough to limit the growth of the mind and soul of a new nation. The inherent qualities, the native impulses, of those early Colonists, wrought out even more than they understood. They compelled intellectual, spiritual, political, industrial, commercial and social opportunity. They assured equality of right to all. They opened the way for that unprecedented expansion of all the self-activities which constitute the soul of a nation. The American colonies did more than win independence. They won freedom, absolute freedom for themselves and enlarged freedom for the people of all lands. It is that which brought the sagacious prophecy of the Spanish statesman of 1777 to realization so swiftly and so strongly.

But so much had to be settled through human instrumentalities and expressed in human action. And it transpired that more of that heroic human action which determined that America should be civilized rather than savage, English rather than Bourbon, republican rather than monarchial, and completely free in a New World rather than bound by the laws, usage, and thought of the Old World, was expressed along the mighty thoroughfare which follows the Hudson from the sea to its source, and then winds along the shores of Lake George and Lake Champlain to the Sorel and the St. Lawrence rivers. It is truly the greatest street ever cut through a wilderness for the mental and moral progress of mankind. A decade before the Pilgrims came to Plymouth Rock, the great forerunners of American exploration, Champlain and Hudson, in the same year, working from the north and from the south, and without knowledge of each other, laid down this first great highway upon the map of the western world. It was the bloody warpath of the Iroquois and the Algonquin, of the French and Indian, and of the Revolutionary, wars. It is so level and so watered that one may float a boat almost the entire distance. It encounters but one elevation and that of but a hundred and fifty feet. It has come to be a great national highway of commerce and of pleasure. With the Berkshires and the Green mountains overhanging it upon one side, and the Catskills and the Adirondacks upon the other, it must always remain surpassingly wild, picturesque, impressive and sublime. It is the easy roadway to the very heart of nature in America, but even that is not its chief attraction. It is the chief roadway over which the new-born soul of the nation fought its way to that freedom of opportunity which has attracted all the peoples of the earth and here gathered and assimilated the great new nation of modern history. Every rod of it has been crimsoned with heroic and patriotic blood. Every nook and vista of it has its true story of struggle and accomplishment, of daring and of sorrow. At its foot the first

American settlement that has endured was established, and there the foremost city of the land, very soon to be the foremost city of the world, sits in confidence and glory. In that city the first rich blood of the Revolution was spilled, and there, eight years after, Washington bade his official farewell to the officers of the patriot army he had led to complete victory. Retreating along this road, under the protection of the army, the New York Convention wrote the first Constitution of the State. In sight of it Arnold proved many times what a fine soldier he was, and once he showed what a contemptible traitor he could be. And in sight of it too American literature had its birth. So too did American unity, for at Albany, in 1754, the first Congress of the American Confederation was assembled, and at Poughkeepsie the State Convention gave to the Federal Constitution that vital support which it had to have. Fort Edward, Fort William Henry, Fort Ticonderoga, Crown Point, which are a little farther up along this roadway, signify pleasant resting places to us, but they ought to portray thousands of men in the bloody agonies of death for English liberty and American independence. Plattsburg, at the far end of it, makes us think of a thrifty city and a pleasant people, but it might well make us think of an old sailor calling his officers to the quarter-deck of his flagship and kneeling down and praying for the victory such men clearly deserved and were very soon to win. A special paper, perhaps a book, would be needed to specify the events of real and often of supreme significance to American nationality and to human freedom in the world, which have transpired along this magnificent highway of more than three hundred miles.

Midway upon this great thoroughfare so close to nature, so created by and so consecrated to the country, stands Saratoga. It is rightfully at the center of the line, for it marks the high tide of the Revolutionary War, the site of one of the great decisive battles of the world; it assured the life of the first great republic that has long endured to give opportunity to the many-sided phases of the spiritual, social, industrial, and political life of mankind.

RESPONSE TO ADDRESS OF WELCOME AT THE MEETING HELD IN SCHUYLERVILLE, FRIDAY MORNING, SEPTEMBER 20, 1912

By Dr. William O. Stillman, Albany, N. Y.
Second Vice-President of New York State Historical Assn.

Mr. President, Ladies and Gentlemen:

It is my privilege on behalf of the New York State Historical Association to thank you for the generous welcome which has been given us in Schuylerville. We appreciate the courtesies which have been shown and have greatly enjoyed looking over the historic sites which are to be found in this locality. No American should forget the importance of the great battle which was fought and won within gunshot of the spot where we are now assembled. In the annals of the human race it has already been numbered by a disinterested English historian as one of the fifteen great decisive battles of the world. In the history of personal freedom and representative government it is, perhaps, fraught with more memorable consequences than any other battlefield which history records. This battle was the turning point in our national struggle for freedom and in our rebellion against unjust government.

The immediate result of the battle of Saratoga was the establishment of a republican form of government in the United States, which has found imitators in other sections of the world, not infrequently, since that day. The French Revolution came as a natural child of the American revolt, and the great French Republic of today was largely called into existence as the result of the successful experiment in self government in this country, which had been carefully studied in France. Since then, national governments have been constantly becoming more democratic. Spain enjoyed a brief period of democracy. Portugal has now a republican form of government and former Spanish possessions in North and South America have gradually thrown off the monarchial yoke and become republics.

Recently Persia has clamored for a representative democratic form of government and only yesterday the Republic of China was born, and that great nation has begun its majestic onward march to fulfill its destiny and infinite possibilities as a democracy, with its unrivaled population, its enormous natural wealth and with opportunities almost unequalled elsewhere on earth. Such have been some of the important outcomes of the struggle which was held on this spot not much over one hundred years ago. The armies on this field were relatively small, compared with those engaged on the vast battle struggles of recent history. The results accomplished in the direction of winning human rights and in enfranchising the world have been wholly beyond computation.

I desire most earnestly to invite the attention of all present to the desirability of giving greater attention in our public schools to our national history. In New York State I feel that we have been lukewarm in this respect. Over in New England every school child can tell you all about Bunker Hill and the "Boston Tea Party." How many children in New York State schools know about the actual occurrences at the battle of Saratoga and the momentous consequences which have resulted from them. New York State is rich in historic memories. We are citizens of no mean commonwealth. From Rouses Point to Staten Island, our territory is crowded with historic memories which should make any state or nation proud. Our ancestors fought well in the battles which determined human progress and the richest possibilities of our national life. From the Green Mountains and the Berkshires to Lake Erie, how many historic events have taken place? Is it not time that more attention should be given to the study of these great occurrences so that our school children shall be stimulated to a more fervent patriotism and possess a memory of the past which shall consecrate them in their future life to the best services of their country?

The New York State Historical Association has an important mission to perform. It has already done a considerable number of things and done them well. I will not take your time by recounting its record of deeds accomplished, but I most earnestly request your co-operation in making the future of our work more effective and richer with results than it has been in the past. There are many historic spots which have, as yet, not been properly studied. There are memorable sites which are yet to be properly marked and to have their importance clearly pointed out. Until history shall lose its magic interest and patriotism shall have become a name for which no response can be evoked in American breasts, there will be a work for this State Historical Association to perform, with ever increasing interest as the generations come and go. I again thank you for your kind welcome and for the attention which you have given.

GENERAL SCHUYLER'S PART IN THE BURGOYNE CAMPAIGN

Francis Whiting Halsey, New York City.

At the outbreak of the Revolution the Province of New York, on whose soil near Saratoga was fought the decisive battle of the war, was one of the least important of the colonies—least in population, least in wealth, least in enthusiasm for the popular cause. That New York had not already shown the commercial supremacy she was afterwards to acquire, was owing to several causes; but first to the constant state of unrest prevailing on her northern and western frontiers, due to French aggressions from Canada and to uncertainties as to what the powerful Iroquois Indians, rightful owners of the soil, might do; and secondly to the system of large colonial land grants by which thousands of acres were still held in single families, so that immigration was discouraged.

That the whole mass of the population was less patriotic than the population of other colonies, was due to the conditions in which, as an English colony, New York had grown. New York was a crown colony,—that is, its governor was a royal appointee. Its administration was directly in charge of men who were responsible only to the governor, or to the British Cabinet in London. Of responsibility to the people of the colony itself there was none. In society was maintained what might very properly be called a small court, modelled after the Court of St. James, and from which fashionable circles and public life derived their tone.

It was entirely outside this official, but extremely influential class, that one had to look for such patriotic sentiment as then existed in New York. While the patriotic party was less influential than the other, it was much more numerous. Some of its component parts were of English stock, but these were men of the small tradesmen and artisan classes. The larger numbers were of other racial origins. First of all, came the descendants of the original settlers of Manhattan Island and Albany—the Dutch. Then came the Scotch-Irish, the Palatine Germans, and the Huguenots. Descendants of these people still lived in some numbers on Manhattan Island, but in the main they inhabited the upper Hudson, the Mohawk, the Champlain and the upper Susquehanna valleys. Eminent among them in Revolutionary services was the Palatine German, Nicholas Herkimer, the hero of Oriskany; but chief among them all was the Dutchman, Philip Schuyler.

That Schuyler did not command the American army at the battle of Saratoga constitutes one of the most pathetic personal incidents in the story of the Revolution. A man of stainless character, public as well as private; of inestimable services to America, not only in the early years of the Revolution, but in the French War; a man also of fine abilities, who had probably made larger personal sacrifices for the American cause than any other man in the country except Washington or Franklin, he was deprived of the Northern command on the very eve of the battle, for causes wholly free from any imputation on his character or his abilities, and was superseded by a man of inferior abilities, one given to secret intrigue, of questionable character and to whose efforts the final success of the American army in the battle itself, was in no wise due. John Fiske has well said that Gates went to Saratoga "to reap the glory earned by other men." Historians no longer accord to Schuyler anything but praise for his work in promoting the cause of the Revolution and nothing but sympathy is extended to him for the wrong Congress did him in sending Gates to take his place. Sir George Otto Trevelyan, the nephew and biographer of Macaulay, in his recent work on the Revolution, not yet completed, has given expression to the universal judgment in these words:

"In the capacity of a military administrator, though less able and experienced than Washington, he was as industrious and unselfish as the commander-in-chief himself. Schuyler loved his country sincerely and singly and he gave her the whole of his time and strength, besides great quantities of money, and (for many years afterwards) all his peace of mind and his happiness. He was fiercely calumniated while alive and since his death he has met with some unfair treatment at the hands of history; but his good fame has survived all assaults whether contemporaneous or posthumous, and he now is almost universally recognized as an honest and devoted friend to America."

"Schuyler was deprived of his command. He received his successor in a friendly manner and with proffers of council and support, which were churlishly rejected. It has been well said that the supreme of good taste rarely had more perfect illustration than in Philip Schuyler's conduct at this trying moment, and throughout the many years of life which still remained to him. Schuyler's modest self-effacement under the infliction of a cruel wrong, and his continued devotion to the national cause, when the triumph of that cause could no longer bring glory or profit to himself, are an indisputable title to the respect of posterity."

How cruel was this wrong done to Schuyler may best be judged from a survey of his earlier services to his country. These have nowhere been better presented than by Bayard Tuckerman, in his "Life of Schuyler." On that book I must often rely in here briefly presenting them.

The family to which Philip Schuyler belonged had been settled in New York for several generations. It was of pure Dutch stock and was one of the four great families which owned vast tracts of land and were eminent in public affairs, the others being the Livingstons, Van Cortlandts and Van Rensselaers. All except the Livingstons were Dutch. Before 1750 the Schuyler family had given to the town of Albany six mayors. One of these was the famous Peter Schuyler, a noted friend of the Indians who, in their inability to pronounce his name, made a "bluff" at it by calling him "Quider."

By inheritance Philip Schuyler early came into possession of a large landed estate, in the administration of which he soon became an experienced man. Much of this land was undeveloped, and called for his activities in finding tenants, building sawmills, and marketing lumber. In this way the valleys of the Hudson and Mohawk became from his youth familiar highways to him as to Sir William Johnson, his close friend. He learned to know the Indians as perhaps no other man, except Johnson, knew them. They were often entertained at his spacious and hospitable home in Albany, and he manifested unusual skill in influencing and controlling them.

During the war with France, Schuyler became a leader, although still quite young. At Albany he raised a company of soldiers. In 1755 his house had become a rendezvous for soldiers on their way north to defend the Champlain valley. He accompanied Sir William Johnson on his expedition to Lake George and with General Bradstreet went to Oswego. Schuyler emerged from this war with the rank of major, a well-earned tribute to services not only as a soldier, but in collecting and forwarding supplies. This experience gave Schuyler in the Revolutionary period a rank which belonged also to Washington, Putnam and Stark. All were veterans of the French war.

The first year of the conflict with England found Schuyler in Philadelphia, where Congress appointed him a Major-General in command of the Revolutionary forces in New York. Contemporary with his appointment was that of Richard Montgomery, as a Brigadier. After the appointment of Washington as commander-in-chief, Schuyler and General Charles Lee accompanied him on his famous journey to Boston by way of New York. While in New York, Washington gave to Schuyler specific instructions as to what he should do in preparing the Northern frontier for defence against an expected descent from Canada by the British. These responsibilities were great. There existed at that time in New York no machinery for raising a patriot army, or providing supplies for one. The official life of the colony, as already stated, was British. Schuyler therefore had to start from the ground.

When an expedition into Canada was decided upon, the conduct of it was confided to him. One of the chief difficulties that met him was the reluctance of New England men, and especially those from Connecticut, to serve under him. Schuyler, as a New Yorker of Dutch stock, had always been unpopular in Connecticut. Another serious difficulty was the spirit of personal independence and equality which prevailed in Connecticut as perhaps nowhere else in America. Volunteers from that province resented military discipline. Schuyler after heroic efforts finally organized and sent forward the expedition. Its melancholy failure, ending in the lamented death of Montgomery at Quebec, was not Schuyler's fault, but the fault of circumstances, which neith-

HIGH ROCK SPRING. (Circa 1840)
Courtesy of Frank J. Wilder

RAILROAD DEPOT, SARATOGA SPRINGS, 1840
Courtesy of Frank J. Wilder

or he nor any other man could then have surmounted. That he employed not only his talents but his personal credit in doing what he could to make it successful has been repeatedly acknowledged. Schuyler used his own and to obtainment supplies, and he declared in a letter to Washington that he had used it to "the full extent of his resources." At one time the obligations he had assumed amounted $70,000, a sum which, according to the standards of our day, would be several times that amount.

Having in mind such services and similar ones rendered by Schuyler during a war period of nearly two years, the question confronts us, why was Schuyler displaced at Saratoga in favor of a man like Gates, his inferior and in inferior? Inferior Gates was in military he best than in personal merit.

It commonly weakens a man's cause in life in his defence zealous on the part of others, but in Schuyler's instrument there can be no question that it was the jealousy of animosity of New England toward New York and the dislike of New England men for Schuyler as a New York Dutchman that finally accomplished his humiliation. Before the Revolution, Schuyler had taken some part in the violent disputes between New York and New England over the Hampshire Grants, which alone was enough to make him unpopular in New England. The additional fact that he was a Dutchman contributed still further to extend the prejudice against him. Prejudice in New England against the Dutch dated far back.—In fact, it reached almost to the beginning of settlements in New York and Connecticut, and in that state of civil war over the "Grants," which prevailed in the territory we now call Vermont, became intense in bitter. Schuyler was never an expressive person in this dispute. It has been well shown that he personally had little to do with the pursuit, except as the colonel of a force of local militiamen, whose duty it was to preserve order and as member of a commission which had to deal with the insurgency.

The failure of the expedition to Quebec gave New England men an opportunity they were not slow to employ for Schuyler's injury. It mattered not that the cause of the failure was the inferiority of the American army, as compared with the British; it mattered not that Quebec was a fortress which only the finest and best trained soldiers could ever hope to capture. The Dutchman er he nor any other man could then have surmounted. That he employed not only his talents, but his personal credit, in doing what he could to make it successful has been commonly acknowledged. Schuyler used his own credit in obtaining supplies, and he declared in letters to Washington that he had used it to "the full extent of his resources." At one time the obligations he had assumed reached $50,000, a sum which, according to the standards of our day, would be several times that amount.

Having in mind these services, and similar ones rendered by Schuyler during a war period of nearly two years, the question confronts us, why was Schuyler displaced at Saratoga in favor of a man like Gates, an intriguer and an inferior? Inferior Gates was in military no less than in personal merit.

It commonly weakens a man's cause to cite in his defence jealousy on the part of others, but in Schuyler's displacement there can be no question that it was the jealousy, or animosity, of New England toward New York and the dislike of New England men for Schuyler as a New York Dutchman, that finally accomplished his humiliation. Before the Revolution, Schuyler had taken some part in the violent disputes between New York and New England over the Hampshire Grants, which alone was enough to make him unpopular in New England. The additional fact that he was a Dutchman contributed still further to extend the prejudice against him. Prejudice in New England against the Dutch dated far back,—in fact, it reached almost to the beginning of settlements in New York and Connecticut, and in that state of civil war over the "Grants," which prevailed in the territory we now call Vermont, became intensely bitter. Schuyler was never an aggressive person in this dispute. It has been well shown that he personally had little to do with the quarrel, except as the colonel of a force of local militiamen, whose duty it was to preserve order and as member of a commission which had to deal with the boundary.

The failure of the expedition to Quebec gave New England men an opportunity they were not slow to employ for Schuyler's injury. It mattered not that the cause of this failure was the inferiority of the American army as compared with the British; it mattered not that Quebec was a fortress which only the finest and best trained soldiers could ever hope to capture. The Dutchman had failed and hence criticism spread far and wide. It reached at last a point where loose accusations were made against him as actively connected with the Conway Cabal to displace Washtions of disloyalty. These accusations were sent to Congress and to Washington, but Washington's knowledge of Schuyler's character was sufficient to prevent them from having any influence with him. Schuyler begged that a Court of Inquiry might be set up and the merits of the case thoroughly investigated, but Washington did not favor it; his confidence in Schuyler was so absolute that he wished not in any way to countenance criticism. Never through all this controversy did Washington's faith in Schuyler waver for a moment.

An opportune time eventually came for an intriguer like Gates to promote his cause. It was not, however, until a year at least had passed that his purpose was accomplished and Schuyler displaced. All through that year Schuyler retained his command, continued to augment his army, to resist the approach of Burgoyne and to gather supplies. Schuyler's policy towards Burgoyne was much in line with the policy Washington himself always followed, and in the employment of which was so successful. That was the policy of wise retreat. Except for it, one may well doubt if the American cause ever could have been won. The more a British army was drawn away from its base of supplies the more did its difficulties increase. The American army on the other hand found friends in the back country wherever it went.

Schuyler was much criticized because of the retreat from Ticonderoga, but the larger view of it ever since has confirmed the wisdom of the step. Once Burgoyne had been drawn south of Lake Champlain, his difficulties in the matter of supplies rapidly multiplied. The battle of Bennington, by which he was seriously weakened, was the result of an attempt on his part to obtain supplies. Moreover, the American victory on that field had a distinct moral effect throughout New England. As a consequence of it, large numbers of militiamen now pressed forward to join the American army in spite of the New England dislike of Schuyler.

Contemporary with Bennington was the battle of Oriskany and the retreat of the British from Fort Stanwix. In that serious disaster to Burgoyne, so serious in fact that Horatio Seymour has ranked it as the decisive battle of the Revolution, Schuyler's hand was potent. It was he who sent out the small force under Arnold that co-operated with the Tyron County militiamen and, by a skilful use of military strategy, forced St. Leger into a precipitous flight from Fort Stanwix.

But all this was overlooked, misjudged or perverted in New England. The abandonment of Ticonderoga was represented as an act of cowardice, if not of treason, and Schuyler was openly accused of treachery. Meanwhile, Gates and his New England friends, among whom curiously enough, were some of the foremost patriots of the time, eagerly sought to use the event to Schuyler's injury. They could not see, as Schuyler saw, how the further advance of Burgoyne southward would multiply his difficulties. Schuyler's original force had been totally inadequate to stay the progress of Burgoyne. Had an engagement taken place near Ticonderoga, or even at Fort Edward, it must have ended in disaster to the American cause and the full possession of the Hudson valley by an English army. Schuyler's policy of delay postponed the engagement with Burgoyne until Bennington and Oriskany had been fought, and the people of New York and New England had been so aroused that an army of 10,000 men rallied to Schuyler's support several weeks before Burgoyne reached him. A litle later this force was augmented to nearly 20,000 and as such was turned over to Gates.

Meanwhile, in Congress the subject of the Northern command was constantly under discussion. We must remember that in those days, when neither railroads nor the telegraph made communication easy, Congress could not know the extent to which militiamen were gathering around Schuyler. Instead of learning these facts, Congress was again and again told that New England men would not serve under Schuyler. Samuel Adams drew up a memorial to Congress, which nearly all of the New England delegates signed, and in which he recited the condition of affairs as New England saw it, and asked for the appointment of Gates in place of Schuyler. Congress now yielded to the pressure and asked Washington to make the change, but Washington refused, saying the whole matter must rest with Congress.

When Gates arrived in Albany, armed with his commission, Schuyler received him with all the politeness due to Gates's rank.

It is matter of record that he gave him all the information he possessed as to his own army and Burgoyne's advance and offered to render Gates any assistance in his power. Gates's character is well revealed in the want of grace with which he received these advances. When his first council of war was called, Schuyler was not asked to attend it—an act of supreme folly, not to say, atrocious manners, on which the best comment ever made was that made by Gouverneur Morris, who said that Gates might disdain to receive advice, but those who knew him best well understood how much he stood in need of it.

Schuyler's efforts for a court of inquiry were finally successful, but not until more than a year after the battle, when he was acquitted on every count. Congress approved the verdict "with the highest honor." In displacing Schuyler, Congress probably acted as best it could in the circumstances. Philadelphia in those days was further away from Albany than London is now. Indeed, if we remember the telegraph and the cable, nothing like that situation exists in present day conditions, except perhaps the difficulty of reaching Central Africa or the North Pole. Congress unquestionably made an error in removing Schuyler, yet the circumstances are generally thought to have made the act fairly excusable. In any case, it resulted in a further accession of New England men and a great deal of enthusiasm on their part for the campaign. Had a really fit man for commander been chosen instead of Gates, probably no great criticism would have occurred.

Gates was the last man in the army of high rank whom Congress should have chosen. Historians are thoroughly in accord nowadays with this judgment. The victory won at Saratoga was in no sense due to him. Moreover, his later career, when the scene of conflict was transferred to Georgia and South Carolina, shows how incompetent a commander he was. His personal character was also set forth conspicuously, when he became actively- connected with the Conway Cabal to dispace Washington from the supreme command.

Gates at Saratoga not only had no share in gathering the forces that opposed Burgoyne, or in conducting the strategy by which Burgoyne was led into the trap that ruined him, but on the field of battle did nothing to secure the victory. The honors of this fight belong to Benedict Arnold and General Morgan, who attacked the British without help from Gates. The best remembered fact about Gates is that during the fighting he was occupied with quarreling in his tent with a wounded English prisoner. The summary of the whole matter that accords well with modern historical judgments has been made by Mr. Tuckerman, whose words I quote:

"The credit for the destruction of Burgoyne's expedition belongs to no one man. Schuyler contributed largely to it by the courage and energy with which he held together the little army left after the loss of Ticonderoga, kept up a bold front toward a greatly superior enemy, delayed and harassed his advance. To Schuyler's prompt action, as to Herkimer and Arnold, was due the safety of the Mohawk Valley. Stark's victory at Bennington contributed much. Lincoln's aid in raising the New England militia was of great value. Looking at the military operations which together constitute the battle of Saratoga, it is impossible to credit Gates with any definite plan of campaign, or to trace the orders of his in any important movement. On the contrary, he obstructed Arnold as much as he could, and at decisive moments was complaining and arguing to no purpose."

"The two battles were fought on the part of the Americans according to no plan but that of attacking the enemy whenever he moved. Arnold, Morgan and Lincoln were partisan leaders, acting on the spur of the moment, agreeing among themselves and assisting each other, but under direction of no single authority. Arnold, indeed, had been deprived of all command by Gates, and was no more than a private citizen when he led the impetuous and decisive charge on Fraser's line at the second battle of Freeman's Farm. It is certain that Schuyler's intimate knowledge of the country where the battles were fought, his energy of character, his readiness to work with and for his fellow officers, his confidential relations with Lincoln, Morgan and Arnold, would have made him a more useful man than Gates at the head of the Northern army. After Burgoyne had been defeated by Morgan and Arnold with their unorganized but hardy followers, Gates first appeared as a real commander-in-chief."

Mr. Tuckerman's appraisal of the honors at Saratoga will be questioned by no careful student of the subject. Those honors belong first to Schuyler, and then to Arnold, to Morgan, to Herki-

mer, to Stark, while to Gates belongs the empty and ironical eminence of having commanded in one of the decisive battles in the
world's history, a battle comparable only to Marathon, Philippi,
Waterloo and Gettysburg, and yet contributing nothing to the
winning of it.

New York has added to her roll of public men senators and
congressmen who have notably influenced the course of this western empire; presidents and cabinet officers, who have deserved
well of later generations; soldiers who have given their talents,
shed their blood and lost their lives for the Republic; administra-
tors who have conserved the work of the statesmen and the soldiers; but she discovers among them all no finer public servant,
no manlier human spirit, no more devoted, more unselfish, soul
than Philip Schuyler.

GENERAL DANIEL MORGAN'S PART IN THE BURGOYNE CAMPAIGN

Rev. John H. Brandow, A. M., Albany.

To fully appreciate the Morgan who wrought so efficiently at Saratoga one should at least have an inkling of the part he previously played in Virginia, in Pennsylvania, in Canada and in the Jerseys, and also of how he behaved after he had there distinguished himself. Until recent years the birthplace of Daniel Morgan was not known for a certainty, and hence nothing was known about the conditions under which his youth was passed. Graham in his otherwise admirable Life of Morgan can say but little about his early environment. But modern methods of historical research have thrown much light on what for long was very obscure. Prof. Charles Laubach, of the University of Pennsylvania, who was born and reared in the same neighborhood where our hero first saw the light, spent much time following up every clue and discovered convincing evidence to prove that Morgan was born at Durham, Bucks County, Pa., in 1736, near the banks of the Delaware River. Previously it was supposed that his birthplace was somewhere in Hunterdon County, N. J.

His grandfather, John Morgan, came from Wales and settled at Darby, Pa. His father, James, became an ironmaster at the Durham Iron Works. A special interest attaches to these works because a large proportion of the cannon and balls used in the Revolution were cast there. Sarah, a sister of James Morgan, married Squire Boone and became the mother of one whose name is writ large in Kentucky's history. So Daniel Boone and Daniel Morgan were first cousins. The name of Daniel Morgan's mother was Elinora ———. Her family name has been lost. The log house in which Morgan was born was stand-

ing till about 1812 at the junction of Durham creek with a smaller stream. No records have been discovered of his boyish days.
His personal story begins when he was nearly grown. This
much he himself disclosed. When sixteen years of age,—because of some disagreement with his father,—he ran away from
home, and went to Virginia. He settled in the Shenandoah
valley, worked on a farm and in a sawmill for a while, then he
hired himself to one Ashley as a teamster. This work proved
quite to his liking as it involved travel and risk. The task was
to haul merchandise from the Virginia seaports over the Blue
Ridge Mountains for the frontiersmen in the valley. Within
two years he had saved enough to purchase an outfit of his
own and start as an independent wagoner.

The sense of ownership and responsibility helped greatly
to develop those qualities of mind and physique which afterward distinguished him:—Strength, agility, the love of fair
play, frankness, good humor, a ready wit, all of which served
to make him a favorite and a leader among the hardy pioneers
west of the Blue Ridge.

At the beginning of the French and Indian war, in 1755,
as we all know, Gen. Braddock landed a fine army on the Virginia coast for the conquest of the regions beyond the Alleghanies. But he was greatly delayed through lack of the means
of transportation. Braddock's advertisements offering big pay,
together with a native love of excitement and conflict, easily
won young Morgan for this his first taste of military life. He
and his team enlisted for the war.

The wagon train was a long way in the rear of the fighting
line when the Indians and French sprung their surprise on
Braddock's unwary host. But the frightened fugitives just from
the front, with their blood curdling tales of Indian atrocities soon
created a panic among the teamsters, most of whom dumped their
cargoes, turned about, and started at top speed for home. But
Morgan was one of the few who did not lose his head. He stuck
by his commander, Col. Dunbar, and brought back a full load of
the sick and wounded.

He had seen war now and his belligerent spirit made him
long for soldiering. Ere long he gave up teaming and enlisted,
starting off with the rank of ensign. His exploits in the wild,

perilous border warfare of the south rival those of Putnam in the north. Did space permit many thrilling encounters and hair breadth escapes might be recounted. Suffice it to say that twice the grisly terror death well nigh had him in his grip, once as the result of a most unjust and brutal flogging by the command of a British officer, and the second at the hands of an Indian who shot him through his neck and mouth, the ball extracting all his teeth on one side. Only an opulence of vitality can account for his recovery in either case.

As a result of a daring and successful exploit in the defense of Edward's Fort, Washington sought his acquaintance and began a friendship which lasted with life. Morgan's experiences and doings in the army were widely published and served to exalt him greatly in the esteem of his neighbors.

The evil associations of the army, however, had a demoralizing effect upon his tastes and habits. He gained the unenviable reputation of being a leader in all sorts of dissipation. He became a gamester, hard drinker, and a sort of swashbuckler generally. This was not because he was in any sense naturally base and vicious, but because he lived in a comparatively rude age, and among a rough people. Moreover, such behavior was mainly the misdirected outgushing of superabundant animal spirits. In addition to all this he became known as the best shot, the keenest hunter, and hardest rider of that region.

As the years advanced Morgan began to see the folly of his conduct and gradually withdrew from his riotous associations and formed more orderly habits. Doubtless the appeals of the master passion aided greatly in enabling him to see a new light. For about this time he chanced to meet a most worthy young woman whose tastes and ideals gave him a vision of nobler things for himself. She was Abigail Bailey, the daughter of a farmer of Berkeley County. Though bereft of the opportunity for education and culture, yet in the truest sense she was a lady, one to the manner born. The denouement of this chance meeting was the one quite natural. In this quiet unbellicose lady, Morgan found his conqueror. Henceforth she led him whither she would, but her "would" was always toward the things that are "lovely and of good report." Although from this time Morgan became a sober and studious man he did not at once become meek and mild, for in the first weeks of his new life he felt called upon to thrash all and every one of those who presumed to joke him about his sudden conversion.

After marriage Morgan settled down to be a farmer, and in this, as in all else he undertook, he made a great success, constantly multiplying his herds and his acres. He christened his home, "The Soldier's Rest." The records show that he took an active part in the Pontiac and Lord Dunmore's wars as a commissioned Captain. Lord Dunmore's war with the Indians ended just as the fires were kindling for the war of the Revolution. In the exciting questions at issue between Great Britain and her colonies, Morgan, who had kept himself posted on current events, made it very clear to his neighbors that his sympathies were wholly with the Colonies, and, if need be, he was ready to draw his sword in their defense. His resolute stand doubtless influenced many in that region to side with the patriots.

The climacteric events of Lexington and Bunker Hill induced the Continental Congress to raise and equip an army. One of the details of this measure was the calling into its service of ten companies of riflemen to be raised in the States of Pennsylvania, Maryland and Virginia. By unanimous vote Daniel Morgan was selected and commissioned to command one of Virginia's two companies.

Morgan's company was raised in the Shenandoah valley and the circumjacent mountains. Ordinary inducements would not have enlisted a man of them. But their devotion to Morgan was that of a Highland Clan to its Chief; so when he cried: "Come boys, who is for the camp before Boston?" the mountaineers turned out to a man. Short was their "note of preparation." The blanket buckled to their backs, a supply of food in their pouches, scanty as an Indian would take for a long trail,— they grasped their rifles and were off for the north, 600 miles away. And think of it; they made it in twenty-one days, an average of twenty-eight and one-half miles per day, and not a man of the ninety-six missing at the final muster. And, too, this was the first of the rifle corps to report. The next day at inspection Washington passing down the lines came to this company. Morgan, in saluting said, pointing to his men: "General, from the right bank of the Potomac." Washington immediately dismounted, passed down the company front and heartily shook the hand of every man.

The siege of Boston was now on. The comparative inactivity of this type of warfare proved irksome to Morgan and his men. It being intimated to him by Washington that an important expedition was afoot and that several companies of riflemen would be needed Morgan at once volunteered his company. His request was finally granted. In due time he found himself in command of a part of Benedict Arnold's force designated to co-operate with General Philip Schuyler for the conquest of Canada.

The force detailed for this service started from Cambridge September 13th, 1775. The hardships and horrors of that six hundred miles march through an uncharted wilderness have often been described. It is a depressing tale. But when they arrived at Point Levi they mustered only six hundred of the eleven hundred that started. Accident, desertion, sickness and starvation had done gruesome work with that intrepid host. However only one of Morgan's men was missing, and he was drowned.

Nor will the design of this paper allow a description of the siege of Quebec. Suffice it to say that Morgan and his men were the first to set foot on the north shore of the St. Lawrence. And had Arnold listened to Morgan, who urged an immediate assault, they would have found its defenders wholly unprepared to oppose them, and in all human probability Quebec would have been theirs. But when the assault was ultimately made they found the garrison greatly strengthened, the weather most bitter and icy, and what is more significant, in the study of that event, one finds an aggregation of apparently insignificant happenings which clearly indicate that "the Divinity who shapes our ends" had decreed that Canada should not be a part of the United States.

In the final assault Morgan with his corps were made prisoners. They found in Sir Guy Carleton a most humane and generous conqueror. He proved this first, by discharging them, on their parole, in August, '76; second, by clothing the naked and the ragged; and third, by shipping them all to New York.

While a prisoner in Quebec Morgan relates that he was approached with a very flattering offer to enter the British service. This he spurned with indignation. On the 11th of September, one year from their setting out from Cambridge, they were landed at Elizabethtown Point, N. J. It is also related that only twenty-five of the ninety-six who started with him ever reached their homes.

Morgan at once reported to Washington, and expressed the wish that through an exchange of prisoners he might be released from his parole, then he would re-enter the service.

Washington had been fully apprised of Morgan's rare qualities and fearless conduct during the Canadian campaign. He at once urgently recommended Congress to promote him to the command of a regiment, such to take effect on his liberation from his parole.

Morgan then started for his home, where he was received with every token of respect and affection, for the story of his exploits had preceded him there. Before the end of that year, '76, he was freed from the obligation of his parole, and had also received his commission as Colonel of the 11th Virginia Regiment. At once he began recruiting for his new command, but he found this a slow business, as most of the desirable men had already been picked up. However, about the 1st of April, 1777, he reported at headquarters with 180 men. Washington was overjoyed to see him.

Washington's previous military experience had taught him the value of a select corps of rangers, composed of hardy, active men, familiar with woodcraft and skilled with the rifle. A body of 500 picked men was accordingly formed from the different regiments of the army. The command of this corps was given to Morgan.

Morgan and his corps in every respect met Washington's high expectations. They proved of invaluable service in the preliminary collisions between Washington and Howe during the early summer of '77 in the Jerseys. In his reports to Congress he took occasion to speak in the highest terms of the "conduct and bravery" of Morgan and his men.

The advance of Burgoyne from Canada and the fall of Ticonderoga resulted in a most urgent call by Schuyler for reinforcements from Washington. The terror caused by the murderous raids of Burgoyne's Indians needed especially to be counteracted, and Washington knew of no better antidote for them than Morgan's rangers; so, with great reluctance he, on the 16th of August, ordered them north. In a few days they were on the march and soon reported themselves to Gen. Gates, who had just succeeded Gen. Schuyler in command of the Northern Department. Gates had already been notified of his coming by Washington, and of the character of the man and his regiment. Hence on his arrival he received from the General a most cordial welcome and every mark of deference. Moreover, as a special token of regard his corps was designated as "the advance of the army," and he was directed to receive orders only from the General-in-Chief. Also under Morgan was placed an additional battalion of 250 men, selected from the Northern Army in the same way his own had been from the Southern. This battalion was led by Maj. Dearborn, a New Hampshire man, who had been a comrade of Morgan in the attempt on Canada. As we may suppose this was mutually agreeable, as an ardent friendship had already developed between these officers on that expedition.

On the 8th of September Gen. Gates abandoned his camp at the mouth of the Mohawk and began the movement toward the north. Morgan and his men were placed in advance as a corps of observation, with orders to report the first signs of the enemy. At this time it was supposed that Burgoyne had already crossed the Hudson; but this did not occur till the 13th and 14th. On the 12th, Gates and his army reached Bemis Heights where Kosciuszko, his Polish engineer, had decided that the lay of the land offered the best natural defence against an enemy. The following day the army began erecting defenses. Morgan's command was placed with Gen. Arnold's division, which formed the left wing of the army, and was stationed about a mile and a quarter west of the river, in the most exposed quarter.

On the morning of the 19th of September Gates, though apprised by his scouts that Burgoyne was pressing forward to attack him, had planned to await the enemy from behind his defenses. But Arnold, divining the intention of Burgoyne, urged Gates to permit him to go out with his men and assail the enemy before he could reach the camp, urging as arguments that if beaten in the open they would still have their intrenchments to fall back on, but if Burgoyne should get near enough to the camp to use his artillery, it would be impossible to hold their position.

Finally Gates yielded so far as to permit Morgan and Dearborn to go out with their rangers to observe and harass the enemy. They sallied forth and about 12:30 P. M. ran foul of Burgoyne's Indians and Canadians scouting near the Freeman cottage. These they drove back with considerable loss, every officer in the party being either killed or wounded. Morgan's men eagerly pursued, but were greatly surprised to find themselves up against the main body of the enemy just within the edge of the woods northeast of the house. In turn they were of course soon routed and became badly scattered in the woods. Morgan, though for a while greatly disconcerted by this accident, was soon able by the vigorous use of his "turkey call" whistle to rally his men about him. Having been strengthened on his left by the arrival of Cilley's and Scammel's regiments they renewed the attack, but with indifferent results.

Burgoyne formed his line of battle in the woods on the north side of a clearing owned by one Isaac Freeman. It contained twelve or fifteen acres and extended east and west about sixty rods. This clearing, called Freeman's Farm, was the principal scene of the action of the 19th. Fraser with the right wing had reached the line of low hills just west of Freeman's Farm when the action began. After the termination of the first skirmish, and when the battle had been vigorously renewed, Fraser wheeled to his left for the purpose of flanking Morgan and the other regiments when, to his surprise, he encountered in the woods, Arnold at the head of several regiments. It is needless to add that the dogs of war were unleashed at once, and a furious struggle ensued, for the two most fiery leaders in either army were here pitted against each other. Fraser was saved this time by the timely appearance of Col. Breyman with his Hessians. Soon he was able to form his junction with Burgoyne, after which the struggle centered on and about the Freeman clearing and the open woods to the west. The Americans attacked the British furiously and drove them into the woods on the north side, where they were rallied, and charging with bayonets drove the Americans back across the same field into the cover of the woods to the south where in turn they recovered themselves and hurled the redcoats back with great slaughter. Many of Morgan's riflemen, posted in trees, did terrible execution among the British officers as well as he rank and file. The bulk of them, however, threw themselves into the charges where the most desperate valor was exhibited, and hand to hand encounters were frequent, especially about the British field battery, which was taken and retaken at every charge.

For four consecutive hours this fierce and bloody battle raged, each side being alternately re-enforced, till finally Riedesel, the German, came with Pausch's battery, which succeeded in folding back the American right wing, after which night compelled a cessation of actual fighting. Result: the Americans retired to their camp for the night, and the British held the ground, sleeping on their arms.

As to the question of victory: Since it was Burgoyne's purpose to advance and not simply to hold his ground, while Gates' purpose was to hold his ground and check the advance of Burgoyne, each can judge for himself to whom the palm should be given. And among the several who distinguished themselves that day we have no hesitancy about mentioning the name of Daniel Morgan. His regiment was the first on the field and the last to leave it. Where it was engaged the strife was more deadly and less interrupted than in any other position. Its loss was greater than that of any American regiment engaged, while the number which fell by its hands was nearly half of those admitted by Burgoyne to have fallen in the battle. Moreover after this battle, in which Morgan's men had been specially pitted against the Indians in the British army, most of them discovered that some very pressing business called them home, and they went.

It is noteworthy, however, that Gates in his report of the battle to Congress had nothing to say about either Arnold or Morgan. This slight with one or two other unfortunate incidents resulted in a rupture between Arnold and Gates, wherein Arnold was deprived of his command.

A few days before the second battle Gates received a request from Washington that Morgan and his corps be returned if he could possibly be spared. From his reply to Washington one can easily draw Gates' real estimate of Morgan's worth. After describing the two armies as still facing each other, and ready to renew the struggle, Gates says: "In this situation your Excellency would not wish me to part with **the corps that the army of Gen. Burgoyne are most** afraid of."

For nearly three weeks Burgoyne and his army had remained quietly in their fortified camp hoping to hear from Clinton, who had promised to come up from the south to their relief. But hearing nothing further from him and the commissariat running low, a council of war was called. Two courses were open before them, to fight or retreat. Finally Burgoyne on his own responsibility decided to make a reconnaisance in force of the American left. If the outlook proved favorable he would fight, otherwise he would retreat.

With a body of 1500 picked men, two 12-pounders, six 6-pounders and two howitzers, he left his camp. It was between 10 and 11 o'clock on the morning of the 7th of October. They moved toward the southwest about two-thirds of a mile to a clearing where they deployed and sat down to give time for a detail of teamsters and batmen to forage in a wheatfield. The place is just north of the Middle ravine. The road now running from Bemis Heights to Quaker Springs passes through the British position. The light infantry under the Earl of Balcarras was stationed on the right, Riedesel and his Germans and a battery of two 6-pounders held the center, Majors Ackland and Williams with the grenadiers and the balance of the artillery were posted on the left. General Fraser with 500 grenadiers occupied some high ground in advance with the intention of stealing around to the left of the American works and holding their attention while the main body could gain the high ground to to the west, from whence they could observe and shell the American camp.

Gates was quickly apprised of this move by some of Morgan's scouts. At once he bade his Adjutant, Wilkinson, to go and ascertain its purport. On his return he reported that Burgoyne apparently offered battle. Gates said, "What would you

GLENS FALLS (1826.)
Courtesy of Frank J. Wilder

U. S. HOTEL (Circa 1840)
Courtesy of Frank J. Wilder

suggest?" Wilkinson replied, "I would indulge him." "Then," said Gates, "order out Morgan to begin the game."

After a short conference with his officers it was decided that Morgan should make a circuit to the west and strike the enemy on his right flank, Gen. Poor with his brigade was to assail the left flank, while Learned's brigade and Dearborn's riflemen were to engage their center and right center. Sufficient time was to be given Morgan to reach his position before an attack should be made.

About 2:30 P. M. the advance began and Poor's men descended into the Middle ravine and ascended the opposite bank with all the steadiness of veterans. After receiving the first volley they rushed forward and closed with the enemy and never slacked the contest till a twelve-pounder was theirs, Major Williams a prisoner, Major Ackland left seriously wounded, and the leaderless grenadiers driven from the field.

Nearly contemporaneous with Poor's attack, Morgan, having discovered Fraser in his advanced position, managed to gain the ridge to the west, and then rushing down upon him like an avalanche, compelled him to retire to the main body; then by a quick move to his left Morgan soon placed himself where he could flank the British right, and then struck with such momentum as to fold them back and compel Balcarras to change front. Nearly simultaneous with Morgan's flank attack, Dearborn with his men, who were now in touch with Morgan, leaped the fence in his front and charged with such effect as to force his opponents back.

But where is Arnold all this while? Arnold the thunderbolt? Why, he is being held in leash by the jealous Gates. Deprived of his command, and refused the privilege of serving even as a volunteer, he is chafing up there in the camp like a caged lion who has had a sniff of blood. The stress proves too much for his unruly spirit. He suddenly mounts his splendid bay, rushes through the sally port and is off for the fray determined to put in at the first opening. This offers itself at the British center. Placing himself at the head of a detachment of Learned's brigade he charged the Germans, broke their lines and compelled them to retire in confusion.

But let us glance at the struggle from the British stand-point. Burgoyne was evidently disconcerted by the promptness and vigor of the American attack. Fraser, having been forced back from his advanced position by Morgan, put in where he could be of the most service. Nor was there any lack of oppor-tunity. Under the withering fire and tremendous pressure of the American attack the lines were being constantly broken. Fraser, finely mounted, rushed fearlessly here and there, rally-ing and animating the men, and directing their movements. When the right wing was disorganized and in danger of being cut off Burgoyne ordered Fraser to form a second line to cover and re-enforce them. This he did with such promptness and energy that Morgan's men were effectually held in check. The falling back of both wings uncovered the center, but the Germans stubbornly held their ground. It was at this juncture that Ar-nold's desperate charge forced them into disorderly retreat. Fraser noticing their peril hastened to their relief with the 24th regiment, which soon brought order out of chaos. Indeed, wher-ever Fraser appeared everything seemed to prosper for King George, for the men believed in him and would follow wherever he led. Morgan, who was directly opposed to Fraser's brigade, noticing that the conflict seemed to be wavering in the balance, chiefly because of Fraser's masterly leadership, called a few of his best riflemen to him and directing their attention toward the enemy, said: "That gallant officer on the grey horse is Gen. Fraser; I admire and respect him, but it is necessary to our suc-cess that he be put out of the way,—take your station in that clump of trees and do your duty." Not many minutes after Gen. Fraser fell mortally wounded and was tenderly borne from the field by a detail of his brave grenadiers.

After the fall of Fraser the men lost heart. Burgoyne tried to rally them, but in vain. Beaten at every point they retreated to their camp, chased by the victorious Americans. This camp they assaulted furiously at various points, and finally under the lead of Arnold at the head of Learned's men they broke through and captured the redoubt which defended the right wing of the British army. In this assault Col. Breyman, its com-mander, lost his life and Arnold was wounded in the same leg hurt at Quebec. A blessed thing for his memory had that bullet pierced his heart instead.

The Americans thus possessed of this right flank defense found it an open gateway to the whole British camp. The British, on the other hand, recognizing the significance of its capture, knew that the game was up for them. But the night was now fallen and put an end to this struggle as it did to the battle of the 19th of September. During that night Burgoyne withdrew his army to the low ground near the river, retaining, however, so much of the heights as lay north of Wilbur's Basin ravine. From here he began his retreat to the north on the night of the 8th, immediately after the burial of Fraser.

Graham in his biography of Morgan relates how, upon his return to headquarters that night to report, he was met by Gates who immediately embraced him, saying, "Morgan you have done wonders today. You have immortalized yourself, and honored your country; if you are not promoted immediately I will not serve another day!" But we will see later how Gates seemed to suffer a lapse of memory.

The behavior of both Gates and Burgoyne after this battle seems well nigh inexplicable. At such a moment the chief concern of the one should have been to save his army from capture, that of the other to immediately follow up his victory and complete the destruction of his enemy. As it was both of them proved themselves masters of the art of inaction. From Wilbur's Basin to Saratoga (now Schuylerville) it was only nine miles, yet Burgoyne and his suite did not cross Fish Creek, a large stream flowing from the west, till the 10th. Until the 12th there was open to him a way of escape on the west side of the Hudson and Lake George, but he dawdled till the gap was closed. Had he possessed the energy and spirit of either Gens. Phillips or Riedesel, his subordinates, Gates would never have felt the touch of Burgoyne's surrendered sword.

Through mismanagement in the commissary department Gates was led to delay his pursuit of Burgoyne till the afternoon of the 10th, or about three days after the battle, and when he reached Saratoga Burgoyne should, by rights, have been two days march further north. When the pursuit did occur Morgan and his corps as usual led the advance and camped that night

(the 10th) just to the south of Fish Creek, Burgoyne occupying
the north side.   Gen. Fellows with some 3000 New Hampshire
and Massachusetts militia held the east side of the Hudson.   On
the 12th Gates's lines of circumvallation were completed; Bur-
gogyne was hopelessly enmeshed and the work of starving him
into surrender was begun.   A Pennsylvania force, Learned's brigade and Morgan with his rangers occupied the ground to the
west and northwest of Burgoyne. Gates with New England, New
York and New Jersey troops held the south, while the redoubtable Stark with Vermont and some New Hampshire men blocked
the way toward the north.

The Americans now made it very interesting for the Britons.
Fellow's batteries on the bluffs east of the river were echoed by
Gates from the heights south of Fish Creek, and a battery on a
hill to the north bellowed "Amen! we are with you," while Morgan's sharpshooters to the west, and the Yankee marksmen
from all sides else, popped at any hostile head that dared show itself from behind a tree or above the breastworks.   All this with
the answering thunders of Burgoyne's heavy artillery in their
effort to silence Fellows must have made terrific music such as
those Saratoga hills never heard before or since.

But this, like all other dramas, however thrilling or tragic,
came to an end.   Burgoyne quickly saw the futility of attempt-
ing to hold out against such a host as now beleaguered him,
which by the way, was the largest American army that assembled at one time and place during the Revolutionary war, about
25,000 men.

On the 13th Burgoyne made the first overtures looking toward surrender.   After some delay and an evident effort at playing for time Burgoyne finally signed what he chose to call "the
treaty of Convention" on October 16th.   The next morning at 11
o'clock the British army left its fortified camp, marched down
the hill to the river flat and piled their arms just to the east of
the Champlain canal.   The only Americans present to witness
this transaction were Colonels Wilkinson and Morgan Lewis
who had been appointed by Gates for the purpose.

In due time Gen. Burgoyne and his subordinates crossed the
creek and passed down between the lines drawn up on either side
of the road to the marquee of Gen. Gates, where he was introduc-

ed, and where in turn Gates introduced his principal officers. When Col. Morgan was presented Burgoyne took his hand and said: "Sir, you command the finest regiment in the world." And as to that matter Burgoyne was about then fully competent to judge.

After this and other encomiums passed upon him by many British officers it is surprising to note that Morgan's name nowhere appears in the official account of the surrender, by Gen. Gates, to the securing of which consummation he contributed so conspicuously and effectively.

Soon after the surrender it was noted by officers that Morgan was being treated by Gates with marked coolness and neglect. This to them was unaccountable, but a clue to the mystery is furnished by Morgan himself in an incident he later saw fit to tell. Immediately after the surrender Morgan visited Gates on business, when he was taken aside by the General and confidentially told that the main army was extremely dissatisfied with the conduct of the war by the Commander-in-Chief, and that several of the best officers threatened to resign unless there was a change. Morgan quickly caught Gates' drift in this talk, and though he was then a stranger to the intrigues of Conway and others, he sternly replied: "I have one favor to ask of you, General, which is this: never mention that subject to me again; for under no other man than Washington, as Commander-in-Chief, would I consent to serve."

Though Gates deliberately ignored Morgan and in a covert way hindered his promotion, yet Washington, and others who knew him, were unstinted in their praise and admiration. Moreover the pen of unprejudiced history has not failed to do him justice as it also has the name of Schuyler and other neglected worthies of that day. For example the late Col. Carrington in his "Battles of the American Revolution," says: "The student of history must write with Sparks, and Irving, and Marshall in the general sentiment that Morgan only, of American officers, can compete with Arnold for the brightest laurels of the Saratoga campaign."

With his command Morgan started from Albany on the 1st of November, following the surrender, to join Washington. He reached headquarters at Whitemarsh, Pa., on the 18th, his force depleted in number and sadly worn from the strain and hardships of the last three months. Nevertheless he took active part in the operations about Philadelphia, and, as might be expected, the enemy soon learned that Morgan with his hornets were in the game against them.

The end of the campaign of '77 found his men placed as usual nearest the enemy to guard the approach to Valley Forge from the south.

During the winter that followed Morgan deemed it best to seek rest and retirement at his home. The fatigues and sufferings experienced by him during the Canadian and Saratoga campaigns had seriously impaired a constitution naturally robust. Moreover at this time he felt the first twinges of an ailment that ultimately forced his retirement from the public service.

In the spring of 1778 he again appeared at the front ready for duty. His command was fully occupied in the movements connected with the evacuation of Philadelphia by the British. At the battle of Monmouth on June 28th his corps chanced to be so placed and occupied that they could take no part in the action. This was a cause of great disappointment and chagrin to him and his men.

Shortly after this battle Morgan was assigned by Washington to the command of Woodford's Brigade. This terminated his connection with the gallant rifle corps. Feelings of deepest regret filled the minds of all concerned. The rest of the year '78 was spent in the maneuvers for the defense of the lower Hudson. Nothing of special moment in connection with Morgan occurred during this period.

Gen. Woodford returned to his command in June, '79, whereat Morgan found himself without any command, unless he chose to accept Congress' offer of the Colonelcy of the 7th Regiment of Virginia. Here in his own case Morgan, like other able officers, was forced to see foreign adventurers, and men of little experience, but possessed of political or social influence, placed above them in command, while the men who had made the sacrifices, won battles, as also the idolatrous homage of their men, were being wholly ignored and treated as unworthy. Therefore, because of this open affront in addition to the aforementioned fact that his health was sadly undermined, and still further, because his finances were greatly depleted, Morgan decided to resign from service. This he did to the infinite regret of the army and of Washington in particular, who while arguing against it was free to acknowledge the justice of his claims. His resignation was accepted about July 1st, 1779. The recovery of his health, the mending of his fortune, and the rejuvenation of his farm with its appurtenances now occupied his time.

In the meanwhile the seat of war had been transferred by the British to the south. Things looked pretty dark for independence in that quarter. The redoubtable Gates had been sent to exterminate Cornwallis, but was himself practically wiped out at the battle of Camden. Prior to this battle Congress had pleaded with every available Southerner to enlist for the final struggle. Among others it bethought itself of Col. Morgan, lately resigned, and, as an inducement for his going to the rescue, again offered him a Colonelcy! Think of it! The pettiness, yes, the indignity of such proposal seemingly did not occur to those men. Quite naturally Morgan proved invulnerable to such a dazzling offer and stayed at home.

But the disaster at Camden stirred the deeper man within. In the presence of that he felt that for him the time was come to sacrifice every private consideration to the public good, so he with a few friends betook themselves to the camp of Gates at Hillsboro, N. C., arriving there in September, 1780.

Gates had already made amicable advances toward Morgan, and was clearly desirous of a reconciliation. Morgan magnanimously smothered his old resentment against Gates, met him half way, and peace between them was restored.

In December following Gates was superseded in command by Gen. Greene. Soon thereafter the affairs of the patriots took on a brighter complexion. About this time at the urgent request of Washington, and other influential officers, Congress repented of its folly and commissioned Morgan a Brigadier General. Almost immediately Greene gave Morgan a thousand men and sent him south to harrass the left flank of Cornwallis' army. Not many days elapsed before the Briton felt the sting of this scorpion in his side. At once Cornwallis sent after him his ablest and mose energetic chieftain, Gen. Tarleton. Learning that Tarleton was after him, Morgan, though outnumbered, decided to give battle. The opposing forces met at an isolated place called the Cowpens on the brink of the Broad river near the line between North and South Carolina. The result of the collision was that Tarleton's force was practically annihilated. This affair in its plan, execution, and denouement was then, and still is, considered the most brilliant battle of the Revolution. And thus Washington's estimate of Morgan and that of all others who knew him, was justified. Even Congress sat up, rubbed its eyes, scratched its dull pate, and concluded that there must be something in this man Morgan after all. As an evidence of its awakened appreciation that body voted him a gold medal. But he had to wait years before he got it.

Soon after this battle a return of his old malady, sciatica, compelled him to withdraw from the army. And though he longed to be back, and actually attempted to rejoin his command, he was forced to yield and make his first surrender to an enemy. This recalls a story his friends used to like to relate, because it is altogether characteristic of him. Soon after the close of the war the War Department sent out blanks to all officers who had served asking detailed information as to the when, the where, and the how of their services. Morgan, impatient of the many categorical questions, siezed his pen and wrote across the sheet: "I fought everywhere and surrendered nowhere."

To us New Yorkers it is interesting to note that on his return to Virginia in 1778 he rechristened his home "Saratoga" as a reminder of the most important battle in which he had been engaged. And in this he forestalled the judgment of modern historians, who by common consent affirm that Saratoga was the decisive battle of the Revolution, and one of the sixteen of all times, in all the world.

Gen. Morgan proved himself to be a born leader of men. And yet one wonders how he was able to collect and hold together so large a body of men, most of whom were known to be high spirited, and often reckless and uncontrollable. It was because he had originally been one of their kind, hence he knew their nature and how to appeal to them. But he had early learned how to control himself, and so could exercise patience with others. However, he had little patience with the shirk or coward. Proximity to Morgan was an uncomfortable place for such, but he was ever ready to share all hardships and work with the men who were worthy. Moreover he was accessible to every man who had a grievance and was always fair in his judgments. It is related that on one occasion he sent a Corporal with a couple of privates to mend a bad place in a road leading to camp. An hour or so later having occasion to pass that way he saw the two men straining to remove a large stone, while with hands in pockets the Corporal stood looking on. Morgan stopped and asked him why he didn't take hold to help the men. "What," said the Corporal, "an officer do such work?" "Oh, beg your pardon," replied Morgan, "I didn't think." And leaping from his horse he gripped the stone saying, "Now boys, together, heave!" and in a trice that stone was out of the way. Without another word he mounted his horse and was off.

Morgan's life typifies in a remarkable way what was won for the world of common men by our war for Independence. As we have seen he was born a peasant in a monarchy, but he became a great leader and moral force in a republic, a government by the citizenship. Such a thing could not have occurred in the Europe of that day.

He was a sort of first fruit of a time, which he helped to make possible, that should give to every one, even a rail-splitter, as Lincoln, a chance to prove to the world "that a man's a man for a' that."

In later years he assisted materially in ending the Whiskey Rebellion in Pennsylvania. This he accomplished more by masterly diplomacy than by actual force. Later still his neighbors voted to have him represent them in Congress, but his enfeebled health effectually hindered him from serving in this way.

Gen. Daniel Morgan died July 6th, 1802, aged 67, and his honored remains lie buried in beautiful Mt. Auburn Cemetery at Winchester, Virginia.

Among the authorities consulted in the preparation of the above paper the following were found specially helpful:

Graham's Life of Gen. Daniel Morgan.

Lives of the Heroes.

Rogers' Biographical Dictionary.

Headley's Washington and His Generals, Vol. II.

Col. Carrington's Battles of the Revolution.

Magazine of American History. Vol. IX.

Custis' Washington.

Outing. Vol. XLVIII.

Special thanks are due Mrs. Delia A. McCulloch, of Point Pleasant, W. Va., for the loan of her volume of the West Virginia Historical Magazine, containing her valuable and informing paper on Gen. Daniel Morgan.

BENEDICT ARNOLD—PATRIOT

By Edgar W. Ames, M. A., (Williams),

Head of the Department of History, Troy High School, Troy, N. Y.

The halos of our Revolutionary sires are sadly askew. No longer can our noble ancestors pose in stony calm above the common herd, for the bright light of historical research has been turned on them and the result is that we find today that these men were just as intensely human as we are. The problem the present day teacher of history must face,—and the one, by the way, that is not faced, and so history becomes to the long suffering boys and girls, a series of dry and unrelated facts,—the problem the teacher must face is the one of humanizing history. The boys and girls must understand that the men whom they study about were just as real, just as full of life and passion, influenced by the same motives as the modern man is. They were not mere registering automatons, never doing evil, never going astray. Washington could use a good round oath if it seemed to relieve his feelings, but more than that, he could wrestle all night in prayer with the Lord as did Jacob of old. Only within the last few years have we understood the human side of our great men. Is it more than reasonable to expect that the greatst evil doer of the time should be painted in the blackest colors when those of small worth were shown to us as demi-gods? The treachery of Benedict Arnold was a terrible thing, but even Arnold the traitor was human. Well might he have paraphrased Shylock, "Hath not a traitor, hands, organs, dimensions, senses, affections, passions?—If you wrong us shall we not revenge? The villany you teach me I will execute, and it shall go hard but I will better the instruction."

The Arnold family was one well known in New England. Among the first settlers of Rhode Island was William Arnold, a name somewhat noted in the annals of the state. A Benedict Arnold was governor of the state for several terms. From this family was descended the man more notorious for his treachery than noted for his patriotism, whose dastardly act overshadowed all the good and patriotic deeds he accomplished, Benedict Arnold. His father had removed to Norwich, Conn., and not being a success as a cooper, engaged in trade and later became a merchant carrying on an extensive business. Sparks, Hill, and others in their biographies of Arnold speak of him as a man little respected by his neighbors, "a drunkard, and a burden on the public mind." Yet it seems strange if this is true, for he held several public offices, selectman, collector, assessor, and surveyor of the port, and if he had been a man of "suspicious integrity" his fellow townsmen would hardly have conferred these honors upon him. He married a Mrs. Hannah King, who seems to have been a splendid woman, a devout Christian of the strictest sect of the Presbyterians. To them was born January 3, 1740, a son. An elder brother had died shortly before, and now as the eldest son, his parents gave him the name borne by the eldest of the family for many generations, Benedict. Of the other children born to this couple, only one daughter, Hannah, survived infancy. She lived for many years after the Revolution, part of the time in Troy, N. Y., with Benedict Arnold's sons, Richard and Henry, who were in business there.

Many of the older biographers of Arnold attempt to show that as a boy he was thoroughly bad and depraved in character and that his whole career was one of evil instincts. They tell of his robbing birds' nests, and that he delighted in hearing the old birds wail for "the destruction of their innocent offspring." They say he used to throw broken bottles and pieces of glass on the road near the school house, in order to cut the feet of his barefooted playfellows. They claim he used to lay traps for unsuspecting youths that he might rush out and belabor them with a whip he kept concealed near by, calling them thieves, as he lashed them over their shoulders. It would seem however that if young Arnold did these reprehensible things, that in the light of modern child study it would not necessarily follow that he would grow up a bad man. I do not doubt if those in this presence should look over their youthful days, but that some of the doings of youth would be construed as an indication of future wickedness. These old biographers tell how at the age of sixteen, he ran away to fight in the French and Indian war, and picture the grief of his poor mother at his wilfulness. This event also is turned to show the bent of the boy's mind toward evil from his early youth. Yet how many boys of that age ran away to fight during the Civil War, and is it not treasured up to them for righteousness, rather than an indication of an evil mind? I can find that the boy Arnold was no more evil than many boys, adventurous, brave, full of tricks, but no such monster of wickedness as he has been painted.

When he was twenty-one years old, he finished his term of service to a firm of druggists, to which he had been bound out some years before. At his coming of age he went to New Haven and set up in business for himself. Not many years ago there was found in the garret of a house he used to occupy, a sign painted black, and with white letters which reads as follows —:

B. ARNOLD, DRUGGIST,
Bookseller, etc.,
FROM LONDON.
Sibi Totique.

"For himself and for all."

It is evident that he soon became a rising, prosperous, young man. He became a merchant and ship owner, commanding his own ships. He had a large trade with Canada, often visiting Quebec, where he purchased the horses and cattle he shipped to the West Indies. He was made a Mason, and elected Captain of the Governor's Foot Guards, one of the two military organizations of the colony. On the 22nd of February, 1767, he married the reigning belle of New Haven, Miss Margaret Mansfield, daughter of the high sheriff of the county. The marriage was a happy one, rudely broken by the death of his wife.

While in New Haven Arnold got into trouble by soundly thrashing an informer who reported to the authorities that he, (Arnold), was smuggling goods into the country. In an open letter to the Connecticut Gazette he explains his share in the trouble: "The informer having been a voyage with me, in which he was used with the greatest humanity, on our return was paid his wages to his full satisfaction, and informed me of his intention to leave town on that day, wished me well, and departed the town as I imagined. But he, two days after, endeavored to make information to a Custom House Officer: but it being holy time, was desired to call on Monday, early on which day I heard of his intention, and gave him a little chastisement, on which he left town; and on Wednesday returned to Mr. Beecher's where I saw the fellow who agreed to and signed the following Oath:

" 'I, Peter Boyle, not having the fear of God before my eyes, but being instigated by the Devil, did on the 24th instant, make information or endeavor to do the same, to one of the Custom House Officers for the Port of New Haven, against **Benedict Arnold,** for importing contraband goods, do hereby acknowledge I justly deserve a Halter for my malicious and cruel intentions. * * * * * **So help me God.**' "

Arnold ends his letter with this query: "Is it good policy; or would so great a number of people, in any trading town on the continent (New Haven excepted) vindicate, protect, and caress an informer, a character, particularly at this alarming time, so justly odious to the Public? Every such information tends to suppress our trade, so advantageous to the Colony and to almost every individual both here and in Great Britain, and which is nearly ruined by the late detestable stamp, and other oppressive acts,—acts which we have severely felt, and so loudly complained of, and so earnestly remonstrated against, that one would imagine every sensible man would strive to encourage trade and discountenance such useless, such infamous informers. I am, Sir, your humble servant, Benedict Arnold."

This was during the excitement caused by the Stamp Act. Smuggling was common throughout the colonies, and in the eyes of the generality of people at least, those who smuggled their goods into the country were not considered law-breakers. We look upon John Hancock as a noble type of patriot. What about his ship "Liberty"? What shall we say of those who burned the "Gaspé" which was patrolling the coast to prevent smuggling? If it is an evidence of patriotism in one to resist the law, we can make no discrimination in regard to another.

From the very beginning of our troubles with the mother country Arnold ardently took the part of the colonies. Not only is this shown in the query just noted, but also in a letter to a friend written soon after the so-called Boston Massacre. Writing from the West Indies where he had gone on a trading expedition, he said, "Good God, are the Americans all asleep and tamely yielding up their liberties, or are they all turned philosophers that they do not take immediate vengeance on such miscreants?"

When the Battle of Lexington was fought, Arnold was thirty-five years old. The news of the battle reached New Haven by pony express the next day after the fighting, and Arnold as Captain of the militia at once called out the Foot Guards. In a fiery and patriotic speech he asked for volunteers, and offered to lead them at once to Boston. A band of sixty, a few of them Yale students, volunteered and the next morning they were ready to march.

The town committee had collected a supply of powder, flints and lead for possible emergencies, and Arnold asked Colonel Wooster, leader of the committee, for enough to supply his men. This Colonel Wooster refused to do, without regular orders from the competent authorities. "Regular orders be d—d," cried Arnold, "and our friends and neighbors being mowed down by redcoats. Give us the powder or we'll take it." Under protest the keys were given up, and the needed supply taken, but Arnold had laid in train the events which brought about his final downfall. His impetuous nature would brook no interference, and the idea of the Irishman at the Donnybrook Fair, "Whenever you see a head, hit it," led to the useless hatred which was the great factor in bringing about his treachery. Wooster never forgot the insult offered him, and Arnold by his defiance of the selectmen, aroused a spirit of unfriendliness at home which exerted a most disastrous effect on his fortunes.

Reaching Cambridge, he laid before the Massachusetts Committee of Safety a plan for the capture of Fort Ticonderoga. Whether he had learned of such plan as he passed through Hartford on his way to Boston is a disputed question, but this project had been conceived by the Connecticut Committee of Safety, which had induced Colonel Ethan Allen and a band of Green

Mountain Boys to join with the force sent by Connecticut. Arnold's proposition had been received with favor by the Massachusetts Committee, and he was hastening forward to its execution, when he heard of the other expedition. Thinking to have the two forces join themselves under his command, he left his men and went on to Castleton, about twenty-five miles from Fort Ticonderoga, where he found a council of war had decided that Allen should have chief command. Arnold showed his commission and instructions, but the Green Mountain Boys would have none of him, and he was forced to submit. Though bitterly disappointed he said, "If I cannot fight as a leader, I'll serve as a private" and joined the ranks as a volunteer. The results of the expedition are too well known for comment.

He now demanded that he should be placed in command of the captured fort, but again his desires were ignored and the Connecticut Committee of Safety appointed Allen as commander. Though once more disappointed, he did not sulk, but setting forth down the lake, he sailed as far as the British post at St. John, and captured it together with a large amount of stores, returning in triumph to Fort Ticonderoga. Hearing that the British were to attempt the recapture of their lost forts, he at once set about the fortifying of Crown Point. While he had been serving his country, messengers and letters were sent to the Committees of Safety of Massachusetts and Connecticut in which Arnold's presumption and arrogance were subjects of censure, but his help in accomplishing the main objects of the expedition was entirely overlooked. His treatment of Wooster, his expedition down the lake when Allen was in chief command, the jealousy between various colonies, all had raised a clique of enemies behind his back, and now to his astonishment, a committee appeared at the fort to investigate the charges made against him.

Naturally, Arnold was very indignant when he was superseded by Colonel Hinman who had been appointed in the interest of peace. He had spent £100 of his own money and contracted debts on his personal credit in procuring necessaries for the army which he was bound to pay or leave in dishonor. On his return to Cambridge he had no difficulty in proving to Congress and to Washington that the charges against him were base-

VIEW OF CONGRESS & COLUMBIAN SPRINGS (Circa 1840)
Courtesy of Frank J. Wilder

BALLSTON (1815). (See Grose's Ballston p. 54)
Courtesy of Frank J. Wilder

less. Washington believed him and always stood his friend until his treachery. Silas Deane wrote from Cambridge, August 10, 1775, "Colonel Arnold has been in my opinion, hardly treated by this (Connecticut) colony, through some mistake or other. He has deserved much, and received little or less than nothing." Deane's brother had previously written from Ticonderoga in June, "Arnold has been greatly abused and misrepresented by designing persons. Had it not been for him everything here would have been in disorder; people would have been plundered of their private property, and no man's life would have been safe that was not of the Green Mountain party." To add to all his other troubles, his wife had died while he was in the camps, leaving him with three small children.

Even with such misuse and hard treatment from the authorities, Arnold now proposed to Congress and to Washington, a plan for the capture of Canada. While serving on Lake Champlain, he had sent spies to Montreal and the surrounding country to bring back information of the British troops in that section. When he returned to Cambridge he proposed that an expedition be sent by way of the Maine wilderness to join with the force under General Schuyler who had been ordered by the Continental Congress to invade Canada by way of Lake Champlain. It was reported that Carleton was about to try to recover Ticonderoga and that intrigues with the Iroquois were taking place to induce them to harry the frontier. Under these circumstances the proposed plan was agreed upon, and the very flower of the army was chosen to go under the leadership of Arnold.

Many men who afterward became noted in the affairs of the nation were included among those who accompanied the expedition; Aaron Burr, notoriously immoral then as in later life, grown to a youth of twenty from the "little dirty, noisy boy, very sly and mischievous" as his mother called him, Daniel Morgan, chief in command of the "riflers" from Pennsylvania, Virginia and the mountains farther south, and Private John R. Henry, who wrote an account of the expedition. With these were eleven hundred men.

The march through the wilderness was one of titanic toil. Stumbling over rocks and fallen trees, dragging their bateaux over one carry after another, living on raw pork through fear of building a fire because of the Indians, facing starvation, boiling and eating their moccasons and even the Captain's dog, nevertheless they pushed on through "the direful howling wilderness not describable," as Dr. Senter calls it in his dairy. Arnold spent the greater part of his time with the advance guard, helping to prepare the way for the toiling soldiers. Todd in "The Real Benedict Arnold" says, "There has been nothing quite like this march before and there has been nothing since with the possible exception of Sherman's march to the sea. But Sherman had the resources of a great nation behind him; he marched through a civilized country of supplies, toward an objective point where powerful allies awaited him. Arnold on the contrary had no nation, no organization behind him. He marched through wilderness in the teeth of approaching winter into an enemy's country, his objective the most strongly fortified post in America. That the expedition came out of the wilderness alive was attributable largely to his courage, patriotism, magnetism and power over his men, and credit was cheerfully accorded him by Washington and his contemporaries."

Before leaving Cambridge, Washington had supplied Arnold with printed copies of a proclamation which urged the Canadians to join the Americans against the British. This manifesto was cordially received by the people, and when Arnold went on to Quebec, he left behind many admirers of the Bostonians." He paid promptly for all he took, and received the ready and willing co-operation of the population in return.

He now hastened toward Quebec, and daybreak of the 14th of November, 1775, found five hundred men drawn up on the Plains of Abraham, where sixteen years before the English had wrested from the French the supremacy of the New World. Arnold at once issued a somewhat bombastic proclamation calling upon the city to surrender, but the British commander recognized him as the man who had been there as a trader in horses some years before, and refused to pay any attention to the horse jockey."

It soon became necessary to get into communication with the force led by Montgomery, an officer who had served with distinction under Wolfe, and who had now succeeded Schuyler. He was supposed to be somewhere near the outlet of Lake Champlain. A volunteer was asked for, to traverse the eighty miles of forests, infested not only with wild beasts, but also with parties of Indians and royalists whose purpose in that section was to cut off all communication between the two forces. Aaron Burr stepped forward, and in the guise of a priest reached Montgomery and delivered his message. Montgomery reached Arnold on December 3, and took command of both forces. Not until December 31 was the attack made, and in a blinding snow storm, Montgomery met his death, and Arnold was severely wounded, his left leg being broken by a musket ball. On January 6, he wrote from his sick bed, "I received a wound by a ball through my left leg at the time I gained the first battery at the lower town. As soon as the main body came up I retired to the hospital, near a mile on foot, being obliged to draw one leg after me, and a great part of the way under the continued fire of the enemy from the walls at a no greater distance than fifty yards," and yet he adds, "I have no thought of leaving this proud town until I first enter it in triumph."

His desire however was not destined to be fulfilled, for the army, worn out by privation and smallpox, was compelled to withdraw. Wooster, Arnold's old enemy from Connecticut, had arrived and taken command, and as there was bad feeling between the two, and also because Arnold's horse had fallen with him and again injured the wounded leg, he obtained leave from Wooster to go to Montreal, of which he took command. For six weeks nothing was done, and as Quebec was now abandoned, acting on the advice of a committee sent by Congress to see how matters stood, the whole force came up Lake Champlain to Crown Point. Arnold went on to Albany where he took part in a council of war which decided to abandon the advanced post and fall back to Fort Ticonderoga.

Lodge in his "Life of Washington" says of the expedition to Canada, "The scheme was bold and brilliant, both in conception and in execution, and came very near severing Canada forever from the British crown."

While at Ticonderoga, Arnold's capacity for getting into trouble was again in evidence. During the stay in Canada, he had made many enemies, among whom was a certain Colonel John Brown, with whom had had also quarreled at the taking of

Ticonderoga. Brown had been busy circulating scandalous stories of Arnold, and in December, 1776, filed formal charges against him, the most important of which related to the seizure of goods from certain Montreal merchants. These goods were taken in such a hurry and the confusion of the departure from Canada was so great, that either through the enmity to Arnold of Hazen, the second in command, or through carelessness, many of the goods were lost or destroyed. In the court-martial of Hazen for disobedience of orders, Arnold became involved in a quarrel with the members of the court, which showed him great unfairness, so much so in fact that General Gates dissolved the court-martial, thus exonerating Arnold. In explaining the matter to Congress, Gates said he had been obliged to act dictatorially when the court demanded Arnold's arrest, for the "United States must not be deprived of that excellent officer's services at this important moment." Sparks in his "Life of Arnold" somewhat reluctantly admits that from the facts and from Arnold's letters to Generals Schuyler and Sullivan, "that he was not practising any secret maneuvre in the removal of the goods or for retaining them in his possession." This charge against him is another link in the chain of events leading to his final ruin, although a subsequent committee of Congress after an exhaustive investigation reported it groundless.

The British under Sir Guy Carleton were now planning to come up the lake to recapture the forts at Crown Point and Ticonderoga. A force of soldiers and sailors together with a thousand Indians, had been collected and was prepared for an invasion of the Champlain Valley. Gates appointed Arnold to command the opposing force. He had twice seen service along the lake, and more than this it was felt his voyages in command of his trading vessels would be a valuable help in directing a naval force. In spite of the fact that there was no ship carpenter in the whole force, and that tools, sails, shrouds, iron-work, guns and ammunition must be hauled from Albany, and that the lumber for the ships must be cut from the forests and be hewed into shape, Arnold imparted so great life and spirit to every stroke of ax and maul, that two weeks before the British sailed, there were ready to oppose them three schooners, two sloops, three galleys, and eight gunboats, fitted out with seventy guns. Arnold reported that he had five hundred half-naked men, and wrote asking for one hundred more, "no land-lubbers." "We have a wretched motley crew in the fleet," he wrote, "the marines the refuse of every regiment, and the sailors few of them ever wet with salt water." He placed his little squadron in ambush behind Valcour Island (near Plattsburg) and waited the oncoming British fleet. "The rascals won't give us a chance to burn powder," said Pringle the commander of the English ships. "Wait and see," said Carleton who stood near by. He remembered the fighting at Quebec, and knew something of the mettle of the commander of the Americans. As the British sailed by the island, Arnold issued forth and attacked. The fight raged all day. When the flagship "Royal Savage" sank, Arnold transferred his flag to the "Congress." At night the ships that remained escaped up the lake. The story goes that as the Americans slipped away through the fog, the British fleet bombarded them all night, as they supposed, but when morning came, and the sun burned off the mists, they saw they had been cannonading a small island with a tall pine tree at each extremity, and to this day the little islet is named "Carleton's Folly," or the "Englishman's Folly."

Arnold in the "Congress" sailed up the lake as far as Otter Creek, which winds its way in and out near the lake shore on the Vermont side. Sailing up this a short distance, he hoped to hide until the British should give up the search; but they drew up their ships off the mouth of the creek thinking that thus they would force him to surrender. Arnold, however, was not to be captured in any such manner, and that night he set his men to digging a ditch from the creek to the lake, as here the creek so winds about, that the stream was not more than a hundred yards from the lake although its mouth was a mile distant. The "Congress" was quietly warped out, and silently shifted across the lake to the north shore of the West Bay into a little inlet now called Partridge Harbor. Again being discovered Arnold fought a running fight across the lake and beaching the "Congress" in Panton Harbor, escaped with his followers to Crown Point.

The whole country rang with Arnold's praises. "The event was so gallant a demonstration of the resolute courage and ardor of the American troops, that it inspired universal confidence and hope at a very gloomy crisis of the Revolution.'' (Sparks.) ''By the display of so much courage and gallantry in times of peril, and by his superior address in deceiving and defying an enemy so much his superior in all particulars, Arnold's name was passed over the country with accompaniments of the highest praise. None spoke of him but in terms of the highest admiration. His popularity was now secure. If he had rested under a cloud of public prejudice before, his recent bravery had served to dissipate all its darkness. From this day he began to be a popular idol, and whenever his name was publicly mentioned it was only to call up recollections of some bold and daring deed, for which that name had now become justly celebrated.'' (Hill.)

During the winter of 1776-1777 while Arnold was engaged in drilling the raw troops he had raised about Boston and in Rhode Island, he was forced to undergo another act of rank injustice. Congress appointed five new major-generals. The whole country, Arnold included, expected he would be one of them because of his services rendered to the country, and on account of the priority of his rank; but when the selection was announced, it was found that his enemies in Congress were successful and that he had been passed over. The reason assigned for ignoring him was that Connecticut had already two major-generals and that it was not fairly entitled to any more. The cabal headed by Lee, Gates and others of that calibre who were conspiring against Washington and Schuyler, together with the New England men whose enimity Arnold had formerly aroused, were really responsible for this. He was left in the position of a veteran too good to be removed from the public service, but ''notoriously unequal to the emergencies of a command in the field.'' When it became known that he had been passed over, everyone was thunderstruck. Washington was amazed and fearing lest he lose the services of one whom he considered among his ablest generals he wrote to Arnold, ''I am at a loss to know whether you have had a preceding appointment, as the newspapers announce, or whether you have been omitted through some mistake. Should the latter be the case I beg you will not take any hasty steps but allow proper time for reflection, which I flatter myself will remedy any error that may have been made; my endeavors to that end shall not be wanting.''

Trevelyan in his "American Revolution" commenting on this event says, "The blow was cruel; and it was felt by Washington not less keenly and resented more openly, than by Arnold himself. The Commander-in-Chief let Congress know that, in his opinion, they had put an inexplicable and unpardonable slight upon an officer who was second to none in all the qualities of a military leader. * * * * * Arnold evinced his sense of Washington's friendliness, in the manner most acceptable to his correspondent, by maintaining an attitude of self-control." In his reply to Washington's letter quoted above, Arnold said, "Every personal injury shall be buried in my zeal for the safety and happiness of my country, in whose cause I have repeatedly fought and bled, and am ready at all times to risk my life." For the present the injustice he had suffered did not weaken his patriotic spirit and his words were soon put to the proof. Governor Tryon sailed from New York to overrun Connecticut, and capture the stores the patriots had collected at Danbury. A small force of five or six hundred militia had been collected to oppose them, and Arnold, who had gone to New Haven on a visit to his sister and his children, who had been cared for by her since the death of Mrs. Arnold, enrolled himself as a volunteer. As usual he distinguished himself for his dashing bravery and his skill in attack. In the forefront of the fight he saved his life by his pistol, after a volley from the enemy at a distance of thirty yards that killed his horse under him. Tryon was forced to retreat leaving a tenth of his men killed or wounded.

When the story of his part in the battle of Danbury became known Congress could not withhold the promotion so long due, and presented him with a horse "properly caparisoned as a token of his gallant conduct," but he was not restored to his seniority in rank. Arnold declined to be pacified with the tardy honor, and he was still quarrelling over his seniority with the War Board, when Washington, who "understood him better than he did himself," (Trevelyan) arranged for him to be sent to Schuyler to assist in opposing Burgoyne who was now on his way up Lake Champlain. He at once said he would be willing to obey not only General Schuyler, but also General St. Clair who was one of the five generals who had been promoted to higher rank over his head. He passed the night with Washington and together they attended a neighboring Masonic Lodge as brother Masons. The autographs of the two were entered in the visitors' book of the Lodge. Today Washington's name may still be read, but through that of Arnold has been drawn a thick black line. On his arrival at Fort Edward, he agreed with Schuyler that it would be better to withdraw the forces southward, and the army marched to Stillwater, and under Arnold's direction, Kosciusko threw up intrenchments on Bemis Heights.

To the westward, in the Mohawk Valley, the affairs of the Americans were in desperate straits, and a messenger was sent to Schuyler from Colonel Peter Gansevoort asking for help. Schuyler asked for a Brigadier to volunteer to lead the rescuing force and as none stepped forward Arnold, though a Major-General, quietly said, "I have been sent north to make myself useful. I'll lead the force." His relief of Fort Stanwix by the stratagem of the half witted Tory boy is too well known to need telling.

Just before he left for the Valley, he received a letter from Congress stating that the matter of his restoration to rank had been brought before that body, and by an aye and nay vote, the first it is said ever taken in that body, his request for restoration to his proper position had been denied. Naturally Arnold was angry and hurt, and asked permission of Schuyler to resign, but was persuaded to wait until the crisis caused by the near approach of Burgoyne's forces was past. In a letter from Arnold to Gates he said, "No public or private injury or insult shall prevail on me to forsake the cause of my injured and oppressed country, until I see peace and liberty restored to her or nobly die in the attempt."

When he returned from his successful expedition for the relief of Fort Stanwix, he found that the machinations of Gates had been successful and that he had superseded Schuyler. Gates and Arnold had always been the best of friends. Now because of Washington's friendship for Arnold and because he was also in the confidence of Schuyler, and particularly on account of his splendid record just made in the Mohawk Valley, Gates became intensely jealous of his subordinate, especially after his brilliant work at the battle of Bemis Heights. Burgoyne had pressed forward slowly from Fort Edward, and now on the 19th of September, 1777, his forces were massed ready to attack the American lines. Gates however, would give no orders and did not act as if he desired to fight. Washington, Morgan, Greene and Arnold were always in the thickest of the fray, but it is stated that Gates throughout the whole of his northern campaign did not so much as hear the whiz of a bullet.

Together with the other generals, Arnold begged and entreated their commander to give orders that would permit them to arrange the troops for the coming fight. For a long time Gates refused, but at last the pressure became so great that he could not longer withstand it; he gave the order and Arnold rushed to the front. A fierce fight raged all day, but the victory finally rested with Burgoyne, as he gained the mile and a half of ground over which the struggle took place. Arnold was the life of the fighting. He did all that a man could do, but Gates refused to send up re-enforcements, and the technical advantage remained with Burgoyne. He however did not consider it much of a victory for in his testimony given afterward before the House of Commons, he said his plan of attack had been utterly spoiled by the bold and skillful attacks of "Mr." Arnold. Lossing in his "Life of Schuyler" says, "but for Arnold on that eventful day, Burgoyne would have marched into Albany at the autumnal equinox, a victor." In the report of the battle Gates sent to Congress, he did not even mention Arnold's name, and when he protested, Gates contemptuously resented it, and began to persecute him in a most cowardly fashion. He insulted him to his face, sneered at him behind his back, and the feeling between the two men became so bitter, that after a stormy interview, Arnold asked Gates for permission to leave the camp and go to Philadelphia. When this became known in the army, a storm of protest arose, and all the officers, with the exception of Lincoln, signed a round-robin asking Arnold to reconsider his determination. Touched by this mark of confidence, and influenced also by the fact that this might be considered desertion in the face of the enemy, as another battle was daily expected, he resolved to stay; but the command of his division was taken from him, and he was no longer invited to the councils of war. "He still continned to haunt the camp as if he were an amateur civilian curious to see what a battle was like" (Trevelyan) and "Gates took no more notice of him than if he had been a dog." (Fiske.)

Not until October 7 was battle again joined. For a long time Arnold kept to his tent, raging because he had no right to be in the midst of the fighting. At last he could stand it no longer, and exclaiming that no power on earth could keep him in his tent that day, he leaped upon his black thoroughbred, and rushed away to the front, pursued by an aid from Gates with orders to return, "lest he do something rash." Fortunately the aid could not catch him. Back and forth along the lines raced the black horse and its rider. Hill says, "He rode with lightning speed up and down the lines, throwing himself into the very jaws of death, as if he were willing on that day to become a sacrifice. His horse was covered with foam and seemed to partake of the fiery desperation of its rider. Again and again he led the troops on the charge, attacking the Hessians in the center with such fury that their solid lines gave way. He brandished his sword like a glittering flame. His shouts and cries imparted to the troops a great share of his own madness. The frenzy that possessed him many of the soldiers declared they had never before seen equalled by mortal man. So uncontrollable was his excitement, he struck an officer over the head wounding him severely; and when told of it afterwards, he declared that he was not aware of having done anything of the kind."

At last as he rode his horse into a sally-port of the British fortifications, the Hessians fled in dismay, believing him in league with the Evil One. As they retreated they fired a last volley, and the black horse went down carrying its rider with it. At the same instant a wounded soldier within the fortifications, propping himself up, shot Arnold in the same leg which had been wounded at Quebec. A rifleman who saw the incident, rushed upon the German with his bayonet and would have run him through the body but Arnold cried out, "For God's sake don't hurt him, he's a fine fellow" and the soldier was spared. The ludicrous side to the event is that as Arnold lay on the ground, Gates' aid who had been trying to catch him rode up and delivered his message to "do nothing rash." The works thus captured formed the key to the British position, and with these in the hands of the Americans, the British were forced to retreat.

Arnold was carried to Albany on a litter, as his unfortunate leg was found to be badly broken. The doctors wished to amputate it, but Arnold fought them off, and the leg was saved. He remained in Albany until spring, and then proceeded by slow stages to New Haven. While here he received from Washington a set of epaulettes and a sword-knot, together with the following letter:

"Valley Forge, 7 May, 1778.

Dear Sir:—A gentleman in France having very obligingly sent me three sets of epaulettes and sword-knots, two of which professedly to be disposed of to any friends I should chose, I take the liberty of presenting them to you and General Lincoln, as a testimony of my sincere regard and approbation of your conduct. I have been informed by a brigade major of General Huntington's of your intention of repairing to camp shortly; but notwithstanding my wish to see you, I must beg that you will run no hazard by coming out too soon.

I am sincerely and affectionately,

Your obedient, etc.,

GEORGE WASHINGTON.

Congress could no longer withhold recognition of his rank, for although it gave the credit of the victory to Gates, yet the soldiers who fought the battle knew to whom the victory was due, and Congress yielded, though somewhat ungraciously.

This was the zenith of Benedict Arnold's fame. From the time of his taking command of Philadelphia, to which he was now appointed, he began to turn himself to plots against the integrity of the country he had done so much to help. It may be well in passing to note another side of his patriotism, shown while he was in New Haven. He learned that the children of his friend Joseph Warren had been unprovided for by the state, and sent five hundred dollars to the lady who had them in charge, also saying he would try to induce Congress to provide for them. In a letter written a little later when he was obliged to curtail his help, he says, "It has not been want of inclination, but want of ability which has prevented my remitting you the balance for the expenses of the children. The Public are indebted to me for a considerable sum which I advanced for them in Canada, and for four years pay which I cannot obtain."

In two of the many poems, if they may be dignified by that name, which Burgoyne's expedition called forth, we find references to Arnold and the position he held in the eyes of the people at this time. In "The Lamentations of General Burgoyne," published in 1778, we read:

"Arnold with wings our line flew o'er,
The like I never saw before.
He threatened death to every one,
That dared to fire another gun."

Another called "Burgoyne's Defeat, An Ancient Ditty," published in the same year, contains this reference:

"At length our gracious Lord inspired our noble
Gates' mind,
To send out General Arnold, to see if he could find
A passage through the enemy, and make them for
to flee;
Which quickly he obtained and set his country free."

No other general in the Continental forces was held in higher esteem than Benedict Arnold with perhaps the exception of Washington. The Commander-in-Chief considered him one of his ablest assistants, showing him his confidence again and again. He wrote him encouraging letters and calmed his chafing spirit with kind words. When the news of the attempted surrender of West Point was told him, for one of the few times in his career he broke down, and with tears coursing his cheeks, exclaimed "My God! Arnold is a traitor! Whom can we trust now!"

Schuyler loved and trusted him. Both he and Washington knew what it meant to be surrounded by treacherous enemies. They, too, suffered from the political chicanery of Congress, and the attacks of scandal mongers and petty politicians. Theirs, however, was a different temperament than Arnold's. Proud, arrogant, impetuous both in peace and in war, he was not able to withstand the attacks of his enemies as did those of stronger character.

His soldiers adored him. One of the New Englanders who followed him at Bemis Heights said of him, "There wasn't any waste timber in him. He was our fighting general. It was 'Come on boys!' It wasn't 'Go boys!' He didn't care for nothing. He'd ride right in."

In the life of no man are the contrasts so great. How in the face of all his glory, all the love of his superiors and equals in office, the adoration of those who followed him through the wilderness of Maine, who fought by his side in the driving snow at Quebec, or who cheered him at Saratoga,—he could have descended to the infamy of betraying these his friends is a problem in psychology too difficult for me to solve. It is pleasant to know that on that last day of his life he called for the Continental uniform he had worn on the day of his escape to the "Vulture," and which he had kept, and also for the sword-knot and epaulettes Washington had given him as the bravest of the brave. "Let me die in my old American uniform," said he, "the uniform in which I fought my battles. God forgive me for ever putting on any other."

Nothing can extenuate his treachery, his fall was too great, but when we see the vacant niche in the noble monument on the battle field of Saratoga, let us remember that before he was Benedict Arnold—Traitor, he was Benedict Arnold—Patriot.

"Lifted up so high
Is dained subjection, and thought one step higher
Would set me highest, and in a moment quit
The debt immense of endless gratitude,
So burdensome, still paying, still to owe."

* * *

"Me miserable! which way shall I fly
Infinite wrath, and infinite despair?
Which way I fly is hell; myself am hell;
And, in the lowest deep, a lower deep
Still threatening to devour me opens wide,
To which the hell I suffer seems a heaven.'"

* * *

"So farewell, hope, and, with hope, farewell fear,
Farewell, remorse! all good to me is lost;
Evil be thou me Good: by thee at least
Divided empire with Heaven's King I hold."

ST. LEGER'S INVASION AND THE BATTLE
OF ORISKANY

By Freeman H. Allen, Ph. D., Colgate University, Hamilton, N. Y.

Even in prehistoric days, Nature had predestined the Mohawk valley to be the scene of unusual human activity. When
the white man first came on the scene, his predecessor, the Redman, had long followed the paths already made by the deer and
the buffalo, or plied its waters in his canoe. The pioneer followed
the Redman's routes, widening the trail, enlarging the clearings,
and bringing the batteaux. Thrifty farmer and villager traded
with the native and slowly but steadily transformed the forest
into homes of a young but vigorous nation. With all this came
a steady advance in the means of travel and communication
which in turn have included the turn-pike and toll-road, the
canal, the railroad, the trolley, and the automobile, until today
steam and electricity propel through this valley, on its waters,
its state roads, or its bands of steel, the commerce of a mighty nation. Its thriving towns, farms and cities are connected by telegraph and telephone, so that former isolated individuals or
groups have become one vast community, the hum of whose business life is heard day and night. I repeat,—Nature predestined
the Mohawk valley to be the scene of unusual human activity,
and its occupants to play a large part in the history of this portion of the world.

What is now central New York was in 1777 the far frontier.
Westward from Albany County was the newly organized Tryon
County, extending from the extreme southern part of the state
to the St. Lawrence, and westward to about the present site of
Rome. Indian trails connected the Mohawk valley with the

Susquehanna and the Delaware valleys, and with Oswego and the St. Lawrence. Forests well nigh impenetrable, save to the woodsman or hunter, stretched in every direction. The colonists,, who for more than a generation had been increasing in the principal valleys, knew the hardships and dangers of the frontier in an Indian country; yet their relations with the Redmen had been, in the main, friendly and mutually advantageous. During the conflicts between the English and the French colonists, the English had succeeded in winning the friendship of the Iroquois —especially of the Mohawks, Oneidas and Onondagas. This friendship was not so much given to the English colonists as to the government which had opposed their common enemy, the French, and especially to the agents of that government. The Johnsons of Johnstown and vicinity were conspicuous examples of the influential agents of the English government, most of whom had little sympathy with the revolutionary party in 1776 and 1777. Through the influence of these agents the Redmen of the Long House were inclined to the English during the last of the struggles with the French for possession in the New World. Sir William Johnson was capable, tactful and successful both in restraining and in protecting them. Through his influence the settlers were kept from encroaching upon the lands of the Iroquois; but with his death the murders and land grabbing by colonials multiplied and increased. While the Johnsons (Sir William, Sir John, his son, and Sir Guy Johnson, his nephew and son-in-law) had long been and still were a powerful influence in what was now Tryon county, it was impossible to prevent sympathy with the revolutionary spirit which grew rapidly after the death of Sir William in 1774 and after England's retaliatory acts of the same year became known in this region. In August of that year a meeting was held at the home of Adam Loucks, Esq., at Stone Arabia and resolutions were adopted in which the patriots of the Palatine district pledged their support to their brethren of Boston, and affirmed their allegiance to the cause of the colonies. This meeting also proceeded to organize a Committee of Safety for Tyron County. From then until two years after the surrender of Cornwallis the region now known as Central New York knew no peace. The Committee endeavored to induce the Indians to at least a neutral attitude, while the Johnsons urged them to an active alliance with the King. In 1776 the young Mohawk Chief, Joseph Brant (Thay-en-da-ne-ga), was sent to England where he was treated as a hero and was made the recipient of many honors and gifts. On his return to America he began organizing the Indians to aid the British. Early in 1776 he and his tribesmen became threatening in various parts of Tyron County, especially in the upper Susquehanna and Mohawk valleys. The Committee of Safety was kept anxious and busy, and the lines became sharp and feelings bitter between those who adhered to the cause of the patriots and those who remained loyal to the king. Probably one-third of the white men of the county were Loyalists and many more were ready to go with whichever might give the greater promise of being "the winning party." To the Committee of Tryon County which called upon Sir John Johnson in October of 1775 to declare himself, he affirmed that "before he would sign any Association, or would lift up his hand against his King, he would rather suffer that his head be cut off." (Minutes of Committee of Safety for Tryon County, page 84.) Already the leading Tories, Sir John's relatives and friends, had abandoned the valley and had found their way to Montreal. Sir John remained however and bade defiance to the Committee of Safety, and began to arm his tenants. General Schuyler marched to Johnstown with some 3000 troops, disarmed the tenants and took Sir John prisoner. He was soon liberated on parole. He soon violated the parole, however, for which General Schuyler, in May, 1776, ordered Colonel Dayton with his regiment just returning from Canada to arrest him. Learning of this Sir John escaped with his Highlanders and other tenants and fled to Montreal. There he was immediately commissioned a colonel in the British service, and raised two batallions of loyalists, composed largely of his retainers. They were called the Royal Greens, and became one of the most active, cruel and vindictive foes with which the patriots had to reckon. Col. John Butler who had long been in close official connection with the Johnsons, and who followed their political fortunes, entered the military service of the King and organized a corps known as Butler's Rangers. They, too, were composed mainly of Tories from Tyron County. The character of this corps, and its methods and spirit, are fairly reflected by the story of the Wyoming massacre, with which the name of their leader is disgracefully but inseparably connected.

As early as March, 1776, James Dean obtained from the Iroquois chiefs the renewal of a pledge of neutrality, but his efforts and those of Samuel Kirkland, the missionary, were only partly effective; for only the Oneidas and the Tuscaroras remained friendly to the Americans, while the larger part of the Iroquois Confederacy, including the fiercest tribes, espoused the King's cause, doubtless believing that it would speedily triumph and that he would richly reward them.

I have dwelt thus on the character of the New York frontier because it furnishes the chief reasons for an important part of the general plan of the English for invading the state in 1777. The strength of the Loyalist party, the experience and standing of the powerful leaders of that party, their influence with the Six Nations, the geography of the region with its few routes of communication and these through the heart of the Indian country—all these seemed to promise that ardent patriots in that part of the province would speedily be crushed and the luke-warm would be won or forced to support the King's cause. The arming of his Highlanders by Sir John Johnson, the fortifying of Guy Park, the visit of Joseph Brant to England in 1776, the threatening attitude and activity of the Indians on the upper Susquehanna and in the Schoharie and upper Mohawk valleys, all seem to have been a part of the preliminary work preparatory to the coming of St. Leger and his army.

The British plan for taking possession of New York was by a concerted movement by three distinct armies operating upon converging lines. While Sir William Howe was to ascend the Hudson, and General Burgoyne was to advance from Canada by the way of Lake Champlain and the Hudson River, Col. St. Leger was to go up the St. Lawrence to Lake Ontario, land at Oswego, and with the aid of Sir John Johnson and his Royal Greens and the Indians, reduce Fort Stanwix on the Mohawk at the eastern end of the "carry" connecting that river with Wood Creek, a tributary of Oneida Lake. This army, it was expected, would be augmented by Tory sympathizers as it marched with little opposition down the valley of the Mohawk to Albany, where the three armies of invasion were to meet. Had these plans prevailed, New

York State would have been in the hands of the British, and it doubtless would have proved very disastrous to the American cause. It is doubtful if this was a wise plan to accomplish its purpose, but if it were to be undertaken, the invasion through the Mohawk valley was a vital part of the general campaign.

About the middle of July, St. Leger landed at Oswego where he began organizing his motley force consisting of 900 or 1000 Indians and about 700 white men; the latter made up of a few companies of British regulars, some Hessians, Johnson's Royal Greens, and Col. John Butler's Rangers. Advancing cautiously they invested Fort Stanwix on the third of August. This frontier fort had fallen into decay since the last war with the French, but had recently been repaired and was now garrisoned by some seven hundred and fifty men, now under the command of Col. Peter Gansevoort. (When the old fort was thus repaired and occupied its name seems to have been changed to Fort Schuyler; but as there are several places in the valley thus designated at various times, I shall, in this paper, continue to refer to it by its earlier name.) The approach of St. Leger was made known to the occupants of the fort by friendly Indians and by the ambushing of some parties who had strayed from the fort in search of game or berries. Shortly before the enemy appeared Lieutenant-Colonel Mellon arrived with two hundred men of the Massachusetts line and a convoy of boats loaded with supplies. News of the invasion had roused the patriots of the valley and General Herkimer, commander of the Militia of Tryon County, a veteran over sixty years of age, summoned all the male inhabitants between the ages of sixteen and sixty. Eight hundred responded to the call mostly Germans and Low Dutch, whose presence in the valley was evidenced by thrift and advancing civilization, and whose homes and loved ones must be defended or fall a prey to the dreaded Indians and to their former neighbors, now with St. Leger.

On the fourth of August this party under Herkimer started from Fort Dayton (now Herkimer village) for the relief of Fort Stanwix. On the evening of the fifth he encamped at Whitesboro. From here he sent three trusty men to acquaint Colonel Gansevoort of his approach and arrange plans of co-operation. The plan was to overwhelm St. Leger by a concerted attack in front and rear. The garrison was to make a sortie, while Herkimer, advancing through the forests, was to suddenly attack the enemy from behind. It was believed that the forces of St. Leger, thus surprised and surrounded, might be crushed and captured at a single blow. To insure complete co-operation, Colonel Gansevoort was to fire three guns as a signal for Herkimer to begin his march from Oriskany, some six miles distant, and the garrison was to keep the attention of the enemy concentrated on the fort until the proper time to sally forth in full force.

Instead of reaching the fort before daybreak of the sixth, the three messengers were compelled to make a wide detour to avoid the enemy, and it was nearly eleven o'clock of that day when Col. Gansevoort was made acquainted with Herkimer's whereabouts and plans. The signal guns were fired, but it was then too late to accomplish the plans of Herkimer.

At daybreak that morning Herkimer's men were ready for the fray. Impatiently they waited for the signal guns from the fort. Hours passed and the impatience manifested itself in murmurings which grew more intense as their commander insisted on waiting for the signal from the fort. Remembering that several of their leader's relatives were Tory sympathizers and that one of his brothers was a leading loyalist, they began to express their belief that he was not anxious to punish the enemy. Persistently he held out against the urgent appeals of many of his officers and men, insisting that it was unwise to move until he was assured by the signal guns that the garrison was ready to co-operate. Finally Colonels Cox and Paris accused him of being a coward and a Tory. Stung by the unmerited taunt he gave the order to march.

Information of the approach of General Herkimer reached St. Leger on the evening of the 5th and he sent a detachment of the Royal Greens under Major Watts and the entire body of Indians under the Mohawk Chief Brant, with Sir John Johnson in supreme command, to intercept his approach. W. Max Reid (The Mohawk Valley, page 419) gives a correct and vivid description of the place and plans for defeating the intrepid defenders of the Mohawk valley. He tells us that about two miles west from Oriskany "were two short ravines separated by a level plateau of perhaps ten acres about fifty feet above the bottom of the ravines. This plateau gradually narrowed to a rounded

point as the ravines opened out and gradually merged into the
swampy flats that stretch north to the Mohawk River three-quarters of a mile away. The westernmost ravine was the rendezvous
of the British troops, who were stationed along its upper eastern
edge, effectually concealed by its fringe of low trees and bushes.
The Indians rapidly took their positions around the south, north,
and eastern edge of the easterly ravine, nearly enclosing it except where the rude road of logs (constructed earlier in the year
by Colonel Gansevoort for easier carriage of cannon and supplies for Fort Schuyler, six miles away) ran down and over the
swampy bottom of the fatal ravine. All around were trees and
low bushes and the attendant rotting logs and tree trunks, while
tangled masses of dead branches and underbrush bordered each
side of the rough road that stretched out east and west until lost
in the gloom of the forest, while the swampy flats, dimly seen
through the mouth of the ravine, were covered with tall swamp
grass and the long, flat leaves of cat-tail and calamus, with here
and there a scrub pine or willow, making a treacherous conceal-
ment for the naked savages. Occasionally a group of pond lilies
and other aquatic flowers added color and beauty to the diversi-
fied landscape.''

Into this trap came the unsuspecting Herkimer followed in
a joyous rollicking manner by three regiments and the baggage
train. The van had crossed the ravine and had nearly reached
the top of the western slope and the major part of the troops
were huddled together at the narrow crossing while the baggage
train was waiting for an opportunity to cross. The rear guard,
under Col. Visscher had not yet descended into the ravine. Suddenly the report of a rifle was heard and Col. Cox fell. Instantly
swarms of Indians dashed upon the rear guard separating them
from the troops below. These were overwhelmed by superior
numbers and most of them were slain or driven back, while the
cordon that was drawn about the doomed patriots in the ravine
was completed. From every tree and bush rang out the report
of rifle and the war-cry of the savages. The battle has been described many times, and many of its incidents detailed. Mr.
Fiske seems to have the support of contemporary narrators in his
brief summary as follows:

"At this moment they were greeted by a murderous volley from either side, while Johnson's Greens came charging down upon them in front, and the Indians, with frightful yells, swarmed in behind and cut off the rear-guard, which was thus obliged to retreat to save itself. For a moment the main body was thrown into confusion, but it soon rallied and formed itself in a circle which neither bayonet charges nor musket fire could break or penetrate. The scene which ensued was one of the most infernal that the history of savage warfare has ever witnessed. The dark ravine was filled with a mass of fifteen hundred human beings, screaming and cursing, slipping in the mire, pushing and struggling, seizing each other's throats, stabbing, shooting, and dashing out brains. Bodies of neighbors were afterwards found lying in the bog, where they had gone down in a death-grapple, their cold hands still grasping the knives plunged in each other's hearts.

Early in the fight a musket-ball slew Herkimer's horse, and shattered his own leg just below the knee; but the old hero, nothing daunted and bating nothing of his coolness in the midst of the horrible struggle, had the saddle taken from his dead horse, and placed at the foot of a great beech-tree, where, taking his seat and lighting his pipe, he continued shouting his orders in a stentorian voice and directing the progress of the battle." (Fiske, The American Revolution, Vol. I., page 289.)

Observing that when a patriot had discharged his gun a savage warrior usually ran to him and tomahawked him before he could reload, General Herkimer gave order that the men should fight in pairs, so that one might defend the other while he was reloading. This soon proved disastrous to the Indians. When the Indians seemed to be getting the worst of the fight a company of Johnson's Royal Greens was brought up. At the sight of these Tryon County loyalists—their former neighbors— Herkimer's men left the shelter of the trees in their eagerness to be avenged and rushed upon them with bayonets, spears and clubbed muskets, and desperate hand to hand fighting ensued. A terrific storm of lightning, wind and rain interrupted the battle for a time, during which the Americans selected better ground. When the fight was renewed, the Indians had become wary and were not so ready to expose themselves or come into close quarters; but when Butler's Rangers and the Royal Greens appeared terrible fighting again ensued.

At length while the fighting was desperate the long delayed signal guns were heard, and the patriots took courage as they thus learned that the messengers had reached the fort. Discouraged by the stubborn resistance and at their severe losses, and alarmed at the uncertain meaning of the booming cannon, the Indians raised the cry "Oonah! Oonah!" their word for retreat, and nearly all fled. Perceiving that their allies had deserted them, the Tories soon followed, leaving the field to the militia who were too weak to pursue them. Due credit must be given to the sturdy yeomen, men and boys, for the determined stand they made that day for home and country; but the hero of the day—the one man without whom the bloody work of that day would doubtless have been followed by speedy and wholesale slaughter and devastation throughout the Mohawk valley, with its dire results upon the campaign along the Hudson—was General Nicholas Herkimer. In the hours of severest conflict the superiority of his character shone out and steadied his men. The rebellious spirit of the morning was forgotten and his orders were obeyed with promptness and with the utmost confidence in his judgment and loyalty. It was he, Herkimer, who saved the day and the cause.

> "Heroes are born in such a chosen hour;
> O'er common men they rise and tower;
>   Like thee, brave Herkimer!
> Who wounded, steedless, still beside the beech
> Cheered on thy men, with sword and speech,
>   In grim Oriskany."
>   (Poem by Rev. Charles D. Helmer, D. D.)

With the other wounded patriots, Herkimer was carried from the field of battle, and under an escort of men he was borne for thirty miles to his home, where after ten days of patient suffering he died, an example of Christian heroism in his last hours.

In the meantime the men at Fort Stanwix had not been idle. After receiving the message from General Herkimer and firing the signal guns, the garrison hastily prepared for a sortie and an attack upon the enemy's camp. The sallying force of 250 men were under Col. Willett, and they fell upon the partially denuded camp of Sir John Johnson and the Indian encampment near it. The occupants of these camps were taken by surprise and hastily abandoned everything in their precipitate flight. Many of the enemy were killed in this attack and in their effort to prevent the return of the sallying party to the fort. Col. Willett lost no men in this enterprise, while he secured several prisoners and much plunder, including provisions, "upwards of fifty brass kettles, and more than a hundred blankets, with a quantity of muskets, tomahawks, spears, ammunition, clothing, deerskins, a variety of Indian affairs, and five colors—the whole of which," writes Col. Willett, "were displayed on our flagstaff under the Continental Flag." This continental flag was doubtless the first one made in accordance with the resolution adopted by Congress on the 14th of June that year, and floated over a besieged garrison. It was hastily made on the morning of the third of August and floated in the face of St. Leger's men when they began the investment of the fort on that day.

For a time it was difficult to tell the results of this fierce and disorderly day. Both sides claimed a victory and St. Leger vainly tried to scare the garrison by the story that their comrades had been destroyed. On the day following the battle, three British officers, one of them Col. Butler, came to the fort under the protection of a flag of truce. They brought word from St. Leger, Major Ancrum delivering the message, to the effect that if the garrison would surrender at once all lives would be saved, and the private property of the officers and men should be secured to them. As an alternative he threatened the destruction of the garrison, and the carrying of torch and tomahawk throughout the Mohawk valley. He assured the garrison that General Burgoyne was already at Albany, and that a mere waiting would place the fort in their hands. To all this trickery, Col. Willett, who was designated by Col. Gansevoort to receive the messengers, replied: "Do I understand you, Sir? I think you say that you come from a British colonel, who is commander of the army that invests this fort, and, by your uniform, you appear to be an officer in the British service. You have made a long speech, on the occasion of your visit, which, stripped of all its superfluities, amounts to this, that you come from a British Colonel to the commandant of this garrison to tell him that if he does not deliver up the garrison into the hands of your Colonel, he will send his Indians to murder our women and children. You will please to reflect, Sir, that their blood will be on your head, not on ours. We are doing our duty; this garrison is committed to our charge, and we will take care of it. After you get out of it, you may turn round and look at its outside, but never expect to come in again, unless you come a prisoner. I consider the message you have brought a degrading one for a British officer to send, and by no means reputable for a British officer to carry. For my own part, I declare, before I would consent to deliver this garrison to such a murdering set as your army, by your own account, consists of, I would suffer my body to be filled with splinters and set on fire, as you know has at times been practised by such hordes of women and children killers as belong to your army." (Diefendorf, The Historic Mohawk, P. 187.)

On the evening of the tenth, Col. Willett and Major Stockwell set forth without blankets or firearms to seek relief from the army under General Schuyler at Stillwater. These two skillful woodsmen crawled through St. Leger's lines and speedily made their way to the hadquarters of the Northern department. Schuyler at once assembled a council of war and advocated immediate relief for the garrison at Fort Stanwix. The unpopularity of the commander rather than the disapproval of his plans caused a negative vote. Overhearing an insinuating remark to the effect that he only wished "to weaken the army," the patriot General indignantly closed the council meeting. "Enough!" he cried, "I shall assume the whole responsibility. Where is the brigadier who will command the relief?" The brigadiers sat in silence; when Arnold, who was a Major General, but who never stood on his rank when work was to be done, suddenly jumped up. "Here!" said he. "Washington sent me here to make myself useful. I will go." The commander seized him by the hand, and the drum beat for volunteers. Like many another leader, Arnold's unpopularity was mainly with the politicians. The common soldiers admired his impulsive bravery and had unbounded faith in his resources as a leader. Accordingly, 1200 Massachusetts men were easily enlisted, and the relief expedition was soon on its way up the Mohawk valley. A week's march brought him to the German Flats, within thirty miles of the beleaguered garrison. The patriots of the valley gathered round him as he advanced and Col. Gansevoort, who was conducting the defence of the fort with diligence and resolution, was gratified by receiving assurance that the garrison would be relieved long before he had "served out his last biscuit."

Desire for revenge on his former neighbors induced Sir John Johnson to send an expedition down the valley in an endeavor to enlist the aid of any sympathizing inhabitants—who, however, were doubtless less numerous than he believed. Several of these men were captured and held as spies at Fort Dayton. On the arrival of Arnold a few days afterward these prisoners were tried by court martial and condemned to be hanged. Among them were Walter Butler (son of Sir John) and a certain Han Jost Schuyler, a queer fellow, with a misty brain. The Indians regarded him with that mysterious awe with which lunatics are wont to inspire them, and he was allowed to come and go among them at will. He was not, however, without a considerable degree of cunning, as the sequel shows. His brother and mother came to the camp and pleaded for his life. Arnold offered to pardon him if he should go and spread a panic in St. Leger's camp by giving an exaggerated account of the approaching army, and so alarm the Indians that they would leave. His brother meanwhile was held as hostage pending the results of his message. Having had several bullets shot through his clothing to make the story of his escape look more plausible he set out.

His story caused consternation in the camp of St. Leger. Han Jost represented the relief party as several thousand strong, and his story was confirmed by some friendly Oneida Indians who arrived soon afterwards. At this confirmation of the story the Indians in a panic took to flight, and as this fear seized St. Leger's men, they, too, became uncontrollable. By noon the next day St. Leger fled and his whole army was dispersed. All his tents, artillery and stores fell into the hands of the Americans, who sallied forth and pursued for a while. The faithless Indians, disappointed at not having secured more scalps, now mercilessly cut off all stragglers whether American prisoners or British. Hardly a remnant of the army was left to return with St. Leger to Montreal. The Mohawk valley was saved, the armies of Clinton, Burgoyne, and St. Leger failed to keep their appointment at

Albany, and the siege of Fort Stanwix was at an end. News of this failure reached Burgoyne before he had time to recover from the news of the disaster at Bennington.

Notwithstanding the weakness of the general plan of the British campaign for possession of New York State in 1777, due to the great distances, the lack of ready communication between the three co-operating armies, and to the fact that the Americans were operating on inner lines and where roads were better, communication easier, and supplies more readily obtainable, still the campaign under St. Leger seems to have been well planned, and it is rather a marvel than otherwise that it failed. It seems that the numerical strength and the spirit of the patriots in the Mohawk valley were both underrated by the planners of the invasion. Military critics have pointed out the fatal elements of weakness and blunder on the part of the British during the Northern Campaign of 1777—and no critics have been more severe than British writers—but many of these would have been forgotten if St. Leger had not failed. August 6th was the time and the battlefield of Oriskany was the place which seemed to determine the issues of the campaign. Benson J. Lossing, the historian, writes:

"I turned from that battlefield, and in contemplating its far-reaching effects upon the campaign in Northern New York in 1777, was satisfied that it was the chief event that caused the Indians to desert St. Leger, and that boastful young leader to raise the siege of Fort Stanwix and fly for refuge to the bosom of Lake Ontario. It was the first fatal shock given to the hopes of Burgoyne, and caused him to despair when his expedition toward Bennington was defeated ten days after the Battle of Oriskany.

The events of Oriskany and Bennington, in August, 1777, caused the flood-tide of invasion from the north to ebb. They led immediately to the important results at Saratoga in October; also to the appreciation by the courts of Europe of the powers of the American soldiery and the ability of the colonists to maintain the cause of Independence. They led to an open treaty of alliance between the United States and France which was signed just six months to a day after the Battle of Oriskany. That battle was the first upon which the fortunes of the old war for independence turned in favor of the American patriots. It was the prophecy of the surrender at Yorktown.

We have, moreover, the declaration of Washington himself that "when all was dark in the north, it was Herkimer who first reversed the gloomy scene."

Lieutenant-Governor Dorsheimer in his speech at the centennial celebration of Oriskany said:

"Herkimer and his men were ambushed by the Indians. That was a favorite device in Indian warfare, but it did not succeed with these sturdy Germans. Most, although simple farmers without military training, not only stood their ground, but quickly adapted themselves to the occasion, adopted the Indian tactics, posted themselves behind trees, and fought with such skill and endurance all through the summer day that the Indians, to use the language of one of their chiefs, had enough, and did not want to fight 'Dutch Yankees' any more."

Ellis H. Roberts, the historian of our State, (New York, Vol. II., page 417), says:—

"The battle broke up the plan of the grand campaign, and it proved that the colonists would fight, and fight well, against the veterans of the British armies and their allies. It turned the tide of defeat and of despondency which the events of the preceding year had raised. It not only prevented co-operation by St. Leger with Burgoyne, but enabled the militia of Tryon and Schoharie counties to join the army at Saratoga. Every available element of strength was imperatively needed there."

Many others might be quoted in confirmation of the opinions thus expressed, and which seem warranted by the facts which are well established relative to this invasion and the Battle of Oriskany.

Rev. Henry Belcher, author of the First American Civil War, is not the first to point out the fact that the struggle of our forefathers for British rights and finally for Independence, was a civil war. But not even in the Carolinas, Maryland, New Jersey or Pennsylvania was this more emphatically true than in the Mohawk valley. Neighborhoods were divided, even families sundered, and the war was the more bitter because the invaders were former friends and neighbors.

BURGOYNE

By Rev. Henry Belcher, M. A., LL. D., Fellow of Kings College, London, and of the Royal Historical Society; Rector S. Michael in Lewes, Sussex, England.

In 1749, on the conclusion of the Peace at Aix la Chapelle, the French government revised their military organization, and among novelties introduced into their army system 16 regiments of mounted infantry on an establishment of 480 men for each regiment. Their weapon was the carbine, even then a piece of a respectable antiquity, but cumbrous and of little value to a mounted man as a killing implement. With each of these mounted men was associated a man on foot; a running companion, trained either to replace his mounted colleague in case of casualty, or to fight on foot. There is to this French organization of the Eighteenth Century a sufficiently close analogy to be found in a brief account of the German system of mounted infantry as described by Julius Caesar in his notes on the Gallic war, to which further reference is unnecessary.[1]

At the time of this reconstruction of the French army Burgoyne was in France. During his stay in Preston in Lancashire with his troop of the 13th Dragoons, he had formed an attachment for Lady Charlotte Stanley, who consented to elope with the young officer, and with him repaired to France, where they appear to have found much happiness during seven years of an exile due to their comparative poverty.

Burgoyne had attained his commission at an early age and was in his 23rd year at the time of the marriage, which compelled him to retire from the army. His known mental activity and his

---

[1] C. J. C. de Bello Gallico, i p. 48.

BURGOYNE'S SURRENDER

Courtesy of Glens Falls Insurance Co.

military training would induce him to notice very carefully the changes going on in the French army and while studying those works on strategy and tactics of which at that time French soldiers were prolific, to devise plans by which this new model might be adapted to the service of the British army.

At the age of thirty he became anxious to resume his former profession, and to rejoin a service which he had quitted with reluctance. By what process of good fortune he regained his rank as captain of a cavalry regiment needs not be examined here. It is well known that for a man to try to recover his status in the army after a voluntary retirement followed by many years inexperience of military life, is an almost hopeless undertaking. Yet Burgoyne was appointed with junior rank as a captain of the 11th dragoons. This was in 1756, the opening year of Pitt's (Chatham's) first ministry.

Having a good name as a smart officer and much interested in his profession, he was also reputed to be a fine French scholar, in days when among the English a little French went a long way. The glamour of the French court and army was still powerful. Rossbach and Minden and Quebec were yet to occur. Madame de Pompadour, highly flattered by the patronage of the Empress Maria Theresa, counted for much in the councils and fashions of Western Europe. In high English quarters, Burgoyne's French experience, his reputation as a French scholar and his presumed study of French military organization were regarded with a favorable eye. At any rate when George the Second had resolved to raise two regiments of light cavalry, Burgoyne appeared to be the man best fitted for the work; he was promoted to be lieutenant-colonel with the task of bringing into shape the 16th Light Dragoons, then newly enrolled. Dragoons were originally light infantry (that is, little men) mounted on quick and wiry cattle, whose moderate size gave the name *dragooner* to any horse capable only of carrying light weights. It is not necessary here to follow the many changes by which the *dragoon*, the mounted ruffians of the persecution consequent on the Revocation of the Edict of Nantes (1665), has merged into the highly trained cavalry man of today. But it appears to be certain that Burgoyne played no inconspicuous part in the process of change.

To train a cavalry regiment for purposes of protection as well as of attack, to increase its mobility, without impairing its discipline or sense of solidarity, belonged to the suspected innovations of those days.

Burgoyne, who rarely denied himself the pleasure of literary composition, took very great pains in drawing up a code of instructions which he embellished with the finest language at his command.

He told his subalterns that, "There are occasions, such as during stable or fatigue duty, when officers may slacken the reins so far as to talk with soldiers, nay, even a joke may be used, not only without harm but to good purpose, for condescensions well applied are an encouragement to the well disposed, and at the same time a tacit reproof to others."

He also recommends his officers to cultivate a taste for drawing, "As a very pleasing and useful qualification," and "to take views from an eminence, and to measure distances with his eye. This would be a talent peculiarly adapted to the light dragoon service."

The Instructions extended over numerous pages, filled with reflections and literary ornaments after the style of Miss Elizabeth Sewell of Lichfield—the ill-fated André's friend. At a period when swearing and cursing were not uncommon among women of rank to say nothing of the foul language prevalent among men of every calling and profession, Burgoyne's gentle caution and fond reminders appear almost maternal. Perhaps his most remarkable effort in this department of his activities was his famous address to the Indian contingent in the early days of the Expedition from Canada.

But whatever be the affectations of his style in framing instructions, there can be little question as to the excellent results of his energetic management, and example. Burgoyne's Light Horse was prominent among the minor features of the British army in 1760, and it is on record that the young King (George III.) was highly pleased with the performances of this corps.

In 1762 the Kings of France and Spain—together with the King of the Two Sicilies—formed a triple alliance of which the chief object was to curb the ambitious projects of Great Britain. Burgoyne in consequence was sent abroad with local rank of Brigadier-General to support Portugal's resistance to a Spanish invasion. His capture of Valencia by a well planned raid which lost nothing in its execution, is perhaps the chief, as it was the most admirable exploit of his life, winning for him very warm encomiums both from the King of Portugal, his superior officer, as well as from the military critics of the day.

An order of the day, August 29th, mentions the glorious conduct of Burgoyne, who—after marching without halting 15 leagues—captured the enemy's headquarters, and with them the officer commanding the Spanish army of invasion, as well as three stands of colors and many other trophies of successful war. The three standards, according to the wish of the King of Portugal, were to be presented to General Burgoyne for transmission to England, to the credit of the 16th Dragoons. In fact, Burgoyne's fame as a good cavalry officer, who must ever be a rare combination of courage and dash, was thoroughly established.

"The British troops," says the Gentleman's Magazine,[2] "behaved upon this occasion with as much generosity as courage; and it deserves admiration that in an affair of this kind the town and the inhabitants suffered very little, which is owing to the good order Brigadier Burgoyne kept up even in the heat of action."

But as it was the first so it was the last detail of his experience as a cavalry commander.

After much fighting the high contending powers grew weary and came to terms. In England the peace was most unpopular. Frederick (the Great) being, as he thought, thrown over by the Whigs, who were bent on peace at any price, adopted towards George III. an unfriendly attitude, which during the War of Independence in America exercised an adverse effect on England's fortunes.

Of this brief and obscure defensive campaign in aid of Portugal against the combined enmity of France and Spain, perhaps, for interest, the leading episode is, that Colonel Charles Lee was an officer of Burgoyne's command, placed in charge of a small mixed force composed of infantry and of the 16th Light Dragoons, which executed a surprise operation of some importance on the right bank of the Tagus a few weeks before the cam-

---

2 1762. p. 443.

paign closed. Fourteen years later Lieutenant-General Charles Lee, no longer in British pay, but an insubordinate second-in-command of the Continental army, was captured by a detachment of this same regiment of Light Dragoons. This exploit is reckoned by Mr. Charles Francis Adams[3] as the only serviceable deed of the British cavalry during the campaign under Howe in 1777.

Burgoyne afterwards submitted to the great Earl a series of casms of Carlyle and Thackeray, he became one of the group of Bond Street generals of whom Lord North is reported to have said he lived in greater dread than of any force of Britain's enemies. The acidulated strictures of Carlyle[4] and Thackeray appear to be due to their unconscious deference to Horace Walpole's sustained disparagement of Burgoyne, and his hatred for George III., Burgoyne's patron. It is quite contrary to the facts that Burgoyne then became a mere wayfarer, on the roads capricious fashion makes for its own entertainment. Neither Bond Street nor Bath detained him in England. He went abroad in 1766, furnished with letters credential from the Earl of Chatham to the renowned Ferdinand of Brunswick.

Chatham's letter to Burgoyne covering this introduction, is couched in terms which might have seemed extravagant if addressed to Hannibal after the Battle of Cannae. Americans will bear in mind how Chatham spoke of the debates in Congress in 1774 and 1775. He said they were equal to the finest oratorical efforts ever achieved in the history of the human race. But Chatham's portentous and exaggerated courtesy was not the least source of the terror he inspired. Lord Rosebery notes how, on his meeting a bishop, Chatham's eagle nose came down with his bending form below the level of his knees. Men did not know how to interpret such salaams; they appeared ironical and aroused apprehension.

Burgoyne returned to London, where according to the sar-observations on the Prussian, the Austrian, and the French armies, which are esteemed valuable memoranda on the matter in review, independently of the fact that they are fruits of his personal observation.

---

3 Military Studies, p. 70.
4 Frederick the Great, Book xx. c. 10. Thackeray. The Four Georges, Geo. III.

The great Earl, who to use a famous expression, lost no time in perusing these despatches, assured Burgoyne in reply, that he was counting the minutes until he could have the pleasure of seeing him.

This high flown way of speech was personally most agreeable to Burgoyne, who was a handsome man of good address and deportment, united by a marriage, of which the irregularity had been condoned, to the Stanleys, a family of high position and influence among the nobles and territorial aristocracy of England, and master of a literary style both of pen and of speech which was at that time much admired. His reputation as a soldier stood very high, and his courage and honour beyond reproach; he was thought to have a pretty wit, which cheered him somewhat before and during and after his sinister experiences of war in America. He proposed to adapt "As You Like It" to the taste of the Macaronis of Bond Street, and among other efforts composed some verses of which one finds an echo in the glee our grandfathers sang so cheerily "What shall he have that killed the deer?" and in a much appreciated verse of Mrs. Leo Hunter's Ode to an Expiring Frog.

These verse compositions were, however, but the by-products of a man of taste and fashion, now verging on the age of fifty. He engaged in more serious undertakings and by accepting the duties of chairman of a committee of enquiry into Clive's conduct in India, did somewhat to break up the energies and ruin the life of that great man. It is now well known that the British ministry had under consideration the appointment of Clive to the military supremacy of the pending Colonial war. Too late, however, for shattered in health and spirit, the founder of the British Empire in India perished by his own hand.[5]

The lapse of a few years brought Burgoyne himself to the same bar of enquiry and disparagement, where on his return from America with reputation tarnished and courage impeached he underwent the degradation and misery of a special enquiry into his own conduct of the expedition from Canada.

---

5 In 1912 a statue of Lord Clive was erected in London.

Burgoyne arrived at Boston in May, 1775, in company with Howe and Clinton in a ship whose name gave much occupation to the jesters of Boston, while the more serious were comforted by the reflection that the Cerberus had quitted British waters during a tempest of thunder and lightning. Being now 53 years of age Burgoyne was bitterly disappointed at his inconspicuous position in connection with this British force. In rank a Major-General, he was occupied with no higher duty than that of looking after a small brigade. Prior to his departure he thought there was good reason to imagine the King's favour had secured for him the post of Commander in Chief in America. Failing this he had hopes of being sent to supersede Tryon in the government of the province of New York. In support of this desired promotion he paid many visits in Whitehall and St. James, and Germain told him that no man was more proper than himself to be sent to New York as governor. But the Howes were too strong for him, their friends were indefatigable in opposition to Burgoyne, whom they did not wish to see in an independent position. After weeks of intrigue the announcement was made that all American appointments must be committed to the discretion of General Gage, then virtually the viceroy of the Atlantic colonies. Burgoyne's disappointment was extreme. He wrote from Portsmouth to tell the King he had received His Majesty's commands for America with regret, spoke of himself as one meditating death as he wrote, and made an emotional claim on the royal consideration for Lady Charlotte Burgoyne, his wife, who in the case of his contemplated suicide would be left penniless. Burgoyne had enjoyed emoluments worth in all about £3,500 a year, his wife had to her fortune £25,000 and an annuity of £400. But after 1766, on his return from his German tour, the allurements of fashionable society had made of him a reckless gambler and a frequenter of the abodes of dicing and drink; the fashionable clubs. He then entered parliament as a nominee of the great Whig house of Stanley, to which his wife belonged, and entangled himself in all the political intrigues of the times.

For the difficult and dangerous work he was now called upon to share, this way of life was an unsuitable preparation. It is certain that his commitments and entanglements made him most reluctant to leave London, not to say still more unwilling to fill an obscure American command. He speaks of the levities, the inattention, the dissipation of his common course of life, and of his leaving his widow only a legacy of his imprudences.

Grant that this language may be somewhat inflated, yet there can be little doubt that Burgoyne quitted London in a state of acute mental despondency, which culminated in the contemplation of suicide.

A voyage over the Atlantic in company with Sir William Howe who, he had reason to consider, had acted treacherously, did not help much to sweeten his bitter reflections.

This feeling affects all his ensuing correspondence with friends at home. It was then a custom of high subordinates to write private and confidential letters about their local superiors to Secretaries of State or to similar government officials of high rank. Burgoyne writes to Lord Rochford, Colonial Secretary, Clinton writes to Dartmouth, American Secretary, de Riedesel writes of the affair at Bennington and Knyphausen writes to Germain after Brandywine.[6] In fact, they were encouraged by their official superiors to use this backdoor way of communication which the usages of recent days disallow. In this spirit Burgoyne offered the most candid criticism of General Gage and of Howe to Lord Rochford in a letter of portentous length. He says of himself, with some justice, that he is a mere cypher as a Major-General, there is not enough work to go round the triumvirate, and as he explains

"My rank only serves to place me in a motionless, drowsy, irksome medium or rather vacuum, too low for the honour of command, too high for that of execution."

Howe is sometimes indicted for giving Burgoyne nothing to do, but with an army well furnished with brigadiers there was nothing for him to do. Hence he solaced himself with letter writing, with some literary efforts as a playwright, gambling, and acting as a kind of prompter to General Gage. "You will see in a moment," wrote Germain to General Irwin,[7] "that Burgoyne composed Gage's proclamation. It is very like the last speech we

---

6 Burgoyne to Rochford, to Lord North and other letters are in de Fonblanque's Burgoyne, p. 180, (undated.) Clinton to Dartmouth in Firle papers (my history of the First American Civil War, Vol. I, p. 199), De Riedesel to Germain, R. O. C. O. F. p. 236. Knyphausen in same folio.

7 Germain to Gen. Irwin, July 26, 1775. (Stopford-Sackville Mss. Vol. I.)

heard him make." Among other doings, which to our ideas would appear quite inadmissible, he opened up a correspondence on his own authority with Lieut.-General Charles Lee, whose service in Portugal under Burgoyne's command has already been noticed.

Gage, it was commonly reported, had consented to this action of Burgoyne's, which proceeded so far as to include a proposition that Burgoyne and Charles Lee should meet in conference with a view to some settlement of points in dispute. These irregular negotiations were, however, summarily quashed by a message from Congress snubbing Lee's officiousness, and forbidding further correspondence.

Lee's letter as a broadside appeared in the New York Gazetteer before Burgoyne received it and was largely circulated in both armies. Burgoyne comes out of this correspondence rather badly.

De Fonblanque, whose sentiments towards Burgoyne's memory and reputation are always on the friendly side, remarks:

"With every desire to do justice to Burgoyne's motives, in which zeal for the public service undoubtedly predominated, it is difficult to reconcile his adoption of a friendly and familiar tone with the opinion he at the time expresses of his former companion in arms and the vile use to which he had hoped to turn him had he succeeded in obtaining the proposed interview."[8]

Burgoyne soon became weary of Boston, and his increasing acerbity tells of his weariness. He characterizes Gage as unfit for his post, as in fact an amiable nobody, and his indictment of the criminal inaction of the Admiral on the station ends with a statement that the Admiral (Graves) is controlled by mere Quaker-like scruples, and that under such influences insult and impunity had, like righteousness and peace, kissed each other.[9] All this may be pardoned in a despondent and disappointed man, but his implied censure of the British troops for cowardice at Bunker Hill, an implication which Barré afterwards expanded into invective, is not so easily overlooked. It is true that Burgoyne subsequently in the House of Commons endeavored to mollify the sting of his statements, but the mischief was done, and to this day the supposed pusillanimity of the British troops is defended on the

8 De Fonblanque, p. 173.
9 Burgoyne to Germain, 20 Aug., 1775.

ground of their Whig sentiments and their unwillingness to fight strenuously for a corrupt ministry. No greater libel on brave men was ever penned.[10] The unpopularity in England of the war, is frequently alleged by Whig historians. It was regarded by the patricians, and by some city magnates with intense disfavour; but the Squires were Tories to a man, and hated the high nobles, even then, as Hanoverian rats, while in the Commons notwithstanding the pocket borough members, the nominees of the high nobles, the Address in favour of Coercion of the Rebel Colonies was carried by a majority of 179. There was no Irish contingent in the House in 1775, hence the majority was enormous. So far as the Commons represented British opinion, the war was popular from Helston to Inverness.

After a few weeks' stay in Boston Burgoyne applied for leave of absence. He ardently wished to get away. He was in a false position. His wife was very ill. It was and is still surmised that a well placed officer of the British army gets as much out of life's pleasures as do most men, and Burgoyne, an elderly man of fashion, was no whit behind the times in his love of elegance and ease. It is reported of a young British officer of our own times that he urged on his superiors the desirability of making such terms with any foe in the field that all afternoons might still be devoted to polo and other delights. Burgoyne was drawn to London by many ropes. Howe and he were doubtless very glad to see the last of each other. Burgoyne and Gage quitted Boston about the same time in the autumn of 1775. Under somewhat altered circumstances and two years later it was his destiny to revisit that turbulent city.

It forms no part of my present undertaking to describe in detail the course of that ill-advised, ill-equipped and unhappy expedition from Canada which Burgoyne, at the age of 55, was appointed to command. Being now a widower, he was more addicted to loose personal habits than is compatible with the vigorous prosecution of any enterprise. Of Madame de Riedesel's strictures on Burgoyne's moments of relaxation most investigators know something. They are to be read with caution, as obviously the baroness had a deep dislike for Burgoyne and took no pains to conceal it.

10 See my History of the First American Civil War, Vol. 1; p. 172 ff.

She mentions how she once publicly rebuked Burgoyne for his neglect of duty. It appears that a number of staff officers came to her clamouring for food. There was, she alleges, plenty of meat to be had, if the commissaries had distributed provisions. Her own larder, which was usually kept in good supply by her cook, a skilled thief and depredator, was just then empty. As these British gentlemen were crying to the German lady for something to eat the Adjutant-General Lord Petersham happened to be passing, to whom she called out with all the indignation she could master:

"Come, sir! see these officers who have shed their blood for the common cause, and who are in want of everything, because they do not receive what they ought to receive; it is your duty to call the General's attention to all this."

Lord Petersham was much affected by this salutation, as he might well be, and within a quarter of an hour up came Burgoyne himself to thank this pretty little German vixen for her reprimand. "He thanked me most pathetically for having reminded him of his duty," writes she in her journal, which also reports that the night before this remarkable incident had been spent by Burgoyne in singing, drinking, dicing and other diversions according to his usual nightly custom. These doings took place in Saratoga itself a few days before the capitulation.

Were the Baroness de Riedesel the sole witness to Burgoyne's personal habits, her charges might be brushed aside, but the subsequent tenor of his life leads to the inference that he was too self-indulgent to be fitted to cope with the difficulties of this expedition.[11]

These were, according to a hackneyed phrase, the defects of his qualities. All portraits of him, notably that by Hollyer, depict a remarkably good looking man. His affability and pleasing deportment were matters of ordinary comment among the men of his command. Lamb, Digby, Hadden and others speak of him as being kindly and good natured, with a full sense, too, of the value to his soldiers of his keeping satisfied that part of their economy

---

11 At 60 years of age he took for his mistress Miss Susan Caulfield, a singer of repute, who became the mother of four of Burgoyne's children, whom he left quite unprovided for. The Stanley family, however, provided for these orphans, of whom one was Sir John Fox Burgoyne, K. C. B., Bart.: father of Captain Burgoyne, R. N., drowned in October, 1870, by the foundering of H. M. S. Captain.

on which an army is said to march. This matter caused him unceasing anxiety.

"It is unfair," he wrote, "to compare or judge an American campaign according to European ideas; how zealously so ever a General in such an undertaking as mine may be served by the chiefs of departments, for one hour he can find to contemplate how he shall fight his army, he must allot twenty to contrive how to feed it." Yet his measures seem to have been fairly satisfactory. Until they were penned up in Saratoga there was plenty of meat to be had. Digby's remarks on the condition of the cattle after their arrival at Saratoga, and Madame de Riedesel's complaints that there was an ample supply of provisions, had the commissaries done their duty, are confirmed by other evidence. In fact, up to October 3rd, there was no shortage of supply of any kind. Hostilities ceased on October 13th, 1777. Of wine and other stimulants there was never any failure. Madeira in large quantities formed an important and difficult item for transit. Officers brought their own private supplies with them as part of the military baggage. Madame de Riedesel had always enough and to spare. She tells of the therapeutic value of her own private supply of Rhenish wine. "I also took care of Major Bloomfield, who was wounded by a musket ball which passed through both cheeks, knocked out his teeth, and injured his tongue. He could retain nothing in his mouth, and soup and liquids were his only nourishment. Fortunately we had some Rhenish wine, and in the hope the acidity would contribute to heal his wound, I gave him a bottle of which he took a little now and then, and with such effect that he was soon cured."

How wine and other stores were forwarded at the public expense for the private benefit of officers is obvious from a notice in Burgoyne's Orderly Book dated August 13, 1777.

"Whereas, two barrels of Madeira wine, three barrels of rum, one bag of coffee, one bag of barley, two kegs of butter, and two rolls of tobacco have been put clandestinely into the provision carts of the army," they are confiscated to the use of the army. A month later there is a complaint that "enormous mismanagement had been committed in respect to the King's carts" and a field officer of each wing is to be responsible for a review of the train of carts as they pass off and to cause all articles improperly introduced into a load to be thrown off and abandoned. But complaints as to the irregularities of officers and others as to conveyance of goods culminated in the charge that the worst offender was Burgoyne himself! Digby reports that officers employed three or four horses apiece to haul their personal baggage. In his examination before the House of Commons Lieut.-Col. Kingston, Burgoyne's Adjutant-General, offered the most evasive evidence, when closely questioned about the misuse of the King's carts.

126.   Q.   Do you know what allowance of wagons was made to a regiment?

A.   I don't recollect any wagons we had to allow.

127.   Q.   Was none of the baggage brought down in wheeled carriages?

A.   Several officers, I believe, brought wagons and carts of the country people for their own use, but I do not remember any of the King's carts or wagons being appropriated to the carriage of officers' baggage.   It might be, but I don't recollect it.

This was the evidence of the Adjutant-General; of the officer who, being the commander in chief's private secretary, and most trusted assistant, professes to know nothing of the contents of an Orderly Book, which is full of complaints of disorder.

Contrast this evasive and suppressive method of statement with Brigadier Phillips' order insisting upon the ammunition wagons being used on the line of march for their obvious purposes and not for officers' kits and belongings. He actually threatens to burn all the stuff he finds in the cart loads, other than the material of the artillery. The order is repeated ten days later, emphasizing the General's displeasure. Two days later he complains that officers being driven from the artillery carts, have seized the provision carts with their horses to carry their own personal baggage, and for other purposes.[12]

General Phillips was not examined during the course of this Commission of Enquiry; yet had he appeared it is doubtful

---

12   Capt. Money's replies (E-3 to Q-15) in the Enquiry by the House of Commons. Kingston himself kept as many horses as he could secure for his own servants: see also Hadden, p. 307; Phillips' complaints and cautions, 1 July, 1777, repeated a week later, and three times in August. Hadden mentions the story about 30 carts appropriated to Burgoyne's own use.

Stedman says that in preparation for this Expedition no steps were taken to collect these carts or wagons before 10 June, 1777; that they were knocked up in a hurry of unseasoned wood, and that before reaching Fort Edward all these vehicles were destroyed. He imputes the long delay at Fort Edward to the shortage of carts.

whether his evidence would not have been given in the same spirit of evasion which characterizes the evidence not only of Lieut.-Col. Kingston, but of that of Sir Guy Carleton.

Kingston for instance "has no information on the subject" of one question. "The matter did not belong to his department" is his reply to other questions, "I had no leisure to pay attention to the point," "I own I don't recollect," "I am not quite positive," "I never had any report made to me;" and so on in the same spirit. As the evidence of the other officers examined is marked by the same fixed reserve whenever Burgoyne's conduct was under review, it may be surmised that a tincture of resentment actuated these gallant officers at the treatment meted out to Burgoyne. All the men who served with him were under the cloud of this misfortune. Most of the rank and file never again saw the shores of their native land. After the Convention of Saratoga the regiments melted away, a disintegration which left few traces anywhere in the districts of their exile. The officers, however, of higher rank who are heard of again considered their just claims to preferment, as compared with the rest of the Army, imperilled.

Burgoyne was sorely distressed that these gallant men should be placed at a disadvantage in the King's service. On his return on parole from Boston in 1777, the King had refused to see him, the Ministry had declined to allow him a court martial; he was deprived of his preferments and of most of his professioual income, and became the pariah of the political and military circles, because as a prisoner of war, it was alleged, he had no rights.

His letter to Lord Amherst is pathetic in appeal on behalf of the officers of his command in this unhappy expedition.[13] "There is not a British officer who served with me during the campaign of 1777 to whom I can impute blame." He also urged that the instances were very numerous wherein particular distinction is due. All his advances were coldly received. Some feeling of umbrage at the action of the Crown and of the Ministerial Party, biased the evidence of the officers, of whose personal attachment to Burgoyne there can be no reasonable doubt. Hence the evi-

---

13   Phillips to Burgoyne, Sept. 29, 1778. Burgoyne to Amherst, Nov. 6, 1778.

dence appears to be of no considerable weight, and does not justify the strain on it which Burgoyne in his review of the evidence, a kind of *apologia pro gestis suis,* subsequently imposes.

The preceding remarks point to a state of indiscipline pervading the little mixed army. The composition of the forces, consisting of so many heterogeneous units, suggested indiscipline. It was an aggregate of British, Germans, Provincials, Canadians and Indians. Of the Indians it is now generally agreed they were worse than useless.

"They," said Lord Harrington to the Committee of the House of Commons, "are little more than a name; if indulged for interested reasons, in all the humours and caprices of spoiled children, like them they grow importunate, and unreasonable upon every new favour."

As a matter of fact, after the murder of Miss McCrea their presence as auxiliary to this force excited unappeasable odium throughout America. Burke, speaking more to the point than his personal knowledge warranted, had said: "I ever believed their services to be over-valued. Sometimes insignificant, often barbarous, always capricious." They were poor scouts, and if Lamb and others are to be credited, deficient in courage. Mr. A. M. Davis is of opinion that "The Indians engaged upon the American side produced no material influence upon Military Movements." They proved to be a mischievous influence, both they and their women. They lurked in the woods and bush through which the one road to Albany passed; a set of thieves and marauders, ever on the lookout for the drink, while their women caused other darker irregularities and scandals.[14] Burgoyne's own opinion of them after all was over and the time of cooler reflection had supervened, is summed up.

"The apparent causes of their change of temper were the resentment I had shown upon the murder of Miss McCrea, and the restraints I had laid upon their disposition to commit other enormities, but I never doubted passions were fomented and their defection completed by the cabals of the Canadian interpreters. Rapacity, self-interest and presumption are the characteristics of these men. The acquisition of the Indian language has usually

---

14 Digby (p. 121) says "they came into our tents without the least ceremony, wanting Brandy or Rum for which they would do anything".

been a certain fortune to a man with an artful head and a convenient conscience." Of these interpreters he goes on to say, their profligate policy was to promote dissension, revolt and desertion.[15]

From the Canadians and Provincials, Burgoyne says he got very little support. The Canadians were mostly of French extraction; Canada had become British dominion only 14 years previously, and was naturally somewhat lukewarm to the King's cause. Of the two thousand auxiliaries expected by him to act as boatmen, portagemen, coureurs de bois, and in such like services, not 500 turned up for duty. He plainly says that his distrust of the armed Canadians was so great as to make him reluctant to put them in any firing line. He thought it prudent to treat them as a stage manager does his supers in the alarums and excursions of a Shakesperian play. He shewed them occasionally at a distance, and considered them in very unfavourable light as compared with Daniel Morgan's Rangers, the far famed Virginian Rifles.

Of Provincials, those most unhappy men whose miserable lot it was to be the object of the supercilious regard and continual disparagement of the English, and unmitigated hatred by the Americans it is difficult to speak with conviction. That they were brutally treated on capture by the patriots is beyond all doubt[16]: that they got a full share of that insolent hauteur for which high European society was then notorious is equally certain. Burgoyne taxes them with gross insincerity: he impeaches them of joining his Army to serve their private ends. After making these strictures on his local allies, the Loyalists, he adds in a footnote, "I would not be understood to infer that none of the Provincials with me were sincere in their loyalty: perhaps many were so." He is not sure of their sincerity, but is certain of their inefficiency. To this somewhat peevish complaint about men who had no friends, and were for the most part ruined by their adherence to the Royal Cause, a forcible rejoinder is to be found in Note LX of de Lancey's edition of Jones's New York—a rejoinder based upon the resentment aroused by "the

15 Burgoyne's Remarks on the Evidence in the Enquiry into the Expedition from Canada.
16 My History as cited above, ii p. 318. C. K. Bolton, Private Soldier under Washington, gives instances connected with the action at Bennington. Cf. Charles Neilson (whose father served, I think, with Gates at Stillwater). Burgoyne's Campaign, p. 127.

overbearing pride of the Regulars, and their contempt for Volunteers.'' The dispute remains in that limbo of recrimination, in which failure is explained by the unsuccessful.

From the Germans, who were merely hired troops, enthusiasm for the cause could not reasonably be expected. The conditions of this warfare were to them novel in quality and application. The German brought with him neither a liking for England nor a dislike for America. Burgoyne confesses that the purpose of the Expedition demanded the impulse of a good deal of enthusiasm, and hints that the German troops were not exactly afire in the cause. They had no humiliations connected with failure, nor was their Empire threatened with disruption. Most of the rank and file were embarked by violence: immature men, disheartened by their prospects, and despondent. "The Germans," says Anburey, "to the number of twenty and thirty at a time will in their conversations relate to each other that they are sure they shall not live to see home again, and are certain they shall soon die.''[17] He adds that these young men, who were certainly as brave as any soldiers in the world, were taken off a score at a time by a mere phantom of their own brain: a circumstance, he says, known to every one in the Army. The equipment of the Germans was to the last degree unsuitable for the service of this Expedition. Pigtails, pomatum (or any greasy substitute), pipe clay, gorgets that choked, cross belts that checked breathing, tight gaiters, much brass ornament, hats, and swords, that, according to an ancient jest, outweighed the whole kit of a soldier in the Federal War, reduced the German soldier's marching progress to the rate of about two miles an hour. Breymann, sent to the relief of Baum at Bennington, compassed 24 miles in 16 hours. De Riedesel's Chasseurs, who were never mounted, marched in huge boots. Other impediments to progress and efficiency crippled this ill stared Expedition from its commencement.

Thus the material conditions and the constitution of the Expeditionary Force were the parents of indiscipline and desertion. Following the custom of European armies, a large number of women attached themselves to the battalions. A question

17   Anburey, a volunteer in Burgoyne's Army, was in captivity after Saratoga fell, 1841. His signature as Captain is last of the Captain's signatures to the Parole of 13 Dec., 1777. His Reminiscences appeared in 1789.

put to Lieut.-Col. Kingston in the Enquiry suggested their total number to be about 2000. Kingston made an evasive reply according to his custom. These poor creatures lived on the soldiers' rations. There were on the strength of the regiments a certain proportion of married women, of whom some followed their husbands into action. The allowance in this Expedition was three to each company; the Boston allowance had been four women. Both Howe's and Burgoyne's Orderly Books testify to the mischievous influence of these camp-followers. They are impeached of selling liquor clandestinely to Indians, and of plundering with violence everywhere. Some of them had come away from Ireland and Southern England as stowaways, misled doubtless by the reports of the good times and wealth awaiting success on the other side. Others according to one authority followed the troops from Montreal. The majority of these unauthorized women were of a class much sung about in the ballads of those days: poor wretches of whom it is presumable that after the Convention of Saratoga the majority perished in the woods. The opinion of the period connived at, if it did not actually approve of, this addition to the comforts of the forces.[18] Madame de Riedesel, for instance, had an enormous coach which conveyed herself, and her three infants, her two women attendants, her bundle of summer dresses, (her winter clothing being left behind at Ticonderoga), and her temporary supply of wine. Her suite also comprised a cook, a kind of handyman as butler, and a young gentleman of the German Army told off as equerry to the General's lady. It appears from Kingston's evidence before the House of Commons that the presence of women in considerable numbers was considered as a matter of course. He had conversed with commanding officers on the matter without noticing any objection being raised to the custom.

Grave disorders and indiscipline[19] ensued from these conditions of Burgoyne's Army. That the march to Albany was by many anticipated to be one of a festive character, as when a great

---

18   The society of women on service was not restricted to the Army. On the foundering of the Royal George at Spithead (28 June, 1782) 100 women perished. Have seen somewhere an authentic statement that women were present in the Victory at Trafalgar, but cannot localize the statement. For further statements about the plague of women in ships cf. Gardner, vol. xxxi., Naval Records Society, pp. 23, 28, 33, etc.

General traverses a country full of a yeomanry and peasantry ardent to welcome a Deliverer, is not without considerable evidence. All Burgoyne's plans were known and discussed in the social circles of Montreal before he quitted the town. He issued an order at the opening of the campaign restricting the officers' kits to the articles of a summer campaign, no leggings nor heavy outer clothing were to be carried, nor anything else beyond absolute necessities. No attention was paid to this order. Six weeks later, the General mentions in a further order that his injunctions have been neglected and adding a warning as to the penalties of further neglect. Two months later at Saratoga he published an order alleging the "enormous mismanagement of "the King's carts," which had been all the time turned into private baggage wagons for the gentlemen of the Army, or for the use of the women. Complementary to this neglect of general orders about baggage, is the evidence of neglect of sentinel duty and of desertion, and of the General's partiality towards his commissioned officers. For instance, a man of the 47th and another of the 9th are punished, the former by one thousand lashes, the latter by death, for desertion. A few days later an officer, whose name and regiment are not mentioned, being guilty of the same offence, "the General forgives, and will forget the fault in question, convinced it is impossible it should happen twice"; on which it may be a just comment that most commanding officers would have made repetition of the offence by that particular offender impossible.

Desertions were numerous. The Americans estimated that 300 men joined their ranks; at least as many perished in the woods. Embarrassment was caused by unauthorized foraging parties. Burgoyne complains in general orders that as many men had been lost to his Army by the casualties attending the search for a few potatoes as would be caused by an engagement of importance. While the "savages" were still well inclined towards him he issued instructions that if soldiers or

---

19 Orderly Book 12 July and 14 Sept., 1777; quoted in Kingston's Evidence, Q-6. After the surrender at Saratoga the captured battalions were marched to Boston where they caused much trouble. They frequently insulted and assaulted the American sentinels. Reprisals ensued. A British officer was killed by a sentinel and some private soldiers wounded. Naturally the British got the worst of it. Gen. Phillips wrote that "every principle of Justice had fled from Boston.

camp followers from the British Army were caught adrift in the woods, the Indians were to deal with them at their discretion "with the utmost rigor."[20] But the call from the woods appears to have been too imperative for any restricting measures to be successful. Emissaries hung round the camps and solicited the men to desert. According to an eye witness in Baum's camp, Patriots under the flimsiest show of friendship were permitted by that easy going man to move about on little tours of inspection at their leisure. They came—they saw, and two days after, they conquered.

The frequent complaints made against the habit of firing muskets and at all hours of the working day within the camp; repeated directions that loaded muskets were not to be kept in tents, and other cautions concur to shew that the discipline of the troops was lax, and its fighting value not so high as customary estimates would suggest. Burgoyne's command is traditionally described as a fully equipped, highly disciplined, veteran army, but on closer examination these various epithets cannot be fully justified. With it marched no cavalry: no mounted infantry: no trained scouts: while the men of the Army were mostly of tender age. Digby speaks of the numerous recruits in the force; Anburey of the lamentations of the German soldiers, that they should never see their homes again. Three officers killed at the second battle of Freeman's Farm were laid in the same grave. Their collective ages did not exceed fifty years. In fact, of Burgoyne's *Veteran Army* both the British and German contingents had been recruited in the good old style: the English kidnapped, or pressed, or sold into the service, by the parish authorities of Merrie England; the Germans torn from their homes to fill with their hire the pockets of their reigning Prince.[21]

The final scene discloses that after the second engagement at Freeman's Farm, the British troops, of whom according to the Adjutant-General's report a bare eleven hundred effectives had

20 "Not only the Discipline and Honour, but also the safety of the troops, require the strictest prohibition from straggling and plundering, and the Savages as well as the Provost will have orders to punish offenders in these respects instantly, and with the utmost rigour." An order of Burgoyne's at the beginning of the Expedition.
21 I have called attention to the sources from which our Armies were drawn during this Century in Chapters on Forces of the Crown in My History of the First American Civil War, Vol. i.

been brought into action, were absolutely exhausted. The 62nd Regiment, or rather its remains, were quite incapable of further exertions: the 47th could not be depended on: the men in general had got into their heads that surrender under a Convention was desirable. Wounds or sickness had deprived all the corps of some of the best company officers. There was no artillery: near-ly every artillery man had fallen in the recent engagements. A victorious effort could not have saved the army, for no provisions remained, while, as every one admitted, the life and property of every non-combatant dependent on the Army were in imminent peril. Consequently the Convention was in many quarters hailed with delight as a supreme deliverance. " 'Twas easy," writes Madame de Riedesel, "after months of anxiety, and I read the same happy change in the countenances of those around me."

Thus ended, after about six months' duty, the command of Lieut.-General Burgoyne in North America. His previous experience of warfare is comprised in a few weeks unsuccessful raiding on the French coast near Cherbourg (1758) and a few weeks active and successful cavalry warfare in Portugal during the second half of 1762. One year would contain all the active service of Burgoyne's military experience, that is even if his few weeks stay in Boston be taken into account. Of his merits as a commanding officer, it is exceedingly difficult to form any just estimate. His hands were tied by his superiors at home; the expedition was a month late in starting; he was ill served in all the minor details of his undertaking; his force was mixed, torn by international jealousies and dissensions, his local allies were at least of doubtful value; his means of transport were insufficient, and his force was too small to hold its lines of communication; its medical arrangements were the most elementary, and even of these the efficiency may be estimated from the fact that after an important engagement it was found the medical stores and comforts had been left behind at Ticonderoga[22], add to this his easy going nature and his regard for his own class did not

---

[22] After the Battle of Hubbardton there was no means of getting the wounded to Ticonderoga except in biers and wheelbarrows, which the wounded found to be as Kingston says "incommodious, preferring to take "their chances out in the open with rattlesnakes, musquitoes and vermin "for company." Lamb's experience, in his Journal of the American war. The Medical Department consisted of 16 persons, inclusive of Surgeons and Hospital Mates.

BURGOYNE'S SURRENDER TO GATES. (Made in 1826.)

Courtesy of Frank J. Wilder

permit him to punish anyone of gentle birth or good official position.

In general terms one quite concurs in Mr. S. G. Fisher's summary of the situation, or again with that of Mr. F. S. Oliver.[23] The censures on Sir Wm. Howe in this connection do not appear to me to be justified, otherwise Howe deserves, I think, all that has been said of him by responsible writers both in America and in England—but for the failure of this expedition he is not responsible: the expedition was from the very first doomed to fail. "It is only dream strategy which attempts to cut off a province by drawing a line, which is immediately rubbed out behind the pencil."

Stedman's criticism of Burgoyne is worth repeating:[24]

"In the whole of Burgoyne's vindications of himself it was observed his method was to state a necessity for every one of his measures taken singly, and not as links of a chain or system of action; taking care to pass over one material circumstance that that necessity invariably originated on his own part in some previous omission or blunder." One is not sure that the ancient censure "*censensu omnium capax imperii, nisi imperasset*," passed on an unsuccessful man, applies fully to Burgoyne, but in such hands as his, this ill digested project was doomed to failure.

All the great captains of antiquity, and those who later have marched in their footsteps, have only done great deeds by conforming to the principles of war, and whatever may have been the audacity of their enterprise and the extent of their success, they have only succeeded by conforming to those principles. Among those principles is that known as Economy of Force: by using mass, rapidity and security in combination.

Major General Townsend[25] points out how the Japanese violated the principle of Economy of Force in connection with the victories of Liao Yang and the Sha Ho by detaching 150,000 men to capture Port Arthur, and thus weakening their mass with the consequence of rendering both those engagements incomplete

23 S. G. Fisher, ii p. 86 ff., F. S. Oliver's Life of Alex. Hamilton, Chapter V.; also C. F. Adams and Worthington C. Ford in Vol. 44 Massachusetts Hist'l Society, pp. 13 ff., 94 ff. and 020 ff.

24 Stedman: Hist. of the American War, 2 vols. 17-94. Vol. 1, pp. 353 to 357. Chas. Stedman served under Howe, Clinton and Cornwallis in this War as Commissary. There is a good notice of him in the Dictionary of National Biography.

victories. Napoleon himself by detaching 30,000 men at Waterloo so far weakened his mass as finally to break it up: he was
driven into the same error at Leipsic; and Baum's disaster at
Bennington was due to the violation of the same principle. Burgoyne having had no real experience of war even as a subordinate and having no breadth of mind to embrace a course of exact
study of war, and being despatched, and having undertaken to
do in a few weeks, what in similar country and under somewhat
parallel circumstances occupied Julius Caesar in Gaul at least
three years, was from the first virtually, if unconsciously, riding
for a fall.

The following letter, written immediately after the disaster
at Saratoga, throws light on Burgoyne's opinion of his auxiliaries, and may be read in connection with certain statements
above:

1777, October 20.—Separate and private. Conscious that
"the precision of my orders both in the letter and spirit left me no
"latitude in abandoning my communications on the 13th of Sep-
"tember, that the corps of troops I commanded was in the inter-
"est of government, a corps to be hazarded for the great purpose
"of forcing a junction, or at least of making a powerful diver-
"sion in your favor, by employing the forces that otherwise
"would join General Washington, convinced that I can justify
"myself to my profession and to the world upon these points, I
"am in no pain concerning them.

"What I feel upon the unfortunate issue of my efforts is
"more easily to be conceived than described. For your private
"consideration, I have to add to the circumstances of my public
"letter, others of a very melancholy nature, viz.: a scandalous de-
"fection of the Indians, a desertion or timidity worse than deser-
"tion of provincials and Canadians, a very few individuals ex-
"cepted, and a strong disposition in the Germans to be prisoners
"rather than endure hard blows. Had all my troops been Brit-
"ish, I, in my conscience, believe I should have made my way
"through Mr. Gates's army. At Saratoga, destitute as I was of
"provisions I was not without resources to have opened a pass-
"age to Ticonderoga had my whole army been in a temper for

---

25   Major Gen. Townsend, C. B. D. S. O., on the Strategical Employment
of Cavalry.   Journal of R. U. S. Institution, August, 1912, p. 1171 ff.

"hardy enterprise—even British troops declined. The utmost "that the officers gave me to hope from the complection of their "men, was, that they would fight upon that ground if attacked. "The Germans fell short of that—it was notorious that they "meant to have given one fire and then have clubbed their arms.

"In short, my army would not fight and could not subsist."

This unfortunate man's remains lie unnoticed and unrecorded somewhere in the North Cloister of Westminster Abbey.

SOME BURGOYNIANA

Presented to Association by Rev. Henry Belcher, M. A., LL. D.

A letter from General Lee, to General Burgoyne, dated June 7, 1775; received at Bofton, July 5. Printed from the New York Gazetteer, July 6. In Broadside form.

My Dear Sir:

'We have had twenty different accounts of your arrival at Bofton, which have been regularly contradicted the next morning; but as I now find it certain that you are arrived, I fhall not delay a fingle inftant addreffing myfelf to you. It is a duty I owe to the friend-fhip I have long and fincerely profeffed for you; a friendfhip to which you have the ftrongest claims from the firft moments of our acquaintance. There is no man from whom I have received fo many teftimonies of efteem and affection; there is no man whofe efteem and affection, could, in my opinion have done me greater honour. I entreat and conjure you therefore, my dear Sir, to impute thefe lines not to a petulent itch of fcribbling, but to the moft unfeigned folicitude for the future tranquility of your mind, and for your reputation. I fincerely lament the infatuation of the times, when men of fuch ftamp as Mr. Burgoyne and Mr. Howe can be feduced into fo impious and nefarious a fervice, by the artifice of a wicked, and infidious court and cabinet. You, Sir, muft be fenfible that thefe epithets are not unjuftly fevere. You have your felf experienced the wickedneff and treachery of this court and cabinet: You cannot but recollect their manoeuvres in your own felect committee, and the treatment yourfelf as prefi-dent received from thefe abandoned men. You can not but recol-lect the black bufinefs of St. Vincents, by an oppofition to which you acquired the higheft and moft deferved honour. I fhall not trouble you with my opinion of the right of taxing America without her own confent, as I am afraid, from what I have feen of your fpeeches, that you have already formed your creed upon this article; but I will boldly affirm, had this right been eftablished by a thoufand ftatutes, had America admitted it from time immemorial, it would be the duty of every good Englifhman to exert his utmoft to diveft Parliament of this right, as it muft inevitably work the fubverfion of the whole empire. The malady under which the ftate labours is indifputably deprived from the inadequate reprefentation of the fubject, and the vaft pecuniary influence of the crown. To add to this pecuniary influence and incompetency of reprefentation is to infure and precipitate our deftruction. To wifh any addition, can fcarcely enter the heart of a citizen who has the leaft fpark of public virtue, and who is at the fame time capable of feeling confequences the moft immediate. I appeal, Sir, to your own confcience, to your experience and knowledge of our court and parliament; and I requeft you to lay your hand upon your heart, and then anfwer with your ufual integrity and franknefs, whether, on the fuppofition America fhall be abject enough to fubmit to the terms impofed, you think a fingle guinea raifed upon her would be applied to the purpofe (as it is oftentatioufly held out to deceive the people at home) of eafing the mother country? Or whether you are not convinced that the whole they could extract would be applied folely to heap up ftill further the enormous fund for corruption which the crown already poffeffes, and of which a moft diabolical ufe is made. On thefe principles I fay, Sir, every good Englifhman, abftracted of all regard for America, muft oppofe her being taxed by the Britifh Parliament; for my own part I am convinced that no argument (not totally abhorrent from the fpirit of liberty and the Britifh conftitution) can be produced in fupport of this right. But it would be impertinent to trouble you upon a fubject which has been fo amply, and, in my opinion, fo fully difcuffed. I find by a fpeech given as your's in the public papers, that it was by the King's pofitive command you embarked in this fervice. I am fomewhat pleafed that it is not an office of your own feeking, tho', at the fame time, I muft confefs that it is very alarming to every virtuous citizen, when he fees men of fenfe and integrity, (becaufe of a certain profeffion) lay it down as a rule implicitly to obey the mandates of a court be they ever fo flagitious. It furnishes, in my opinion, the beft argument for the total reduction of the army. But I am running into a tedious effay, whereas I ought to confine myfelf to the main defign and purpofe of this letter, which is to guard you and you colleagues from thofe prejudices which the fame mifcreants, who have infatuated General Gage, and ftill furround him, will labour to inftil into you againft a brave, loyal, and moft deferving people. The avenues of truth will be fhut up to you. I affert, Sir, that even General Gage will deceive you as he has deceived himfelf; I do not fay he will do fo defignedly, I do not think him capable; but his mind is fo totally poifoned, and his underftanding fo totally blinded by the fociety of fools and knaves, that he no longer is capable of difcerning facts as manifeft as the noon day fun. I affert, Sir, that he is ignorant, that he has from the beginning been confumately ignorant of the principles, temper, difpofition, and force of the colonies. I affert, Sir, that his letters to the miniftry, at leaft fuch as the public have feen, are one contiued iffue of mifreprefentations, injuftice, and tortured inferences from mis-ftated facts. I affirm, Sir, that he has taken no pains to inform himfelf of the truth; that he has never converfed with a man who has the courage or honefty to tell him the truth.

I am apprehenfive that you and your colleagues may fall into the fame trap, and it is the apprehenfion that you may be confiderately hurried by the vigor and activity you poffefs, into meafures which may be fatal to many innocent individuals, may hereafter wound your own feelings, and which can not poffibly ferve the caufse of thofe who fent you, that has prompted me to addrefs thefe lines to you.—I moft devoutly wifh, that your induftry, valour, and military talents, may be referved for a more honourable and virtuous fervice againft the natural enemies of your country, (to whom our court are fo bafely complacent) and not be wafted in ineffectual attempts to reduce to the wretched eftate of fervitude, the moft meritorious part of your fellow fubjects. I fay, Sir, that any attempts to accomplish this purpofe muft be ineffectual. You cannot poffibly fucceed. No man is better acquainted with the ftate of this continent than myfelf. I have ran through almoft the whole colonies, from the north to the fouth, and from the fouth to the north. I have converfed with all orders of men, from the firft eftated gentlemen to the loweft planters and farmers, and can affure you that the fame fpirit animates the whole. Not lefs than an hundred and fifty thoufand gentlemen, yeomen, and farmers, are now in arms, determined to preferve their liberties or perifh. As to the idea that the Americans are deficient in courage, it is too ridiculous and glaringly falfe to deferve a ferious refutation. I never could conceive upon what this notion was founded. I ferved feveral campaigns in America laft war, and cannot recollect a fingle inftance of ill behaviour in the provincials, where the regulars acquitted themfelves well. Indeed we well remember fome inftance of the reverfe, particularly where the late Colonel Grant, (he who lately pledged himfelf for the general cowardice of America) ran away with a large body of his own regiment, and was faved from deftruction by the valour of a few Virginians. Such prepofterous arguments are only proper for the Rigby's and Sandwich's from whofe mouths never iffued, and to whofe breafts truth and decency are utter ftrangers.

You will much oblige me in communicating this letter to General Howe, to whom I could wifh it fhould be in fome meafure addreffed, as well as to yourfelf. Mr. Howe is a man for whom I have ever had the higheft love and reverence. I have honored him for his own connections, but above all for his admirable talents and good qualities. I have courted his acquaintance and friendfhip, not only as a pleafure, but as an ornament: I flattered myfelf that I had obtained it. Gracious God! is it poffible that Mr. Howe fhould be prevailed upon to accept of fuch an office! The brother of him, to whofe memory the much injured people of Bofton erected a monument, fhould be employed as one of the inftruments of their deftruction! But the fafhion of the times it feems is fuch, as renders it impoffible that he fhould avoid it. The commands of our moft gracious Sovereign are to cancel all moral obligations, to fanctify every action, even thofe that the Satrap of an Eaftern defpot would ftart at. I fhall now beg leave to fay a few words with refpect to myfelf and the part I act. I was bred up from my infancy in the higheft veneration for the liberties of mankind in general. What I have feen of courts and Princes convinces me, that power cannot be lodged in worfe hands than in theirs; and of all courts I am perfuaded that ours is the moft corrupt and hoftile to the rights of humanity. I am convinced that a regular plan has been laid (indeed every act fince the prefent acceffion, evinces it) to abolifh even the shadow of liberty from amongft us. It was not the demolition of the tea, it was not any other particular act of the Boftonians, or of the other provinces which conftituted their crimes. But it is the noble fpirit of liberty manifeftly pervading the whole continent, which has rendered them the object of minifterial & royal vengeance. Had they been notorioufly of another difpofition, had they been "homines ad fervitudinem paratos," they might have made as free with the property of the Eaft India company as the felonius North himfelf with impunity. But the Lords of St. James's and their mercenaries of St. Stephen's well know, that as long as the free fpirit of this great continent remains unfubdued, the progrefs they can make in their fcheme of univerfal defpotifm, will be but trifling. Hence it is that they wage inexpiable war againft America. In fhort, this is the laft afylum of perfecuted liberty. Here fhould the machinations and fury of her enemies prevail; that bright goddefs muft fly off from the face of the earth, and leave not a trace behind. Thefe, Sir, are my principles; this is my perfuafion, and confequentially I am determined to act. I have now, Sir, only to entreat that whatever meafures you purfue, whether thofe of your real friends (myfelf amongft them) would wifh, or unfortunately thofe which our accurfed mifrulers fhall dictate, you will ftill believe me to be perfonally, with the greateft fincerity and affection,

Your's, &c.

C. LEE.

A Copy of General Burgoyne's Answer to General Lee, dated July 8th, 1775.

Dear Sir,

When we were laft together in fervice, I fhould not have thought it within the viciffitudes of human affairs that we fhould meet at any time, or in any fenfe, as foes. The letter you have honoured me with and my own feelings, combine to prove we are ftill far from being perfonally fuch.

I claim no merit from the attentions you fo kindly remember in the early periods of our acquaintance, but as they manifeft how much it was my pride to be known for your friend; nor have I departed from the duties of that character, when, I will not fcruple to fay, it has been almoft general offence to maintain it: I mean fince the violent part you have taken in the commotions of the Colonies.

It would exceed the limits and the propriety of our prefent correfpondence to argue at full the great caufe in which we are engaged. But anxious to preferve a confiftent and ingenuous character and jealous I confefs of having the part I fuftain imputed to fuch motives as you intimate, I will ftate to you as concifely as I can the principles upon which, not voluntarily, but moft confcientioufly I undertook it.

I have, like you, entertained from infancy a veneration for public liberty. I have likewife regarded the Britifh conftitution as the beft fafeguard of that bleffing to be found in the hiftory of mankind.

The vital principle of the conftitution, in which it moves and has its being, is the fupremacy of the King in Parliament—a compound, indefinite, indefeafible power, coeval with the origin of the empire and co-extenfive over all it's parts.

I am no ftranger to the doctrines of Mr. Locke, and other of the beft advocates for the rights of mankind, upon the compacts always implied between the governing and governed, and the right of refiftance in the latter when the compact fhall be fo violated as to leave no other means of redrefs. I look with reverence almoft amounting to idolatry upon thofe immortal whigs who adopted and applied fuch doctrine during part of the reign of Charles the Ift, and in that of James IId.

Should corruption pervade the three eftates of the realm fo as to pervert the great ends for which they were inftituted and make the power vefted in them for the good of the whole people operate, like an abufe of the prerogative of the Crown, to general oppreffion, I am ready to acknowledge that the fame doctrine of refiftance applies as forcibly againft the abufes of the collective body of power, as againft thofe of the Crown or either of the other component breuches feparately: Still always underftood that no other means of redrefs can be obtain'd: A cafe I contend much more difficult to fuppofe when it relates to the whole than when it relates to parts.

But in all cafes that have exifted or can be conceived, I hold that refiftance, to be juftifiable, muft be directed against the ufurpation or undue exercife of power; and that it is most criminal when directed againft any power itfelf inherent in the conftitution.

And here you will immediately difcern why I drew a line in the allufion I made above to the reign of Charles I. Towards the clofe of it the true principle of refiftance was changed and a new fyftem of government projected accordingly. The patriots previous to the long Parliament and during great part of it, as well as the glorious revolutionifts of 1688, refifted to vindicate and reftore the conftitution; the republicans refifted to fubvert it.

Now Sir, lay your hand upon your heart, as you have enjoined me to do on mine, and tell me to which of thefe purpofes do the proceedings of America tend?

Is it the weight of taxes impofed, and the impoffibility of relief after a due reprefentation of her burthen, that has induced her to take ARMS? Or is it a denial of the right of Britifh legiflation to impofe them and confequently a ftruggle for total independency? For the idea of power that can tax externally, and not internally, and all the fophiftry that attends it, tho' it may catch the weaknefs and the prejudice of the multitude in a fpeech or pamphlet, it is too prepofterous to weigh ferioufly with a man of your underftanding; and I am confident you will admit the cafe to be fairly put. Is it then from a relief of taxes, or from the controul of Parliament "in all cafes whatfoever" we are in war? If for the former, the quarrel is at end—there is not a man of fenfe and information in America who does not know it is in the power of the Colonies to put an end to the exercife of taxation immediately, and forever. I boldly affert it becaufe fenfe and information will alfo fuggeft to every man, that it can never be the intereft of Britain after her late experience to make another trial.

But if the other ground is taken, and it is intended to wreft from Great Britain a link of that fubftantial, and I hope perpetual, chain by which the empire holds—think it not a minifterial mandate; think it not a mere profeffional ardour; think it not a prejudice againft a part of our fellow fubjects, that induces men of integrity, and among fuch you have done me the honour to claſs me, to act with vigour; but be aſſured it is a conviction that the whole of our political fyſtem depends upon the prefervation of its great and eſſential parts diftinctly, and no part is fo great and eſſential as fupremacy of legiſlation.—It is a conviction, that as a King of England never appears in fo glorious a light as when he employs the executive powers of the ftate to maintain the laws, fo in the prefent exertions of that power, his Majeſty is particularly entitled to our zeal and grateful obedience not only as foldiers but as citizens.

Thefe principles, depend upon it, actuate the army and fleet throughout: And let me at the fame time add, there are few, if any gentlemen among us who would have drawn his fword in the caufe of flavery.

But why do I bind myfelf to the navy and army? The fentiments I have touched are thofe of the great bulk of the nation. I appeal to the landed men who have fo long borne burthens for America; I appeal to thofe trading towns who are fufferers by the difpute and the city of London at the head of them, notwithſtanding the petitions and remonftrances which the arts of party and faction have extorted from fome individuals; and laft becaufe leaft in your favour, I appeal to the majorities in the houfes of Parliament upon American queftions this feffion. The moft licentious news writers want affurance to call thefe majorities miniſterial; much lefs will you give them that name when you impartially examine the characters that compofe them.—Men of the moft independent principles and and fortunes, and many of them profeffedly in oppofition to the court in the general line of their conduct.

Among other fupporters of Britifh rights againft American claims, I will not fpeak pofitively, but I firmly believe, I may name the man of whofe integrity you have the higheft opinion, and whofe friendfhip is neareft your heart—I mean Lord Thanet, from whom my Aid de Camp has a letter for you, and alfo one from Sir Charles Davers: I do not inclofe them, becaufe the writers, little imagining how difficult your conduct would render our intercourfe, defired they might be delivered to your own hands.

For this purpofe as well as to renew, "the rights of fellowfhip," I wifh to fee you; and above all, I fhould find an interview happy if it fhould induce fuch explanations as might tend in their confequence to peace. I feel in common with all around me, for the unhappy bulk of this country; they forefee not the diftrefs that is impending over them. I know Great Britain is ready to open her arms upon the firft overture of accommodation; I know fhe is equally refolute to maintain her original rights; and if the war proceeds, your one hundred and fifty thoufand men will not be a match for her power.

The place I would propofe for our meeting is the honfe upon Bofton neck, juft within our advanced centuries, called Brown's houfe,—I will obtain authority to give my parole of honour for your fafe return. I fhall expect the fame on your part that no infult be offered to me. If this plan is agreeable to you, name your day and hour. At all events, accept a fincere return of the affurances with which you honour me, and believe me in all perfonal confiderations, affectionately yours.

P. S. I obeyed your commands to Generals Howe and Clinton. I alfo communicated your letter and my anfwer to Lord Percy. They all join me in compliments, and authorize me to affure you they do the fame in principles.

A Copy of General Lee's letter, declining the interview propofed by General Burgoyne.

Cambridge, Head Quarters, July 11.

General Lee's compliments to General Burgoyne. Would be extremely happy in the interview he fo kindly propofed. But as he perceives that General Burgoyne has already made up his mind on this great fubject; and as it is impoffible that he (Gen. Lee) fhould ever alter his opinion, he is apprehenfive that the interview might create thofe jealoufies and fufpicions, fo natural to a people ftruggling in the deareft of all caufes, that of their liberty, property, wives, children, and their future generation. He muft therefore, defer the happinefs of embracing a man, whom he moft fincerely loves until the fubverfion of the prefent tyrannical miniftry and fyftem, which he is perfuaded muft be in a few months, as he knows Great Britain cannot ftand the conteft. He begs General Burgoyne will fend the letters which his Aid de Camp has for him. If Gardiner is his Aid de Camp, he defires his love to him.

A copy of letter written by Baron de Reidesel.

C. O. 5—236

p. 132.

Camp near Jones's Farm
28 August 1777
Baron de Reidesel
R 31st Oct''
*(5 Inclosures)

Milord.

Me flattant que votre Excellence daigne encore se souvenir de son très humble Serviteur, qui certainement serve avec Zèle pour le Service de La Majesté quoique ses Fecultés sont si foibles qu'il ne puet pas être d'antant d'Utilité comme il le souhaite luimême.

L'Evacuation de Ticonderoga, le Gain de l'Affaire de Hoperton, la Prise de Skeensborough, et la Retraite de l'Enemi jusqu' à Stillwater 22 Miles en deca d'Albance, etoient des Succès si rapides, qu' à peine nous pouvions suivre l'Ennemi. Le Manque de Chariage rallentit beaucoup le Transport de nos Provisions, pour remedier à ces Inconveniens le General Burgoyne projettait d' enlever le considerable Magazin de Bennington à l'Ennemi, dans l'Esperance d'en faire vivre notre Armée un certain Tems. L'Issue de cette Expedition n'a pas été selon nos Souhaits. Pour prouver à Votre Excellence que ni les Troupes employés dans cette Expedition, ni les deux Commandeurs, ont manqué dans leur Conduite, ni agit contre leurs Orders, j'ai l'honneur de presenter à Votre Excellence une courte Relation de cette triste Affaire, avec les rapports et Instructions.

J'espére que nous trouverons bientôt l'Occasion de reparer cet Echec, et que les premières Nouvelles que Votre Excellence recevra de notre Armée seront plus satisfaisantes.

Me recommandant dans les Bontés de Votre Excellence.

J'ai l'honneur d' être &c.

REIDESEL.

*Not here given.

NOTE.—The following addresses by Horatio Seymour and George William Curtis, made at Schuylerville at the celebration of the one hundredth anniversary of the Surrender of Burgoyne, are included in these Proceedings because of their direct bearing on the subject of this meeting and their standing as classics in the historical literature of America.

ADDRESS OF HON. HORATIO SEYMOUR

One hundred years ago, on this spot, American Independence was made a great fact in the history of nations. Until the surrender of the British army under Burgoyne, the Declaration of Independence was but a declaration. It was a patriotic purpose asserted in bold words by great men, who pledged for its maintenance their lives, their fortunes and their sacred honor. But here it was made a fact, by virtue of armed force. It had been regarded by the world merely as an act of defiance, but it was now seen that it contained the germs of a government, which the event we celebrate made one of the powers of the earth. Here rebellion was made revolution. Upon this ground, that which had in the eye of the law been treason, became triumphant patriotism.

At the break of day one hundred years ago, in the judgment of the world, our fathers were rebels against established authority. When the echoes of the evening gun died away along this valley, they were patriots who had rescued their country from wrong and outrage. Until the surrender of the British army in this valley, no nation would recognize the agents of the continental congress. All intercourse with them was in stealthy ways. But they were met with open congratulations when the monarchs of Europe learned that the royal standards of Britain had been lowered to our flag. We had passed through the baptism of blood, and had gained a name among the nations of the earth.

The value of this surrender was increased by the boastful and dramatic display which had been made of British power. It had arrayed its disciplined armies; it had sent its fleets; it had called forth its savage allies, all of which were to move upon grand converging lines, not only to crush out the patriotic forces, but to impress Europe with its strength, and to check any alliances with the American government. It made them witnesses of its defeat when it thought to make them the judges of its triumph. The monarchs of Europe who watched the progress of the doubtful struggle, who were uncertain if it was more than a popular disturbance, now saw the action in its full proportions, and felt that a new power had sprung into existence—a new element had entered into the diplomacy of the world.

The interests excited in our minds by this occasion, are not limited to a battle fought, or an army captured; they reach even beyond the fact that it was a turning point of the revolutionary struggle. We are led to a consideration of a chain of events and of enduring aspects of nature, which have shaped our civilization in the past, and which now and throughout the future, will influence the fortunes of our country. Burgoyne did not merely surrender here an army, he surrendered the control of a continent. Never in the world's history, was there a transfer of a territory so vast, and of influences so far reaching, as that made a century ago where we now stand.

We meet to-day to celebrate the surrender of Burgoyne, by appropriate ceremonies, and to lay the corner stone of a monument which will commemorate not only that event, but every fact which led to that result. The reproach rests upon the United States, that while they stand in the front ranks of the powers of the earth, by virtue of their numbers, their vast domains and their progress in wealth and in arts, they give no proof to the eyes of the world that they honor their fathers or those whose sacrifices laid the foundations of their prosperity and greatness. We hope that a suitable structure here will tell all who look upon it that this was the scene of an occurrence unsurpassed in importance in military annals. And it will also show that a hundred years have not dimmed its lustre in our eyes, but that the light shed upon its significance by the lapse of time, has made deeper and stronger our gratitude to those who here served their country so well, and by their sacrifices and sufferings, achieved its independence and secured the liberties, the prosperity and greatness of the American people.

All that throws light upon the scope and policy of the designs of the British government are, on this day, proper topics for consideration. When we trace out the relationships which these designs bore to preceding occurrences; and when we follow down their bearing upon the present and future of our country, we shall see that a suitable monument here will recall to all thoughtful minds the varied history of our country during the past two centuries. It will do more. For the enduring causes which have shaped the past, also throw light upon the future of our government, our civilization and our power.

The occurrences which led to the surrender of the British army, have been appropriately celebrated. The great gatherings of our people at Oriskany, at Bennington and at Bemis's Heights, show how this centennial of what has been well termed the year of battles, revives in the minds of the American people an interest in the history of the Revolution. These celebrations have tended to make our people wiser and better. It is to be hoped that they will be held on every battle field in our country. They will not only restore the patriotism of our people but they will teach us the virtues of courage and patient endurance. This is a time of financial distress and of business disorder, and we have lost somewhat of our faith with regard to the future, and we speak in complaining tones of the evils of our day. But when we read again the history of the war for our independence; when we hear the story of the sufferings of all classes of our citizens; when we are reminded that our soldiers endured from want, and nakedness, and hunger, as no pauper, no criminal suffers now; when we think that the fears which agitated their minds were not those which merely concerned the pride of success, the mortification of failure, or the loss of some accustomed comfort, but they were the dread that the march of hostile armies might drive their families from their homes, might apply the torch to their dwellings, or worse than this, expose their wives and children to the tomahawks and scalping knives of merciless savages, we blush at our complaints. In view of their dangers and sufferings, how light appear the evils of our day.

But there is something more than all this to be gained by these celebrations. Before the Revolution the people of the several colonies held but little intercourse. They were estranged from each other by distance, by sectional prejudices, and by differences of lineage and religious creeds. The British government relied upon these prejudices and estrangements to prevent a cordial co-operation among the colonists. But when the war began, when the men of Virginia hastened to Massachusetts to rescue Boston from the hands of the enemy and drive them from New England; when the men of the east and south battled side by side with those from the middle states, and stood upon this spot as brothers to receive with a common pride and joy the standards of a conquered foe; when Greene and Lincoln went to the relief of the southern colonies all prejudice not only died away, but more than fraternal love animated every patriot heart from the bleak northernmost forests of New England to the milder airs of Georgia. And now that a hundred years have passed, and our country has become great beyond the wildest dreams of our fathers, will not the story of their sufferings revive in the breast of all the love of our country, of our whole country, and all who live within its boundaries? Men of the east and men of the south, or you who can trace your lineage back to those who served their country a century ago upon the soil of New York, we do not welcome you here as guests; you stand here of right, by virtue of a heritage from our fathers, who on this ground were common actors in the crowning event of the war waged for the liberties, the glory, and the prosperity of all sections of our great country.

At this celebration of the grand conclusion of the campaign of Burgoyne, we have a broader field of discussion than that of a battle, however stirring it may have been. The occasion calls not only for praise of heroic courage, not only for a deep interest in every statement showing the influence of its victories over the judgment of the world as to the strength of our cause, but also for its importance as one of the links in the chain of events reaching back more than two centuries, and which will continue to stretch down into the future far beyond the period when human thought or conclusion can be of value.

Influence of the Topography of Our Country.

The speaker and others who have addressed the public with regard to American history, have made frequent references to the extent that it has been shaped by the topography of this part of our country. On this occasion it forces itself upon our attention, and we must again outline its relationship to events. We cannot, if we would, separate the design of the campaign of Burgoyne, nor the military aspects of its progress, from the character of the valleys through which its forces were moved, nor from the commanding positions at which it was aimed. Our mountains and rivers have been the causes of so many of the great facts in the history of this continent; they are so closely identified with its political and social affairs, that they seem to become sentient actors in its events. We are compelled to speak of their bearings upon the course of war, of commerce and of civilization, to make a clear statement of the scope and significance of the events we celebrate. This cannot be given if we speak only of the things which relate to the British invasion of 1777, and of its signal defeat.

Those who would learn the causes which have shaped the course of military and political affairs on this continent, which have given victory in war and prosperity in peace, must spread out before them the map of our country. Having traced its grand system of mountains, rivers and lakes, they will be struck with the fact that for a thousand miles the Alleghanies make long ranges of barriers between the Atlantic and the great plains of the interior. About mid-way of their lengths these lofty mountains are cut down to their bases by the gorge of the Hudson, through which the tides of the ocean pour their floods in triumph. Towering cliffs overshadow the deep waters of the river. Had but a single spur of those rocky buttresses which crowd upon either shore been thrown across the narrow chasm, had but one of the beetling cliffs which stand upon its brink been pushed but a few feet across its course, the currents of events would have been changed as completely as the currents of the floods. The nations who controlled the outlets of the Mississippi and the St. Lawrence would have been the masters of this continent. No one who has marked the physical character of our country, and who has studied its history, can pass through the highlands of the Hudson and note how at every turn of its stream the cliffs threaten to close its course, without feeling that the power which made the mountain chains to stop abruptly at its brink, was higher than blind chance—

something more than the wild, unreasoning action of convulsed nature.

The valley of the Hudson does not end when it has led the ocean tides through the mountain passes. It stretches its channel northward to the St. Lawrence, and holds within its deep basin not only the Hudson flowing south, but Lake Champlain, which empties its waters into the ocean far north through the gulf of St. Lawrence. It thus not only connects the harbor of New York with the basins of the great lakes, but by the Mohawk branch of the Hudson it has also channeled out another level passage, stretching westward to the plains watered by the confluents of the Mississippi. These valleys of the Hudson and Mohawk have been the pathways of armies in war and the routes of commerce in peace. They have been the highways through which the nations of Europe and the people of the Atlantic coast have poured their hosts of emigrants into the vast regions which stretch out from the Alleghanies to the base of the Rocky mountains. But nature did not stop in her work when she gave to the regions in which we meet advantages of deep valleys, making the easy communication from the sea coast to the interior of our country. From the outward slopes of highlands which guard these channels of intercourse, the waters flow by diverging valleys into almost every part of our Union. These highlands make, in many ways, the most remarkable watersheds to be found on the face of the earth. There is not elsewhere an instance where interlocking sources of rivers pursue courses diverging in so many directions, forming so many extending valleys, and at length find their outlets into the ocean at points so distant from each other, and from the headwaters on the ground where they had their common origin. For these reasons the valleys of the Hudson and the Mohawk, and the mountain strongholds which command them, have ever been the great central points of control in the wars of both civilized and savage races. Once when in company with General Scott, we overlooked from an elevated point the ground on which we stand and the confluence of these rivers, and the range of highlands which marked their courses, the old warrior with a kindling eye, stretched out his arm and said: ''Remember this has been the great strategic point in all the wars waged for the control of this continent.''

The mountains and valleys of New York not only make channels for commerce in peace, but a grand system for defence and attack in war. They are nature's commanding works, which dwarf by comparison all human monuments of engineering skill into insignificance. Their influence is most clearly shown by the power they gave to the Indian tribes who held them when Europeans first visited our continent. The rivers which flowed in all directions from their vantage ground on the highlands, first taught the Iroquois the advantage of united action, and led to the formation of their confederacy. Pouring their combined forces at different times into the valley of the Delaware, or the Susquehanna, or the Alleghany, they were able to subdue in detail the divided tribes living upon these streams. Thus gaining courage and skill by constant victories, they boldly pushed their conquest into remote sections of our country. The British ordnance maps published during the colonial period, make the boundaries of their control extend from the coast line of the Atlantic to the Mississippi river and from the great lakes to the centre of the present state of North Carolina. There is no instance in history where a region so vast has been conquered by numbers so small. Their alliance with the British government was one of the grounds on which the latter contested the claims of the French to the interior of our continent, by virtue of its discoveries on the St. Lawrence and Mississippi. Thus the victories gained by the Iroquois, through their geographical position, had a great influence in deciding the question, whether the civilization of North America should be French or English in its aspects, laws and customs.

It is a remarkable fact, that with a view of overcoming the British power on this continent, nearly a century before the campaign of Burgoyne, its plan was forecast by Frontenac, the ablest of the French colonial commanders. He proposed to move against the colony of New York by the same routes followed by the British forces in 1777. He was to lead his army through the valley of Lake Champlain and Upper Hudson to Albany. At that point he designed to seize vessels to pass down the river, and there to act with the French ships of war, which were to meet him in the harbor of New York. Nothing can show more clearly the strategic importance of the valley in which we meet, than the fact that he urged this movement for the same reasons which led the British king to adopt it after the lapse of so many years. Frontenac saw that, by gaining control of the course and outlet of the Hudson, the French would command the gateway into the interior, that they would divide the British colonies, and New England thus cut off, would, in the end, fall into the hands of the French. He also urged that in this way the Iroquois would be detached from the English alliance.

The influence of the valleys of our country has not been lost in the wars of our day. "We should have won our cause," said Governor Wise, a distinguished leader of the Southern confederacy, "had not God made the rivers which spring from the highlands of New York, to flow from the north to the south, thus making by their valleys, pathways for armies into all parts of our territories. Had their courses been in other directions, their streams would have made barriers against Northern armies instead of giving avenues by which they could assail us." Nor have they been less controlling in peace than in war. They make the great channels of commerce between the east and the west, and enable us to draw to the seaboard the abundant harvests of the valley of the Mississippi, and to send them to the far off markets of Europe. Numerous and varied as have been the movements of armies along these watercourses, even they sink into insignificance compared with the vast multitudes which have poured through them from Europe and the Atlantic coast to fill the west with civilized states. Through them we draw armies of immigrants, prisoners of peace captured from Europe by the strength of the inducements held out to them by the material and political advantages of our country.

We are in our day the witnesses of a greater movement of the human race, both as to numbers and influence upon civilization, than is recorded in past history. It can tell of no such continued and great transfer of population from one continent to another. Unlike other invasions, it does not bring war and rapine, but it bears peaceful arts and civilization into vast regions heretofore occupied by scanty tribes of warring savages. Familiar with this great movement, we are prone to look upon it with some degree of indifference. But through the centuries to come it will be regarded as one of the greatest events in the history of mankind.

I have not dwelt upon these hills and valleys merely because they have been the scenes of the most dramatic and important events in American annals, but because they have given birth to these events. I have spoken of them, not because they have been associated with history, but because they have made history. They gave to the Iroquois their power; they directed the course and determined the result of the war between France and Britain for domination on this continent. Neither the surrender of the British army on these grounds, the causes which preceded nor the consequences which flowed from it, can be appreciated until the enduring influences of the great features of our country are clearly brought into view. Elsewhere rivers and mountains mark the lines which make enemies of mankind. Here they form the avenues which bind us together by intercourse. They give not merely to a country, but almost to our whole continent, a common language, customs and civilization. The world has never before seen a social structure with foundations so broad. Time may make many changes, but there will ever be a unity in the population of North America, a community of interests upon a grander scale than has yet been seen among mankind. He who studies the map of our continent and doubts this, does not merely lack political faith, but is guilty of impiety when he closes his eyes to the truths which God has written by streams and valleys, upon the face of this continent.

It was the design of the British government in the campaign of 1777 to capture the center and stronghold of this commanding system of mountains and valleys. It aimed at its very heart—the confluence of the Mohawk and Hudson. The fleets, the armies, and the savage allies of Britain were to follow their converging lines to Albany. Its position had made that city the place where the governors and agents of the colonies had been used to meet with reference to their common interest. Here the agents of the New England and southern provinces came to consult with the chiefs of the Iroquois, and to gain their alliance in their wars with the savages of the west, who threatened the European settlements. In the expressive language of the Indians, Albany was called the "Ancient Place of Treaty." It was also the point at which the military expeditions against the French at the north and west were organized. Even before Benjamin Franklin brought forward his plan at Albany for colonial union, the idea of such alliance was constantly suggested by the necessity of common action in attack or defence against savage or civilized enemies.

There was much to justify the boastful confidence of the British that they could thus crush out American resistance. To feel the full force of this threatened blow, we must forget for a time our present power; we must see with the eyes of our fathers, and look at things as they stood a century ago. The care with which the army of Burgoyne was organized, its officers and men selected, and its material for an advance and attack provided, has been made familiar to our people by this year's addresses. The progress of the British navy up the Hudson to a point west of the Alleghany range, its seizure in its course of Stony Point and Fort Clinton, its success in forcing a passage through the highlands at West Point, the capture and burning of Kingston, where the British admiral awaited communication from Burgoyne, have all been clearly narrated on the pages of history. Had the commander of the expedition gone to Albany he might have saved the army of Burgoyne. General Gates saw if this had been done he would have been forced to retreat into New England. But it was not known at the time how great a peril was averted by an act of negligence in the British war department. It appears that orders were prepared, but not sent to General Howe, directing him to co-operate with Burgoyne with all his forces. If this had been done, there is reason to fear the result would have been fatal to our cause. This is one of those strange occurrences recognized in the lives of individuals as well as in the affairs of nations, showing that there is an over-ruling Providence that watches over both.

The importance of the movement from the west by St. Leger and his Indian allies is not generally understood by our people. It was made with confidence of success; and when its commander wrote to Burgoyne that he would be able to sweep down the valley of the Mohawk and place himself in the rear of the American army, there was much to justify that confidence. The address of Mr. Roberts and others, at the Oriskany celebration, are valuable contributions to the history of St. Leger's invasion. The Palatines who inhabited the valley of the Mohawk were, by their position, language and usages, severed from the body of the American colonies. The wise policy of Sir William Johnson had done much to attach them to the British crown. To enable them to worship God in accordance with their own creed and in the faith of that part of Germany from which they came, aid was given to them for the erection of churches for their use. Many of these were strong stone churches, which were afterwards fortified and used as places of refuge and defence during the Revolution by the families of the settlers against the ruthless warfare of savages. Most of these churches still stand, monuments of the past, and are now used for the sacred purpose for which they were built. The heirs and representatives of Sir William were with the army of St. Leger, and assured him that the dwellers upon the Mohawk would respond to their appeals, and rise in arms to uphold the cause of the crown. No stronger proof can be given that the love of liberty and of democratic principles were engendered and born upon our soil and not imported in some latent form in the ships which brought over the first colonists, than the fact that these settlers from the Palatinates of Germany, who had not known of republican usages in their native land and who could not, from their position and their language, receive impressions from the other colonists, had yet, amidst the trials and perils of border life and warfare, gained the same political convictions which animated the colonists in all parts of our country. It was the most remarkable fact of the revolutionary war, and of the formation of state and general governments, that, although the colonists were of different lineages and languages, living under different climates with varied pursuits and forms of labor, cut off from intercourse by distance, yet, in spite of all these obstacles to accord, they were from the outset animated by common views, feelings and purposes. When the independence was gained, they were able, after a few weeks spent in consultation, to form the constitution under which we have lived for nearly one hundred years. There can be no stronger proof of the fact that American constitutions

were born and shaped by American necessities. This fact
should give us a new faith in the lasting nature of our government. In the case of the Palatines of the Mohawk this truth
shines out more clearly than elsewhere. Isolated by language,
lineage and position, the great body of them fought for the
American cause, and showed a sturdy valor from the outset.
They endured more of suffering and danger in its most appall-
ing form, than were felt elsewhere. With the loss of their
language and from the great inflow from other states and countries into Central New York, many of the incidents and traditions of the valley of the Mohawk are lost. It is due to them
from the whole country that, as far as possible, its history
should be developed and made familiar to our people. The
most telling blow to the cause of the crown, and to the hopes of
St. Leger, was that the mustering of the men under Herkimer,
their desperate valor in the fight at Oriskany showed that he was
to be met with undying hostility where he had looked for friends
and allies. From that day the hope which animated him when
he promised to aid Burgoyne faded away.

The defeat of St. Leger and their allies was given by Burgoyne as one of the great causes of his failure to reach Albany.
While the hostile Indians inflicted great evils upon the American
settlements, their prestige was lessened in the eyes of the world.

Indian Allies.

The importance of the Indian alliance with the British during
the Revolution, has been undervalued by most of those who
have written the histories of the Revolution. We look upon
Indian wars as mere savage outbursts, which may cause much
misery and suffering, but which threaten no danger to governments. We are apt to think that the savages were merely
used to divert and distract the American forces. But such
was not the import of their alliance, in the judgment of the
contending parties or of the nations of Europe, who watched
with interest the course of military events on this continent.
We must bear in mind the estimation in which the Iroquois were
held at the close of the French war. They had done much to
give the victory to the English. At times, the hostility of
these savage confederates would have been fatal to the British

cause. Their position made them conquerors of their kindred races. Victories inspired them with heroism. Extended conquests had taught them much of the policy of government. In the councils of their confederacy, orators and statesmen had been formed. They extorted from their French enemies expressions of admiration and statements of virtues, which we should do well to imitate in our own day and in our own councils. Colden, who was familiar with their polity, states that the authority of their rulers consisted wholly of the estimation in which they were held for integrity and wisdom, and they were generally poorer than the rest of the people. He adds, "there is not a man of the Five Nations who has gained his office otherwise than by merit." Their enemies, the French, testified in their histories, that while they were the fiercest and most formidable people in America, they were politic and judicious in the management of their affairs. For nearly a century the French and English struggled to gain their friendship by every influence of religion, of diplomacy and display of power. Even as late as 1754, George Washington, then a colonial officer, called upon them for assistance in his movements against the French on the Ohio river, and claimed that he went forth to fight for their rights, because the French were occupying territories which belonged to the Iroquois. Only twenty years before the revolutionary war, the British ministry insisted in its correspondence with the French government, that the Iroquois were the owners, by conquest, of the Ohio territory, and that they were the subjects of the British crown. This was the claim set up against the French rights of discovery. It is a remarkable fact, that the French did not deny the right of conquest by the Iroquois, but denied that they were the subjects of Britain in these strong words: "Certain it is that no Englishman durst, without running the risk of being massacred, tell the Iroquois that they are the subjects of England." One of the first acts of the continental congress was designed to secure the alliance of the Six Nations. In this they were unsuccessful, except as to the Oneidas. The co-operation of their savage allies was deemed of the utmost importance by the British.

I do not speak of the action at Bennington nor of the battle of Bemis's Heights. The late celebration upon the grounds upon which they took place, have made the public familiar with all their aspects and results.

Influence of Burgoyne's Surrender.

France saw that upon the very theatre of war where Britain had wrested from it the control of this continent, its ancient enemy had been beaten by the new power which was springing into existence. To the French government this victory had a significance that no like victory could have had upon other fields. It knew better than others the commanding features of this region. Its missionaries were highly educated men, who marked with care the character of our mountains, lakes and streams. Impelled by religious zeal and devotion to the interests of their native land, they boldly pushed into the remote portions of the continent in advance of commercial enterprise or military expeditions. Their narratives are to this day of great value and interest. The surrender of Burgoyne had also a marked effect upon the tone and policy of the British cabinet; it no longer fought for conquest, but for compromise. Its armies were moved with a view of saving a part if it could not hold all of its jurisdiction. It was able to take possession of the principal cities, but it could not find elsewhere positions, like that aimed at by Burgoyne, which would enable it to sunder and paralyze the patriot forces. It exhausted its armies in campaigns which produced no results, even when successful in repulsing our forces or in occupying the points at which they were directed. Its commanders were animated by only one gleam of hope. The proud power which at the outset called upon the world to witness its strength in crushing rebellion, stooped to dealings with a traitor, and sought to gain by corruption what it could not gain by force. The treason of Arnold excited the deepest feelings, because the loss of West Point, the key of the Hudson, would have given the British a position from which they could not have been dislodged at the center of the strongholds of defence and the commanding basis for attack of the Hudson and its guardian mountains. The fact that the loss of West Point would have been deemed a fatal blow to the American cause places the strategic importance of this region in the strongest light.

The surrender of Burgoyne not only gave new hope to the patriots, but it exerted a moral influence upon our soldiers. The colonists up to that time had been trained in the belief that British soldiers were irresistible. To hold them superior to all others in arms had been American patriotism. Through the century of the French wars, precedence had always been yielded to the officers of the crown; and the colonists looked mainly to the British army to protect their homes from invasion. Colonial papers showed an extravagance of loyalty which is frequently exhibited in the outlying and exposed settlements of all nations. The Revolution, while it made a revulsion of feeling, did not at the outset destroy this sense of the superior skill and power of British arms. The early engagements in the open fields had not been fortunate for the patriot cause. The armies of the crown were still buoyed up by that sense of superiority, which, in itself, is an element in martial success. Burgoyne did not doubt his ability to destroy any army he could reach. The battle of Bemis's Heights was a fair and open contest on equal terms. In strategy, in steadiness, in valor, the continental troops proved themselves in all ways equal to the picked and trained men against whom they fought.

From the day that victory was won, the American soldier felt himself to be the equal of all who could be brought against him, and he knew that he was animated by higher and nobler purposes than those which moved the ranks of his enemies. The whole spirit of the contest was changed. Our armies reaped a double triumph on this field. There was much in the contempt which had been shown by their enemies of their qualities as soldiers, much in the taunts and sneers of the British cabinet, much in the pillage and destruction which ever attend the march of invading armies, to excite the victors to exhibitions of triumph over fallen foes. But they bore themselves, not as men intoxicated by successful fortunes in war, but as men who felt it was in them to win victories there or elsewhere. There was a calmness in the hour of triumph, which more than even courage upon the battlefield, impressed the defeated army with the character of those of whom they had spoken so contemptuously. The enemy were twice conquered, and in many ways the last victory over them was most keenly felt. The moral and the military advantages of the surrender of the British army was marred by no act which lessened the dignity of the conquerors. And he who reads the story of the contest, finds himself most triumphant in his feelings over the moral rather than the martial victory.

General Schuyler.

When we read the story of the event which we now celebrate, whether it is told by friend or foe, there is one figure which rises above all others upon whose conduct and bearing we love to dwell. There is one who won a triumph which never grows dim. One who gave an example of patient patriotism unsurpassed on the pages of history. One who did not, even under cutting wrongs and cruel suspicions, wear an air of martyrdom, but with cheerful alacrity served where he should have commanded. It was in a glorious spirit of chivalrous courtesy with which Schuyler met and ministered to those who had not only been enemies in arms, but who had inflicted upon him unusual injuries unwarranted by the laws of war. But there was something more grand in his service to his country than even this honor which he did to the American cause, by his bearing upon this occasion. The spirit of sectional prejudice which the British cabinet relied upon to prevent cordial co-operation among the colonies, had been exhibited against him in a way most galling to a pure patriot and a brave soldier. But, filled with devotion to his country's cause, he uttered no murmur of complaint, nor did he for a moment cease in his labors to gain its liberties. This grand rebuke to selfish intriguers and to honest prejudices did much to discomfit the one and to teach the other the injustice of their suspicions and the unworthiness of sectional prejudices. The strength of this rebuke sometimes irritates writers who cannot rise above local prejudices, and they try to lessen the public sense of his virtue by reviving the attacks, proved to be unjust upon investigation, and which, by the verdict of men honored by their country, were proved to be unfounded. The judgment of George Washington and of the patriots who surrounded him, with regard to men of their own day and affairs with which they were familiar, cannot be shaken by those who seek to revive exploded scandals and unfounded suspicions. The character of Gen. Schuyler grows brighter in public regard.

The injustice done him by his removal from his command, at a time when his zeal and ability had placed victory almost within his reach, is not perhaps to be regretted. We could not well lose from our history his example of patriotism and of personal honor and chivalry. We could not spare the proof which his case furnishes, that virtue triumphs in the end. We would not change, if we could, the history of his trials. For we feel that they gave luster to his character, and we are forced to say of Gen. Schuyler that, while he had been greatly wronged, he had never been injured.

Saratoga Monument.

The association formed under the laws of this state to erect a suitable monument to commemorate the defeat of the British army under Burgoyne, has selected this spot upon which to place it, because here it will recall to the mind not only the final act, but every event which led to the surrender. It will carry the thoughts of him who looks upon it back to the first and fierce fight at Oriskany. It will remind him of the disaster to the British forces at the battle of Bennington. It will excite the deepest interest in the contest on the hills at Bemis's Heights. It will do more. It will bring before the public mind that great procession of events, which for two centuries have passed through the valleys of the Hudson and the Mohawk. When it shall excite the interests which attach to the occasion which we celebrate linked history will lead the public mind back, step by step, to the earliest period of the French and English settlements on this continent. We shall be taught what made the savage tribes of this region superior in war and polity to their kindred races. We shall be reminded of the forays of savages, the march of disciplined armies, the procession of Christian missionaries, which exceed in dramatic interest and in far reaching consequences, all other incidents of war, of diplomacy, and of religious zeal exhibited on this continent. The events which have occurred in these valleys have also been closely connected with the most important facts of European history. The ambition of Louis the fourteenth of France aimed at supremacy on two continents. The prolonged war over the balance of power in Europe, concerned the civilization of America. The genius of Marlborough, and the victory of Blenheim, were of more enduring consequence to us than to the parties engaged in the contest. They did not foresee that they were shaping the civilization of a continent, or the destinies of a people at this day exceeding in numbers the united population of the countries engaged in the war. Where else in our country can a monument be placed, from which will radiate so much that is instructive? Where else can a structure be erected which will teach such varied history? Elsewhere, great achievements in peace or war, make certain spots instinct with interest. Elsewhere, the great features of nature have influenced the fate of nations. But it is not true that elsewhere mountains and rivers have been such marked and conspicuous agents in shaping events. Here they have directed the affairs of this continent. In selecting a place where a monument should stand, this association has not been embarrassed by any questions as to the comparative importance of the act of surrender of the British army, or of the battles which made that surrender inevitable. Each has its peculiar interest, and each should be marked by suitable monuments. But the last scene in the drama unfolds to the mind the plot and incidents which reach their conclusions at the close. A monument on this ground not only commemorates what occurred here, but it recalls to the mind all the incidents and battles which preceded it, and gives to each a deeper interest, than when they are considered separately. Each is viewed not only in the light of the wisdom, valor or patriotism displayed, but of its bearing upon the grand result. He who visits the scene of the bloody fight at Oriskany, or looks over the hills where the men of Vermont drove back the troops of Burgoyne, or studies the movements of the armies at the battle of Bemis's Heights, finds that his thoughts do not rest until they dwell upon the grand conclusion reached upon this spot. When his mind is kindled with patriotic pride upon either of the battle fields to which I have alluded, he will turn to the ground upon which we now meet, and thank God for the event we now celebrate.

The surrender of Burgoyne marks the dividing line between two conditions of our country; the one the colonial period of dependence, and the other the day from which it stood full armed and victorious here, with a boldness to assert its independence, and endowed with a wisdom to frame its own system of government. From this review of the past we instinctively turn our minds and try to scan the years that are to come. It is not given to us to forecast the future. But when we study the great natural features of our country, and see how they have directed the past, we learn from the silver links of rivers and the rocky chains of mountains that God has written and stamped on the face of this continent, that it shall ever be held by those speaking a common language, with a common civilization, and living together with that freedom of intercourse which shall forever, under some forms, make them one people.

A monument upon this spot will not merely minister to local pride; it will not foster sectional prejudices; every citizen of every state of this union will feel as he looks upon it that he has a right to stand upon this ground. It will tell of the common sacrifices and common trials of the fathers of the republic. Men from all parts of our union will here be reminded that our independence as a people was wrought out by the sufferings and sacrifices of those who came from every quarter of our country to share in this valley in the perils of battle and in the triumphs of victory. Here sectional passions will fade away; and the glorious memories and the fraternal feelings of the past will be revived.

We are told that during more than twenty centuries of war and bloodshed, only fifteen battles have been decisive of lasting results. The contest of Saratoga is one of these. From the battle of Marathon to the field of Waterloo, a period of more than two thousand years, there was no martial event which had a greater influence upon human affairs than that which took place on these grounds. Shall not some suitable structure recall this fact to the public mind? Monuments make as well as mark the civilization of a people. Neither France, nor Britain, nor Germany, could spare the statues or works of art which keep alive the memories of patriotic sacrifices or of personal virtues. Such silent teachers of all that ennobles men, have taught their lessons through the darkest ages, and have done much to save society from sinking into utter decay and degradation. If Greece or Rome had left no memorials of private virtue or public greatness, the progress of civilization would have been slow and feeble. If their crumbling remains should be swept away, the world would mourn the loss, not only to learning and arts, but to virtue and patriotism. It concerns the honor and welfare of the American people, that this spot should be marked by some structure which shall recall its history, and animate all who look upon it by its grand teachings. No people ever held lasting power or greatness, who did not reverence the virtues of their fathers, or who did not show forth this reverence by material and striking testimonials. Let us, then, build here a lasting monument, which shall tell of our gratitude to those who, through suffering and sacrifice, wrought out the independence of our country.

GEORGE WILLIAM CURTIS' ORATION

Within the territory of New York, broad, fertile and fair, from Montauk to Niagara, from the Adirondacks to the bay, there is no more memorable spot than that on which we stand. Elsewhere, indeed, the great outlines of the landscape are more imposing, and on this autumnal day the parting benediction of the year rests with the same glory on other hills and other waters of the imperial state. Far above, these gentle heights rise into towering mountains; far below, this placid stream broadens and deepens around the metropolis of the continent into a spacious highway for the commerce of the world. Other valleys with teeming intervale and fruitful upland, rich with romantic tradition and patriotic story, filled like this with happy homes and humming workshops, wind through the vast commonwealth, ample channels of its various life; and town and city, village and hamlet, church and school, everywhere illustrate and promote the prosperous repose of a community great, intelligent and free. But this spot alone within our borders is consecrated as the scene of one of the decisive events that affect the course of history. There are deeds on which the welfare of the world seems to be staked; conflicts in which liberty is lost or won; victories by which the standard of human progress is full high advanced. Between sunrise and sunset, on some chance field the deed is done, but from that day it is a field enchanted. Imagination invests it with

"The light that never was on sea or land."

The grateful heart of mankind repeats its name; Heroism feeds upon its story; Patriotism kindles with its perennial fire. Such is the field on which we stand. It is not ours. It does not belong to New York; nor to America. It is an indefeasible estate of the world; like the field of Arbela, of Tours, of Hastings, of Waterloo; and the same lofty charm that draws the pilgrim to the plain of Marathon resistlessly leads him to the field of Saratoga.

The drama of the Revolution opened in New Egland, culminated in New York, and closed in Virginia. It was a happy
fortune that the three colonies which represented the various
territorial sections of the settled continent were each in turn
the chief seat of war. The common sacrifice, the common struggle, the common triumph, tended to weld them locally, politically
and morally together. Doubtless there were conflicts of provincial pride and jealousy and suspicion. The Virginia officers
smiled loftily at the raw Yankee militia; the Green mountain
boys distrusted the polished discipline of New York; and the
New York Schuyler thought these boys brave but dangerously
independent. In every great crisis of the war, however, there
was a common impulse and devotion, and the welfare of the continent obliterated provincial lines. It is by the few heaven-
piercing peaks, not by the confused mass of upland, that we measure the height of the Andes, of the Alps, of the Himalaya. It is
by Joseph Warren not by Benjamin Church, by John Jay not by
Sir John Johnson, by George Washington not by Benedict Arnold, that we test the quality of the revolutionary character. The
voice of Patrick Henry from the mountains answered that of
James Otis by the sea. Paul Revere's lantern shone through the
valley of the Hudson, and flashed along the cliffs of the Blue
Ridge. The scattering volley of Lexington green swelled to the
triumphant thunder of Saratoga, and the reverberation of Burgoyne's falling arms in New York shook those of Cornwallis in
Virginia from his hands. Doubts, jealousies, prejudices, were
merged in one common devotion. The union of the colonies to
secure liberty, foretold the union of the states to maintain it, and
wherever we stand on revolutionary fields, or inhale the sweet-
ness of revolutionary memories, we tread the ground and breathe
the air of invincible national union.

Our especial interest and pride, to-day, are in the most important event of the Revolution upon the soil of New York.
Concord and Lexington, Bunker Hill and Bennington, the
Brandywine and Germantown, have had their fitting centennial
commemorations, and already at Kingston and Oriskany, New
York has taken up the wondrous tale of her civil and military
achievements. In proud continuation of her story we stand
here. Sons of sires who bled with Sterling on the Long Island

shore; who fought with Herkimer in the deadly Oneida defile; who defended the Highland forts with George Clinton; who, with Robert Livingston and Gouverneur Morris, were driven from town to town by stress of war, yet framed a civil constitution, all untouched by the asperity of the conflict and a noble model for all free states; sons of sires who, leaving the plough and the bench, gathered on this historic war-path—the key of the then civilized continent; the western battle ground of Europe; the trail by which Frontenac's Indians prowled to Schenectady, and crept to the Connecticut and beyond; the way by which Sir William Johnson and his army passed in the old French war, and humbled Dieskau at Lake George; the road along which Abercrombie and his bright array marched to disaster in the summer morning, and Amherst marshaled his men to co-operate with Wolf in the humbling of Quebec; sons of sires, who, mustering here on ground still trembling with the tread of armies, where the air forever echoes with the savage war whoop, or murmurs with the pathetic music of the march and the camp—

"Why, soldiers, why
Should we be melancholy, boys,
Whose business 'tis to die?"

even here withstood the deadly British blow and enveloping the haughty Burgoyne, compelled not only him to yield his sword, but England to surrender an empire; sons of such sires, who should not proudly recall such deeds of theirs and gratefully revere their memory, would be forever scorned as faithless depositaries of the great English and American tradition, and the great human benediction, of patient, orderly, self-restrained liberty.

When King George heard of the battle of Bunker Hill, he consoled himself with the thought that New York was still unswervingly loyal; and it was the hope and the faith of his ministry that the rebellion might at last be baffled in that great colony. It was a region of vast extent, but thinly peopled, for the population was but little more than one hundred and sixty thousand. It had been settled by men of various races, who, upon the sea shore, and through the remote valleys, and in the primeval wilderness, cherished the freedom that they brought and transmitted to their children. But the colony lacked that homogeneity of population which produces general sympathy of conviction and concert of action; which gives a community one soul, one heart, one hand, interprets every man's thought to his neighbor, and explains so much of the great deeds of the Grecian commonwealths, of Switzerland, and of Old and New England. In New York, also were the hereditary manors— vast domains of a few families, private principalities, with feudal relations and traditions—and the spirit of a splendid proprietary life was essentially hostile to doctrines of popular right and power. In the magnificent territory of the Mohawk and its tributaries, Sir William Johnson, amid his family and dependents, lived in baronial state among the Indians, with whom he was allied by marriage, and to whom he was the vicar of their royal father over the sea. The Johnsons were virtually supreme in the country of the Mohawk, and as they were intensely loyal, the region west of Albany became a dark and bloody ground of civil strife. In the city of New York, and in the neighboring counties of Westchester upon the river and sound, of Richmond upon the bay, and Queens and Suffolk on the sea, the fear that sprang from conscious exposure to the naval power of Great Britain, the timidity of commercial trade, the natural loyalty of numerous officers of the crown, all combined to foster antipathy to any disturbance of that established authority which secured order and peace.

But deeper and stronger than all other causes was the tender reluctance of Englishmen in America to believe that reconciliation with the mother country was impossible. Even after the great day on Bunker Hill, when, in full sight of his country and of all future America, Joseph Warren, the well-beloved disciple of American liberty, fell, congress, while justifying war, recoiled from declaring independence. Doubtless the voice of John Adams, of Massachusetts, counseling immediate and entire separation, spoke truly for the unanimous and fervent patriotism of New England; but doubtless, also the voice of John Jay, of New York, who knew the mingled sentiment of the great province whose position in the struggle must be decisive, in advising one more appeal to the king, was a voice of patriotism as pure, and of courage as unquailing.

The appeal was made, and made in vain. The year that opened with Concord and Lexington, ended with the gloomy tragedy of the Canada campaign. On the last day of the year, in a tempest of sleet and snow, the combined forces of New England and New York made a desperate, futile onset; and the expedition from which Washington and the country had anticipated results so inspiring was dashed in pieces against the walls of Quebec. The country mourned, but New York had a peculiar sorrow. Leaving his tranquil and beautiful home upon this river, one of her noblest soldiers—brave, honorable, gentle—the son-in-law of Livingston, the friend of Schuyler, after a brief career of glory, died the death of a hero. "You shall not blush for your Montgomery," he said to his bride as he left her. For fifty years a widow, his bride saw him no more. But while this stately river flows through the mountains to the sea, its waves will still proudly murmur the name, and recall the romantic and heroic story of Richard Montgomery.

The year 1776 was not less gloomy for the American cause. Late in November Washington was hurriedly retreating across New Jersey, pursued by Cornwallis, his army crumbling with every step, the state paralyzed with terror, congress flying affrighted from Philadelphia to Baltimore, and the apparent sole remaining hope of American independence, the rigor of winter, snow, and impassable roads. Ah, no! It was not in winter but in summer that that hope lay, not in the relentless frost of the elements, but in the heavenly fire of hearts beating high with patriotic resolve, and turning the snow flakes of that terrible retreat into immortal roses of victory and joy. While Howe and his officers, in the warm luxury and wild debauchery of the city they had captured, believed the war ended, gaily sang and madly caroused, Washington, in the dreary Christmas evening, turned on the ice of the Delaware, and struck the Hessians fatally at Trenton; then in the cold January sunrise defeating the British at Princetown, his army filed with bleeding feet into the highlands of New Jersey, and half starved and scantily clothed, encamped upon the frozen hills of Morristown. "The Americans have done much," said despairingly one of their truest friends in England, Edmund Burke, "but it is now

evident that they cannot look standing armies in the face."
That, however, was to be determined by the campaign of 1777.

For that campaign England was already preparing. Seven
years before, General Carleton, who still commanded in Canada,
had proposed to hold the water line between the gulf of St.
Lawrence and the bay of New York, to prevent a separation of
the colonies. It was now proposed to hold it to compel a separation. The ocean mouths of the great waterway were both in
complete possession of the crown. It was a historic war path.
Here had raged the prolonged conflict between France and
England for the control of the continent, and in fierce war upon
the waters of New York, no less than on the plains of Abraham,
the power of France in America finally fell. Here, also, where it
had humbled its proud rival, the strong hand of England grasping for unjust dominion was to be triumphantly shaken off.
This region was still a wilderness. Seventy years before, the
first legal land title in it was granted. In 1745, thirty years
before the Revolution, it was the extreme English outpost. In
1777, the settlers were few, and they feared the bear and the
catamount less than the Tory and the Indian. They still built
block houses for retreat and defence like the first New England settlers a hundred and fifty years before. Nowhere during
the Revolution were the horrors of civil war so constant and so
dire as here. The tories seized and harassed, shot and hung
the whigs, stole their stock and store, burned their barns and
ruined their crops, and the whigs remorselessly retaliated.
The stealthy Indian struck, shrieked and vanished. The wolf
and the wildcat lurked in the thicket. Man and beast were
equally cruel. Terror overhung the fated region, and as the
great invasion approached, the universal flight and devastation
recalled the grim desolation in Germany during the thirty
years' war.

Of that invasion, and of the campaign of 1777, the central
figure is John Burgoyne. No name among the British generals
of the Revolution is more familiar, yet he was neither a great
soldier nor a great man. He was willing to bribe his old comrade in arms, Charles Lee, to betray the American cause, and
he threatened to loose savages upon the Americans for defending
it. Burgoyne was an admirable type of the English fashionable

gentleman of his day. The grandson of a baronet, a Westminster boy, and trained to arms, he eloped with the daughter of
the great whig house of Derby, left the army and lived gaily
on the continent. Restored to a military career by political
influence, he served as a captain in France, and returning to
England was elected to parliament. He went a brigadier to
Portugal, and led a brilliant charge at Valentia d'Alcantara,
was complimented by the great Count Lippe, and flattered by
the British prime minister. For his gallantry the king of
Spain gave him a diamond ring, and with that blazing on his
finger he returned once more to England, flushed with brief
glory. There for some years he was a man of pleasure. He wrote
slight verses and little plays that are forgotten. Reynolds painted his portrait in London, as Ramsay had painted it
in Rome. Horace Walpole sneered at him for his plays, but
Lord Chatham praised him for his military notes. Tall and
handsome, graceful and winning in manner, allied to a noble
house, a favorite at court and on parade, he was a gay companion at the table, the club and the theatre. The king admired his dragoons, and conferred upon him profitable honors,
which secured to him a refined and luxurious life. In parliament, when the American war began, Burgoyne took the
high British ground, but with the urbanity of a soldier, and he
gladly obeyed the summons to service in America, and sailed
with Howe and Clinton on the great day that the British troops
marched to Concord. He saw the battle of Bunker Hill, and
praised the American courage and military ability, but was very
sure that trained troops would always overcome militia. The
one American whom he extolled was Samuel Adams. He
thought that he combined the ability of Caesar with the astute-
ness of Cromwell; that he led Franklin and all the other
leaders, and that if his counsels continued to control the continent, America must be subdued or relinquished.

Burgoyne saw little actual service in this country until he
arrived at Quebec on the 6th of May, 1777, as commander of
the great enterprise of the year. The plan of campaign was
large and simple. One expedition led by Burgoyne, was to
force its way from Quebec to Albany, through the valley of the
Hudson, and another, under St. Leger, was to push through the

valley of the Mohawk, to the same point. At Albany they were to join General Howe, who would advance up the river from the bay. By the success of these combined operations, the British would command New York, and New England would be absolutely cut off. This last result alone would be a signal triumph. New England was the nest of rebellion. There were the fields where British power was first defied in arms. There were the Green mountains from which Ethan Allen and his boys had streamed upon Ticonderoga. There was Boston bay where the tea had been scattered, and Narragansett bay where the Gaspe had been burned, and the harbors of Machias and of Newport, from which the British ships had been chased to sea. There were Faneuil Hall and the town meeting. There was Boston, whose ports had been closed— Boston with the street of the massacre—Boston, of which King George had bitterly said that he would "as lief fight the Bostonians as the French." There were the pulpits which preached what Samuel Adams called liberty, and Samuel Johnson sedition. The very air of New England was full of defiance. The woods rustled it, the waters murmured it, the stern heart of its rugged nature seemed to beat in unison with the stout heart of man, and all throbbed together with the invincible Anglo-Saxon instinct of liberty. To cut off New England from her sisters—to seize and hold the great New York valleys of Champlain and the Hudson—was to pierce the heart of the rebellion, and to paralyze America. Here, then, was to be the crucial struggle. Here in New York once more the contest for the western continent was to be decided. Burgoyne had airily said in London, that with an army of ten thousand men he could promenade through America, and now the brilliant gentleman was to make good his boast.

While he was crossing the ocean to begin his task, and when every possible effort should have been made by congress to meet the ample and splendid preparations for the British invasion, wretched intrigues displaced General Schuyler in the northern department, and it was not until late in May that he was restored to the command. The peril was at hand, but it was impossible to collect men. By the end of June, the entire garrison of Ticonderoga and Fort Independence, the first great barrier against the advance of Burgoyne, consisted of twenty five hundred continentals and nine hundred militia, barefooted and ragged, without proper arms or sufficient blankets, and lacking every adequate preparation for defence. But more threatening than all, was Sugar-loaf hill, rising above Ticonderoga, and completely commanding the fort. General Schuyler saw it, but even while he pointed out the danger, and while General St. Clair, the commandant of the post, declared that from the want of troops nothing could be done, the drums of Burgoyne's army were joyfully beating in the summer dawn; the bugles rang, the cannon thundered, the rising June sun shone on the scarlet coats of British grenadiers, on the bright helmets of German dragoons, and on burnished artillery and polished arms. There were more than seven thousand trained and veteran troops, besides Canadians and Indians. They were admirably commanded and equipped, although the means of land transport were fatally insufficient. But all was hope and confidence. The battle flags were unfurled, the word was given, and with every happy augury, the royal standard of England proudly set forward for conquest. On the 1st of July, the brilliant pageant swept up Lake Champlain, and the echoes of the mighty wilderness which had answered the guns of Amherst and the drum-beat of Montcalm, saluted the frigates and the gunboats that, led by a dusky swarm of Indians in bark canoes, stretched between the eastern shore, along which Riedesel and the Germans marched, and the main body advancing with Phillips upon the west. The historic waters of Champlain have never seen a spectacle more splendid than the advancing army of Burgoyne. But so with his glittering Asian hordes, two thousand years before, the Persian king advanced to Salamis.

At evening the British army was before Ticonderoga. The trained eye of the English engineers instantly saw the advantage of Sugar-loaf, the higher hill, and the rising sun of the 5th of July glared in the amazed eyes of the Ticonderoga garrison, on the red coats entrenched upon Sugar-loaf, with their batteries commanding every point within the fort, and their glasses every movement. Sugar-loaf had become Mount Defiance. St. Clair had no choice. All day he assumed indifference, but quietly made every preparation, and before dawn the next day he stole away. The moon shone, but his flight was undetected, until the flames of a fire foolishly set to a house suddenly flashed over the landscape and revealed his retreat. He was instantly pursued. His rear guard was overtaken, and by the valor of its fierce but hopeless fight gave an undying name to the wooded hills of Hubbardton.

Ticonderoga fell, and the morning of its fall was the high hour of Burgoyne's career. Without a blow, by the mere power of his presence, he had undone the electric deed of Ethan Allen; he had captured the historic prize of famous campaigns. The chief obstruction to his triumphal American promenade had fallen. The bright promise of the invasion would be fulfilled, and Burgoyne would be the lauded hero of the war. Doubtless his handsome lip curled in amused disdain at the flying and frightened militia, plough boys that might infest but could not impede his further advance. His eager fancy could picture the delight of London, the joy of the clubs, of parliament, of the king. He could almost hear the royal George bursting into the Queen's room and shouting, "I have beat all the Americans." He could almost read the assurance of the minister to the proud earl, his father-in-law, that the king designed for him the vacant Red Ribbon. But his aspiring ambition surely anticipated a loftier reward—a garter, a coronet, and at last, Westminster Abbey and undying glory.

Ticonderoga fell, and with it, apparently, fell in Europe all hope of the patriot cause; and in America, all confidence and happy expectation. The Tories were jubilant. The wavering Indians were instantly open enemies. The militia sullenly went home. The solitary settlers fled southward through the forests and over the eastern hills. Even Albany was appalled, and its pale citizens sent their families away. Yet this panic stricken valley of the upper Hudson was now the field on which, if anywhere, the cause was to be saved. Five counties of the state were in the hands of the enemy; three were in anarchy. Schuyler was at Fort Edward with scarcely a thousand men. The weary army of St. Clair, shrunken to fifteen hundred continentals, all the militia having dropped away, struggled for a week through the forest, and emerged forlorn and exhausted at the fort. Other troops arrived, but the peril was imminent. New

York was threatened at every point, and with less than five thousand ill-equipped regulars and militia to oppose the victorious Burgoyne, who was but a single long day's march away, with only the forts and the boom and chain in the Highlands to stay Clinton's ascent from the bay, and only the little garrison at Fort Stanwix to withstand St. Leger, General Schuyler and the council of state implored aid from every quarter. A loud clamor, bred of old jealousy and fresh disappointment, arose against Schuyler, the commander of the department, and St. Clair, the commander of the post. The excitement and dismay were universal, and the just apprehension was most grave. But when the storm was loudest it was pierced by the calm voice of Washington, whose soul quailed before no disaster: "We should never despair; our situation has before been unpromising and has changed for the better; so I trust it will be again." He sent Arnold to Schuyler, as an accomplished officer, familiar with the country. He urged the eastern states to move to his succor. He ordered all available boats from Albany to New Windsor and Fishkill, upon the Hudson, to be ready for any part of his own army that he might wish to detach. While thus the commander-in-chief cared for all, each cared for itself. The stout-hearted George Clinton, and the council of New York were thoroughly aroused and alert. Vermont called upon New Hampshire, and the White mountains answered to the Green by summoning Stark and Whipple, who, gathering their men, hastened to the Hudson.

While this wild panic and alarm swept through the country, Burgoyne remained for a fortnight at the head of Lake Champlain. He, also, had his troubles. He was forced to garrison Ticonderoga from his serviceable troops. His Indian allies began to annoy him. Provisions came in slowly, and the first fatal weakness of the expedition was already betrayed in the inadequate supply of wagons and horses. But the neighboring tories joined him, and counting upon the terror that his triumphant progress had inspired, he moved at the end of July from Lake Champlain toward the Hudson. His march was through the wilderness which Schuyler had desolated to the utmost, breaking up the roads, choking with trees the navigable streams, destroying forage, and driving away cattle. But

Burgoyne forced his way through, building forty bridge's and laying a log-wood road for two miles across a morass. The confidence of triumph cheered the way. So sure was victory, that as if it had been a huge pleasure party, the wives of officers accompanied the camp, and the Baroness Riedesel came in a calash from Fort George to join her husband with Burgoyne. But before that slowly toiling army, the startled frontier country fled. Almost every patriot house west of the Green mountains and north of Manchester was deserted. The tories, proud of British protection, placed signs in their hats and before their doors, and upon the horns of their cattle, wearing the tory badge, as Gurth wore the collar of Cedric the Saxon. To us the scene is a romantic picture. The scarlet host of Burgoyne flashes through the forest with pealing music; the soldiers smooth the rough way with roystering songs; the trains and artillery toil slowly on; the red cloud of savages glimmers on his skirts, driving before him farmers with wives and children, faint and sick with cruel apprehension flying through a land of terror. To us it is a picture. But to know what it truly was, let the happy farmer on these green slopes and placid meadows, imagine a sudden flight to-night with all he loves from all he owns, struggling up steep hills, lost in tangled woods, crowding along difficult roads, at every step expecting the glistening tomahawk, the bullet, and the mercies of a foreign soldiery. Not many miles from this spot, the hapless Jane MacCrea was killed as Burgoyne's savages hurried her away. Her story rang through the land like a woman's cry of agony. This, then, was British chivalry! Burgoyne, indeed, had not meant murder, but he had threatened it. The name of the innocent girl became the rallying cry for armies, and to a thousand indignant hearts, her blood cried from the ground for vengeance. We come with song and speech and proud commemoration to celebrate the triumph of this day. Let us not forget the cost of that triumph, the infinite suffering that this unchanging sky beheld; the torture of men; the heart-break of women; the terror of little children, that paid for the happiness which we enjoy.

Burgoyne reached the Hudson unattacked. As he arrived, although he had no tidings from below, he heard of the successful advance in the valley of the Mohawk. St. Leger had reached Fort Stanwix without the loss of a man. It was necessary, therefore, for Burgoyne to hasten to make his junction at Albany with Howe and St. Leger, and on the 6th of August he sent word to Howe that he hoped to be in Albany by the 22d. But, even as he wrote, the blow fatal to his hopes was struck. On that very day the patriots of Tryon county, men of German blood, led by Nicholas Herkimer, were hastening to the relief of Fort Stanwix, which St. Leger had beleaguered. The tale has just been eloquently told to fifty thousand children of the Mohawk valley gathered on the field of Oriskany, and it will be told to their children's children so long as the grass of that field shall grow, and the waters of the Mohawk flow. In the hot summer morning, Herkimer and his men marched under the peaceful trees into the deadly ambush, and in the depth of the defile were suddenly enveloped in a storm of fire and death. Ah! blood-red field of Oriskany! For five doubtful desperate hours, without lines, or fort, or artillery, hand to hand, with knife and rifle, with tomahawk and spear, swaying and struggling, slipping in blood and stumbling over dead bodies, raged the most deadly battle of the war. Full of heroic deeds, full of precious memories; a sacrifice that was not lost. The stars that shone at evening over the field, saw the Indian and the white men stark and stiff, still locked in the death grapple, still clenching the hair of the foe, still holding the dripping knife in his breast. The brave Herkimer, fatally wounded, called for his Bible and tranquilly died. He did not relieve the fort, but it held out until Benedict Arnold, sent by Schuyler, coming up the valley, craftily persuaded St. Leger's Indians that his men were as the leaves of the forest for number. The savages fled; St. Leger's force melted away; the Mohawk expedition had wholly failed, and the right hand of Burgoyne was shattered.

Every day lost to the English general was now a disaster. But his fatal improvidence forced him to inaction. He could not move without supplies of food and horses, and an expedition to secure them would also serve as a diversion to favor St. Leger. Three days after Oriskany, and before he had heard of that battle, Burgoyne detached the expedition to

Bennington. New England was ready for him there as New York had been at Stanwix. Parson Allen from Pittsfield came in his chaise. Everybody else came as he could, and when the British advance was announced, John Stark marched his militia just over the line of New York, where the enemy was intrenched on the uplands of the Walloomsac, and skillfully surrounding them, the Yankee farmers who had hurried away from their summer work, swept up the hill with fiery and resistless fury, seized the blazing guns, drove the veteran troops as if they were wolves and wild cats threatening their farms, and after a lull renewing the onset against fresh foes, the New England militia won the famous battle of Bennington, and the left hand of Burgoyne was shattered.

So soon was the splendid promise of Ticonderoga darkened. The high and haughty tone was changed. "I yet do not despond," wrote Burgoyne on the 20th of August, and he had not yet heard of St. Leger's fate. But he had reason to fear. The glad light of Bennington and Oriskany had pierced the gloom that weighed upon the country. It was everywhere jubilant and everywhere rising. The savages deserted the British camp. The harvest was gathered, and while New England and New York had fallen fatally upon the flanks of Burgoyne, Washington now sent Virginia to join New York and New England in his front, detaching from his own army Morgan and his men, the most famous rifle corps of the Revolution. Indeed, Burgoyne's situation was worse than he knew. It now appears that the orders of co-operation with him were not sent to Lord Howe. Lord Shelburne in a memorandum upon Lord George Germaine, recently published, says of the inconsistent orders, given by the two Generals in America, that Lord George was very impatient of trouble, and that he had appointed to call at his office and sign the despatches, but by some mistake those of Lord Howe's were not fairly copied; Lord George would not stop and the clerks promised to send them to the country. But then ensued forgetfulness and delay, and the packet sailed without Lord Howe's orders. Of this, however, Burgoyne knew nothing. He was still counting upon the active co-operation of Lord Howe, while he chafed under his own mishaps. But while the American prospect brightened, General Schuyler, by order of congress, was superseded by General Gates. Schuyler, a most sagacious and diligent officer whom Washington wholly trusted, was removed for the alleged want of his most obvious quality, the faculty of comprehensive organization. But the New England militia disliked him, and even Samuel Adams was impatient of him; but Samuel Adams was also impatient of Washington. Public irritation with the situation, and jealous intrigue in camp and in congress procured Schuyler's removal. He was wounded to the heart, but his patriotism did not waver. He remained in camp to be of what service he could, and he entreated congress to order a speedy and searching inquiry into his conduct. It was at last made, and left him absolutely unstained. He was unanimously acquitted with the highest honor, and Congress approved the verdict. General Schuyler did not again enter upon active military service, but he and Rufus King were the first senators that New York sent to the senate of the United States. Time has restored his name and the history of his state records no more patriotic name among her illustrious sons than that which is commemorated by this village, the name of Philip Schuyler.

Largely re-enforced, Gates, on the 12th of September, advanced to Bemis's Heights, which the young Kosciussko had fortified, and there he awaited Burgoyne's approach. Burgoyne's orders had left him no discretion. He must force his way to Albany. With soldierly loyalty, therefore, he must assume that Howe was pushing up the Hudson, and that his own delay might imperil Howe by permitting the Americans to turn suddenly upon him. On the 11th of September he announced to his camp that he had sent the lake fleet to Canada, that he had virtually abandoned his communications, and that his army must fight its way or perish. On the 13th he crossed the Hudson, and then received his first tidings from Howe, in a letter from him written long before, and which did not even mention a junction. Burgoyne had already felt himself deserted if not betrayed, and he comprehended his critical situation. Howe was on the Delaware and Carleton would give him no aid from Canada. The country behind him was already swarming with militia. He was encamped in a dense forest, with an enemy hidden in the same forest before him, whose drum-beat and morning gun he could hear, but whose numbers and position he did not know. Yet while he could see nothing, every movement of his own was noted by an eagle eye in a tree top on the eastern side of the Hudson, and reported to Gates. And when at last Burgoyne marched out in full array, with all the glittering pomp of war, to find the foe in the forest, Gates instantly knew it. Burgoyne boldly advanced, his communication with Canada gone, the glory of Ticonderoga dimmed, the union with Howe uncertain, disaster on the right hand and on the left, the peerage and Westminster Abbey both fading from hope, and he suddenly confronted breastworks, artillery and an eager army. He must fight or fly, nor did he hesitate. At eleven o'clock on the morning of the 19th of September, he advanced in three columns towards Gates's line on Bemis's Heights. At one o'clock the action began; at four it was general and desperate; at five, Burgoyne's army was in mortal peril; at nightfall the Germans had stayed the fatal blow, and the battle ended. Both sides claimed the victory, and the British bivouacked on the field. As on Bunker Hill, the first battle in America which Burgoyne had seen, if this were a British victory another would destroy the British army.

Burgoyne huddled his dead into the ground, hastily intrenched and fortified a new position, soothed his discouraged army and meditated a fresh assault. But receiving the good news of Howe's success at the Brandywine, and of the immediate advance of Clinton to break through the highlands of the Hudson and fall upon the rear of Gates, he decided to wait. He was encamped in the wilderness without communications, but he sent word to Clinton that he could hold out until the 12th of October. Again through the forest he heard the morning and evening gun and the shouting of the American camp, and once the joyful firing of cannon that he could not understand, but which anounced American victories in his rear. The alarm of the British camp was constant. The picket firing was incessant. Officers and men slept in their clothes, rations were reduced, and the hungry army heard every night the howling of the wolves that hunted the outskirts of the camp as if making ready for their prey. At last, with provisions for sixteen days only, and no news from Clinton, Burgoyne summoned his generals for a final council. It was the evening of the 5th of October, and, could he but have known it, Howe at Germantown, had again succeeded and Sir Henry Clinton was just

breaking his way through the Highlands, victorious and deso-
lating. On the very morning that Burgoyne fought his fatal
battle the river forts had fallen, the boom and chain were
cleared away, the marauding British fleet sailed into Newburgh
bay, Clinton sent word gaily to Burgoyne, ''Here we are!
nothing between us and Albany,'' while Putnam was hastening
up along the eastern bank and George Clinton along the western, rousing the country and rallying the flying citizens from
their alarm. Of all this Burgoyne knew nothing. In his extremity, his own plan was to leave boats, provisions and magazines, for three or four days, and falling upon the left of the
Americans, to attempt to gain the rear. The German General
Riedesel advised falling back toward the lake. The English
Fraser was willing to fight. The English Phillips was silent.
Compelled to decide, Burgoyne at last determined to reconnoi-
tre the Americans in force, and if he thought that an attack would
be unwise, then to retreat toward the lake.

On the morning of the 7th of October, at ten o'clock, fifteen
hundred of the best troops in the world, led by four of the most
experienced and accomplished generals, with a skirmishing van
of Canadian rangers and Indians, moved in three columns toward the left of the American position into a field of wheat.
They began to cut forage. Startled by the rattling picket fire
the American drums beat to arms, and the British approach
was announced at headquarters, Morgan and the Virginian sharpshooters were thrown out beyond the British right. Poor, with
the New York and New Hampshire men, moved steadily through
the woods toward the British left, which began the battle with
a vigorous cannonade. The Americans dashed forward, opened
to the right and left, flanked the enemy, struck him with a
blasting fire, then closed and grappling hand to hand, the mad
mass of combatants swayed and staggered for half an hour, five
times taking and re-taking a single gun. At the first fire
upon the left, the Virginia sharp-shooters, shouting, and blazing with deadly aim, rushed forward with such fury that the
appalled British right wavered and recoiled. While it yet staggered under the blow of Virginia, New England swept up, and
with its flaming muskets broke the Engilsh line, which wildly
fled. It reformed and again advanced, while the whole American force dashed against the British center, held by the Ger-

mans, whose right and left had been uncovered. The Germans bravely stood, and the British General Fraser hurried to their aid. He seemed upon the British side the inspiring genius of the day. With fatal aim an American sharp-shooter fired and Fraser fell. With him sank the British heart. Three thousand New Yorkers, led by Ten Broeck, came freshly up, and the whole American line, jubilant with certain victory, advancing, Burgoyne abandoned his guns and ordered a retreat to his camp. It was but fifty-two minutes since the action began. The British, dismayed, bewildered, overwhelmed, were scarcely within their redoubts, when Benedict Arnold, to whom the jealous Gates, who did not come upon the field during the day, had refused a command, outriding an aid whom Gates had sent to recall him, came spurring up; Benedict Arnold, whose name America does not love, whose ruthless will had dragged the doomed Canadian expedition through the starving wilderness of Maine, who volunteering to relieve Fort Stanwix had, by the mere terror of his coming, blown St. Leger away, and who, on the 19th of September, had saved the American left,—Benedict Arnold, whom battle stung to fury, now whirled from end to end of the American line, hurled it against the Great Redoubt, driving the enemy at the point of the bayonet; then flinging himself to the extreme right, and finding there the Massachusetts brigade, swept it with him to the assault, and streaming over the breastworks, scattered the Brunswickers who defended them, killed their colonel, gained and held the point which commanded the entire British position, while at the same moment his horse was shot under him, and he sank to the ground wounded in the leg that had been wounded at Quebec. Here, upon the Hudson, where he tried to betray his country, here upon the spot where, in the crucial hour of the Revolution, he illustrated and led the American valor that made us free and great, knowing well that no earlier service can atone for a later crime, let us recall for one brief instant of infinite pity, the name that has been justly execrated for a century.

Night fell, and the weary fighters slept. Before day dawned, Burgoyne, exhausted and overwhelmed, drew off the remainder of his army, and the Americans occupied his camp. All day the lines exchanged a sharp fire. At evening, in a desolate autumn rain, having buried solemnly, amid the flash and rattle of bombs and artillery, his gallant friend, Fraser; leaving his sick and wounded to the mercies of the foe, Burgoyne who, in the splendid hour of his first advance had so proudly proclaimed "this army must not retreat," turned to fly. He moved until nearly day-break, then rested from the slow and toilsome march until toward sunset, and on the evening of the 9th he crossed Fish creek and bivouacked in the open air. A more vigorous march—but it was impracticable—would have given him the heights of Saratoga, and secured the passage of the river. But everywhere he was too late. The American sharpshooters hovered around him, cutting off supplies, and preventing him from laying roads. There was, indeed, one short hour of hope that Gates, mistaking the whole British army for its flying rear-guard, would expose himself to a destructive ambush and assault. When the snare was discovered, the last hope of Burgoyne vanished, and unable to stir, he sat down grimly north of the creek, where his army, wasted to thirty-four hundred effective men, was swiftly and completely encircled by the Americans, who commanded it at every point, and harassed it with shot and shell. Gates, with the confidence of overpowering numbers, purposely avoided battle. Burgoyne, deserted by his allies, his army half gone, with less than five days' food, with no word from Clinton, with no chance of escape, prepared honorably to surrender.

On the 14th of October, he proposed a cessation of arms to arrange terms of capitulation. His agent, Lieutenant-Colonel Kingston, was received at the crossing of the creek by Adjutant-General Wilkinson, and was conducted by him, blindfolded, to General Gates. Gates's terms required an unconditional surrender of the army as prisoners of war. Burgoyne, anxious to save his army to the king for service elsewhere, insisted that it should be returned to England, under engagement not to serve again in North America during the war. Gates had no wish to prolong the negotiations. He had heard from Putnam that the English army and fleet were triumphantly sweeping up the river, and that he must expect "the worst," and he therefore hastened to accept the proposition of Burgoyne. But Washington, with his Fabian policy, scorned even by Samuel and John Adams, had made "the worst" impossible. Hanging upon the army of Howe, engaging it, although unsuccessfully,

at the Brandywine and at Germantown, he had perplexed, delayed and disconcerted the British general, gaining the time
which was the supreme necessity for success against Burgoyne.
By reason of Washington's operations, Howe could not strengthen
Clinton as they both expected, and Clinton could not move until
his slow re-enforcements from over the sea arrived. When
they came, he burst through the Highlands indeed, with fire
and pillage, and hastened to fall upon the rear of Gates. But
before he could reach him, while still forty miles away, he
heard the astounding news of Burgoyne's surrender, and he
dropped down the river sullenly, back to New York, he, too,
baffled by the vigilance, the wariness, the supreme self-command
of Washington.

For a moment, when Burgoyne heard of Clinton's success, he
thought to avoid surrender. But it was too late. He could
not, honorably, recall his word. At nine o'clock on the
morning of this day, a hundred years ago, he signed the convention. At eleven o'clock his troops marched to this meadow,
the site of old Fort Hardy, and with tears coursing down
bearded cheeks, with passionate sobs and oaths of rage and defiance, the soldiers kissing their guns with the tenderness of
lovers, or with sudden frenzy knocking off the butts of their
muskets, and the drummers stamping on their drums, the
king's army laid down their arms. No American eyes, except
those of Morgan Lewis and James Wilkinson, aids of General
Gates, beheld the surrender. As the British troops filed afterwards between the American lines, they saw no signs of exultation, but they heard the drums and fifes playing "Yankee
Doodle." A few minutes later, Burgoyne and his suite rode to
the headquarters of Gates. The English general, as if for a
court holiday, glittered in scarlet and gold; Gates plainly clad
in a blue overcoat, attended by General Schuyler in citizen's
dress, who had come to congratulate him, and by his proud and
happy staff, received his guest with urbane courtesy. They
exchanged the compliments of soldiers. "The fortune of war,
General Gates, has made me your prisoner." Gates gracefully
replied, "I shall always be ready to testify that it has not been
through any fault of your Excellency." The generals entered
the tent of Gates and dined together. With the same courtly
compliment the English general toasted General Washington,

the American general toasted the king. Then, as the English army, without artillery or arms, approached on their march to the sea, the two generals stepped out in front of the tent, and standing together conspicuous upon this spot, in full view of the Americans and of the British army, General Burgoyne drew his sword, bowed, and presented it to General Gates. General Gates bowed, received the sword, and returned it to General Burgoyne.

Such was the simple ceremony that marked the turning point of the Revolution. All the defeats, indeed, all the struggles, the battles, the sacrifices, the sufferings, at all times and in every colony, were indispensable to the great result. Concord, Lexington, Bunker Hill, Moultrie, Long Island, Trenton, Oriskany, Bennington, the Brandywine, Germantown, Saratoga, Monmouth, Camden, Cowpens, Guilford, Eutaw Springs, Yorktown,—what American does not kindle as he calls the glorious battle roll of the Revolution!—whether victories or defeats, all are essential lights and shades in the immortal picture. But, as gratefully acknowledging the service of all the patriots, we yet call Washington father, so mindful of the value of every event, we may agree that the defeat of Burgoyne determined American independence. Thenceforth it was but a question of time. The great doubt was solved. Out of a rural militia an army could be trained to cope at every point successfully with the most experienced and disciplined troops in the world. In the first bitter moment of his defeat, Burgoyne generously wrote to a military friend, ''A better armed, a better bodied, a more alert or better prepared army in all essential points of military institution, I am afraid is not to be found on our side of the question.'' The campaign in New York also, where the loyalists were strongest, had shown, what was afterwards constantly proved, that the British crown, despite the horrors of Cherry Valley and Wyoming, could not count upon general or effective aid from the Tories or from the Indians. At last it was plain that if Britain would conquer, she must overrun and crush the continent, and that was impossible. The shrewdest men in England and in Europe saw it. Lord North himself, King George's chief minister, owned it, and grieved in his blind old age that he had not followed his conviction. Edmund Burke would have made peace on any terms. Charles Fox exclaimed that the ministers knew as little how to make peace as war. The Duke of Richmond urged the impossibility of conquest, and the historian Gibbon, who in parliament had voted throughout the war as Dr. Johnson would have done, agreed that America was lost. The king of France ordered Franklin to be told that he should support the cause of the United States. In April he sent a fleet to America, and from that time to the end of the war, the French and the Americans battled together on sea and land, until on this very day, the 17th of October, 1781, four years after the disaster of Burgoyne, Cornwallis, on the plains of Yorktown, proposed a surrender to the combined armies of France and the United States. The terms were settled upon our part jointly by an American and a French officer, while Washington and La Fayette stood side by side as the British laid down their arms. It was the surrender of Burgoyne that determined the French alliance and the French alliance secured the final triumph.

It is the story of a hundred years ago. It has been ceaselessly told by sire to son, along this valley and through this land. The later attempt of the same foe and the bright day of victory at Plattsburgh on the lake, renewed and confirmed the old hostility. Alienation of feeling between the parent country and the child became traditional, and on both sides of the sea a narrow prejudice survives, and still sometimes seeks to kindle the embers of that wasted fire. But here and now we stand upon the grave of old enmities. Hostile breastwork and redoubt are softly hidden under grass and grain; shot and shell and every deadly missile are long since buried deep beneath our feet, and from the mouldering dust of mingled foemen springs all the varied verdure that makes this scene so fair. While nature tenderly and swiftly repairs the ravages of war, we suffer no hostility to linger in our hearts. Two months ago the British governor-general of Canada was invited to meet the president of the United States, at Bennington, in happy commemoration not of a British defeat but of a triumph of English liberty. So, upon this famous and decisive field, let every unworthy feeling perish! Here, to the England that we fought, let us now, grown great and strong with a hundred years, hold out the hand of fellowship and peace! Here, where the English Burgoyne, in the very moment of his bitter humiliation, generously pledged George Washington, let us, in our high hour of triumph, of power, and of hope, pledge the queen! Here, in the grave of brave and unknown foemen, may mutual jealousies and doubts and animosities lie buried forever ! Henceforth, revering their common glorious traditions, may England and America press always forward side by side, in noble and inspiring rivalry to promote the welfare of man!

Fellow-citizens, with the story of Burgoyne's surrender— the revolutionary glory of the State of New York—still fresh in our memories, amid these thousands of her sons and daughters, whose hearts glow with lofty pride, I am glad that the hallowed spot on which we stand compels us to remember not only the imperial state, but the national commonwealth whose young hands here together struck the blow, and on whose older head descends the ample benediction of the victory. On yonder height, a hundred years ago, Virginia and Pennsylvania lay encamped. Beyond, and further to the north, watched New Hampshire and Vermont. Here, in the wooded uplands at the south, stood New Jersey and New York, while across the river to the east, Connecticut and Massachusetts closed the triumphant line. Here was the symbol of the Revolution, a common cause, a common strife, a common triumph; the cause not of a class, but of human nature—the triumph not of a colony, but of United America. And we who stand here proudly remembering—we who have seen Virginia and New York—the North and the South—more bitterly hostile than the armies whose battles shook this ground—we who mutually proved in deadlier conflict the constancy and the courage of all the States, which, proud to be peers, yet own no master but their united selves—we renew our heart's imperishable devotion to the common American faith, the common American pride, the common American glory! Here Americans stood and triumphed. Here Americans stand and bless their memory. And here, for a thousand years, may grateful generations of Americans come to rehearse the glorious story, and to rejoice in a supreme and benignant American Nationality.

F. C. Yohn, Artist   Courtesy of Glens Falls Insurance Co.

THE DEATH OF JANE McCREA

(Calendar for 1912)

INFLUENCE OF DEATH OF JANE McCREA
ON BURGOYNE CAMPAIGN.[1]

By James Austin Holden, A. B.
State Historian of New York State.

As far back as history can be traced by means of signs and symbols of expressed thought, it seems as though the destinies of nations and peoples had been decided, not so much by an ordered plan, as by some rule of chance, some unforseen, unlooked for and almost irrelevant happening that had no apparent bearing upon the questions at issue, or the great matters at stake.

The truth of one old saw so well known to most of you—

> For want of a nail a shoe was lost,
> For want of a shoe a horse was lost,
> For want of a horse a rider was lost,
> For want of a rider a battle was lost,
> For want of a victory a kingdom was lost,
> And all for the want of a horse-shoe nail.

is exemplified in the chance-won victories on many a battle-field.

From Caesar to Napoleon, from Washington to Grant full as many battles have been won by apparent luck, as by well defined and beforehand planning on the chess-board of war.

By all the laws and book-rules of military art, John Burgoyne should have won the battles of Saratoga, IF, that great "IF" the conquerer of so many generals in public and private life, fate had not intervened.

On the American side was the crafty mediocre politician "Gusty and Blustry" Gates, who had succeeded Philip Schuyler, the most brainy man the Americans had in this section, supported by what one of the patriot colonels called "this retreating, raged,

---

1. This is the whole of a paper prepared for the Saratoga meeting of the New York State Historical Association, parts only of which were read at the session held Sept. 19, 1912.

starved, lousey, thievish, pockey army"[1]; on the other Burgoyne a man of parts and of proved ability in foreign wars, with the flower of the English army and some of its best generals, as well as the Hessian contingent, officered by men who had made a business of war.

Viewed from the vantage point of Afterwards, we can now see several reasons why Burgoyne lost; but in those days they were not so readily apparent.

To the decided check at Fort Ann on the 8th of July, when Colonel Pierce Long and Colonel Hendrick Van Rensselaer successfully held the British, giving the main body retreating from Ticonderoga, a chance to escape; to the rear guard skirmish at Hubbardton the day before, which though won by the British over Seth Warner caused the first delay; to the victory of Stark over Baum and the Hessians at Walloomsac or Bennington; to Herkimer's sacrifice, and defeat of St. Leger at Oriskany; to the legendary capture of the spy and his canteen, in which false news was substituted for British consumption; to Schuyler's well planned obstruction of Wood Creek and the old War Trail, by cutting down trees across the pathways, filling the creek with stone, brush and logs, and breaking down bridges, so delaying the army's progress for days; to Burgoyne's alleged drunken revels at Skenesborough, where he was encamped for sixteen days; to the failure of Howe and Clinton to co-operate with him, to a forgotten and pigeon holed order of Lord Germaine; to all of these and to each one of them has been attributed, by orators and writers of history, the defeat of Burgoyne at Saratoga.

That each did its share in that defeat, nearly every writer and critic of that amply documented and abundantly written about affair is ready to acknowledge. But the real contributory causes to the final defeat were Burgoyne's "slick" tongue and fatal, but facile pen, which in that extraordinary proclamation issued from his camp at the River Boquet, June 23, 1777, demanded allegiance to the king, submission to his representative, maintenance and support of his cause, and in default of these threatened the Americans, Whigs and Tories alike with the vengeance of his Indian allies. These although forced upon him by King George and the

---

1. Revolutionary Journal of Col. Jeduthan Baldwin, Bangor, Me. (1906) p. 60.

English ministry, he had accepted and had inflamed by his adroit, specious and stirring oratory at the war feast two days before. At this time after forbidding bloodshed and scalp taking by them he had said :—

" * * * You shall receive compensation for the prisoners you take, but you shall be called to account for scalps.

In conformity and indulgence of your customs, which have affixed an idea of honour to such badges of victory, you shall be allowed to take the scalps of the dead, when killed by your fire and in fair opposition; but on no account, or pretence, or subtlety, or prevarication are they to be taken from the wounded, or even dying; and still less pardonable, if possible, will it be held, to kill men in that condition, on purpose, and upon a supposition, that this protection to the wounded would be thereby evaded."[1]

His bombastic proclamation, copied in the papers and gazettes of the day, the subject of lampoons and witticisms here and in England, paraphrased and burlesqued by American poets, satirists and patriot writers, disgusted his enemies, alienated his friends, and in the sore days to come, was to rise up and smite him in the fatherland he loved and fought for devotedly, whatever his faults might have been.

Both his speech and his proclamation had results he little dreamed of, when arrayed in the grandeur of his Lieutenant General's uniform he stood that bright June day before his savage allies, the present representative of "the great father beyond the great lake"; and received their expressions of fealty, and by their chiefest warrior this promise: "We have been tried and tempted by the Bostonians; but we love our father, and our hatchets have been sharpened upon our affections. * * * With one common assent, we promise a constant obedience to all you have ordered, and all you shall order, and may the Father of Days give you many, and success.[2]

With the death of Montcalm on the Plains of Abraham, the dominance and supremacy of the Anglo-Saxon race had apparently been forever established in the New World. Fear of the Great Father on his English throne, in the Canadas, and love and respect

1. Burgoyne's State of the Expedition. London (1780). Appendix, p. 13.
2. Ibid, pp. 12-14.

for Sir William Johnson and his memory in the great confederacy of the Six Nations, had kept alive the embers of the great peace-fires, east and west, and north and south.

Indian outrages were few and in most cases directly attributable to the passions and vices, to the greed and poor liquor of those whites who may have suffered in these spasmodic raids. Still in the distance were the horrors of Wyoming, or Cherry Valley, of Minisink, of the Mohawk Valley, of Ballston. Not as yet had Walter Butler's "Blue Eyed Indians" and his Mohawk allies swept through the valley making his name a hissing and a reproach in the ages to come. Not as yet had Brant's warriors kissed the skulls of the patriots with their sharp knives. Not as yet had unborn babes been carved from their living mothers to be dashed in white faces piteous with the death agony. Not as yet had the fierce Iroquois surgeons fastened Lieutenant Boyd's intestines to a stake, and driven and dragged him around it, until he hung quivering in the bonds of his own bowels. All these were of a later date, and many of them the savage reprisals for Sullivan's raid, which all but exterminated the highest type of Indian civilization the world has ever known, and as events proved, to little effective purpose from a military or a civil standpoint.

When the King and the British Ministry compelled Burgoyne to enroll the Indians as his allies, they became morally responsible for every crime committed by those allies from that time on, and added the one thing needed to convert to the American cause, many a wavering borderer, who cared more for his scalp than for either the British or Patriot causes. While later to fight "fire with fire" the Americans used those tribes which had remained faithful, as scouts and skirmishers, and while scalping was done under the Stars and Stripes, as well as the English standard, as shown by many a soldier's journal of that time, this fact neither palliates the offenses committed by the British in the name of War, by their red-skinned helpers, nor condones the outrages and murders they perpetrated.[1]

For almost two decades opportunity had been offered, and been seized, for colonization in the great territory opened up by

---

1. In this connection it is to the credit of General Gates that unlike Burgoyne he refused to pay a bounty for scalps to his Indians, at a time when live prisoners were bringing twenty dollars each. Col. Baldwin's Journal; p. 121.

the cessation of the Seven Years' War in 1760. So practically immune for seventeen years from Indian raids and surprises, the "Proclamation" of Burgoyne, and the substance of his grandiloquent speech to the Indians as they became public, aroused a feeling of insecurity, and a sense of military responsibility such as up to that time had not existed in Northern New York, and its nearby neighbors, if we may judge by the Governor Clinton Papers and State records. For up to that time there had maintained a strong Tory sentiment in Albany, Charlotte, Saratoga and parts of old Tryon County, mostly populated with holders of King's grants, former soldiers of the old Indian Wars, emigrants from the British Isles or people from the older counties below Albany, or from the other colonies to which the Boston and Philadelphia ideas of Liberty, Freedom and Equality meant little either from a sentimental or a business standpoint.[1]

The fearsome massacres of Schenectady, of Old Saratoga and Deerfield in the so-called King William's and Queen Ann's wars, in the latter end of the Seventeenth and the earlier days of the Eighteenth centuries, and the later border troubles and bloodshed in the Coos country, and along the great war trails of New England and New York in the French and Indian War following, which had become memories, whose resulting heart pangs affected only those whose near and dear ones had suffered from the savagery of the foe, were now recalled by settlers who had long since ceased to carry a rifle across the plough handles, as they turned long furrows in the virgin sod.

In the final and ultimate analysis it would seem strange to attribute as definite causes of Burgoyne's defeat King James I, his Bible and John Calvin, and still a logical argument can be adduced in support of even so far brought and apparently wide afield statement.

In those days of our youth, when fads and frills in education were as yet unknown, and scholars really learned something from their books that "stood by", many of you will remember that a good working knowledge of English Literature was obtained from the text-books of the day. In the little reddish manual used in the old Academy where the writer prepared for college under

---

1. See State Historian's Minutes of Commissioners for Conspiracies.

the tutorage of that splendid teacher, who later was to become one of the founders of this Association, Daniel Cephas Farr, were quotations to memorize from the standard authors, and one of them occurs to me now as fitting here:

> "There is a Divinity that shapes our ends
> Rough-hew them how we will."

So from the safe and sane view point of Hind Sight we can now see the underlying causes of what must have seemed to our forefathers, to whom their religion meant so much, the immediate workings out of a miraculous intervention of Providence itself.

Those of you who were favored in hearing the scholarly and delightful address of Ex-Chancellor MacCracken at Kingston last year, will remember the stress laid by him upon the influence of the Scotch-Irish in America and New York.[1] This statement of his is of interest:

"King James First coming to the English throne in 1603 first started Scotch emigration to England. As Walter Scott says, quoting an old writer in his 'Fortunes of Nigel': 'A throng of Scotch not only attended the king on his coming first out of Scotland, but through his whole reign, like a fluent spring were found still crossing the Tweed.' "

"Next the king started the Scotch towards North Ireland. This James First was neither a great king nor a great man, yet he gets the credit of two of the greatest translations in history. First, the translation 300 years ago of the Bible into English; second, the translations of myriads of Scotch into the North of Ireland, in what is known as 'The Great Plantation of Ulster'."

"There they lived a hundred years, preparing their sons to become the keystone of America. For while New England was builded by Puritans and Virginia by Anglicans, the Middle States got their chief material for the war of independence and their courage, not from William Penn's people who would not fight, or the Dutch who were not a large element, but from the quarter million and more of Scotch and Scotch-Irish and from their children."

Dr. MacCracken states in another place that "The Scotch-Irish form five-tenths of the Presbyterians in America."[2]   And

---

1. Henry M. MacCracken, D.D., LL. D., in Proceedings N. Y. Hist. Assn. (1912), Vol. XI, pp. 105-106.
2. Idem. pp. 113, 115.

again, that "Many of the New York Scotch-Irish were of the
Covenanter party or of the Associate party, who, like the former,
were advanced champions of religious liberty."

These people were hard workers, good pioneer stuff, inured
to hardships, dour and resolute, and in search of places where
their altars could be set up away from persecution and religious
intolerance.

These conditions prevailing, it seems a natural consequence,
as has been stated, that when the French and Indian wars ended
in 1760, and the whole northern territory of New York and the
Hampshire Grants were thrown open to settlers, we find a goodly
number of patents and tracts of land in this great northern wilderness, especially in Charlotte County, taken up by the Scotch or
their allied brethren the Scotch-Irish.

Between 1760 and 1765 many of the townships in Charlotte
county, of which the present Warren and Washington counties
were then the principal parts, had been settled by colonies of
hard-working, God-fearing pioneers. Salem and Argyle were
dominated by the Scotch-Irish; Fort Edward mostly by Connecticut men and Kingsbury by the same; Hebron and upper Washington and Greenwich by the Scotch, and Whitehall or Skenesborough by a Scot, while Queensbury was occupied by the Wings,
Quakers from Dutchess County, their friends, relatives, and de-
pendants.

So struggling against the natural enemies of frontiersmen,
the forest with its wild beasts and reptiles, the want of necessities, the dearth of supplies; remote from the centers of the then
known civilization; the nearest neighbors perhaps miles away,
except may be in the little hamlets at Wing's, the later Glen's
Falls, Kingsbury, Fort Edward, Fort Miller, Argyle, Greenwich
or Cambridge, or those in Old Saratoga; and unless located on the
old military road laid out by Sir William Johnson in the former
wars, separated by virgin woodlands and high hills and reachable
only by rude Indian trails or horseback paths,—we find the inhabitants of this region, already involved in the meshes of the revolution, and awaiting the advance of Burgoyne, as their loyalty or patriotism predominated, with hope and pleasure, or dismay and fear.

As has been already mentioned the advertised use of Indians
in Burgoyne's pronunciamento, added little to the feeling of

security which the Tories and Great Britain's supporters had during the early summer of 1777, as the red-coated forces dragged their slow way down the Wood creek trail. While the patriots scared at the easy conquest of Ticonderoga, which had a reputation at home and abroad far in excess of its actual value as a military strategic and defensive fortification, at the success of Burgoyne at Hubbardton, and Fort Ann, and not as yet heartened by Bennington and Oriskany, were ready to desert, and give up the fight.

The more we read in contemporary journals and diaries of American soldiers who fought in the Revolution, of their lack of discipline, their extreme youth and inexperience, of the want of military cohesion, of the disregard of the wishes of the officers, their orders and commands, of the contempt of the New Englanders for the "Yorkers," especially Schuyler, of their disobedience to the oaths of enlistment, of the desertions on the eve of battle of men whose only excuse was that they must go home to care for their crops, and get in their harvests, and that if successful they would come back to fight,—the more we are convinced that as the Psalmist sang:

If the Lord himself had not been on our side, now may Israel say; if the Lord himself had not been on our side, when men rose up against us;

They had swallowed us up quick; when they were so wrathfully displeased at us.[1]

Let us shift the scene of action and the persons of the great northern tragedy which made so great an impression on the fate of General Burgoyne, and perhaps changed the destinies of the nations of the earth, to the little commonwealth of New Jersey.

Here in November, 1739, a young Scotch-Irishman by the name of James McCrea, a student of the old Log College, "and a son of William McCrea, a prominent elder in the White Clay Creek Church near Newark, Delaware," [2] was licensed by the New Brunswick Presbytery, and the following April (1740), was called to supply the Presbyterian churches at Lamington, Lebanon, Peapack, Readington, and Bethlehem, thus becoming, ac-

---

1. The Psalter, Psalm CXXIV, vs. 1-2.
2. Henry Race, M. D. Historical Sketch of Jane McCrea, delivered before New Jersey Hist. Soc., May 20, (1886), p. 3.

1. THE ELIJAH SWEET GRAVE (p. 282)
2. THE GRAVE OF REV. JAMES McCREA (p. 257)
3. THE CASE HOME, some 40 rods to the east of which
   Jane McCrea was killed (p. 280)

cording to Webster,[1] "the father and founder of the congregation of Lamington,or Bedminster."

His was an interesting history as a pioneer of the Presbyterian church.

He officiated as pastor at Lamington till October 21, 1766, when he resigned becoming a pastor emeritus, as it were, until his death, May 10, 1769, at the age of 59.

James McCrea was twice married, having, it is said, seven children by his first wife, Mary Graham, and five by his second.[2] Three miles from the Lamington church, on a farm afterwards known as the "Lane Farm," stood until 1883, or 1884, a two story frame building which, burned about that time, has since been replaced by a new house.[3]

In that old framed building was born as the sixth child to James and Mary McCrea, a daughter whom they called Jane;[4] and it is with the subsequent history of that hapless and ill fated girl that the Burgoyne Campaign of 1777 is so intimately concerned and connected.

To the historian the "Story of Jane McCrea" is at once the most alluring and most provoking of all the episodes connected with the Revolutionary War, fact and fancy being so inextricably interwoven. No two authorities agree upon the important points, or upon all of the facts. In the years 1883-84, my father, the late Austin W. Holden, known locally as "Queensbury's Historian," prepared for the Glens Falls Republican a series of articles upon the "True Story of Jane McCrea." At that time he exhausted every known available source of information, and collected a vast volume of facts and data which should be embodied in some more permanent form than the scrap book shape they are now in. He had the assistance in his quest of the late Judge James Gibson of Salem, the late William L. Stone, and other well known historians. In addition to this material preparatory to this series of papers, he had collected information for years from Judge William Hay,

---

1. History of Presbyterian Church, Phila. (1857), pp. 493-494.
2. Dr. Race, Historical Sketch of Jane McCrea, p. 4. James Gibson, Genealogy of McCrea Family, in Salem-Review Press (1888-1890).
3. Letter from Rev. I. Alstyne Blauvelt, Roselle, N. J. (June 15, 1912).
4. The various ways of spelling the Christian and family name of Jane McCrea are as numerous as the accounts of how she met her fate. We find Jennie, Jennett and Janett, Janie, Jenny, Jeanie, and the family name as McCrea, M'Crea, MacCrea, Macree, McRea, and other variants, while Gen. Burgoyne in one place calls her "Miss Mecree".

Dr. Asa Fitch and Dr. E. B. O'Callaghan, well known historical writers of the earlier part of the nineteenth century.

To this collection the writer has added largely in the years that have passed since his father's death. He has accumulated books, pamphlets, monographs and papers on the Burgoyne Campaign, all of which bear in one way and another on the death of Jane McCrea. Lately, through the great kindness of Hon. Edgar Hull of Fort Edward, who has long been an indefatigable investigator in this same field, and through the Rev. O. C. Auringer, the poet, whose last long splendid poem was devoted exclusively to "The Death of Maid McCrea" and who has given years of study to the subject, much valuable information has been obtained.

An attempt was made, but unsuccessfully, to find new and original material in the way of letters, etc., in English archives, but there seems to be no such source matter accessible at present that has not been used.

This paper therefore will perhaps add but little to what has already been written and said about the Fort Edward tragedy, except that it embodies the conclusions of at least three persons, my father, Mr. Hull and myself, who have devoted years of study to the subject.

Returning now to the town of Lamington in New Jersey, we find as before stated that the minister, James McCrea, had seven children by his first wife, Mary Graham, to whom he was married April 8, 1740,[1] and who died September 15, 1753, aged thirty-one years; and five by his second wife, name unknown.

The children by the first wife were John, Mary, William, James, Samuel, Jane, and Stephen; and by the second, Robert, Philip, Gilbert, Creighton, and Catherine.[2]

Of the children John, William, Stephen and Philip were patriots, serving with the American forces; John becoming distinguished in civil life as well as a colonel in that army. Stephen became an army surgeon and we find his name in many of the journals of contemporary patriots. He lived, then, at Stillwater, N. Y.

Robert and Creighton on the other hand became virulent royalists, and prominent later in the English service abroad.

1. New Jersey Archives, Marriage Records, 1665-1880, vol. XXII.
2. Judge Gibson's Manuscript, also R. O. Bascom's Fort Edward Book, pp. 56-60.

Not much is known of the other children that is pertinent here.

The men all seemed to be capable, possessed of ability, well educated and apparently highly esteemed; (Robert, the loyalist, becoming governor of the Channel Islands after the war), and the girls undoubtedly were properly brought up and well taught for those days.

Colonel John McCrea graduated from Princeton, came to Albany in 1766 to practice law but did not like it, married one of "The" Beekmans of Albany, decided to farm it and so removed about 1773 to Northumberland, a few miles below Fort Edward in Saratoga County. Here he established himself upon a farm, where he lived till the Invasion of 1780, when his home was burned by the Tories. He then removed to Salem, N. Y., and became a man of consequence in the new State, having as before stated served acceptably as an officer during the war.

Why Jane McCrea came from "Jersey" to live with her brother John in the Saratoga wilderness, is beyond the ability of the historian of today to say. Her father died in 1769. Whether her home life with a step mother became uncongenial, or whether the latter was also dead "no man knoweth to this day."

Realizing that there were two brothers in Saratoga County with whom she could make a home, we find her in 1777, a member of Colonel John McCrea's household. At this time Jane McCrea must have been at least 24 years old, providing she was a child of the first wife who died in 1753, leaving a younger child, Stephen, who at the time of the Revolutionary War was a practising physician, and therefore necessarily had to be at least twenty-one years old in order to get his license. Of the second wife's children, besides the two who were officers in the British army, one (Philip) was an American lieutenant who later on was accidentally shot and killed by his men. So figure it how we may, the legendary and poetic girl of 17 or 18 must give way to the mature but undoubtedly more capable woman of the middle twenties.

All accounts agree that she was a most attractive girl in her personal appearance, only one man, the unfortunate and so pessimistic General Wilkinson, calling her aught but fair to look upon. She was large of stature, well formed, some say majestic, and strikingly good looking. Her hair seems to have been her crowning beauty, it being so long as to brush the floor when tied in a braid.

Here the conscientious historian pauses appalled, for we find that hair called all the shades there are, from raven black down through the browns, the auburns, the reds and the blondes.[1] It probably, however, would not be making too wild a guess for one to say, remembering she was of Scotch-Irish descent, and that a niece of hers was decidedly fair haired, that she was of the light complexioned type, rather than of the darker Celtish strain. However, aside from the fact that she was not in her teens, the historian does not need to dwell long on the point as to whether she was a blonde or a brunette, since to one man at least she was most "bonny" to look upon.

Living in Lamington at the time of the residence there of the McCrea family, was another family by the name of Jones. A Welshman whose first name is unknown took Sarah Dunham as his wife and to them were born seven sons, Jonathan, John, Daniel, Thomas, Dunham, Soloman and David, also two daughters.[2] They were neighbors and friends of the McCreas according to all accounts. Why or how, other than the workings out of fate, they came to settle in northern New York cannot now be told. Finally, however, we find from the records that the Widow Jones with her sons moved to Charlotte county, and settled in the vicinity of Moss Street, about three miles from Sandy Hill, or as it is now known, Hudson Falls, their homestead being in the northwest corner of the Kingsbury patent.

It is supposed by the earlier historians, who had a chance to verify these matters, that the house on this grant was used by Burgoyne as his headquarters, while at the Pitch Pine Plains encampment on July 29.[3] If so, it was to the house of David Jones' brother that the advance news of Jennie McCrea's fate was brought. But we are getting ahead of the story.

Daniel Jones after the settlement of Queensbury by Abraham Wing in 1763, married Deborah, sixth child of the "Founder" as he is locally known, and his wife Anstis (Wood). Daniel Jones thus became one of the earliest settlers of Queensbury, and was interested in building the first saw and grist mills at Wing's Cor-

---

1. After delivering a paper on "Some Errors Regarding Jane McCrea, Corrected," before Jane McCrea Chapter D. A. R. at Glens Falls, January 17, 1913, I was advised by Mrs. Eber Richards of Hudson Falls, that in her girlhood she saw a lock of Jane's hair, possibly cut off at one of the numerous interments, and it had a decided reddish tinge.
2. R. O. Bascom's Fort Edward Book, pp. 74-79.
3. Burgoyne's Orderly Book, p. 58.

ners, now Glens Falls. The Jones family for some reason espoused the British cause on the breaking out of the Revolution,
and their lands became forfeit to the State after the war. They
all fled to Canada, where they settled and died, never returning to
Kingsbury or Queensbury to live.[1]

We now come to an analysis of that Romance of the Revolution known as the Story of Jane McCrea.

It is claimed that David Jones and Jane McCrea had been
lovers in the old New Jersey days as boy and girl, and that when
she removed to Northumberland the old attachment was revived,
although not looked upon favorably by the brother, John McCrea,
to whom the royalist proclivities of the Jones family were abhorrent, and objectionable.

It is stated by Dr. Holden that the widow Jones, David's
mother, lived in a small house a few rods below the Halsey Rogers place, on the west bank of the river, about a mile below Fort
Edward, thus being in a way a neighbor of the McCreas.[2]

It is also taken for granted by Dr. Holden that David Jones,
who with a brother had remained in New Jersey till his mother
could establish herself in this section, when they too came to
Wing's Falls, worked for his brother Daniel at the Wing saw
mills, and so would have had chances to again meet Jane McCrea
who often visited "Tenty" Higson (nee Wing) the daughter of
Abraham and wife of James Higson, a Wing follower and co-
worker, who lived on the Ridge just outside the present city limits
of Glens Falls; Mrs. Higson being a friend and confidante of Jane.[3]

So time went on and the days of '76 drew near. The Jones
boys went to Canada and took service,[4] John McCrea and some of
his brothers threw in their lot with the Americans. Then came
the Burgoyne Invasion, and in the summer of 1777, the approach
of the British and the fall of Ticonderoga.

We will stop a moment here to get the "lay of the land" that
what follows may be more readily understandable.

For many miles to the north of Fort Edward huge white and
yellow pines, hemlocks, spruces and other evergreens stretched in

1. Holden's History of Queensbury, pp. 72-72. Rev. Conway P. Wing,
D. D. The Wing Family, Carlisle, Pa., (1881) pp. 99-103.
2. Holden's Jane McCrea Scrap Book, p. 9.
3. Holden's History of Queensbury, p. 72; History of The Wing Family, pp. 99-103.
4. Since this article was put in type this statement has been confirmed
by the researches of Prof. W. H. Siebert, as published in his monograph The
American Loyalists *** of Quebec, Ottawa (1913), pp. 7-8.

an almost unbroken forest, called upon the contemporaneous military maps "The Open Pine Plains," and by Burgoyne "The Pitch Pine Plains." [1]   As stated, only a few scattered huts and dwellings with their clearings along the old military trail, broke into the solid woods to the top of the hill overlooking Fort Edward. In 1755, Sir William Johnson had blazed a military road from Fort Lydius, afterwards Lyman and then Edward, to Lake George, which substantially followed the main traveled road of today. This road, however, instead of winding around the Fort Edward hill, as it does at present, and going over the canal and railroad bridges, since in those days there were necessarily neither canals nor railroads, nor bridges, bore easterly past one of the five block-houses erected by Amherst in 1759, all of which with the fort itself, were now in a dilapidated and practically useless condition, as means of defence. The road then went "directly over the crest of the hill, going rather abruptly down the steep declivity, not far from the canal lock and thence on to the Widow McNeil's house by means of a corduroy road over the marshy flat at that spot, and thence along the bank of the river to the fort." [2]   It is said there was a fine plain or clearing around the fort at this time. [3]

The Widow McNeil spoken of, occupied one of the three houses then existing in the hamlet of Fort Edward, the other two being the old Fort House still standing in Moreau, and the Dr. Smyth or Ezekial Baldwin house near the old fort. The McNeil house is thus described in a letter to Dr. O'Callaghan by Dr. Asa Fitch, the noted historian and scientist of Washington county: [4]

"The Widow Campbell house, from which Jane McCrea, Mrs. Campbell and a servant boy living with her, named Norman Morrison, were taken by Indians from Burgoyne's camp, was some 16 feet by 20 in size, built of round logs, with a door on its east side only, an old fashioned fire-place, without jambs at its north end, on one side of which were ladder-like stairs, leading to a loft overhead, and rather south of the center of the floor, a trap door, opening into an unwalled cellar-hole underneath. The building was subsequently the residence of Sheriff Peter B. Tierce, who married a grand-daughter of Mrs. Campbell's. It was demolished some

1.   Burgoyne's Orderly Book, p. 58.
2.   Holden's Scrap Book of Jane McCrea, p. 18.
3.   Baxter's Lieutenant Digby's Journal, Albany (1887), p. 240.
4.   Burgoyne's Orderly Book, pp. 181-182.

fifty years ago (about A. D. 1800). It stood in what is now (1850) the garden of Dr. Norton's, some ten rods south-west of the brick house in which the doctor resides, and was thus equidistant between and about eight rods from the road on one side, and the river on the other, and some sixty rods north of the fort."

The Widow McNeil, who plays a considerable part in the events which are to follow, was a Scotchwoman, of reputed property-worth, who came to this country before the Revolution and settled at Fort Edward. She was said to be an own cousin of the General Fraser, afterwards killed at the battle of Bemis Heights. She married Alexander Campbell, and to them at Argyle, Scotland, was born Catherine, who married Robert Hunter, to whom was born a daughter Polly, afterwards married to Peter B. Tierce or Tearse, a Huguenot and officer in the American army whom she met in New York. He was later on very prominent in the early history of the State in Washington and Warren counties, and some of his and Polly Hunter's descendants live in Glens Falls to this day.

(Edgar Hull is authority for the statement that widow Mc-Niel at one time, and Peter B. Tearse at another, owned the whole of lot 141, Argyle Patent.)

Robert Hunter died, conditions changed, and the family came to America; Mr. Campbell dying during the passage, and Mrs. Hunter a year after coming to New York City, where they had settled.

After a time Mrs. Campbell married a Mr. McNeil and removed to the Town of Queensbury, on a large tract of land; but Mr. McNeil also dying, his widow and her granddaughter, as already stated, settled in Fort Edward, not far from the site near the corner of Bridge Street and Broadway.

She afterwards took again the name of Mrs. Campbell to distinguish her from another "Widow McNeil" in the vicinity, thus explaining some accounts which state a Mrs. Campbell was with Jane McCrea.[1]

For some time Jane McCrea had been very intimate with Mrs. McNeil and her granddaughter, so much so as to call the older

---

woman "aunt," although no relation.[1] I believe a modern descendant of Mrs. McNeil has recently published a private booklet highly eulogizing her ancestress, and claiming on what authority, is unknown, that Jennie McCrea was only a hired seamstress who was at the house, to get Mrs. McNeil ready to go to Albany, where she had been urged to remove by her granddaughter's fiancè, the Lieut.-Captain and later Adjutant Peter Bailey Tearse, of Marinus Willett's company heretofore mentioned, who was soon to make a brilliant record at Oriskany.

Be the reason that, or the more romantic one, that having been visiting at Mrs. Jones's, her prospective mother-in-law, she had come to Fort Edward to meet her lover David when he should arrive with Burgoyne's forces, arrayed in finery which attracted the attention of the ferryman Bitely at Jones's Ferry, we do not know. Suffice it to say that on the morning of Sunday, July 27, 1777, she was in Fort Edward and at the house of Mrs. McNeil,[2] Polly Hunter luckily had been sent to Argyle to a friend's with a message and some valuables, preparatory to the setting out for Albany of Mrs. McNeil and herself. In the house besides the two women was a colored slave woman and her baby, it is said, and also a young man named Norman Morrison, who in some way disappears from the story before the capture.

As to what happened on that bright and beautiful July morning, there are as many versions as there are historians who have attempted to write about the affair, and as many perversions as there are sensible and logical accounts of the death of Jane McCrea.

Every one is familiar with the conventional accounts of the Fort Edward tragedy. How, it is claimed, her lover, David Jones, now an officer in Peters's corps of Loyalists, hired a band of savages with a barrel of rum to come and escort her to the British camp, where they were to be married by the British chaplain Brudenell; how becoming over anxious he sent another band under the "ferocious Chief Le Loup," or the "Wyandotte Panther," the first being under Duluth a "good Indian"; how Jane set out willingly with Mrs. McNeil as a companion, with the escort, on

1. W. B. Tearse, Mss. Account.
2. E. B. O'Callaghan, Burgoyne's Orderly Book, Albany (1860) pp. 188-189.

reading a letter from Jones which has never been seen since, and which no one else ever saw; how the second band of savages came up and on reaching a pine tree and spring near the top of Fort Edward hill the entire body of Indians began to quarrel over the promised reward, and as to which was to conduct the girl to Jones; how in accordance with Indian custom (?) in such cases of dispute, one of the chiefs either tomahawked or shot Jane, and scalped her; and how, then, the band subjected the body to mutilation, it being claimed to have had several knife and hatchet or shot wounds upon it when found by the Americans; how the body was stripped of the wedding finery and hid in the brush; how the two bands then took their way to the British camp dragging Mrs. McNeil, a very corpulent and heavy person with them, in a state of practical nudity, to the horror and dismay of her relative, General Fraser, who found nothing large enough to cover her but his military cloak; how on the delivery of the scalp to Jones he is said to have driven the Indians away in a mad frenzy, then to have become semi-insane; and to have passed the rest of his life in Canada a moody, saddened and misanthropic man, who religiously observed the anniversary of Jane's death in seclusion; how General Burgoyne threatened to hang Le Loup or the chief in command who had done the dastardly deed, and on being prevented by his officers for political reasons curtailed the privileges of the Indians to such an extent that before the next battle they had left him in disgust; how Gates took advantage of the murder to verbally castigate Burgoyne in his messages to him on the subject, and how this death of an unprotected and defenseless woman aroused all America to seek revenge on the British; all this, as is well known, is part of the commonly accepted version of the death of Jane McCrea.

Over seventy-five years ago, however, local and other historians began to find inconsistencies in the tale that puzzled them, and soon other and pretendedly correct versions began to appear, each based upon one of several alleged lines of evidence. These various sources for these differing stories may be briefly mentioned here so as to have their true value in our final summation of the affair.

First Source:

As soon as the news of the death of Jane McCrea reached the

American army, one of the first acts of Gates upon superceding Schuyler, was to address a scathing communication to General Burgoyne, in reply to a request of Burgoyne for kindly treatment of British prisoners by Gates, accusing him of instigating the Indian outrages, and conniving at them. To this General Burgoyne indignantly replied, alleging the affair to have been an accident caused by the fortuitous meeting of the two bands of Indians and their quarreling over the girl.[1]

Second Source:

The story of Albert Baker of Sandy Hill as related in old age by his son Caleb Baker, and published in various forms in the early part of the last century, though full of inconsistencies, had believers for a while. Baker was at Fort Edward at the time, but "under suspicion by Schuyler", was separated by nearly half a mile of dense forest from the spot, and it is extremely doubtful that he ever saw anything of the tragedy.

According to the legend he claimed that he was one of a party sent out from the fort after the attack, and that when they reached the spot the victim was breathing her last.[2] Also that she was shot in the side by the American troops then engaged in a skirmish with the Indians.

Third Source:

The admissions of the Indians themselves, that they had slain Jane. They appeared at the tavern of the Tory William Griffith on a by-road to Sandy Hill, having with them their captive Mrs. McNeil, and exhibiting the reeking scalp of Jane Mc-Crea, recognizable to all who knew the girl, both from the abnudance of the hair, and its striking coloration. It is claimed by Dr. Holden, that the scalp of Jane was also exhibited by the savages, at the old Wing homestead, about where the present "Old Ladies' Home" now stands on Warren Street in the City of Glens Falls. Here it was seen and recognized by Mr. Wing's daughter "Tenty" Higson, who had been Jane's friend and confidante during her love affair with Jones.[3]

---

1. These letters are printed in full in Baxter's Digby's Journal, pp. 261-265, q. v.

2. For Baker's statement see Holden's McCrea Scrap Book, pp. 113-115.

3. Holden's Queensbury, p. 72; also Rev. C. P. Wing's History of the Wing Family, Carlisle, Pa., (1881) pp. 99-102.

Also in this same connection there is the statement made years afterwards to Franklin B. Hough, by Eleazer Williams (the alleged lost dauphin) that Thomas Williams, a Caughnawaga Indian and a descendant of Eunice Williams of Deerfield massacre fame, was offered the reward by Jones to bring Jane to him. He refused, but afterwards two parties, each ignorant of the other's errand, set out, found the maiden as related, and in a quarrel slew her with a tomahawk blow.[1]

Fourth Source:

There are various semi-contemporaneous accounts to be considered, such as the letter of Dr. John Bartlett, surgeon in the American army, written from Moses Creek (now Moses Kill) the night of the 27th;[2] Newspaper Items collected by Frank W. Moore;[3] Dr. Thatcher's entry in his Journal of September 2nd;[4] Memoirs of General Heath under date of August 14th;[5] Rev. Wheeler Case's Poem on Jane McCrea;[6] Annual Register (London) for year 1777;[7] Journal of Sergt. Lamb;[8] Memoirs of Marquis De Chastellux;[9] Gordon's History;[10] Burgoyne's State of the Expedition;[11] Papers of Capt. Rufus Lincoln;[12] Gen. E. Hoyt's Mss. History of Burgoyne's Invasion;[13] Anburey's Travels;[14] Digby's Journal;[15] Andrew's History of the War;[16] and a number of others which need not be mentioned here.

Fifth Source:

Mrs. McNeil who was Jane's companion on this direful day, never saw her alive after the savages and their captives reached the forks at the Fort Edward hill, where the two groups separated. Mrs. McNeil's bulk and lack of agility delaying the band which was conducting her. Her narrative on that occasion, however, has been the basis for many of the printed reports, she stat-

1. Hough's History of St. Lawrence and Franklin Counties, p. 201.
2. Holden's McCrea Scrap Book, p. 55, also New England Genealogical Register, p. 31.
3. F. W. Moore's Diary of American Revolution, pp. 475-476.
4. Dr. Thatcher's Journal, p. 114.
5. Heath's Memoirs, (1798) (reprint of 1904) pp. 135-141.
6. Revolutionary Memoirs, (Dodd Reprint 1852), pp. 37-39, with Asa Fitch Letter, pp. 56-65.
7. Annual Register, London (1781), pp. 156-157.
8. R. Lamb, Journal of American War, Dublin (1809), pp. 145-147.
9. Memoirs of Marquis Chastellux, v. I, p. 417.
10. Dr. William Gordon, D. D. History, v. II, pp. 543-545.
11. Burgoyne's State of the Expedition (ed 1780) pp. 64, 546.
12. Capt. Rufus Lincoln Papers (1904) p. 15.
13. Hoyt's Mss. in Proceedings N. Y. Hist. Soc. June 1, 1847.
14. Anburey's Travels, v. 1, p. 327.
15. Digby's Journal, pp. 262-265.
16. Andrews' History of the War, (London, 1786), pp. 393-394.

ing that Jane was tomahawked by one of the two parties of Indians. Dr. Gordon saying in a foot note: "This is the substance of the relation given by Mrs. McNeil, who was in company with Miss M'Rea when taken by the Indians."[1] This statement of Dr. Gordon's should be borne in mind in connection with the entirely different story told by Mrs. McNeil in her old age.

We now come to one of the strangest turns in this strange tale. Among the prominent men of Warren County and afterwards of Saratoga, during the first half of the last century was the Hon. William Hay; a good lawyer and politician, a judge, a newspaper man, poet, literateur and historian. His only faults were a disposition to write history along his own preconceived ideas and from a somewhat different standpoint than others, and a Scotch obstinacy which prevented him ever receding from a position once assumed. He was a great friend of my father, and many of his letters have given me, as they did my father, valuable hints on local points. He however firmly believed that Jane had been killed by a party of American troops pursuing the Indians from the fort,[2] and claimed to have evidence, which was never submitted to anyone so far as I know, that this was a fact. Had he stopped there, all would have been well, but it seems in some way that this "new information" came to the attention of the late Benson J. Lossing, the most industrious historical publisher, compiler and writer our country has ever seen. Lossing did much valuable work, and rescued many facts from oblivion, but he also did much mischievous work, which from his popularity and presumed ability, will, I fear, place many a stumbling block in the way of accurate historical writing in this State for years to come.

Lossing, about 1848, "discovered" in Fort Edward Mrs. Polly Finn, wife of William Finn, and granddaughter of Polly Hunter and Peter Bailey Tearse, and great great granddaughter

---

1. Dr. Gordon's History, v. II, p. 544.

2. Judge Hay wrote a historical novel concerning 'Burgoyne's Campaign" and containing a Correct Account of its Chief Incident the Decease of Jane McCrea," which was published in the Glens Falls Republican, beginning March 20 and ending May 22, 1860. This work contains much valuable local information in the shape of foot notes to the narrative. The version of Jane's death however was derived, according to Judge Hay, from an interview with Polly Hunter Tearse, in 1827, she being at that time a woman of about seventy. It must be borne in mind however that Polly Hunter's knowledge of the affair, like that of Mrs. McNeil, was derived at the time entirely from others, so must be treated carefully as hearsay.

therefore of Mrs. McNeil. Mrs. Finn was then about sixty years old, and her story entirely traditionary, but so far as I ever knew, with no documentary evidence to support it. Still, relying on it, she having evidently told it so long as to convince herself, Lossing brought out a new version of the McCrea story in which he strongly claimed she was killed by the rifle shots of pursuing Americans, who had come out to rescue Jane and their advanced picket guard.[1] And sad to say this misversion has received the sanction of some of the best historians of the time, including that of the late Judge James Gibson of Salem, in spite of the fact that there is not one single scintilla of evidence I have ever seen to support it.

Later on William L. Stone the younger, gave credence and circulation to the Hay version[2] which closely resembled the Lossing one, so far as the shooting by the Americans was concerned. Thus by his prominence adding to the confusion already created and to the doubts beginning to arise in the minds of historical writers.

During the compilation of my father's articles on the McCrea affair, Mr. Stone, over his own signature, receded from his position in this matter and accepted my father's conclusion, that the Maid of Fort Edward was killed by the Indians; but years after, in the History of Washington County,[3] he returned to his former views.

The question of the shooting by the Americans can briefly be disposed of by considering:

First, That Burgoyne was more bitterly assailed for this one happening of warfare than for anything else in his campaign, not only by the enemies he had made, but by his friends. Edward Burke made it, as is well known, the occasion for one of his most celebrated oratorical efforts before parliament, and was backed by Lord Chatham in his position.

Seeking for every excuse to exculpate himself from blame, one of the readiest debaters, and most powerful of personal advocates,

---

1. Lossing's Field Book American Revolution, New York, (1851), vol I, pp. 96-101; id. Life and Times of Philip Schuyler, New York, (1883), vol. II, pp. 250-254.
2. W. L. Stone's Version of Murder of Jane McCrea in Historical Magazine, (April, 1867); id. in Galaxy (Jan. 1867); in Beach's Indian Miscellany, pp. 379-386; in Burgoyne's Campaign, pp. 338-345.
3. W. L. Stone's History of Washington County, N. Y. (1901), pp. 185-211.

neither at the time, nor later when brought to trial in England, did Burgoyne disclaim responsibility for the killing of Jane Mc-Crea by the Indians, nor modify his indignation at the savages, nor his willingness to punish the perpetrator, even at the expense of losing the Indians' services by so doing. That he would not have grasped with avidity the chance to fling back upon Gates the burning reproaches of that general on this occasion, had the deed been done by the Americans, none but a most prejudiced historian would deny.[1]

Second, Not one of the many authorities consulted by my father or myself, especially the earlier contemporary journals, diaries and papers anywhere state that she was shot by the Americans, but do state positively that she was killed by the Indians.[2]

Third, Fonblanque, Burgoyne's biographer, who searched high and low for letters, papers, and authorities with which to prepare his very exhaustive work, does not deny that Jane McCrea was killed by Burgoyne's Indians, and especially quotes in this connection a letter from one of the McCreas seeking patronage from Burgoyne, and endorsed in the latter's hand as follows: "From Capt. McCrea (1782) brother to Miss McCrea who was murdered by the Indians during the campaign of 1777."

Burgoyne always claimed the killing was accidental, but never that it was not done by the Indians. Why then should American historians seek to show such a deed was done by the Americans?

Fourth, By recently published soldiers' journals we are advised that: "July 23 Fort Edward evacuated & destroyed by our peoples & retired to Moses Creek."[3]   Again "at the aproch of Gen¹ burgoynes Army, Gen¹ Schyler Evacuated Fort Edward and their postes at moses creek and Retreeted on the 28th to Saratoga twenty miles from fort Edward and but 36 above Albany."[4]

By Dr. Holden's researches it was determined that there were but a few men at the fort on the 27th, merely a rear guard to pro-

1.   Burgoyne's State of the Expedition, pp. 98-101; Substance of General Burgoyne's Speeches in Mr. Vyner's Motion, Dublin, (1778) pp. 8-10; also note in appendix to same; E. B. DeFonblanque's Life of Burgoyne, London, (1876), pp. 242-245, 256-260.
2.   Vide Frank Moore's Diary of the Revolution, New York (1860) vol. I, pp. 475-476, for newspaper extracts from Pennsylvania Evening Post of August 12, 1777; in which it is stated that she was shot and mutilated by the savages. Vide note p. 476.
3.   Baldwin's Journal, p. 112.
4.   Capt. Rufus Lincoln Papers, p. 115.

tect stragglers, the main body having gone a few days before. So that even had it been desirable there was no force there to go forth in pursuit of Indians, and in fact at the immediate time no one in the fort knew that Jane McCrea had been killed. Why then should there have been any pursuit?

The whole weight of evidence therefore, is against any theory except the original one regarding the real slayers of Jane McCrea.

Fifth, A contemporary diary showing there was no large number of soldiers at Fort Edward, says:

Saturday 26th. "This morning came an express informing Major Whiting was attacked. A reinforcement was immediately sent off and Gen Larned with 500 men went around to come off the backs of them. But it rained hard and prevented this design. On their return we learnt that an advance guard of twenty men from Major Whiting being posted on a hill was attacked, in which a Lieutenant and seven were killed and a number wounded. They also took two women out of a house, killed and scalpt them; our people repaired to the fort defended it and drove them off.

Sunday 27th. This day the Lieutenant and Miss McCray was brought up and buried here [four miles below Fort Edward], the Lieutenant under arms his name was Van Vacken [Van Vechten] of Vandikes regiment."[1]

It will be noted that this entry is merely heresay evidence but confirms the killing of Jane by the Indians. A rather queer error is the date which this soldier says was Saturday the 26th, it having always been understood to have been on Sunday the 27th.

Sixth, Another argument against the shooting of the girl by the Americans, and that she was killed by the Indians, is furnished by the fact that the Indians took her scalp, and at a time subsequent to their attack on the block house.

I had always understood that while renegades and half breeds might scalp a person whom they had not killed, that chiefs of the pure blood would not stoop to such a deed.

I therefore asked the opinion of the State Archeologist A. C. Parker on this point, and received the following letter partly confirming my belief:

1. Diary of Capt. Benjamin Warren, Journal of American History, (1909), No. II, pp. 204-205.

Geological Hall, Albany, N. Y.,
May 28th, 1912.

Hon. Jas. A. Holden,
State Historian,
Albany, N. Y.

Dear Mr. Holden:

In reply to your letter of the 23rd, relative to the scalping customs of the western Indians and Iroquois, I wish to say that I have never been able to find a record fully authenticated which would establish the fact that any Indians ever scalped dead bodies which they might happen to find. Of course, it is well known that scalping was practised when an enemy had been shot or otherwise killed in battle or on raids against settlements. One of the customs was the first two warriors who reached it first might touch the head of a person just shot and add this fact to their war honors, calling such an act a "coo." With the western Indians especially, feathers were cut and marked to represent the number of "coo's" which might be credited to a warrior's battle honors.

Your statements about the killing of Jane McCrea bring up a number of interesting points and I shall take pains to investigate, as far as I can, the facts of the story and see what may be made out of it from an ethnological standpoint. It always seemed to me that the story was capable of criticism but I had not studied it critically. I presume the picture of this event as published by the Glens Falls Insurance Company[1] has given renewed stimulus to the interest in the story.

Very truly yours,

(Signed)   ARTHUR C. PARKER,
                                      Archeologist.

Seventh, The tradition in the McCrea family was that Jane was killed by the Indians while quarreling over her ransom. And this tradition is given currency both by Wilson,[2] her biographer,

----

1. Mr. Parker's reference is to the very popular and most artistic Historical Calendars of the Glens Falls Insurance Company. These calendars with their sketches of historical events in the vicinity of Glens Falls, painted by the best artists procurable for the work in this country, and their interesting and generally accurate letter-press descriptions of the events, prepared by the able and facile pen and brain of the Company's president, Col. John L. Cunningham, began in 1900 with a picture and sketch of Jane McCrea. This had become so rare and unobtainable, that this year (1912) the company decided to issue another Jane McCrea calendar. A copy of the pictorial design, is given elsewhere.

2. D. Wilson's Life of Jane McCrea, New York, (1853), pp. 105-106.

and by Prof. Benj. Silliman,[1] whose "Tour Between Hartford and Quebec" is considered a standard work.

When an eye witness and family tradition agree it would seem proof conclusive to unbiased minds as to how she met her death.

Eighth, Washington Irving in his Life of Washington claimed to have obtained information from one of the McCrea descendants,

---

1. The McCrea tradition copied in the second edition of Prof. Silliman's "Tour" follows:

"Feby., 7, 1824—The following letters, which have recently appeared in the public prints, are worthy of being preserved in this place:

From the Mohawk (N. Y.) Herald.
MURDER OF MISS McCREA.

Florida, Dec. 27, 1823.

Dear Sir:—

There was no event during our revolutionary struggle with Great Britain, that created more sympathy than the tragical fate of Jane McCrea. The time, and every circumstance attending that transaction, was peculiarly fitted to harrow up the minds of men to resistance and revenge. Wherever the story was told (and it was told throughout the continent with the rapidity of lightning) every bosom was thrilled as by an electric shock, and beat in unison. Young as I was, the horrors of the scene impressed my mind so deeply, that forty-six years have in no part effaced it. But the subsequent writers of that period of our history have related the story very differently. In order to correct in season every mistake, I lately requested Colonel McCrea, of Saratoga, to state all the facts, as they were known and believed in the family. This gentleman was nephew to Jane McCrea, and is distinguished for candor and probity, and is perhaps better able to tell the story than any other living witness. The following is an extract from his letter. I hope you will think with me that it ought to be preserved, and give it a place in the Herald. I am &c.,

S. REYNOLDS.

Ballston, July 15, 1822.

Sir—It is with no small degree of diffidence I undertake to commit to paper that which is known in our family concerning the late Jane McCrea; and in yielding to this, I do it solely with a view of complying with your request of transmitting to posterity, something more of her history than is at present extant. Miss Jane McCrea, who was killed by the Indians at Fort Edward, in July 1777, was the second daughter of the Rev. James McCrea, formerly pastor of a congregation in Lamington, New Jersey, but died previous to the revolution. His eldest son Col. John McCrea, had become a resident of Albany before his father's death, and his sister Jane directly repaired to his house, and resided with him. In the year, seventy three, they removed to that part of this county now known by the name of Northumberland, on the west side of the Hudson River, about three miles north of Fort Miller Falls, and he was here when his sister was killed. This was on Sunday morning, and it was evening before he received the fatal news. Early the next day, he sent his family to Albany, and repaired himself to the American camp, where he found his sister's corpse, shockingly mangled,—Two of the neighboring women, whom he had brought with him, washed and dressed her remains, and he had her interred with one Lieutenant VanVechten, three miles south of Fort Edward. She was twenty-three (23) years of age, of an amiable and virtuous character, and highly esteemed by all her acquaintances. She was at the time on a visit to a family in the neighborhood of Fort Edward. A Mrs. McNeil had persuaded her to remain till the Monday following. Here she was concealed in the cellar, when the Indians arrived, who, after ransacking the house, discovered her retreat, and drew her out by the hair, and placing her on a horse, proceeded on the road towards Sandy Hill. They had gone but a short distance, when they met another party of Indians, returning from Argyle, where they had killed the family of Mr. Bains. This party disapproved of taking Miss McCrea to the British Camp, and one of them struck her with a tomahawk, and tore off her scalp. It was said, and generally believed, that she was engaged in marriage to Captain David Jones, of the British Army. Captain Jones survived her only a few years, and died, as was thought of grief. I am, sir, your most obedient servant &c,

JAMES McCREA.

Dr. S. Reynolds.

then living in Ohio. His version differs from the rest, in that he declares Jane herself to have offered the reward to be conducted to Jones after her capture, which is a plausible theory under the circumstances.[1]

Ninth, While quoted by Sparks, and alluded to in Holden's narrative, it has remained for the Hon. Edgar Hull of Fort Edward to bring forth the most positive evidence yet produced as to the McCrea tragedy—namely, the actual affidavit of the only eye witness of the affair, a soldier by the name of Samuel Standish. All the other accounts of the murder are based generally on pure hearsay. This, however, is the tale of the one man who was present at the time and presumably saw the affair as it was, and who swears that he did so see it.

We are now prepared to bring together the loose ends and give as true version of the "Death of Jane McCrea" as can be adduced from the varied stories which time, tradition and historians have accumulated during the almost century and a half since the commission of the crime.

Some time in the latter part of 1776, David Jones had gathered together a lot of his Tory neighbors and with his brother Samuel had joined the British army, being assigned to Peters' Corps of Rangers.[2] So that Col. McCrea who had gone with Montgomery on his fatal campaign against Quebec and had ever since done what he could for the American cause, opposed the union; but there is reason to believe that "twixt love and duty," love had its way as usual. A certain David Freel, accounted as a neer-do-well of the day, was their go between, and one day it is said brought this letter to the maiden:

Skeensboro', July 11th, 1777.

"Dear Friend: ·

I have ye opportunity to send you this by William Ramsey, hoping through Freel it will come safe to hand. Since last writing, Ty has been taken, and we have had a battle, which no doubt you have been informed of before this. Through God's mercy I escaped destruction, and am well at this place, thanks be to Him. The rebels cannot recover from the blow yt has been struck, and

1. Washington Irving's Works, New York Ed. (1860) v. III, pp. 140-147.
2. Reid's Reminiscences, p. 26.

no doubt the war will now soon end. Such should be the prayer of all of us. Dear Jenny, I do not forget you though, much there is to distract in these days, and hope I am remembered by you as formerly. In a few days we will march to Ft. Edward, for which I am anxious, where I shall have the happiness to meet you, after long absence. I hear from Isaac Vaughn, who has just come in, that the people on the river are moving to Albany. I hope of your brother John goes you will not go with him, but stay at Mrs. McNeil's, to whom and Miss Hunter give my dutiful respects. There I will join you. My dear Jenny, these are sad times, but I think the war will end this year, as the rebels cannot hold out, and will see their error. By the blessings of Providence I trust we shall yet pass many years together in peace. Shall write on every occasion that offers, and hope to find you at Mrs. Mc. No more at present:—but believe me yours aff'tly till death,
                                                    DAVID JONES.''[1]

Now, so far as known, this is the only letter that Jane received from Jones before her murder, and does not even intimate he was to send for her, in fact it is said Jones always denied this part of the story.[2] As the story goes, Col. McCrea who after the evacuation of Fort Edward had charge of the rear guard with headquarters at Moses Creek, or Kill, urged Jennie to go with him and his family to Albany, in fact insisted upon it.[3] She, it is said, as will be seen later, declined to go. Staying all night anyway with Mrs. Jones, she crossed the ferry the next morning, and the ferryman for Philander Doty who ran the ferry at the old Rogers place in Moreau, and who knew she had been visiting Mrs. Jones, noticed especially, evidently being an "observing man," that she was dressed in her best outfit of clothes and wore what he afterwards naturally described as "her wedding cap."[4]

Arriving at her "Aunt" McNeil's house, she found all in confusion. Polly Hunter's lover, Adjutant Peter B. Tearse, had urged them to go to Albany which they had decided to do. Polly Hunter had gone to a neighbor's in Argyle for some things Mrs. McNeil did not want left behind. A colored slave "Eve" and her baby

---

1. D. Wilson's Life of Jane McCrea, pp. 65-66.
2. W. L. Stone's, Burgoyne Campaign, pp. 311-312.
3. Irving's, Life of Washington, New York (1860) v. III, pp. 140-147. Version derived from a niece of Miss McCrea.
4. Letter from Dr. Asa Fitch to E. B. O'Callaghan in Burgoyne's Orderly Book, pp. 188-189.

were at the house and a young man by the name of Norman Morrison had two horses there, although this part of the story is much in dispute. It is said he had gone for a side saddle at a neighbor's. At any rate he comes in and disappears from the scene very mysteriously. However, whether Jane walked or was dragged to her fate, or rode, is immaterial, except for the purpose of adding artistic embellishment to an old tale.

Upon the brow of Fort Edward hill was an old dilapidated block-house, a survival from the days of Amherst. A small picket or squad of Americans commanded by Lieutenant Tobias Van Vechten was in charge of the spot. The number at the fort is variously estimated from 100 to 300 men, too few to either attack or defend from an unknown force. They were anxiously waiting the report of Van Vechten as to the nearer approach of Burgoyne's forces to fall back to Moses Kill, on the rear guard.

This was on Sunday morning. Two days previous a party of Indians said to have been headed by an Iroquois chief named Le Loup, and by others a chief called "The Wyandot Panther," but by later authorities called a Winnebago, were scouting near Argyle.

In revenge it is said for the killing of one of their number by the fort at New Perth or Salem, they attacked a family by the name of Allen on the way to Fort Edward and wiped out the entire household. John Allen was a farmer living three-fourths of a mile north-easterly from the present South Argyle. The family was surprised at dinner and horribly butchered. Allen, his wife and sister-in-law, three children and three slaves belonging to his father-in-law, George Kilmore, fell victims to the Indians' ferocity. Allen was shot, the others knifed and tomahawked, and all scalped.[1] The tragedy was not known till the following Sunday morning, nor by the neighborhood generally until Monday night, when they went into fortified camp at Cossayuna Lake, or found their way through savage-infested woods to the American camp.[2]

This band of savages laid perdu until Sunday, when suddenly to the amazement of the picket at the top of Fort Edward hill they were surrounded by 200 yelling [3] ferocious appearing hostile Indians, who poured in volleys of shot upon them.

---

1. It is also stated that a family by the name of Bains or Baines and one John White were massacred the same day. Holden's Jane McCrea Scrap Book, p. 142. 2. Arthur Reid, Reminiscences of the Revolution, Utica, (1859), pp. 17-23. 3. Edgar Hull, Letter, August 17, 1912.

LIEUT. VAN VECHTEN'S GRAVE
(Near this spot the first interment of Jane's body was made)

THE DR. NORTON HOUSE
(Fort Edward.)
In the rear of this house stood the log cabin of Mrs. McNeil from which
Jane was taken by the Indians to her death

The official report of this affair which was discovered by Dr. Holden in the Revolutionary Papers of the State is as follows:

Extract of a Letter from Albany dated 28th July.

(Miscel. Pap. 39:405.)

"Last Friday arrived here part of Genl. Glover's Brigade, the remainder have arrived since together with Genl. Lincoln— This will give new life to our Army to the northward—We have just had a brush with the Enemy at Fort Edward in which Lt. Tobias Van Veghten was most inhumanly butcher'd and Scalped, two Serjeants and two privates were likewise killed and Scalped —one of the latter had both his hands cut off."[1]

In some way the name of Lieutenant Palmer has become mixed up with the tragedy. Mr. Hull, in an article in the Fort Edward Advertiser,[2] claims from his researches that Lieutenant Palmer was not a myth, but had some part in the skirmish and was also killed.

In one account Lieutenant Palmer [3] was designated to escort Mrs. McNeil and family, and while waiting for her to pack he went up the hill to reconoitre.

Be that as it may, it was only a little while after noon, when a soldier passed the McNeil house on the run, and called out to them that the Indians were coming. Mrs. McNeil looked out, saw the savages[4] approaching, and having hurried the others down into the cellar, tried to climb down herself, but being so fleshy she is said to have caught in the trap-hole where she was discovered by the Indians, who following the flying soldiers, saw the house and turned aside for plunder. Dragging her out of the cellar-way, some of them went down, and catching sight of the light dress of Jane McCrea pulled her out, by the hair of the head, the negress and her baby in the gloom of the cellar escaping capture.

Both Mrs. McNeil and Jane had their clothing torn off by the savages, either at this time or later on. One version has it that the Indians tried to put Jane and Mrs. McNeil on the waiting horses,

---

1. Copied from Calendar of New York Historical Mss. "Revolutionary Papers" vol. II, p. 256. 2. Fort Edward Advertiser, Nov. 18, 1889. 3. Stone's History of Washington County, New York, (1901), pp. 187-188.
4. The words savages and Indians have been used interchangeably in this article without regard to their ethnic values. The loyal Six Nations were with St. Leger under Sir John Johnson. It has always been understood that those with Burgoyne were mostly Canada middle west Indians, of Algonquin origin, or remote Iroquoian stock.

but Mrs. McNeil could not stay on for want of a side saddle, so one of the captors carried or dragged her along, while Jane's horse was led. Another version is that both were dragged along. Now from where the house stood to the top of the hill, where the old military road came out, is about one hundred rods, and from there to the fort is sixty rods [1] or about one half a mile in all, with trees between preventing sight of it from the fort.

Among the plunder taken from the house was a bed, a kettle and a looking-glass. In one account there is mention made of this glass, stating that the Americans next day found the broken mirror hanging on a shrub. The frame of the glass is today in the possession of a lady in Glens Falls, a lineal descendant of Polly Hunter Tearse.

When the two females arrived at the foot of the hill the roads or trails diverged, one going over the hill to the right, the other to the left. Here the two bands were separated and Mrs. McNeil, as has been stated, never saw Jane again alive or dead. She was taken to the British camp, as has been claimed, in an almost naked condition. She lived to a good old age, and being a very gossipy as well as intelligent and interesting talker, although possibly a bit fond of enlargement, according to contemporaries,[2] in the course of time the story grew in her mind, inaccuracies crept in, as they always will with oft repeated stories, especially as old age comes along, and at last the tale of her old days differed in many ways from the one she first told, and which Dr. Gordon recorded in his history.

Now comes the only written contemporary story we have, of how Jane died. In his investigations Mr. Hull some time ago wrote to his then Congressman, the Hon. Wm. H. Draper of the Washington-Saratoga district, asking for a copy of the application for a pension made by Samuel Standish, whose last days were spent in Hartford, N. Y., who was wounded in the affray at the blockhouse, and who was the only living witness of Jane's death.

After unraveling considerable red tape, the Commissioner of Pensions furnished the following letter, which through the courtesy and kindness of Mr. Hull, I insert in its entirety:

----

1. Edgar Hull, Letter, (May 19, 1912).
2. Burgoyne's Orderly Book, pp. 183-184.

August 28, 1911.

IIon. William H. Draper,
    House of Representatives.
Dear Mr. Draper:

In reply to your letter dated the 24th and received the 25th instant, I have the honor to furnish you the following account of the murder of Jane McCrea, related by Samuel Standish in his application for pension, Sur. File No. 28,889.

"The next morning (after the battle of Fort Ann) they marched to Fort Edward and while there he was with others called on to relieve a guard on a hill north of the Fort went and relieved the guard and had not been there long before he heard an Indian scream and Instantly was fired upon by them. he ran towards the River and Fort & before he arrived he met three Indians coming from the River between him and the Fort who all fired upon him, but missed him, where he was taken prisoner by them taken up the hill again near a spring, was there stripped of his hat, coat & handkerchief and pinyoned by them and after a short time he saw a party of Indians coming with two women they came up the hill to a spring and there they seemed to be in a quarrel, they shot one of the women and scalped her, this woman he knew to be Jennet McCrea he had seen her before the Americans offered to take her down the river she refused to go said she was not afraid to stay the other woman was old Mrs. McNeil aunt to Miss McCrea"

                            Very respectfully,
    (Signed)   J. L. DAVENPORT,
                                    Commissioner.

Surely this letter, which confirms some of the accounts of the affair, ought to an unprejudiced mind, settle positively the question of who killed Jane McCrea, and how the deed was done.

The body was then mutilated by the knives of the party and the scalp taken. It is of course very possible and very probable she was also tomahawked, perhaps as she fell, to make sure of her death.

The Indians next rolled the bodies of Van Vechten and Jane down a declivity, and covered them with leaves and brush, hanging her shoes on a branch near by, which the following day led to the discovery of her body. The killing is said to have taken place near an old pine tree and beside a spring.

It is hard to destroy the romance and tradition which have hung around the old spring near the road so long, or to cast a doubt on the pine tree which died about 1849, was cut down by George Harvey in 1853 and made into souvenirs by J. M. Burdick later of Glens Falls, but then of Fort Ann, at his factory soon afterwards, especially as I have been told by one who claimed to be conversant with the facts, that almost a whole pine grove was used up in making these souvenirs so great was the demand. But as a boy I can remember my father pointing out a house with a stone wall on the left side of the road leading down to Fort Edward and saying that Jane McCrea was killed in the old road, not far from a spring and tree several [1] rods (say forty or fifty) over from the supposed place of tradition. It is stated by older historians that this hill was full of springs long since dried up, by the cutting down of the original forest. However no one knows exactly the real place, and if it pleases people to believe the present spring the real one, let no historian no matter what he believes personally take that comfort from them, for she was certainly killed on Fort Edward hill. In this connection, the following extract may be of interest:

"A writer signing himself "A. S." in the New York Mirror for August 15, 1835, throws doubt of the exact locality.[2] He says 'Miss McCrea was found near a spring on the east side of the present road. She had been dragged from near the block-house adjacent to which the road ran; for the blood was on the sand the next morning * * * the spring on the west side of the road, near a tall stump of a tree, is not the spot where she was found.' "[2]

Dr. John Bartlett in his report to the Surgeon General written from Moses Kill the night of the 27th, at 10 o'clock says the report of the killing came to the fort where he was at two o'clock,[3] and he was unable to find any of the camp surgeons to go out.

Caleb Baker, whose father was a putative eye witness, says the men were afraid to go out.[4] While on the other hand Mrs. Mc-

1. See confirmation of this in Gen. E. Hoyt's Statement, Silliman's Tour Between Hartford and Quebec, 1st Ed. pp. 134-138.
2. Charles A. Campbell in The Magazine of American History (for March 1882) pp. 202-203.
3. Article by the late Dr. Gardner Cox of Holyoke, a collateral descendant of Mrs. McNeil, in Springfield Republican (April 12, 1903).
4. Hon. Henry C. Martindale of Sandy Hill, Letter in New England Palladium about Nov. 17, 1830, reprinted in Warren Messenger (June 29, 1831), republished in Glens Falls Republican (March 26, 1861).

OLD FORT EDWARD CEMETERY

(Stake shows where Jane McCrea was rebuned in 1822)

FORT EDWARD CREEK

Shows building standing on site of old Black House

THE McCREA FARM

On the right of this house on the knoll, stood Col. McCrea's house, where Jane lived

OLD BLOCK HOUSE

Taylor's Farm, Moreau. Old ferry posts in distance. Lower part of barn, showing original timbers

Neil could not get any of the Indians who took her to go back and look for Jane, for fear of the Americans.[1]

According to Albert Baker of Bakers Falls, as told by his son Caleb,[2] it was the next morning before a party went out from the fort in search of the bodies of the men killed the day before. And at that time the body of Jane McCrea, which Dr. Holden says had been rolled part way down the hill, and lodged by a pine tree, was found by Colonel, afterwards Governor Morgan Lewis, as shown by the following extract from a letter to Gates:

Under date of July 28th, Dr. Jonathan Potts, a great admirer and henchman of Gates, writes him from Albany at 8 a. m.

"A letter from Col. Lewis this moment arrived mentions that last evening a party of the enemy of about 1,000 attacked our Picquet near Fort Edward of 150 men drove them in Kill'd five men among whom is a Lieut: they also Kill'd a young Lady Dr. McCrea's Sister, all of whom they scalped & butchered."[3]

Col. McCrea was overcome with the tragedy when he heard of it, and it is recorded that he came with Mrs. Bell, a neighbor, who prepared the body for burial at Moses Kill, where it was interred beside Lieutenant Van Vechten's.[4]

I have but recently heard that there is a tradition in the Bell family, whose descendants still live around Glens Falls, that Mrs. Bell's husband and another neighbor (Durkee) built the rough coffin on the farm, in which Jane's remains were placed.

Edgar Hull says, in addition to the official report of the finding of the bodies: "All accounts agree that the next morning after the three tragedies the bodies of Jane McCrea and Lieutenant VanVeghten were taken from the hill under supervision of Morgan Lewis (afterwards governor) on a boat to a point just north of Three Mile creek and buried beside each other. Both were scalped and mutilated—three bullet holes in the body of the girl, according to Governor Lewis, and one through her breast near her heart, according to Mrs. Bell. In April, 1822, the bones of both were uncovered. His was left there but hers were removed. The late Dr. Asa Fitch of Salem interviewed the eye witnesses of the

1. Dr. Cox's Article in Springfield Republican, vide supra.
2. E. Hull, Letter (Aug. 9, 1912).
3. B. F. DeCosta's, Notes on History of Fort George. p. 36; Gates Mss. p. 39.
4. Holden's, Jane McCrea Scrap Book, p. 147.

disinterment, as stated in Bascom's history, pages 70, etc. The bones of Lieutenant VanVechten now lie 'under the embankment thrown up against the abutment at the point where the earth meets the planking of the bridge over which the road passes' and the 'excavation for the Champlain canal passes within a few feet of the spot where his remains are lying.' Her body was originally interred exactly under the east corner of the south abutment of the canal bridge over which the road passes, a few rods north of the site of the old 'black house' and his body beside her. Perhaps, sometime as we cross the canal bridge to observe Decoration day at the cemeteries we might stop and scratch his name on one of the stones of the abutment or at least fling a flower down on the tow path of the canal within a foot or two of his scalped skull.''[1]

Returning to the British camp, after Mrs. McNeil had scolded Gen. Fraser sufficiently, and he had realized that his statement of a few days before, that Indian atrocities must be winked at in a conquered country, had better have been thought than said, he sent a squad of English soldiers to Argyle, and brought back Polly Hunter to camp. Unable to persuade her to return to Scotland he is reported to have told her—''Polly, Polly I am afraid you have a Yankee lover.''[2] All the world it is said loves a lover, so those with sentiment left to spice a bit of dry history, will rejoice that out of this bloody and unhappy affair, this one romance culminated happily.

Two side incidents may be worth recording here, which have turned up in the course of investigation:

In the town of Upper Lisle this state, is a grave kept marked with an American flag, of the soldier who stood guard over the remains of Jane the night before burial. Dr. Cox in his article in the Springfield Republican states the soldier's name was Elijah Sweet.

The other incident is that:—

Garret G. Lansing of Oriskany, then a boy of sixteen enrolled for service that summer, ''and the next week started with a small detachment of militiamen to reach the northern army.

---

1. Fort Edward Advertiser (Nov. 18, 1909). Since that article appeared in print the local G. A. R. post has erected a marker at the spot for VanVechten.
2. Mss. Account given J. A. H. by late W. B. Tearse of Glens Falls.

This reached Fort Edward when the services over the remains of Miss McCrea had just been commenced. After her burial the detachment marched onward toward the rear of the army."[1]

On April 22nd or 23rd, 1822, the remains of Jane were taken up and re-buried in the old Fort Edward cemetery on State street in that village.[2] It was made the occasion of a considerable observance. It is said the remains were placed in the same grave with Mrs. McNeil's. The late Judge Gibson of Salem, wrote my father regarding the event under date of February 21st, 1884, as follows :

"The *Caldwell Guardian* of contemporaneous issue with the event, gave an account of the first removal of the remains of Jane & their re-interment in the grave of Mrs. McNeil at Fort Edward & the sermon preached by the Rev. Hooper Cummings from Micah 2, 10 (I have a copy Ms. of this article in the Guardian and can lend you if you wish). His fate was almost as unfortunate as that of the maiden over whose remains he thus preached. His wife torn from his side and thrown by the wind into the chasm at Trenton & his own reputation & life sacrificed subsequently by his enemies. He is well called the 'Unfortunate & lamented Rev. Hooper Cummings.' I have other notices of this re-interment published about the same time, from which I see the event must have excited considerable interest."

In 1852 the remains were again moved, this time to the Union cemetery between Fort Edward and Hudson Falls, where they still rest, in an enclosure guarded by an iron picket fence erected by popular subscription and the labor of the school children of Glens Falls, Sandy Hill and Fort Edward, about 1895. The grave is marked by a marble slab erected in 1852 by Sarah Hanna Payne a niece of Jane McCrea, which had been badly scarred by relic hunters and souvenir fiends, before the new iron fence was put up.

Regarding Mrs. Payne; it is through the Rev. O. C. Auringer the poetical biographer of Maid McCrea, as well as archeologist and scholar, that I am enabled to present new evidence in this case.

1. Publications of the Oneida Historical Society, No. 5, (January 13th, 1880.)

2. Bascom's Fort Edward Book, pp. 41-45, 70-73.

Mr. Auringer has shared with me his very recently acquired knowledge that all these years a real McCrea side of the story had rested with Dr. Drury S. Sanford of Long Island, Lake George, and Long Island City, whose great grandmother Mary, a sister of Jane, married the Rev. John Hanna of Clinton, N. J. Their second daughter Catherine married Dr. Samuel G. Torbert of New York, whose youngest daughter Jane Elizabeth espoused Dr. S. T. W. Sanford of Long Island City; Drury S. Sanford, being their son.

Sarah Hanna, sister of Catherine and own niece of Jane, was brought up by Jane's brother Dr. Stephen McCrea of Stillwater, married a Colonel Josiah Payne and afterwards lived on the Northumberland Farm once owned by Colonel John McCrea.

It was Mrs. Payne who after Jane's remains, mutilated by shot holes and knife thrusts, naked, covered with leaves and brush had been found near a spring and an old pine tree on the hill the next day, had first been buried by Colonel McCrea just below Fort Edward, beside the body of Lieutenant VanVechten, and after they had been removed thence and buried in April 1822, with appropriate ceremonies in the old Fort Edward cemetery, in Mrs. McNeil's grave, had them taken up in 1852, and placed, let us hope for all time, in the Union Cemetery between Hudson Falls and Fort Edward, and then erected the present tablet to the memory of her aunt, which forever asserts her belief in the cause of Jane's death.

Her version of the affair, as related to me by Dr. Sanford, as firmly impressed on his mind in his youth was, that Jane was murdered by the Indians, who shot, then tomahawked and scalped her. This contradicts flatly the many erroneous ones so commonly seen, one having been printed as late as last year, which were derived originally from Mrs. McNeil the Tory, who told one story to Dr. Gordon the historian, as already stated, after the war, and another to her descendants living in Fort Edward and vicinity, in her failing old age, when she claimed that the Americans shot Jane while pursuing the Indians. Mrs. Payne's evidence added to that of Standish, that Jane was positively killed by the Indians, would seem to be proof positive that the Americans had nothing to do with her death, accidental or otherwise.

D. A. R. MARKER
On the brow of Port Edward Hill

JANE McCREA'S FINAL RESTING PLACE

On an anniversary of the murder, July 27, 1901, a memorial marker, pyramidal in shape, of Kingsbury blue stone, was erected on the top of Fort Edward hill by the members of Jane McCrea Chapter, D. A. R., with elaborate and appropriate ceremonies. It is inscribed:

Memorial to
JANE McCREA
Massacred near this spot by the Indians
July 27, 1777
Erected by Jane McCrea Chapter D. A. R.

I wish I might for romance's sake pronounce to be true, the commonly accepted story of David Jones's love affair with Jane and his sending the Indians after her, and that they quarreled over the reward; but I find no verification of the story, it being apparently ornamental embroidery of an old tale for fireside consumption and amusement, albeit that a love affair existed between them, and that they hoped in event of Burgoyne's presumed triumph, that they would soon be married, is true.

The main inaccuracies in the McCrea story, which I hope I have, however imperfectly, corrected in this article are:

First, her age. I have shown that she was in her early twenties and not her "teens."

Second, there is nothing to show that Jones ever sent for her to meet him at Burgoyne's camp, and her seizure by the Indians must be considered accidental, and her death, barbarous as it was, an accident of war.

Third, she was killed by the Indians and not by the Americans, in spite of all claims to the contrary.

Fourth, the tree and spot so long claimed as sacred to her memory are of doubtful historic worth and open to question.

Fifth, neither track, vestige nor trace are left of the McNeil hut and the house known as the McCrea house in Fort Edward, never was seen by and never sheltered Jane McCrea, but is in reality the Polly Hunter Tearse home of a later day.

So died Jane McCrea, and so was she buried to await the final call, when let us hope that she and her lover torn apart by the cruelties of war, may once more be reunited.

We have now come, perhaps by devious and winding ways, to the title point of our paper, which is the "Influence of the Death of Jane McCrea upon the Burgoyne Campaign".

As soon as the news of the tragedy which even in those days of lack of easy communication, spread like wildfire, had reached New England it stimulated week-kneed communities to send re-inforcements, even to Schuyler, whom the New Englanders dis-liked. Vermont and New Hampshire were also inspired to do something, badly as they hated New York for the Hampshire Grants matter. In a few days the little force of 2700 continentals, not all of whom were effectives, and 1500 militiamen of Schuyler on July 27, had been augmented by a respectable number of fighting men.

The whole of Northern New York now certain that Bur-goyne's promises of safety were worthless, for every day brought its tales of scalping and killing, came over to the side of the Americans.

Neutrals no longer claimed to be neutral, but cast in their lots with the patriots.[1] Burgoyne found it very difficult to get forage or provender for animals and men. Behind him on the old Johnson and Wood Creek trails the men from the New Hampshire Grants took up their station, after the base at Lake George was at last abandoned, and proceeded to help draw the net closer around the doomed army.

The rumors of the McCrea affair, although perhaps grossly exaggerated at home and abroad, caused a shudder to run over the whole civilized world, losing to Burgoyne for the time being, the moral support and friendly feeling of even his allies, albeit he was simply carrying out his King's orders, and against his own wishes, for he never esteemed the Indians of any use.[2]

As has already been fully stated Gates lost no time in giving to the world his ideas of the matter, and sustained by public opinion it aided him in gaining recruits, getting the support of his army, and uniting a rather disheartened people. Later he was to fall to his proper plane of poor mediocrity, but at this time he had the people with him, like many another braggart and blusterer, whom the world takes at his own figures, only to con-sign to obscurity, when found out.

---

1. Digby's Journal, p. 269.
2. See Burgoyne's State of the Expedition, on this point.

Letters in existence show the alarm of the Americans at this time over the situation. Frantic appeals were made to the legislatures, or their equivalent assemblies of the other states of the federation, and at last stirred by these appeals, these bodies came into line and sent all the aid they could give.

In command of the savages was St. Luc de la Corne, a Frenchman who as an officer under Montcalm, had hung like an avenging spirit on the flanks of the English commanders from 1756 to 1759, and who had marked with blood of the English and Provincials, nearly every foot of the old Military Trail and the Great Carry. He persuaded Burgoyne "for motives of policy" not to punish the murderer of Jane McCrea, on account of the evil influence it would exert on the rest of the Indians, but did not like him, nor did Burgoyne care for St. Luc, esteeming him a double-faced and treacherous ally.[1]

Up in New Hampshire, like Ethan Allen later on, another Achilles sulking in his tent, sat John Stark, peeved because he had not been given a general's commission. New Hampshire, however, hearkening to the urgent call for help, persuaded John Stark to take on the independent command of her forces. I am firmly convinced that one of the determining causes for this, was the hope that he might once more meet his old enemy St. Luc, with whom, as an officer of Rogers' Rangers, during the exciting days of 1755-1760, he had had many a bloody meeting in the country around Lakes Champlain and George, and along the old road from William Henry to Fort Edward, and so settle once for all the old scores.

Stark took command August 8, and soon afterward Bennington was won.

The defection of his Indian allies quickly followed the McCrea affair, on account of Burgoyne's stringent management of them, his restriction of their privileges and barbarities, and compelling them to work under British officers.

This was followed too by St. Luc's practical desertion in the face of the enemy, and by the abandonment of St. Leger by his Indians whom even Sir John Johnson could not keep faithful.[2]

---

1. Burgoyne's State of the Expedition, pp. 48-50, 99-101 LXVII. Also Substance of General Burgoyne's Speech, Dublin, (1788) pp. 5-10; also Appendix. Digby's Journal, pp. 253-254.
2. Ibid. pp. 48-50, 99-101.

About this time New York's Committees of Safety plead for assistance with the other colonies as these extracts from the George Clinton Papers show:

Under date of August 11 the Albany Committee of Safety writes to Governor Clinton—"Should Albany fall in the hands of the Enemy, the savages would take an active part against us." (Probably referring to those of the Six Nations who had remained neutral[1].)

Under date of August 12, the following letter was written from the quarters of the Council of Safety at Kingston—

"It would be very advantageous to have some southern troops, acquainted with the Indian mode of fighting, sent to the Northward to rouse the spirits of our Army there, who shudder at the very appearance of Indians and hardly dare Stir out of their camp."[2]

General Washington in response to appeals for help, wrote the following from his headquarters in Buck County, Pennsylvania, to Major General Gates, under date of August 20:

"From the various representations made to me of the disadvantage the army lay under, particularly the militia, from an apprehension of the Indian mode of fighting, I have dispatched Colonel Morgan with his corps of riflemen to your assistance, and presume they will be with you in eight days from this date. This corps I have great dependence on, and have no doubt but they will be exceedingly useful; as check given to the savages, and keeping them within proper bounds, will prevent General Burgoyne from getting intelligence as formerly, and animate your other troops from a sense of their being more on an equality with the enemy."[3]

In the beginning of my article I called attention to the workings of fate, and in no better way can that theory be exemplified than in this action of Washington. For with the 700 men of Morgan came Timothy Murphy and other sharpshooters who accustomed "to knocking out the eye of a squirrel with a rifle", seriously embarrassed the Burgoyne forces, by picking off their officers. The culmination of the matter came on October 7, when

1. Public Papers of Governor George Clinton, Vol. II, p. 210.
2. Id. p. 217.
3. Spark's Washington's Writings, vol V, p. 37.

Morgan at Arnold's order came to Murphy and twelve of his best shots and pointing out a very active officer in full uniform, said: "That gallant officer yonder is General Fraser. I admire and respect him, but it is necessary for our good that he should die. Take your stations and do your duty."

Within a few minutes a rifle ball cut the crupper through his horse's mane. Calling his attention to this, his aide said to him: "It is evident you are marked out for particular aim; would it not be prudent for you to retire from this place?" Frazer replied: "My duty forbids me to fly from danger."

The third shot was from the rifle of Murphy, and Frazer fell, mortally wounded.

His death so disheartened the British that the moment he fell the tide of battle turned against Burgoyne. "He had lost his best subordinate, the only one of his officers who had the slightest influence with him."

The death of Howe at Ticonderoga delayed the British conquest of America for two years. The death of Frazer at Saratoga made America a Republic.

The general condition of the State and country at this particular time can best be exemplified by the following extracts:

Caleb Stark says, in 1860—"Women yet live who can testify of such days, when they lived in fear of the fate of Miss McCrea the bride of Fort Edward—that Gertrude of Wyoming in real life; when every rustle of a shaken leaf seemed an Indian tread, every tree an Indian covert, every window a mark for his rifle, and every hamlet fully assured that it was singled out, above all others, as the victim of the savage."[1]

The Sexagenary writes:

"The savages that remained with Burgoyne were continually for miles in advance of him, on his flanks, reconnoitering our movements and beating up the settlements. Their cruelty was not to be restrained, and after the death of Miss McCrea, whom I have often seen, they were not all checked by the animadversions and threats of Sir John himself.

My father, on learning the fact of their approach, went immediately over to his brother's house, which was about one-fourth

---

1. Caleb Stark's Memoirs of General John Stark, Concord, (1860), p. 331.

of a mile off, to ascertain what was to be done for the safety of
the families. He found him making every exertion to move
away, and the domestics busily engaged in getting everything
ready. During my father's absence my mother, who was a resolute woman, one fitted for the times in which she lived, was in-
dustriously placing the most valuable of her clothing in a cask;
and at her instance I went with some of our servants to catch a
pair of fleet horses and harness them as fast as possible to the
wagon. To those who now sit quietly in their own shady bowers,
or by the fireside long endeared by tranquility and happiness, I
leave it to be imagined with what feelings we hastened to abandon our home and fly for safety, we knew not whither. The men
of this generation can never know what were the sorrows of
those fathers who saw their children exposed to dangers and to
death, and what the agonies of those mothers who pressed their
offspring to their bosom, in the constant apprehension of seeing
them torn from their embraces to become the victims of savage
cruelty."[1]

Dr. Gordon in his history wrote:

"The murder of Miss McRea exasperated the Americans; and
from that and other cruelties occasion was taken to blacken the
royal party and army. The people detested that army which accepted of such Indian aid, and loudly reprobated that government which could call in such auxiliaries. Gen. Gates was not deficient in aggravating, by several publications, the excesses which
had taken place; and with no small advantage to his own military
operations."[2]

In the Annual Register for 1777, the editor says:

"His (Arnold's) forces were daily increased through the
outrages of the savages, who, notwithstanding the regulations
and endeavours of General Burgoyne, were too prone to the exercise of their usual cruelties, to be effectually restrained by any
means. The friends of the royal cause, as well as its enemies, were
equally victims to their indiscriminate rage. Among other instances of this nature, the murder of Miss M'Crea, which happened some little time after, struck every breast with horror.

---

1. The Sexagenary, Albany, N. Y. (1866) pp. 67-68.
2. William Gordon's History of United States, London, (1788), Vol. II,
p. 545.

Every circumstance of this horrid transaction served to render it more calamitous and afflicting. The young lady is represented to have been in all the innocence of youth, and bloom of beauty. Her father was said to be deeply interested in the royal cause; and to wind up the catastrophe of this odious tragedy, she was to have been married to a British officer on the very day that she was massacred.

Occasion was thence taken to exasperate the people, and to blacken the royal party and army. People were too apt to jumble promiscuously, and to place in one point of view, the cruelties of these barbarians, and the cause in which they were exerted. They equally execrated both. Whilst they abhorred and detested that army, which submitted to accept of such an aid, they loudly condemned and reprobated that government, which could call such auxiliaries into a civil contest; thereby endeavouring, as they said, not to subdue but to exterminate, a people whom they affected to consider, and pretended to reclaim as subjects. General Gates, in the course of these transactions, was not wanting by several publications to aggravate and inflame the picture of these excesses; and with no small effect."[1]

Captain Rufus Lincoln of Wareham, Mass., who kept a journal all through the war, made this note at the time:

"It was at this time that this armey Seemed to Carry all before them, That the New England States, as well as the Congress, acted with that vigure and firmness that Convince their Enemyes that they would not Sink under their past Misfortuanes, and the apperhensions of future dangers by turning out the Militia from all Quarters to oppose their farther progress. It was about this time that Mrs. McCrea and many other peasable inhabitance were Crualy murdred by the Indianes.

And indeed the Ravages they Committed aded much to the number of the American Army. as the Inhabitance Rather Chused to turn out and oppose them the (n) to be Cruely Murdered With their famelys and all that was dear to them.—"[2]

R. Lamb, a non-commissioned officer in the British army wrote:

---

1. Second Edition, London, (1781) p. 156.
2. Papers of Captain Rufus Lincoln, (privately printed 1904), p. 15.

"The terror excited by the Indians, instead of disposing the inhabitants to court British protection, had a contrary effect. This was chiefly occasioned by the murder of Miss M'Crea, a young lady of the neighborhood of Fort Edward."[1]

Dr. Andrews, an English historian, said:

"The resentment occasioned by the conduct of the Indians, and no less the dread of being exposed to their fury, helped considerably to bring recruits from every quarter to the American army. It was considered as the only place of refuge and security at present. The inhabitants of the tracts contiguous to the British army, took up arms almost universally. The preservation of their families was now become an object of immediate concern. As the country was populous, they flocked in multitudes to General Arnold's camp; and he soon found himself at the head of an army, which, though composed of militia, and undisciplined men, was animated with that spirit of indignation and revenge which so often supplies all military deficiencies. * * *

This want of resources was an equal motive of discouragement to the British army, and of encouragement to the Americans. It was not doubted among them, that this alone would be an unsurmountable impediment, and totally obviate the exertions that would otherwise have resulted from the British General's well-known abilities and valour."[2]

P. Stansbury, a famous traveler, a native of New York City, who made a pedestrian's tour of over 2000 miles in New York, New England and Canada, visited the Saratoga battle grounds in September 1821. He said:

"The period between the 19th of September and the second engagement on the 7th of October was full of painful anxiety on the part of the British. Not a day passed without the death of some soldier or officer, shot by the American scouts and marksmen."[3]

---

1. R. Lamb, Journal of the American War, Dublin, (1809), p. 145.
2. Andrews, History of the Late War, London, (1786) pp. 394-395.
3. "Burgoyne's army was as good as cut off from its outposts, while in consequence of its proximity to the American camp, the soldiers had but little rest. The nights also were rendered hideous by the howls of large packs of wolves, that were attracted by the partially-buried bodies of those slain in the action of the 19th. On the 1st of October a few English soldiers, who were digging potatoes in a field a short distance in the rear of headquarters, within the camp, were surprised by the enemy, who suddenly rushed from the woods and carried off the men in the very faces of their comrades". Stone's Burgoyne's Campaign, p. 55.

"And at this moment the Indians, when their assistance was most needed, deserted from the cause under which they had enlisted. Their defection was occasioned by the disappointment of their hopes of plunder and by the notice which Gen. Burgoyne was in honor obliged to take of the cruel massacre of Miss McCrea."[1]

Many other authorities might be quoted in this connection to show the effect of the killing of Jane McCrea upon the public mind.

It may be well to close this series of observations by quoting the most recent English view of the matter, that of our honored guest the Rev. Dr. Belcher who in his lately published work the "First American Civil War" says, anent this occurrence:

"The news of this crime spread all over New England and New York with the rapidity of bad news. Burgoyne was held responsible for the murder. The most violently worded accounts of this outrage were diffused by the Patriot press. It was alleged that the murder had been committed in the presence of 300 regulars, and in sight of an advance party of Americans, who could give no assistance. Similar stories were spread all over the Continent. The literature of the murder of "Jenny McCrea" is considerable.[2] The effect was to involve Burgoyne in augmented embarrassments."[3]

Reid, the historian of Argyle, claims that when the bloody scalps of the Allens and Jane McCrea were brought into Burgoyne's camp near Fort Ann, an aged Indian, already preparing to depart to the Happy Hunting Grounds of his race, viewed these gory relics regretfully and said: "That Army cannot prosper that tolerates the taking of scalps of women and little children."[4]

This prophecy might well have been true, for within the month there came to Burgoyne the reverses at Bennington, the repulses and practical defeat of St. Leger at Oriskany, the secession of his Indian allies, the disasters at Freeman's Farm on Septem-

1. W. L. Stone's, Saratoga Battle Grounds, Albany, (1895), pp. 169-170.
2. "J. Fiske, History of the American Revolution, says of this victim: "How she came by her cruel death was never known." The actual facts proved were few, the amplification of them as intentionally mischievous. Mr. Baxter (editor of Digby's Diary) says she was shot accidentally by Americans, and that her remains being exhumed in later years, there was no sign of her having been scalped. But, for all practical purposes, had the crime been a matter of public observation, as was the assassination of the Empress of Austria, the effect on public opinion could not have been greater.—Fiske, i. 276; Baxter in Digby's Journal, a long note, p. 235."
3. Belcher's First American Civil War, London, (1911), v. II, p. 296, n. 1.
4. Reid's Reminiscences, pp. 29-31.

ber 19, followed by the crushing and decisive defeat at Bemis
Heights on October 7, and to the British the ignominious surrender less than two months from the day the "Maid of Fort Edward" met her death.

The pathway of human progress has in almost all ages led
upwards only through the blood of the martyrs. Whether or not
then Jane McCrea's life was so ordered, that through her sacrifice there should come at that time, as there did, a renaissance of
patriotism, a reawakening of the public spirit, an arousing of
the lion-heart in a dormant population, with the ultimate result
of the birth of a new nation, no man today has the omniscience to
say, and conjecture is our only recourse.

Judging however from the view point of the twentieth century, with the knowledge that through wars and through peace
we are today a mighty nation of nearly an hundred millions, with
a dominion from the rising to the setting sun, controlling the destinies not only of our own but of alien peoples, that we belong to
a land of liberty that has been made possible by the struggles,
sacrifices and privations of a comparative handful of patriots, of
whom our own splendid State supplied its sufficient and able
quota at the time of need; that under one flag, the same that
waved at Oriskany and Saratoga, we stand for self-government,
for the equality of races, and for the freedom of men; while we
pause a moment to drop the roses of love and the amaranths of
remembrance on the grave of Jane McCrea, I believe we may also
feel, that in her death she did not die in vain, and that from her
quiet sepulchre beside the majestic Hudson, there came forth
many of the flowers and blossoms of progress, from whose seeds
this then tiny Republic of ours has grown into one of the might-
iest, wealthiest, most powerful and most important of the nations
of the earth.

APPENDIX

JANE McCREA BIBLIOGRAPHY

APPENDIX 1.

The Location of the Jane McCrea Tree and Spring.

There has been so much discussion as to the location of the Jane McCrea tree and spring, that even at the risk of being considered an iconoclast by destroying old traditions, I have thought it best to insert here the testimony of a Fort Edward resident, which confirms the story told me by my father in my boyhood viz: that the place of the maiden's death was several rods to the eastward of the spot where the so called pine tree was cut down, for making into souvenirs, by George Harvey in 1853, and that the present spring near the railroad track, is not the original spring. Again, since this article was prepared for the Saratoga meeting, a file of the Warren Messenger, published at Glens Falls in the year 1833 has come into my possession. In the issue for Friday, July 26, there is a letter from some unknown writer, under date of July 10, at Sandy Hill, with the details of a visit to that vicinity. The writer gives an account of the tragical story of Miss McCrea, and then speaks of the tree and spring as follows:

"I visited to day the pine tree, near Fort Edward, where, during the Revolution, Janet McCrea met her melancholy fate. The tree is apparently of greater age than any in the neighbouring forest, and from its size, it forms a prominent object on the road. The spring which formerly budded up beneath it and rendered it a resting place for the thirsty huntsman and warrior, has dried up and disappeared, as if abashed by the blood which has stained its chaste waters.—"

In my original article will be found a statement by another visitor to the spring, who likewise verifies the fact that it had disappeared at the time of that person's visit. So that if the spring had dried up at as early a date as this, it is manifestly an impossibility that the present one could be the real "Jane McCrea Spring."

I have lately received from the Hon. Edgar Hull of Fort Edward the following statement of John B. Case, living in one of the houses on the brow of the Fort Edward hill, to which I referred at the beginning of this article, as corroborating my views of the location.

John B. Case of Fort Edward states:

I was born Sept. 1st, 1836, in the old house now occupied by Alfred Case, Jr., which then stood a few rods south of its present location. There was a house, in the cellar whereof was a spring of water which stood south of the house now owned by A. D. Wait & about 100 feet east of the dry bridge. It was occupied by John T. Taylor who lived there a good many years & raised a family there.

There was a private road which circled around the hill past this house & terminated on top of the hill at a place where the land was cultivated. It was not a public road but a private road used by Timothy Eddy & others for farming purposes, who cultivated the land on the flat, & it did not connect with any other road. There was a large flowing spring at the foot of the hill near where the stone wall is now located on the east side of upper Broadway about 150 feet north of the dry bridge where my family used to get water for domestic purposes. It was located about the same distance south of the Harvey spring. Above this spring near the bank of the hill were pine trees one of which & in fact two of which pine trees were very large ones & this spring emerged from their roots. These two large pine trees were located a short distance east of the spring on the side or top of the hill. All around in the vicinity of this spring was a black alder swamp. My grandmother's name was

Lavina Case, she died in 1857 aged 63 years. She told me many times that the place where Jane McCrea was killed was about 70 rods east of the spring called the Jane McCrea spring & formerly owned by George Harvey. There used to be a gully wherein there was a spring located about 10 or 15 rods east of the Palser Wait house which was filled up about the time the Palser Wait house was built. My grandmother lived in Fort Edward all of her married life.

JOHN B. CASE.

Dated March 25, 1908.

There was no road which ran west of the Harvey spring up the hill and no road which ran west of upper Broadway up the hill. There was a swamp where the Methodist church now stands extending east to the canal lock and west to the old iron foundry and machine shop which in later years was filled in. There was no red house at the lower end of the village except the one occupied by Nicholas McIntyre Justice of the Peace unless maybe the old Fort House was painted red.

EDGAR HULL.

APPENDIX II.

Jane McCrea's Bibliography.

It was my desire and intention to prepare for this Saratoga book an extensive and inclusive Burgoyne bibliography, but the demands of office in other directions and lack of time at my disposal, with other intervening matters which pressed the project into the background, have prevented this bibliography being made the *magnum opus* that I had hoped it would be.

I have been obliged to content myself therefore with making merely a rough list of the works consulted by me in preparing this sketch of Jane McCrea. It will differ from other bibliographies of the affair in that a larger number of newspaper extracts and scraps will be found in it than in any other place within my knowledge. Incidentally of course each one of the references in this list is a Burgoyne item, for the Mc-Crea tragedy is so inextricably interwoven with the story of the Burgoyne Invasion as to be an integral part of it. A few Burgoyne items which were consulted in the hope that there might be something in them relating to Jane McCrea, have been added to this list although concerned only with the campaign as a whole. The story of Jane McCrea is one which has attracted many newspaper writers as well as historians to the study of its hidden mysteries, in most cases without results, so far as the solving of the problem is concerned.

In addition to the older historians like David Wilson, Benson J. Lossing, William L. Stone, Dr. Asa Fitch, Judge James Gibson, Judge William Hay (of Saratoga Springs) and my father, the late Dr. Austin W. Holden, Queensbury's historian, the most of whom did their investigating and work over half a century ago, there have been in these later days such commemorators of the tragedy as the late Dr. Joseph E. King, one of the poet historians of whom Rev. O. C. Auringer is the latest, the late Robert O. Bascom of Fort Edward, Hon. Edgar Hull, also of Fort Edward, whose indefatigable work has thrown some new light on obscure points connected with the history of Fort Edward and Jane McCrea, Drury S. Sanford of Long Island, Lake George, and Long Island City, a lineal descendant of Jane McCrea's niece, and James T. Holmes, an attorney at law of

Columbus, Ohio a well known historical writer of that state, who became interested in the McCrea matter by accident and has since acquired what is said to be one of the largest collections of books and articles pertain. ing to her in the United States, aside from that of the writer, who has added largely to that left by his father, a specialist in the subject.

To Mr. Hull my indebtedness for many articles, suggestions and help. ful hints is here gratefully acknowledged.

INDIVIDUAL AND FAMILY BIBLIOGRAPHY.

DR. ASA FITCH. Letter on Jane McCrea in Proceedings New Jersey Historical Society [1852], Vol. V, p. 164.

D. WILSON. Life of Jane McCrea, and an account of Burgoyne's Expedition. N. Y. (1853), pp. ix-xi, 2-155.

R. WEBSTER. History of the Presbyterian Church in America. Phila. (1857), pp. 493-494. Sketch of Rev. James McCrea, with mention of Jane's death.

WILLIAM ALLEN, D. D. The American Biographical Dictionary, 3d Ed., Boston (1857), pp. 565-566.

ARTHUR REID. Reminiscences of the Revolution, or LeLoup's Bloody Trail from Salem to Fort Edward. Utica (1859). "Story of Jane McCrea," pp. 24-29.

WILLIAM HAY. Historical novel concerning Burgoyne's campaign, and containing a correct account of its chief incident, the decease of Jane McCrea. Glens Falls Republican, Glens Falls, N. Y., (1860.) from March 20 to May 22, inc.

LORENZO SABINE. Biographical sketches of Loyalists of the American Revolution. Boston (1864), Vol. I, p. 592. "David Jones." Death Jane McCrea mentioned.

A. W. HOLDEN, A. M., M. D. "The Story of Jane McCrea." Published in Glens Falls Republican, serially, from Nov. 20, 1883, to April 22, 1884, in twenty-three "Articles," containing extracts from every printed and local authority available to the author at that time, and the latter's deductions and conclusions.

JUDGE JAMES GIBSON. Letter to A. W. Holden, Salem (N. Y.), Dec 1, 1883. "She was accidently shot by an American party pursuing those with her."

HENRY RACE, M. D. A Historical Sketch of Miss Jane McCrea, read before New Jersey Historical Society, Newark, (May 20, 1886).

JUDGE JAMES GIBSON. "History of Washington County in Review-Press," Salem, N. Y., (1888). "The McCrea Family."

[HARRIET M. WILLIAMS]. Salem Historical Committee. The Salem Book, Salem, N. Y., (1896). Sketch of Col. John McCrea, 73-74.

WILLIAM BEECHER TEARSE Mss. Genealogy of great grand son of Peter Bailey Tearse, adjutant to Col. Willett at Fort Stanwix, and Polly Hunter, friend of Jane McCrea, whose story is given in the Mss.; Glens Falls (1899).

ROBERT O. BASCOM. "The Fort Edward Book," Fort Edward (1903). History Jane McCrea, pp. 43-73; cut Jane McCrea House, p. 53; cut Jane McCrea Marker, p. 69; cut Jane McCrea Headstone, p. 73. History of Jones Family, pp. 74-79.

REV. GEORGE WARNE LABAW. Genealogy of the Warne Family in America, N. Y. (1911), p. 335. Mentions father of Jane McCrea, "who was murdered by the Indians at Fort Edward, N. Y."

GLENS FALLS INSURANCE COMPANY, Glens Falls, N. Y. Historical and Art Calendars for 1900 and 1912, "Jane McCrea Calendars," letter press by Col. John L. Cunningham, President of the company.

EARLY HISTORIES OF THE AFFAIR.

ANON. The Annual Register for the year 1777. London (1781), p. 156.

GENERAL BURGOYNE. Speeches, Dublin, (1778.) Speech of General Burgoyne. Motion by Mr. Vyner, p. 8.

ANON. The History of the War in America. Dublin (1779), Vol. I, pp. 287-288.

LIEUT.-GEN. JOHN BURGOYNE. A statement of the Expedition from Canada. London (1780.) Evidence Earl of Harrington. Mentions McCrea matter, pp. 49, 99.

M. HILLIARD D'AUBERTEUIL. Miss Mac Rae: Roman Historique, Phila. (1784).

JOHN ANDREWS. History of The Late War. London (1786), pp. 394-395. Influence on Campaign.

WILLIAM GORDON. The History of the United States of America. London (1788), Vol. II., pp. 543-545.

MARQUIS de CHASTELLUX. Travels in North America. Translated by an English gentleman. London (1787), Vol. I., pp. 417-419.

[ENSIGN THOMAS ANBUREY]. Travels in America, by an Officer. London (1789), Vol. I., pp. 369-371; Vol. II., p. 184.

ISAAC WELD, JR. Travels Through the States of North America, 1795, 1796 and 1797. London (1800), Vol. I., pp. 278-279.

MRS. MERCY WARREN. History of the American Revolution. Boston (1805), Vol. II., pp. 25-27.

R. LAMB. An Original and Authentic Journal of Occurrences During the Late American War. Dublin (1809), pp. 145-147.

[DANIEL C. SANDERS]. A History of the Indian Wars. Montpelier, Vt. (1812), pp. 131-134.

GENERAL JAMES WILKINSON. Memoirs of My Own Times. Phila. (1816), Vol. I., pp. 230-231.

PROF. BENJAMIN SILLIMAN. Tour Between Hartford and Quebec. New Haven (1820), pp. 134-138.

THOMAS J. ROGERS. A New Biographical Dictionary of the Departed Heroes, Soldiers and Statesmen of America. Third Edition. Easton, Pa. (1824), p. 157.

JOEL MUNSELL. Annals of Albany. Albany (1856), Vol. VII., p. 167. "1822, April 23. The remains of Jane McCrea having been removed to the burying ground at Fort Edward, the Rev. Hooper Cummings attended the ceremonies and preached a sermon on the occasion from Micah 2:10."

G. M. DAVISON. Fashionable Tour. Saratoga Springs (1828), pp. 112-113.

JAMES McCAULEY. History of the State of New York. N. Y. (1829), Vol. III., pp. 202-203.

JANE McCREA
Calendar of 1900

Courtesy of Glens Falls Insurance Co.

ABIEL HOLMES. American Annals. Cambridge (1829), Vol. II., p. 272, note.

AUTHORITIES. 1822—1850.

JOHN H. HINTON. History and Topography of the United States. London (1830), Vol. I., p. 373, note.

JAMES STUART. Three Years in North America. N. Y. (1833), Vol. I., pp. 118-119.

F. S. EASTMAN. A History of the State of New York. N. Y. (1833), pp. 231-232.

JOHN LENDRUM. History of American Revolution. Exeter (1836), Vol. II., p. 16.

JARED SPARKS. Washington's Writings. Boston (1839), Vol. V., p. 37. Influence on Campaign.

WILLIAM DUNLAP. History of the New Netherlands, Province of New York and State of New York. N. Y. (1840), Vol. II., pp. 110-111. Wild and wonderful. Says she was killed by blows of the tomahawk on her head but not scalped.

JOHN W. BARBER. The History and Antiquities of New England, New York and New Jersey. Worcester (1841), pp. 445-446. Second Ed., 1847, pp. 444-446. Wood cut Jane McCrea, p. 444.

SAMUEL G. DRAKE. The Book of the Indians. Boston (1841), pp. 35-36.

[G. HILLS]. Events in Indian History. Phila., March 4, (1842). Murder of Jane McCrea, pp. 207-208.

CHARLES NEILSEN. Burgoyne's Campaign. Albany (1844), pp. 64-80, 223.

[GEORGE N. THOMPSON]. Confessions. Trials and Biographical Sketches of the Most Cold Blooded Murderers. * * * Also * * * Daring Outrages Committed in this and Other Countries. Hartford (1844). Murder of Jane McCrea, pp. 22-24.

JACOB K. NEFF. The Army and Navy of America. Phila. (1845), pp. 364-370.

JOHN W. BARBER AND HENRY HOWE. Historical Collections of the State of New York. N. Y. (1845), pp. 569-570. Wood cut Jane McCrea Tree, p. 570.

NEW YORK HISTORICAL SOCIETY. Proceedings for 1847. Stated meeting June 1, (1847). Extract from Epaphras Hoyt's MS. History of Burgoyne's Invasion.

ROBERT SEARS. Pictorial History of the American Revolution. N. Y. (1847), p. 252. Full page cut, p. 253.

B. J. LOSSING. "1776," or The War of Independence. N. Y. (1847), p. 235, note.

J. T. HEADLEY. Washington and His Generals. N. Y. (1847), Vol. I., pp. 233-235.

JOHN FROST. Remarkable Events in the History of America. Phila. (1848). Cut.

ALLEN COREY. Gazetteer of the County of Washington, N. Y. Schuylerville (1849-1850), p. 45.

AUTHORITIES. 1850—1880.

B. J. LOSSING. New History of the United States. [New York], n. d., p. 278.

EVART A. DUYCKINCK. National Portrait Gallery, n. d., Vol. I., pp. 258-259. (Sketch Horatio Gates).

B. J. LOSSING. Fieldbook of the Revolution. N. Y., (1851), Vol. I., pp. 48, 96-102.

ZADOCK THOMPSON. History of Vermont. Burlington (1853), part III, p. 50.

FRANKLIN B. HOUGH. A History of St. Lawrence and Franklin Counties, New York. Albany (1853), p. 201.

JAMES GRAHAM. Life of General Daniel Morgan. N. Y. (1856), pp. 133-139. Influence on Campaign.

R. HILDRETH. The History of the United States of America. N. Y. (1856), Vol. II., pp. 204-205.

WILLIAM V. MOORE. Indian Wars of the United States. Phila. (1856), pp. 237-238. Gives an account of Jane McCrea.

OFFICIAL. Proceedings of the Convention of the Soldiers of the War of 1812 * * * held at Schuylerville * * * Oct. 17, 1856 * * * to Celebrate Anniversary of Burgoyne's Surrender. Albany (1857), Jane McCrea, p. 15. Oration, Alfred B. Street.

H. B. DAWSON. The Historical Magazine. N. Y. (1858), Vol. II., No. 3, 2d Series. Story of Jane McCrea, pp. 70-71.

J. A. SPENCER. History of the United States. N. Y. [1858], Vol. I., pp. 499, 513-514.

JAMES THACHER. The American Revolution. N. Y. (1860), pp. 95-96.

WASHINGTON IRVING. Life of George Washington. N. Y. (1860), Vol. III., pp. 100-107.

E. B. O'CALLAGHAN. Burgoyne's Orderly Book. Albany (1860), pp. 181-182, 187, 189.

JARED SPARKS. Library of American Biography. N. Y. (1860), Vol. III., First Series, pp. 100-107.

FRANK MOORE. Diary of American Revolution. N. Y. (1860), Vol. I., pp. 475-476.

CALEB STARK. Memoirs of John Stark. Concord (1860), pp. 192, 331.

ROBERT TOMES, M. D. Battles of America by Sea and Land. N. Y. [1861], Vol. II., p. 9. McCrea murder mentioned.

WILLIAM KETCHUM. An Authentic and Comprehensive History of Buffalo. Buffalo (1865), Vol. I., pp. 294-296.

GEORGE BANCROFT. History of United States. Boston (1866), Vol. IX., pp. 371-372. Id. Boston (1879), Vol. V., pp. 579-580.

SEXAGENARY. (JOHN P. BECKER?) Reminiscences American Revolution. Albany (1866), pp. 67, 124.

H. B. DAWSON. Historical Magazine, "G. H. M." The Murder of Jane McCrea, Vol. I., (Jan. 1867), pp. 46-47. Idem, W. L. Stone, (April, 1867). Jane McCrea, pp. 229-230.

HARPER'S NEW MONTHLY MAGAZINE. N. Y. (1867), Vol. XXXV, (June to November, 1867), p. 259.

W. L. STONE. Jane McCrea Tragedy in The Galaxy. N. Y. (Jan., 1867), Vol. III., pp. 46-52.

T. ADDISON RICHARDS. Miller's Guide to Saratoga Springs. N. Y. (1867). Jane McCrea mentioned on pp. 81-82.

[JAMES TERWILLIGER, CLERK OF SENATE]. Calendar of Historical Manuscripts Relating to the War of the Revolution in the Office of the Secretary of State. Albany (1868), Vol. II., p. 256. Death of Lt. Tobias Van Veghten mentioned. He was later buried beside Jane McCrea at Moses Kill.

B. F. DeCOSTA. Notes on History of Fort George in American Bibliopolist. N. Y., April (1871), Chap. 5, p. 224.

HAMILTON CHILD. Gazetteer and Business Directory of Washington County, N. Y. Syracuse (1871), pp. 102-103.

E. P. WALTON. Records Council of Safety State of Vermont. Montpelier (1873), Vol. I., p. 9.

A. W. HOLDEN. History of Queensbury. Albany (1874), p. 452.

CATHERINE V. R. BONNEY. Legacy of Historical Gleanings. Albany (1875), Vol. I., p. 65.

B. J. LOSSING. History of American Revolution. N. Y., n. d., Vol. II., pp. 481-483, 485.

EDWARD B. DeFONBLANQUE. Political and Military Episodes. * * * Life and Correspondence of the Right Hon. John Burgoyne. London (1876), pp. 257-258.

MRS. [E. F.] ELLET. Domestic History of the Revolution. Phila. (1876), pp. 81-84.

NATHANIEL B. SYLVESTER. Historical Sketches of Northern New York and the Adirondack Wilderness. Troy (1877), p. 267.

B. J. LOSSING. Our Country. N. Y. (1877), Vol. II., p. 928. Cut.

WILLIAM L. STONE. Campaign Gen. John Burgoyne. Albany (1877). Note on p. 29; also pp. 227, 302-313, 338.

JAMES R. OSGOOD. Osgood's New England. Boston (1877), pp. 355-356.

WILLIAM L. STONE. Memoirs of the Centennial Celebration of Burgoyne's Surrender. Albany (1878), p. 76.

CRISFIELD JOHNSON. History of Washington County, N. Y. Phila. (1878), p. 249.

N. B. SYLVESTER. Saratoga County. Phila. (1878), pp. 53-56.

THOMAS JONES. History of New York. N. Y. (1879), McCrea matter, Vol. I., pp. 187-281; Burgoyne matter, pp. 674-695.

ALLAN C. BEACH, Secretary of State. Centennial Celebrations of State of New York. Albany (1879). Proceedings at Bemis Heights, pp. 150-192; Proceedings at Schuylerville, pp. 233-356. Jane McCrea mentioned, pp. 271-293, 304.

AUTHORITIES. 1880—1900.

E. J. LOWELL. The Hessians in the Revolution. N. Y. (1881), p. 138.

REV. CONWAY P. WING, D. D. The Wing Family. Carlisle, Pa. (1881), pp. 99-103.

WILLIAM L. STONE. Orderly Book Sir William Johnson. Albany (1882). Appendix p. 106 gives note upon Jane McCrea and Ransom Cook, who delivered note from David Jones.

LAMB'S. Magazine of American History. New York, March (1882). "Story of Jane McCrea," by Charles A. Campbell, pp. 202-203.

B. J. LOSSING. Life and Times Gen. Philip Schuyler. N. Y. (1883), Vol. II., pp. 250-253. Gates' Version, pp. 253-254.

JEPTHA R. SIMMS. Frontiersmen of New York. Albany (1883), Vol. II., pp. 117-118. Cut of tree and "place where Miss McCrea was murdered."

H. P. SMITH. Warren County. Syracuse (1885), p. 160.

HARVEY RACE, M. D. A Historical Sketch of Miss Jennie McCrea. In N. J. Historical Society Proceedings. Second Series, Vol. IX (1886-1887).

JAMES PHINNEY BAXTER. Digby's Journal, 1776-1777. Albany (1887). Gives an account of Jane McCrea, pp. 235-237.

JUSTIN WINSOR. Narrative and Critical History of America. Boston (1888), Vol. VI. Burgoyne Campaign, pp. 291-323; Sources of Information, pp. 346-366. McCrea mentioned, p. 627.

JOHN FISKE. American Revolution. Boston (1891), pp. 324-328.

J. H. PATTON. Four Hundred Years of American History. N. Y. [1892], Vol. I., pp. 473-474. Idem. History of the United States. N. Y. (1860), pp. 429-430.

WILLIAM M. SLOANE. French War and Revolution. London (1893), p. 268.

GRESHAM PUBLISHING CO. History and Biography Washington County. Richmond, Ind. (1894), pp. 46-47.

BRYANT & GAY. Scribner's Popular History of the United States. N. Y. (1896), Vol. III., pp. 569-571. Highly improbable account. Cut of a band of mounted (sic.) savages.

ELIZABETH EGGLESTON SEELYE. Saratoga and Lake Champlain in History. Lake George (1898). Jane McCrea, pp. 51-54.

JUSTIN WINSOR. Readers Handbook American Revolution. Boston (1899), pp. 138-139.

JOHN HENRY BRANDOW. Story of Old Saratoga. Albany (1900), pp. 83-84.

STATE HISTORIAN. Public Papers of Governor George Clinton. Albany (1900), Vol. II., pp. 210, 217. Influence on Campaign.

AUTHORITIES. 1900—1912.

J. P. MAC LEAN, Ph. D. The Story of Jane MacRae in American Monthly Magazine (D. A. R.) Washington (Sept., 1901), Vol. XIX, No. 3, pp. 245-249.

W. L. STONE. History of Washington County. N. Y. (1901), pp. 185-211.

HON. ROBERT EARL. Address before Herkimer County Historical Society. Herkimer (1902), p. 133. McCrea affair cited.

H. H. ROBERTSON. Titus Simons, Quartermaster. Hamilton, Ont. (1903), p. 3.

RUFUS ROCKWELL WILSON. Heath's Memoirs of the American War. N. Y. (1904), pp. 135, 411.

JAMES M. LINCOLN. The Papers of Captain Rufus Lincoln of Wareham, Mass., privately printed (1904), pp. 15-16. Influence on Campaign.

SHERMAN WILLIAMS. Early New York History. N. Y. (1906), pp. 195-196.

SYDNEY GEORGE FISHER. The Struggle for Independence. Phila. (1908), Vol. II., pp. 85-86. McCrea affair and its influence.

DAVID E. ALEXANDER. Diary of Captain Benjamin Warren in Journal of American History. Meriden, Conn. (April-June, 1909), Vol. II., pp. 204-205.

W. MAX REID. Lake George and Lake Champlain. N. Y. (1910), pp. 165, 278, 290, 291-293.

HENRY BELCHER. First American Civil War. London (1911), Vol. II., pp. 295-296.

SIR GEORGE O. TREVELYAN. The American Revolution. N. Y. (1912), Vol. IV., pp. 126-127, 148.

TRAGEDY MENTIONED.

CHARLES BOTTA. History American War. New Haven [1834], Vol. II. Jane McCrea on pp. 5-7.

W. L. STONE. Life of Brant. N. Y. (1838), pp. 203-206, and also mentioned on p. 207.

THEODORE DWIGHT. Northern Traveller. N. Y. (1841), p. 139.

LITTELL'S LIVING AGE. Vol. XVII (1848), pp. 226-233. (From Blackwood's Magazine).

H. B. DAWSON. Historical Magazine. N. Y. (1870), 2d Series, Vol. II., Feb'y. Mentioned p 133.

ELLEN HARDIN WALWORTH. Battle of Saratoga in "Magazine of American History." N. Y. (May, 1877), Vol. I., No. 5. Jane McCrea men-tioned, pp. 285, 273-302.

WILLIAM TRACY. Annual Address. Publications of Oneida His-torical Society at Utica, (Nov. 5-Jan. 13, 1880). McCrea funeral men-tioned, p. 14.

HENRY B. CARRINGTON. Battles of the American Revolution. N. Y. [1888]. Mentioned, pp. 325-326.

MRS. ELLEN HARDIN WALWORTH. Battles of Saratoga. Albany [1891] Jane McCrea mentioned, pp. 19, 162-164.

W. L. STONE. Saratoga Battlegrounds. Albany (1895). Mentions Tragedy on p. 170, and in note on p. 184, also on p. 319, in connection with her brother, Col. John McCrea.

WILLIAM S. OSTRANDER. Old Saratoga and the Burgoyne Cam-paign. Schuylerville (1897), pp. 18-19.

BAYARD TUCKERMAN. Life of General Philip Schuyler. N. Y. (1903). McCrea affair mentioned, pp. 209-211.

A. B. HART. American Nation; C. H. Van Tyne's American Revolu-tion. N. Y. (1905), Vol. IX. McCrea mentioned on p. 164.

W. L. STONE. The Saratoga County Society of New York. Year Book. N. Y. (1905). Jane McCrea mentioned on p. 24. Mentions death of Mrs. Ayres, widow of the late Robert Ayres, who delivered letter to Jane McCrea from David Jones.

HUGH HASTINGS. "Battle of Saratoga" in Transactions of Mont-gomery County Historical Society. Amsterdam (1905), pp. 24-39. Mc-Crea mentioned, pp. 34-35.

SARANAC CHAPTER, D. A. R. Three Centuries in Champlain Valley. Plattsburgh (1909), pp. 232-233.

HENRY MITCHELL MAC CRACKEN. The Saratoga Campaign as a Type of New York History. Dedication Saratoga Battle Monument, October, 1912, in The Penn. Germania. Cleona, Pa. (Jan. 1913), Vol. II., No. 1, pp. 7-19. McCrea mentioned, pp. 7-8.

MARY GAY HUMPHREYS, Catherine Schuyler. N. Y. (1910). McCrea story, pp. 151-154.

HARRY C. AND MARY WOLCOTT GREENE. The Pioneer Mothers of America. N. Y. (1912), Vol. II. Jane McCrea mentioned, p. 91.

M'CREA POEMS AND BALLADS.

PHILIP FRENAU. Poems. America Independent. Phila. (1786). Death of Jane McCrea, p. 160.

REUBEN SEARS. Mineral Waters of Ballston and Saratoga. Ballston Spa (1819), pp. 31-32.

S. COLEMAN. The Bride of Fort Edward. N. Y. (1839). A dramatic story, pp. VII and VIII, 9-174.

REV. WHEELER CASE. Ed. by Rev. Stephen Dodd. Revolutionary Memorials. N. Y. (1852), pp. 37-39. Appendix II, pp. 56-65.

JOHN TRUMBULL. "M'Fingal," a Modern Epic Poem. Hartford (1856). Jane McCrea's death mentioned in note, on p. 147.

LURA A. BOIES. Rural Rhymes. Saratoga Springs (1860). Jane McCrea, pp. 17-28; Defeat of Burgoyne, pp. 28-35.

ALFRED B. STREET. "Burgoyne." A poem written for the Centennial Celebration at Schuylerville, October 17, 1877. Albany (1877). McCrea, pp. 26-27.

"R. R." "The Fate of Jane McCrea," poem. Washington County Advertiser, March, 1887 (?)

W. L. STONE. "Burgoyne's Ballads." Albany (1893). Gives account Jane McCrea, pp. 128-207. Includes poems by Rev. O. C. Auringer, A. W. Holden, Lura A. Boies, Rev. Wheeler Case, Joel Barlow, Sarah J. Hale, Henry Herbert, Jos. E. King and sketch by J. A. Holden.

O. C. AURINGER. The Death of Maid McCrea. Boston (1909). Epic poem, pp. 11-66.

ETHAN ALLEN. Washington, or The Revolution. A drama. N. Y. (1895), Part I, p. 164. McCrea mentioned.

EVARTS A. DUYCKINCK. Cyclopaedia of American Literature. Phila. (1875), Vol. I. Burgoyne Ballads, pp. 466-468; 471-472. Jane McCrea, p. 471.

NEWSPAPER ACCOUNTS.

JANE McCREA DISINTERMENT. Washington County Post, April 25, 1822.

MISS McCREA. Originally printed in Boston Palladium and copied in Warren Messenger (Glens Falls), Oct. 21, 1830.

LETTER dated Sandy Hill, July 10, 1833, describing scene of tragedy, as it was then, in Warren Messenger (Glens Falls), July 26, 1833.

"VERITAS" [Dr. Asa Fitch]. Letter on Jenny McCrea in Union Village (N. Y.) Journal, June 9, 1853.

CORRESPONDENT OF FORT EDWARD LEDGER. Water Works and Pure Water at the Fort Edward Institute. Reprinted 'n Sandy Hill Herald, April 26, 1859. Jane McCrea springs as a water supply.

WILLIAM HAY. Historical Novel Concerning Burgoyne's Campaign, and Containing Correct Account of its Chief Incidents in the Decease of Jane McCrea. In the Glens Falls Republican from March 20 to May 22, 1860.

HENRY C. MARTINDALE of Sandy Hill. Letter on Jane McCrea, dated Nov. 17, 1830, published in New England Palladium. Copied into the Warren Messenger of Glens Falls, June 29, 1831; reprinted in Glens Falls Republican March 26, 1861.

"THE TRUE STORY," in Sandy Hill Herald, Feb'y 18, 1872.

J. DeWITT MILLER. "Some Rambles About Fort Edward." Salem (N. Y.) Press, June 4, 1875.

OBITUARY * * * OF DUNHAM JONES. Some Account of the Jones Family and the Murder of Jane McCrea. Toronto (Upper Canada) Globe, Jan. 5, 1877.

J. WATTS DePEYSTER. Burgoyne in New York. "Anchor's" letter in New York Times, n. d. (Supposed to be in July, 1877).

"FORT EDWARD CELEBRATION." A Peep Behind the Scenes, in Sandy Hill Herald, Aug. 2, 1877.

"SOME NEW FACTS ABOUT THE MURDER OF JANE M'CREA ONE HUNDRED YEARS AGO." Independent, Sept. 12, 1877. Copied from N. Y. World. No date given.

"JANE M'CREA—SOME NEW FACTS." Sandy Hill Herald, Aug. 23, 1877. Copied from New York World, date not given.

REV. JOSEPH E. KING. Poem in Commemoration of Jane McCrea. Fort Edward Gazette, Aug. 3, 1877.

REV. SAMUEL McKEAN. "Address Centennial Commemoration Death of Jane McCrea." In Fort Edward Gazette, Aug. 3, 1877.

JANE M'CREA. HONORS TO HER MEMORY. Sandy Hill Herald, Aug. 2, 1877, with Dr. King's Poem.

ALFRED B. STREET. "Old Fort Edward," in Fort Edward Gazette, March 22 (1878). Part of his Centennial Poem, "Burgoyne."

"NEW VERSION OF AN HISTORICAL INCIDENT," from Plattsburgh Republican, date not given, probably in "the seventies" of the 19th Century.

ROGERS PLACE, * * * Formerly Owned by Jane McCrea's Lover. Troy Daily Press. Date unknown, supposed to be in early 80's.

"M. N. H." Some Historical Trees, in Boston Herald, date unknown, but probably in 80's. Mentions "Jane McCrea pine."

ANON. "The Burgoyne Tree." at Schuylerville, in Albany Argus (1880).

SAMUEL McKEAN. "The Fort Edward Scout," Glens Falls Republican, March 29, 1881. Copied from Troy Morning Telegram. Mentions the McCrea farm.

"MORE ABOUT THE MURDER OF JANE M'CREA." Troy Times, July 21, 1882.

"CAROLUS." "Jennie McCrea," a True Story of the Revolution. Dubuque (Iowa) Times. Oct. 29, 1882.

"INVESTIGATOR." "Fort Edward in the Olden Time." Washington County Post, February 3, 1882.

JULIA C. SMALLEY. A Scrap of Unwritten History. (Jones Family in Canada). Catholic World, December, 1882.

"MORE ANON." An Historical Place. Reminiscences of Fort Edward. David Jones and Jane McCrea, in Troy Northern Budget, Feb'y 16, 1883. Idem. Reminiscences of Fort Edward, One Hundred and Six Years Ago, in Budget, April 14, 1883.

"PAP." "Seen Thro' Southern Eyes." Dated at Fort Edward, Nov. 3, 1885, in New Orleans Daily States. Reprinted in some local paper; no date given.

D. A. HARSHA. "The Death of Jane McCrea." Albany Argus, Oct. 10, 1886.

"MORE ABOUT JANE M'CREA'S BONES." Sunday Ray, Glens Falls, March 20, 1887.

ANON. "Jane McCrea and Her Remains." Salem Press, March 14, 1887. Copied from Albany Journal. Date not given.

"THE LEGEND OF JANE M'CREA." Troy Daily Times, Sept. 1, 1888.

"THE LEGEND OF JANE M'CREA." Glens Falls Republican, Sept. 18, 1888. Copied from Warrensburgh (N. Y.) News. No date given.

ANON. The Hermit of Mt. Ida, "Old Washington County, The Patriotism of the Town of Hartford," in Troy Northern Budget (1888). Men who fought against Burgoyne.

A. W. HOLDEN. Sandy Hill Herald Anniversary Edition, Thursday, June 14, (1888), Vol. LXV, pp. 10-12. Jane McCrea.

JUDGE JAMES GIBSON. History of Washington County, in Salem Review-Press, Dec. 12, 1890. Account mentions the death of Jane McCrea, Allen Massacre, etc.

D. TURNER. "Reminiscences of Fort Edward," in Troy Daily Times, Sept. 29, 1890.

E. F. RICE. Query in New York Mail and Express February 23, 1901, regarding Dr. Norton of Jane McCrea fame, at Fort Edward.

"TO PROTECT A HISTORICAL SPOT," Fort Edward Advertiser. April 1, 1894.

"FENCE AROUND GRAVE OF JANE M'CREA," in Fort Edward Advertiser, Sept. 18, 1894.

MRS. IRVING C. FORTE. Paper on Local Colonial Homes before Jane McCrea Chapter, D. A. R., May 10, 1901, in Fort Edward Advertiser, May 23, 1901.

MEMORIAL TO JANE M'CREA," in The Morning Star (Glens Falls), July 29, 1901.

F. W. HARRIS. "Jane McCrea—Monument Dedication by D. A. R." Glens Falls Daily Times, July 29, 1901.

GARDNER COX, M. D., of Holyoke, Mass. "The Murder of Jane McCrea," in Springfield (Mass.) Sunday Republican, April 12, 1903. Cuts of tombstone, McCrea (?) house and D. A. R. marker.

"JANE M'CREA—HER MURDER RECALLED BY FILING DEED OF ROGERS' PLACE," in Glens Falls Times, June 13, 1903.

"HISTORIC FARM SOLD." Sandy Hill Daily News, June 13, 1903. Regarding sale of "Rogers," formerly "Jones," (?) farm in Saratoga County.

JAMES T. HOLMES, Columbus, Ohio. "Biography Colonel Joseph Holmes," in the Sentinel, Dec. 6, 1906, to Sept. 5, 1907. Treats of Jane McCrea in connection with "Obadiah Holmes, Jr., 1760-1834."

"FORT EDWARD STAGED STIRRING SCENES IN REVOLUTIONARY WAR," in The Knickerbocker-Press, Albany, May 12, 1912, with cuts of alleged McCrea house, the grave, and D. A. R. marker.

EDGAR HULL. "No Dispute Over Location of the Mouth of Bond Creek," in Fort Edward Advertiser, Oct. 29, 1909.

IDEM. "Additional Interesting Facts of Early Fort Edward History," in Fort Edward Advertiser, November 18, 1909.

IDEM. "Jane McCrea; Her Death in Fort Edward." Glens Falls Times, April 7, 1910. Copied from Troy Times of March 15, 1910.

IDEM. "Fort Edward History," in the Troy Times, March 15, 1910.

IDEM. Valuable Historical Article on Location of Old Fort Edward in Fort Edward Advertiser, July 18, 1912. Block house connected with Jane McCrea tragedy located.

IDEM. "Curiosities of Fort Edward Past Historical Literature," in Fort Edward Advertiser, Feb'y 13, 1913.

WILLIAM L. STONE. "The Jane McCrea Tragedy," in Albany Argus. No date given.

MRS. FINDLEY BRADEN. "Poor Jenny McCrea." Poem. In Moreristown (Pa.) Herald. Date not given.

BURGOYNE CAMPAIGN.

ANON. The Substance of General Burgoyne's Speeches on Mr. Vyner's Motion on the 26th of May and upon Mr. Hartley's Motion on the 28th of May, 1778, with an Appendix. Dublin (1778).

ANON. A Letter to Lieut.-Gen. Burgoyne on his Letter to his Constituents. London (1779).

ANON. A Reply to Lieutenant-General Burgoyne's Letter to his Constituents. London (1779).

ANON. A Letter from Lieut.-Gen. Burgoyne to His Constituents Upon His Late Resignation with the Correspondence Between the Secretaries of War and Him Relative to His Return to America. Also, a Letter to Lieut.-Gen. Burgoyne on His Letter to His Constituents and a Reply to Lieut.-Gen. Burgoyne's Letter to His Constituents. Dublin (1779).

ANON. A Letter to Lieut.-Gen. Burgoyne Occasioned by a Second Edition of His State of the Expedition from Canada. London (1780).

ANON. Essay on Modern Martyrs: With a Letter to General Burgoyne. London (1780).

ANON. Remarks on General Burgoyne's State of the Expedition from Canada. London (1780).

ANON. "The History of the Civil War in America," by an Officer of the Army. London (1780), Vol. I., Second Edition. Burgoyne Expedition, pp. 369-397.

JOHN BURGOYNE. Supplement to a State of the Expedition. London (1780). Pamp. 26 pp.

ANON. The Narrative of Lieutenant-General Sir Henry Clinton, K. B., Relative to His Conduct During Part of His Command of the King's Troops in North America, With an Appendix Containing Copies and Extracts of * * * Parts of His Correspondence. London (1783).

C. STEDMAN. The History of the * * * American War. London (1794), Vol. I., pp. 318-357.

M. M. NOAH. "Marian, or the Hero of Lake George." A Drama. New York, January (1822). Burgoyne mentioned, p. 10.

ANON. The Fashionable Tour in 1825. Saratoga Springs (1825), pp. 73-89, 99-100.

CHARLES A. GOODRICH. "A History of the United States of America." Hartford (1833), pp. 254-269.

HUGH MOORE. Memoirs of Col. Ethan Allen. Plattsburgh (1834), pp. 136-137; 174-175, 184, 195. Burgoyne mentioned also in foot note.

ANON. The Wars of America, by a Revolutionary Soldier. Baltimore (1839). Burgoyne's Expedition, pp. 246-254.

CHARLES COFFIN. The Life and Services of Major General John Thomas. N. Y. (1844).

ALEXANDER GRAYDON. "Memoirs of His Own Times * * * of the Revolution." Phila. (1846), pp. 114-297.

MRS. MARIA CAMPBELL. Revolutionary Services * * * of General William Hull. N. Y. (1848), pp. 72-111.

JOHN W. BARBER. Historical, Poetical and Pictorial American Scenes. Boston [1850], pp. 69-114.

HENRY B. DAWSON. Battles of the United States. N. Y. (1858), Vol. I., Chap. XXV, pp. 284-300. Burgoyne Campaign.

ANON. Battle of Saratoga. Historical Magazine. N. Y. (1858), Vol. II., No. 3, pp. 65-80.

FRIEDRICH KAPP. The Life of Frederick William Von Steuben. Introduction by George Bancroft. N. Y. (1859), p. 91.

CHARLES MACKAY. History United States of America. London [1860], Vol. I., pp. 294-324. Forbids Indian atrocities, p. 301.

WILLIAM P. UPHAM. Memoirs of General John Glover of Marblehead, from the Historical Collections of the Essex Institute. Salem (1863),

ANCHOR [J. WATTS DE PEYSTER]. Schuyler and Practical Strategy. Red Hook, (Jan. 27, 1866). Pamp. 8 pp.

GEORGE L. SCHUYLER. Correspondence and Remarks, Etc. Northern Campaign and Maj-Gen. Philip Schuyler. N. Y. (1867), pp. 1-10, 30, 37.

WILLIAM L. STONE. Burgoyne in a New Light. "The Galaxy." N. Y. (Nov. 1868), Vol. V., No. 1, pp. 78-85.

ALFRED B. STREET. The Burgoyne House, "Hours at Home." N. Y. (Sept. 1869), Vol. IX, No. 5, pp. 464-470. Fiction.

E. M. RUTTENBER. Indian Tribes of Hudson River. Albany (1872). Indians with Burgoyne, pp. 273-276.

W. L. STONE (?) An Address to the American People in Behalf of a Monument to be Erected in Commemoration of the Victory * * * at Schuylerville. N. Y. (1874). Pamp. 11 pp.

N. B. SYLVESTER. Historical Address, Saratoga and Kayadrossera. Troy (1876), pp. 38-44.

ANON. Memoirs of Burgoyne, "The Nation." N. Y. (April 13, 1876), pp. 250-251.

J. T. HEADLEY. Burgoyne's Original Order Book, in "The Galaxy." N. Y. (Jan. 1876), Vol. XXII., No. 5, pp. 604-618.

GEORGE G. SCOTT. Historical Address and J. S. L'AMOREAUX, Centennial Address, July 4. 1876. Ballston Spa (1876).

GEN. EDWARD F. BULLARD. History of Saratoga and the Burgoyne Campaign, Schuylerville, July 4, 1876. Ballston Spa (1876).

R. M. DEVEN. Our First Century. Springfield, Mass., pp. 72-80.

W. L. STONE. Campaign of Burgoyne, Harper's Monthly, Vol. LV., New York (1877), pp. 673-693.

JOHN AUSTIN STEVENS. The Burgoyne Campaign. An address delivered on the battlefield * * * of Bemis Heights, Sept. 19, 1877. N. Y. (1877).

GEORGE W. CURTIS. Burgoyne's Surrender and Oration on the 100th Anniversary. N. Y. (1877).

J. WATTS DE PEYSTER. Major General Philip Schuyler and the Burgoyne Campaign, 1777. Address before New York Historical Society. n. d. Pamp., pp. 26.

CHARLES L. DEAN, LL. D. Report of the Council. Proceedings of the American Antiquarian Society, Worcester, Mass., Oct. 22, 1877. Worcester (1878). Discussion of Convention Matter, pp. 9-83.

W. L. STONE (Secretary of Association). History of The Saratoga Monument Association. Albany (1879).

J. WATTS DE PEYSTER. Proofs Considered in Connection with Vindication of Sir John Johnson, Bart. An Address, before New York Historical Society, Jan. 6. 1880. Refers to Burgoyne on p. 20. Idem. In Proceedings New Jersey Historical Society, Vol. II., 1846-1847, pp. 115, 122-127, 128.

ANON. Magazine of American History. New York, March (1882), pp. 222-224.

J. WATTS DE PEYSTER. The Burgoyne Campaign Phila. (1883). Idem. In United Service, October, 1883.

"HISTORICAL JUSTICE." Gates vs. Burgoyne. Saratoga Daily Journal, August 8, 1883. "Anchor" (J. Watts De Peyster). "Who 'Burgoyned' Burgoyne." Saratoga Daily Journal, August 30, 1883. Col. Long at Wood Creek. Saratoga Daily Journal, Sept. 7, 1883, reprint. Pamp. 8 pp.

HON. EDWARD WEMPLE AND HON. SAMUEL S. COX. Remarks in House of Representatives Thursday, Dec. 4, 1884, Saratoga Monument. Pamp. 4 pp.

WILLIAM L. STONE. Saratoga Battleground. Magazine of American History. N. Y. (Nov. 1885), Vol. XIV, No. 5, pp. 510-512.

C. H. CRANDALL. When Burgoyne Surrendered, "The Saratoga Monument." American Magazine. N. Y. (1888), Vol. VIII., pp. 415-430.

JAMES DAVIE BUTLER "Butler Family." Albany (1888), p. 98.

VERMONT STATE CENTENNIAL AT BENNINGTON. Bennington (1891).

N. H. CHAMBERLAIN. In the Footprints of Burgoyne. New England Magazine (N. S.), Vol. IV., Boston (1891), pp. 798-805.

JOHN G. NICOLAY. "The Battle of Saratoga." The Chatauquan. Meadville, Pa. (1892), Vol. XIV, (Jan.), pp. 387-396.

ANON. With Burgoyne at Saratoga. Macmillan's Magazine. London, Nov., (1896), No. 445, pp. 71-80.

WOODROW WILSON. A History of the American People. N. Y. (1902), Vol. II., pp. 268-281.

HENRY W. ELSON. History of the United States of America. London (1905), Vol. II., pp. 68-78.

YEAR BOOK OF THE SARATOGA COUNTY SOCIETY OF NEW YORK. N. Y. (1905). "Burgoyne," pp. 18, 19, 21, 24.

J. W. GARNER AND HENRY C. LODGE. The History of the United States. Phila. (1906), Vol. II., pp. 445-455.

THOMAS WILLIAMS BALDWIN. "The Revolutionary Journal of Col. Jeduthan Baldwin, 1775-1758." Bangor (1906). Allen Massacre referred to, p. 112.

CAPTAIN H. GARBETT. Progress and Failure of the Expedition from Canada June to October, 1777. Journal of the Royal United Service Institution. London, (Jan. 1911), Vol. LV, No. 395, pp. 3-38.

ASA WHEELER. Letter in New York Genealogical and Biographical Record for April, 1913, pp. 124-125. Retreat from Fort Edward. Burgoyne matter.

ANON. Unidentified Magazine, "Capture of General Burgoyne's Army," pp. 433-441.

ANON. The Lamentations of General Burgoyne After He Became the Prisoner of "The Rebels." A Poem, pp. 1-8.

SARATOGA MONUMENT. Remarks of Messrs. Wemple and Cox of New York. Battle of Saratoga, p. 2. Burgoyne, pp. 3-4.

CHARLES MACKAY. The History of the United States of America. London, n. d., Vol. I., pp. 300-324.

LETTERS AND DOCUMENTS

The following letters and documents illustrating some of the customs and problems of the Revolutionary War Period were read by Asahel R. Wing, Fort Edward.

Pawling precinct ye 19th of ye 9th month, 1776.

Dearly beloved Father and Mother after a Salutation of our effectionate love towards you and our beloved brothers and Sisters in them parts we hope these loins May find you all in a state of health as they leave us at present through the goodness of God. We have renewed cause of deep thankfulness and awfull reverence to the Lord in remembrance of the Mercies Dayly bestowed on us poor unworthy Creators for the preservation of our lives in this time of trial and justifys the upholding the Churches and unity of the brotherhood and privilege of the Gospel of light Dispensed to us by ages past and gon—and now beloved parents May the Lord preserve us free from joining in with either party in the present Conflict in the Nation and lead us through this world of trials in the fear of God and in peace with all Men and now most tender parents may we with you be inabled to put up our petitions in prayer to all Mighty God for the reconcileation and releaf of our Distressed Nation who is wandering up and down in a multitude of Confusion, and now beloved parents our Consurn Dayly remains for you all in them remoat parts of the world on account of the Distressed Indians who we hear are killing the people at Chere valy and be pleased to inform us by the first oppertunity of your State of health and how you all fair in them parts. Your loving and dutiful Son and Dater.

NEHEMIAH MERRITT, PHEBE MERRITT.

Saratoga, Nov. 17th, 1777.

I have Considered about your Sons Horse and give him Leave to keep the Same untill some higher Power shall order it otherwise. I also grant you Leave to keep a hunting gun in your house and forbid anyone to take the same without orders from the general.

I am Sir,

Your friend & Servt.
CHRIS P. YATES.

A true Copy.
to Abraham Wing.

This Certifys that in the year 1777 when the Continental army then under my Command retreated from Fort George and Fort Edward, I ordered all horses, Neat Cattle, grain, forage, Carriages and whatever else might facilitate the enemies progress into the Country to be taken for the use of the American Army from those persons as did not remove with their effects, and what Could not be taken away to be destroyed, that many persons from whom such Articles were taken could not remove on Account of Illness or other unavoidable impediments—that in Consequence of those orders horses, Cattle, grain, forage and Carriages were taken or destroyed but from whom particullarly or to what Amount I believe cannot now be determined otherwise than by affidavid of the persons from whom those things were taken or by that of those who were acquainted with the taking or destroying. As It is more than probable that the officers commanding the detachments sent on this service did neither keep an Account of what they took or destroyed, nor gave certificates —That I also ordered all the saw and grist mills to be striped of their Iron work and well recollect that Mr. Ephraim Wings mills were striped but of what particular Articles I cannot say—

Albany, October 10th, 1785.
PH. SCHUYLER.

Sir:

A Number of Milch Cows have been brought down from beyond our lines some of which belong to Mr. Abraham Wyng and his family and as he is so situated that he cannot move I have permitted him to remain and Consented that he should take back

Eight of his Cows. you will therefore please to deliver them to him.

I am Sir Yours

PH. SCHUYLER.

Head Quarters, July 26th, 1777.
  To Major Gray
    D: Commissary.

Mr. Asaph Putnam being sworn before this county affirmeth that he heard Daniel Park Say that King George the 3rd had sent moneys into America to merit the favour of the Americans and that it came to the mare of Albany and through the Hands of the Jassops and that he believed that Abraham Wing had felt of some of it. further the deponant Saith not.

Thomas Bradshaw being sworn before us and Sayeth that Daniel Park thretned Abraham Wing and Sayeth that he wode kill him if that he come over and made motions to strike att him and Damed the authority of the commitay of the County and further the Deponant Saith not. Gilbort Carswell being Sworn deposeth to the aBove writen.

Samuell Harris being Sworn before me Sayeth that Some time last may he was att the Landing or Carrying place operset Said Dan Parks, saw Parks and heard him make free with the caracter of Abraham Wing and Said that Wing was a Rascal and that he had proved himself So and that would vindicate what he had Said. A true Cope of the evedence a test by me.

  THOMAS SHERWOOD, Charman.

County   Persionally before me Albert Jos.
  of   Baker one of the Justices for Said County
Washington   Samuel Younglove of Lawful age

Deposeth and Saith that he saw James Stinslor take out of the House of Abram Wing in the year one thousand Seven hundred and Eighty to the amount of about one hundred panes of glass with the Sashes or near thereabouts and saw him have five saw mill Saws and Sundry other articles which the Said Stinslor told the deponant he had taken from the Said Wing and the deponent farther declares that the Said Stinslor told him the deponant that he had got to the amount of between forty and fifty Pound from old Tory Wing farther more the deponant Saith not.

SAML. YOUNGLOVE.

Sworn before me this 11th June, 1787.

ALBERT BAKER, J. P.

Queensbury, November ye 30th, 1767.

then Received of Abraham Wing twenty three pounds York curency and one Good Cow and Calf and two Good Sutes of Cloathing and my Learning namely Reading, Riting and Sifering to my full Satisfaction Specified in an Endenture wherein I were bound an a printice to the Said Abraham Wing by an Endenture dated May the 25th, 1753—and do by these presents acknowledge the Endenture fuly absolutely and Entirely Satisfied to me on Said 'Wings part and do acquit and Discharge Said Abraham Wing from all Bills Bonds accounts Due Debts and Demands contrevarsies or Quarils or any other Riting that may hereafter arise from the Begining of the world to the above date as witness my hand.

TRUELOVE BUTLER.

Witness present
  Phinehas Babcock
  Asoph Putnam.

GUIDE TO THE SARATOGA BATTLEFIELD

From Schuylerville. If you are a good walker go first by
electric car to Wilbur's Basin. From there walk to Freeman's
Farm, one and one-half miles to the west. After crossing the canal
take first left hand road up the hill. From there it is a straight
road to the battlefield. After crossing the ravine turn in at the
first house on the left. You are then at the place.

If you are not a walker, then take a carriage at Schuylerville.
Perhaps you better go by Quaker Springs and return by the River
road. The scenery from Quaker Springs to the battlefield is superb.
After leaving Quaker Springs, up the second road to your left
came General Fraser on the morning of the 19th of September,
1777, on his way to the battle. Near here he turned southward.
After passing the Quaker meeting house, a half mile farther on
you come to a fork in the roads, keep to the left; then take second road to the left and turn in at the first house you come to on
the right. You are then at the Freeman's Farm House (now Es-
mud's).

From Saratoga Springs. It is nine miles to the battlefield.
You will need to take a carriage, and a lunch, as it will be quite
late before you get back. Drive out Union Avenue to Moon's;
then down the hill back of his place, cross the trestle bridge over
the foot of the lake; then along the shore of the lake for a mile and
a half to the Cedar Bluff house. Take first left hand road beyond
this up the hill. On top of the hill turn to the right, a little
farther on turn to the left, then southwest for half a mile till you
meet a road running directly east, take this over hill and dale for

three miles, passing three cross roads from the north, till you come to a school house and the Quaker meeting house. Arrived at this turn you are on historic ground. It was near here that General Fraser with his brigade, coming up from the river on the morning of the 19th of September, 1777, turned to the south on his way to the battlefield. Now turn up the hill to the right past the school house and church. About half a mile south of the church you come to a fork in the roads, keep to the left; then take second road down the hill to your left, turn in at the first house you come to on your right; this is Freeman's farm (now Esmond's.)

From Mechanicville and the south. Take electric car to Still-water or Bemis Heights; there get a carriage to the battlefield. Turn up the hill at Bemis Heights. About a mile up the hill another road comes in from the north. Follow this road for a mile and a half turning to the right at the second cross road, then down the hill, and turn in to the right at the first house you come to; this is Freeman's farm.

Arrived at Freeman's farm, first obtain permission to look over the grounds. Then as you stand at the front of the house facing the west you are looking out on the field of the first day's battle. The original Freeman's cottage stood to your left near the west line of the barnyard. It was at and about this cottage that Morgan met the British scouts under Major Forbes. He drove them back into the woods just north of the road, and was there in turn driven back and scattered by Burgoyne's main body. Burgoyne formed his line of battle just north of the ravine which runs parallel with and a little to the north of the road. Then he advanced and the battle raged for four hours back and forth across the open clearing both to the east and west of the cottage, but principally to the west. The battle ended when the Germans coming up from the river occupied the knoll to the south of the barns with reinforcements and turned the American right wing, just at dark.

After the battle the British held the field and fortified themselves. See map for location and direction of their lines. Here they remained for seventeen days. Let us now look over the grounds a bit.

FIRST: In the hollow just beyond the barnyard at the south you see the old battle well. About this well many poor fellows were found dead after the battle, who in their last moments had dragged themselves thither to quench their raging thirst, a condition which always follows loss of blood.

SECOND: From the well, climb the knoll and pass to the southwest till you come to the fence. It was on this knoll that Riedesel posted his infantry and cannon whose attack decided the battle of the 19th of September, 1777, for the British. About the knoll the British built a strong redoubt, which served as the southwest defense of their camp. Against this redoubt Arnold led the ineffectual charge after the retreat of the British on the 7th of October. On the little rocky knoll, a few rods to the west of you, the British had an outwork.

THIRD: Should you wish to see the only remains of Burgoyne's camp defenses, take the road one-half mile to the east to Mr. E. R. Wilbur's. The ravine you cross on the way was the line between Hamilton's and Fraser's camps. About a half mile from Mr. Wilbur's to the south, in the bushes, are some well preserved breastworks. Their location and form are marked on the map, as is also the location of Burgoyne's headquarters tent. When there, look for remains of old camp well over the fence to the west.

These are on the land of Mr. Eugene Curtis, and it is hoped that they may be preserved intact, as relics of the historic past are becoming more scarce and more interesting as the years go by.

FOURTH: About sixty rods to the northwest of Freeman's farm, and north of the road, is Breyman's hill, called by the residents Burgoyne's hill, a misnomer. This defended the extreme right of the British camp, and was held by the Germans under Colonel Breyman. The capture of this strong position by Arnold ended the second day's battle, and forced Burgoyne to retreat. Arnold broke through the breastworks between the road and the first clump of trees. Once within the works, he quickly compelled the defenders to retreat. In the contest which followed his entrance he was wounded, and Colonel Breyman was killed. The tablet is placed on the line of the works, while Arnold was doubtless wounded a little to the rear, to the east. Hardly a suggestion of the old earthworks remain here.

FIFTH: Returning to the road, pass up the hill to the west and turn to the left. It was this high ground, over which the road runs, that Fraser occupied and held during the first day's battle. Just after you have passed three houses, look on the right side of the road for the tablet which marks the place where General Fraser was shot. The basswood tree over the tablet grew out of the stump of the original one, under which the tragedy occurred. The man who shot him, Timothy Murphy, doubtless stood some eight hundred or a thousand feet to the west or south-west of this point.

SIXTH: Passing on you will notice, as you descend the hill, a tablet on the right of the road, against the fence. This is about on the line where Burgoyne posted his forces before the second battle. The British grenadiers, under Major Ackland, were posted from near this point around the base of the hill to the left. The British light infantry, with one cannon, occupied the hill over to the right and also a part of the plain this side of the hill. The Germans held the center. The artillery was posted at intervals from the right of Ackland's grenadiers to the center of the German lines. The twelve-pounders, over which there was such a stubborn fight, were posted in the rear of the German left, a little up the hill.

The battle opened with an attack by the Americans under General Poor on the grenadiers at the extreme left; at nearly the same time Dearborn and Learned struck both the British and German lines in front, while Morgan charged up the hill at the rear of the British extreme right, and forced them to retire. Soon Arnold compelled the Germans to give way when, after fifty-two minutes of fiercest fighting the entire force of the British were compelled to hurry back to their camp, which was stormed by Arnold and their right defense taken, as previously stated.

SEVENTH: Leaving the second day's battle ground, you pass toward the south, over a stone bridge. This bridge spans the Middle ravine, which figures so prominently in the history of the hostile camps, and the two battles. Passing on you soon come to an isolated hill crowned with farm buildings. From the top of the log house, which then stood there, Colonel Wilkinson observed the British army deploying into line and apparently offering battle, which fact he reported to General Gates, who at once ordered the attack. At the foot of this hill stands a tablet whose inscription gives the impression that from here General Fraser was shot. This could not be for two reasons: first, because Morgan and his men were not here, but were engaged with the British right, half a mile and more to the north-west; and second, because the shoulder of the hill would prevent seeing General Fraser from here, or if not the hill, the trees, and also the smoke of battle, would screen him at this distance.

EIGHTH: Passing on three-fourths of a mile toward the southeast, and climbing the hill, we come to the site of Fort Neilson, which defended the north-west angle of the American camp. The barns stand on the site of the old log barn about which the ramparts were thrown up. The wing to the rear of the main house is the identical one occupied by Morgan and Poor as their quarters. The interior has been kept intact. From this point Arnold no doubt mounted his horse and rushed into battle without orders. For the location and direction of the American works, and the point of departure of the divisions into battle, see map.

NINTH: After leaving Fort Neilson, as you continue down the road toward the south, somewhere down in the field to your left stood the ammunition magazine of the Americans. At the intersection of the roads, as you turn to the left, you will observe a tablet. A little way back of this in the field was Gates' headquarters, and up to the right of it was the hospital. Here Gates stayed during the second day's battle, and here he had the heated argument with Sir Francis Clerke, a wounded prisoner, over the merits of the questions at issue between the Americans and British, apparently more anxious to win in the battle of words than in the life and death struggle waging beyond the sally port of his camp.

TENTH: When you reach the foot of the hill at the river, you will see on your left, next the fence, a tablet marked Bemis' tavern. Fothem Bemis kept tavern here, and owned part of the heights to the west. Hence the name, Bemis Heights. The old tavern stood over in the fields a little way to the north. Now turning northward, you will soon see another tablet in front of a house to your left. From here ran strong entrenchments to the river, where a floating bridge spanned that stream. Note here the narrowness of the passage between the hill and river. It was a veritable Thermopylae. Burgoyne acknowledged in his testimony before the court of inquiry that he dare not attempt to force it. The crest of the hills, as you pass northward, were crowned with strong breastworks and batteries. Three-fourths of a mile to the north of Bemis', you will see another tablet on the right side of the road in front of a barn. This marks the site of the advance works of the Americans. Those entrenchments, however, were near the river to the south-east. See the map. A little farther on you will notice two houses, some distance off to your right, next the river. The lower farm was Vandenburgh's, and served as a stopping place over night for the frightened inhabitants on their way from the north to a place of safety. The highway ran along the river till after the Revolution.

ELEVENTH: Two miles to the north of Bemis Heights we come to Wilbur's basin. Here just to the north of the buildings Burgoyne had his hospital, his park of artillery, and his magazines. At the river bank were tied his transportation boats, and thrown across the river was a pontoon bridge. Up to the left you will notice three hills. On each of these was placed a battery for the defense of his camp and stores. On the middle one General Fraser was buried, and his body was never removed, so far as is known. Consult map for locations. The fourth house to the north along the river is Ensign's, where Neilson had his struggle with the big Indian described in the chapter of anecdotes.

TWELFTH: Nearly two miles north of Wilbur's basin you come to Searle's ferry. Forty rods above the ferry is a farm house. Turn to the west just north of the barns, pass over the canal bridge, and a few rods to the west of the bridge, on a rise of ground, and a little to your left, you will see a depression in the ground. That marks the cellar of Sword's house, which Burgoyne occupied two days as headquarters, and in the vicinity of which his army was encamped.

THIRTEENTH: Throughout the day you have noticed a high mountain on the east side of the river, about six miles away. That is Willard's mountain, so called from the fact that a Mr. Willard posted himself on that mountain during the latter days of Burgoyne's advance and signaled his observations to General Gates.

OLD SARATOGA,
(SCHUYLERVILLE)

DRAWN BY
JOHN H. BRANDOW,
From U. S. Geological Survey Map, Compared with
Burgoyne's Military-Map

Route Discontinued.
Old Route Still In Use.
Modern Roads.

LEARNED'S

FLEMEN

Canadians

Camp

SCALE.

GENERAL

VER

ON

GUIDE TO REVOLUTIONARY AND COLONIAL SITES AT SCHUYLERVILLE

Copied by permission from J. H. Brandow's "Old Saratoga and The Burgoyne Campaign."

Schuylerville is connected by rail with Saratoga Springs, 13 miles; Fort Edward, 12 miles by electric road; Greenwich, 6 miles; Mechanicville, 16 miles.

Many will doubtless be surprised and pleased to know that a goodly number of relics of Revolutionary and Colonial days are still to be seen at Schuylerville (the original Saratoga), and that many historic sites of the first importance are here pointed out with certainty. Consult the map in connection with guide.

As the multitudes of tourists who visit this hallowed spot naturally turn their steps toward the monument first, we will begin our tour at that point.

FIRST: The monument stands within the lines of Burgoyne's fortified camp. This camp took in the buildings just north of the monument, extended diagonally south-east down the hill across the road to near Chestnut street, thence south along the crest of the terrace into the Victory woods; thence west just over the brow of the hill to a point south of the cemetery; thence north along the western slope of the cemetery ridge to the place of beginning.

SECOND: About sixty rods northwest of the monument on a knoll covered with small trees, and now known as the Finch burying-ground, but owned by James H. Carscadden, are to be seen remains of earthworks thrown up by Morgan's men. This place can be seen from the monument. Look for them on the east side of burying-ground and also in the bushes.

THIRD: In the Victory woods, south of the monument, there are hundreds of feet of the British breastworks in an excellent state of preservation.   The ground never having been permanently cleared nor plowed, these earthworks remain as the British left them, except that the logs, which may have entered into their construction, are rotted away.   To find them, look for two pine trees near the northern end of the woods; between these trees you will find an angle in the works running south and west.   At the upper end of the northern leg of this angle are some rifle pits, plainly' discernible; there are also some in front and south of it.   Next, about 125 feet to the southwest, you will find another angle running west and then south; walk on the crest of these works till you come to an obtuse angle which veers to the southwest; near this some breastworks run directly south on the edge of a clearing.   You can follow these easily for several hundred feet.   Near the southern end of these turn to the left down into the woods and you will find a line of breastworks running from the swampy place through the woods to the crest of the ridge on the east.   These two latter works were doubtless intended to cover their outposts, or advanced pickets.

The writer asked Mr. J. J. Perkins, the custodian of the monument, who was in the artillery service several years during the civil war, to go over the ground with him, and he declares that there is no doubt of their genuineness.

These being the only relics of Burgoyne's defensive works remaining on this side of the river, at Schuylerville, it is earnestly hoped that they may be preserved intact.   They will doubtless remain undisturbed so long as they continue in the hands of the Victory Manufacturing Company.   These woods ought to be owned by the village, or State.

FOURTH: Back of the Victory schoolhouse, on a knoll covered with pines, may be seen remains of earthworks thrown up by the Americans.   These are in a good state of preservation.   This site is visible from the windows of the fourth and fifth stories of the monument.

FIFTH: Above the Victory Mills, on the south side of the creek, is a clump of pines against a hill.   On the top of the hill back of those pines are remains of Gates' works, where he had a battery posted.   This site is also visible from the monument. Just below the Victory stone bridge, on the right bank of the creek, is the site of Schuyler's upper sawmill, the only building spared to him by Burgoyne. That mill sawed the timber in the present Schuyler mansion.

SIXTH: Going down Burgoyne street from the monument, after you cross the railroad, the next street you come to is Pearl street. On either side of this street as you look northward you see the camp ground of several companies of British troops and some Germans who tented in the woods. A few of the ancient oaks may yet be seen in the Reformed Church yard.

SEVENTH: A few rods north of the foot of Burgoyne street, on the east side of Broadway, between the blacksmith shop and the brick store, stood the old elm under which, tradition says, Burgoyne signed the agreement to surrender, or "Convention," as he loved to call it. The tablet which hung on the old elm is now attached to the brick wall.

EIGHTH: Old Fort Hardy was located in the angle of Fish creek and the river. The road to Greenwich crosses its site. It was built in 1757 under the supervision of Colonel Montressor, a royal engineer, and it covered about fifteen acres. It supplanted a wooden or block-house fort which stood in the same angle, but the latter was, of course, a much smaller structure.

NINTH: On the continuation of Spring street, east of Broadway, is the place where Burgoyne had his artillery parked behind strong entrenchments. Directly opposite this on the other side of the river, on the high bluff, now void of trees, is the place where General Fellows had his battery posted, which so seriously annoyed the British. On the wooded bluff just to the north of this stood a Colonial fort built in 1721 (?).

TENTH: On the northwest angle of Spring street and Broadway, and on the high ground west of Broadway, as you go to the north, was the camp ground of the Germans ("Hessians"), under General Riedesel. A few rods northwest of the house on the corner, now owned by Mr. P. McNamara, were the barracks, built before the Revolution, burned by the British, and then rebuilt and occupied at one time by General Stark. Here no doubt the noted spy, Lovelass, was tried and condemned.

ELEVENTH: The Marshall house is the one in whose cellar the Baroness Riedesel (pronounced Re-day-zel), with her children, and the wounded officers, found refuge during the six days' siege of

Burgoyne. This is located about a mile north of Fish Creek and on high ground to the left of the road. It can be reached by electric cars. An iron sign marks the place. This house was built by Peter Lansing of Albany in 1773, as a farm house. In 1785 it came into the possession of Samuel Bushee, who in turn sold it to his brother-in-law, Samuel Marshall, in 1817. His son, William B. Marshall, repaired and altered it somewhat about 1868. He, however, had the good taste to leave the lower rooms and cellar, the really interesting portions, as they were.

The Marshalls relate the visit of an old man to the house in the early part of this (the nineteenth) century. He had not been here since the Revolutionary war, but always wanted to come and visit that house. He said that he was the gunner that leveled the cannon that bombarded the house, that they shot several times before they got the range; finally they saw the shingles fly, and then they kept it warm for that house and its occupants, as well as other points, till Burgoyne showed the white flag. On being asked why they fired on women and wounded soldiers, he replied that they supposed it to be Burgoyne's headquarters.

TWELFTH: A little to the north of the Marshall house, take the road to the east across the Canal bridge to the iron bridge that crosses the Hudson to Clark's Mills. Stop in the middle of the bridge and a little way to the north, on the east side in the rear of Mr. John A. Dix's house, you will see a road running diagonally down the bank. This was cut by the British as an approach to their pontoon bridge, there anchored. This road, together with the cut through the bank on the opposite side, locates the exact point where Burgoyne and his army crossed the Hudson September 13-15, 1777.

THIRTEENTH: Remains of the breastworks thrown up by Burgoyne to defend the bridge are to be seen just north of Mr. Dix's house, and the board fence which starts from the bridge, and runs north to the barn, is built on the crest of a portion of these old defenses.

FOURTEENTH: Looking east from this bridge, and a little to the left, are two rounded and bare knolls or hills. On the crest of the eastern one Captain Furnival posted his battery from which he began the cannonade of the Marshall house.

FIFTEENTH: Returning to and through Schuylerville, place yourself on the bridge that crosses Fish creek, near the south end. The stream which this bridge spans figures largely in both Colonial and Revolutionary history. It was the south line between the British and American armies during the siege of Burgoyne. Looking down stream the old ford crossed just this side the canal aqueduct, or about opposite the Schuyler mansion. There the French and Indians crossed on the night of November 27, 1745, to the massacre of Saratoga. There the armies in Colonial times crossed on their expeditions into Canada. There the British army crossed before and after the battles, and again after the surrender on October 17, 1777. A few rods below the bridge on the right side of the stream, in a recess in the bank, is the probable site of the early sawmill mentioned by the French in their story of the massacre of Saratoga, and also the site of one of General Schuyler's sawmills burned by Burgoyne. On the opposite side or left bank of the creek, just this side of the brick grist mill, stood General Schuyler's grist mill, also burned by Burgoyne. Turning around to your right you observe some cotton mills just above the bridge, and to the south of the creek. There stood several of the mills of General Schuyler burned by Burgoyne. Here was erected the first flax or linen mill in America, put up and run by General Schuyler. The tall mill nearest you and covered with vines, is the oldest cotton mill in New York State. It was erected by Philip Schuyler, 2d, in 1828.

SIXTEENTH: Leaving the bridge we come next to the Schuyler mansion, embowered in its grove of ancient trees. This was erected by Gen. Philip Schuyler in the month of November, 1777. The main house was put up in seventeen days by the artisans of Gates' army. This house has sheltered as guests, 'Washington, Alexander Hamilton, Gov. George Clinton, and Lafayette, and many other notables of our country. It remains substantially as General Schuyler left it. Its predecessor was burned by General Burgoyne on the 11th of October, 1777. That house stood about twelve rods southeast of the present one. The lilac bushes at the bottom of the excavation are the descendants of the ones that stood in the garden of mansion No. 2.

The original house, the one burned by the French and Indians at the time of the massacre, stood twenty rods directly east of the present one on the bank of the canal. That one was built of brick. In it Capt. Philip Schuyler, uncle of the general, was shot and a number of other occupants perished in the flames. To the east of the canal on the flats were the wheat fields set on fire by Mrs. General Schuyler to prevent them becoming forage for the British army.

SEVENTEENTH: Retracing your steps to the road near the bridge, and looking south you see at a little distance a brick house. Back of this house is a gravel hill which originally extended to the east across the road. On the eastern brink of that hill, as it then was, the noted spy Lovelass was hung, on the limb of an oak tree. He was buried underneath it in a sitting posture; John Strover saw him hung and buried, and told his son George all about it. When the Waterford and Whitehall turnpike was built this gravel hill was partially dug away. George Strover was present and waited until Lovelass' remains were unearthed, when he appropriated the skull. This gruesome relic is still kept in the Schuyler mansion.

EIGHTEENTH: About one-third of a mile south of the creek, and in the fork of the River and Victory roads, stood the old Dutch Reformed Church. It was built in 1771. Here after service on the 30th of April, 1775, the people of this neighborhood heard the news of Lexington and Concord from the lips of General Schuyler. That church was used by the British for a hospital. A young woman while sitting at one of the north windows was shot by an American sharpshooter, and her blood stained the floor as long as the building stood. The church was damaged a few days later by several cannon balls shot from the British batteries. It was afterwards used by the Americans as a commissary depot. This church was taken down in 1822.

NINETEENTH: Pass down the road a few rods till you stand under the rocks, and in front of a small house on the hill. Right east of you on the river bank you see the site of two, and perhaps four Colonial forts. The last two which stood there were the only ones of the eight, built in this vicinity, that saw any fighting. The first of the two was known as "the fort at Saratoga," and was burned by the French on the night of the massacre in 1745. Without the walls of the last one, or Fort Clinton, several bloody and disastrous encounters took place with the French and Indians.

This fort experienced at least one successful mutiny. It was soon after dismantled and burned by orders of Gov. George Clinton in October, 1747. The location of these interesting forts was lost for many years, but was discovered by the writer of this guide, Rev. John H. Brandow in the spring of 1900. Loose stones and brickbats cover the site of the forts.

TWENTIETH: Somewhere between the above mentioned house and the canal bridge, and south of where you stand, is the place where Burgoyne went through the formal act of surrender by drawing his sword and delivering it to General Gates.

The exact location has been irretrievably lost. The tablet that purports to mark the place should probably stand several rods to the north. The old road is said to have run where the canal now is.

TWENTY-FIRST: About ten rods below the canal bridge is a little ravine where a Tory waylaid Colonial Van Veghten, of Coveville. Screened by some trees he waited till the Colonel passed along a-horseback on his way up to visit General Schuyler. The Tory had his rifle leveled at him, and was about to pull the trigger, when his nerve failed him and he allowed the Colonel to pass unharmed. He related this incident after the Revolution.

TWENTY-SECOND: On the east side of the river, a mile or more south of the bridge, on the edge of a high bluff facing the south and overlooking a ravine, are some breastworks thrown up by the Green Mountain boys during the siege of Burgoyne. They are in an almost perfect state of preservation, still being breast high. They are on the farm now owned by Nathan Corliss. These were identified as Revolutionary remains by the writer during the summer of 1900, after his attention had been called to them by Mr. Robert Coffin, who lives in the neighborhood.

TWENTY-THIRD: About one and one-third miles below Fish creek, on the east side of the road, stands the house which was probably used by General Gates as his headquarters from the 10th to the 15th of October, 1777, and again used by him after the surrender. On the 14th or 15th of October he moved up to the place south of the old Dutch Church, where the formal surrender occurred on the 17th. The house was enlarged after the Revolution and is now owned and occupied by Edward Dwyer, who has the good taste to keep the house in its ancient form.

TWENTY-FOURTH: Looking off to the southeast from almost any point in or about Schuylerville one sees a mountain about ten miles away. That is Willard's Mountain; so called from the fact that a Mr. Willard posted himself on its top during the advance of Burgoyne, and signaled his observations to General Gates. This mountain is about 1,400 feet above sea level, and affords the finest and most extensive view to be had from any point within thirty miles from here.

Old Saratoga, destroyed by the French and Indians in 1745, was situated, mainly, just below the fort marked No. 17 on the map.

Schuylerville is well supplied with excellent hotels and well-equipped liveries. Carriage drives hereabouts are unusually numerous and attractive: To the battlefield, two ways, 9 miles; to Saratoga Lake, 9 miles; to Fort Miller, 5 miles; to Cossayuna Lake, 12 miles; to the magnificent Dianondahowa Falls, 3 miles; to Greenwich, 5 miles; to Bald Mountain, the deserted village, 4 miles, and to the top of Willard's Mountain, 12 miles. The roads are unusually good.

MAP OF
THE AMERICAN & BRITISH
FORTIFIED CAMPS

Also Showing the Saratoga Battlefields, of
September 19th and October 7th, 1777

Drawn by *JOHN H. BRANDOW*

From the U. S. Geological Survey Sheets. Compared with
Burgoyne's and other Military Maps, and after a personal
Survey of the Grounds.

Scale

Hudson River

Champlain Canal

KEY TO MAP

1. About Swart's house and vicinity the British camped from the 17th to 19th Sept.
2. Site of the original Freeman cottage.
3. Old battle well.
4. Present house at Freeman's farm.
5. Where Frazer was shot.
6. Here second battle ended, and Arnold was wounded.
7. Here Major Ackland was wounded, and so many Grenadiers fell.
8. Hill from which Col. Wilkinson observed movements of the British just before the second battle.
9. Where house stood in which Frazer died.
10. Hill on which Frazer was buried.
11. The remains of Burgoyne's camp defenses.
12. Burgoyne's pontoon bridge.
13. Fort Nelson, and house used by Morgan and Poor for headquarters.
14. Gates' headquarters.
15. American hospital.
16. Ammunition magazine.
17. Bemis' Tavern.
18. Gates' floating bridge.
19. Van Denbergh's house where the unsuspected inhabitants tarried at night, on their way to safety.
20. Enoka's where Neilson and the big Indian had their life and death struggle.

ST. LEGER'S INVASION AND THE BATTLE OF ORISKANY

FIRST PRIZE ESSAY

Wm. R. Stevens, North Tonawanda High School.

There are so-called "battles" occurring in the early part of the American Revolution which have been so related and studied, so emphasized and so lauded, that engagements which were literally battles and really of importance from a military point of view, have been overshadowed and obscured. Lexington was a mere skirmish, and in the battle of Bunker Hill the grossest ignorance of military science was displayed. In our own Empire State was fought a battle of greater consequence and of far more importance than either Lexington or Bunker Hill. That battle was the bloodiest of the war, the battle of Oriskany.

Oriskany was fought on the sixth of August, 1777. The year previous, the Declaration of Independence had been signed and given to the world. That the colonies were no longer fighting for the "immemorial rights" of Englishmen, was evident. They were fighting for freedom from governance by Great Britain. There had been many failures and defeats, such as the unfortunate loss of Ticonderoga, the abandonment of Long Island and the lower Hudson, and the British occupancy of New York. Washington's brilliant stroke at Trenton had arrested the downward-sinking hopes and restored the flagging confidence on the part of the patriots. Boston, that "hotbed of sedition," had driven the soldiers of England forever from her shores. The States, moreover, were universally supporting the cause. Georgia and South Carolina both had proved their loyalty, as had Virginia by furnishing many civil leaders. In the latter State all semblance of British control had been destroyed when the commander-in-chief formally struck the flag of Great Britain from the State House. In many of the States a State Constitution had been adopted. Among these was New York. In July of this same eventful year of seventeen hundred and seventy-seven, George Clinton had been duly inaugurated as Governor. Aid and alliance with France had been sought with assiduity. The generous and noble-hearted Lafayette had offered his services and had been appointed a major-general. Some of the generals had shown their inefficiency and jealousies and political intrigues were creating havoc. The people were poor. Paper money was depreciating. Derogatory comment was heard regarding Washington's slowness. Times were hard. New York was especially a sufferer. Burgoyne had advanced from Canada to the Hudson with the loss of only two hundred men. Clinton might at any moment move up the river. The success of the division penetrating inland from Oswego would mean the ultimate defeat of the Americans.

In England, Burke had plead the cause of America without result. William Pitt, by this time Earl of Chatham, had two years before declared that America could not be conquered. London's surging populace had demanded that the King stop this "unnatural and unfortunate" war.

The foregoing conditions composed the situation which confronted the British ministry and the difficult problem of defeating the rebels must, of necessity, be solved before the sun would again rise and set on territory actually ruled by King George, south of the St. Lawrence.

The British plan to again become pilots of these turbulent colonies was to enter upon a campaign for the capture of the Hudson Valley. The failure of Montgomery's Invasion would enable Burgoyne to proceed through the old Champlain route. Howe had been forced to leave New England where nearly one-third of the population and resources of the colonies was centered, but from there had gained a foothold at New York and the lower Hudson. Since they held a firm and assured position at Montreal, from there and New York as bases for operations, they intended to cut off New England from the other States and grasp the country between Lake Ontario and the Hudson. Here they thought, by adroit management, they might defeat the Americans in a decisive battle and gain New York, the key to the military position. Hence the plan was, specifically, Burgoyne was to start from Montreal up Lake Champlain to the headwaters of the Hudson; Howe, with Clinton, was to ascend the Hudson from New York; a third force composed of Indians, Tories, and regulars, was to advance from Montreal under Barry St. Leger, by way of Oswego, to the Mohawk Valley, from there making its way east and joining Burgoyne. Up to this time Burgoyne's march had been the march of a Napoleon. His capture of the fortress which had been considered impregnable had been a great blow to the States, especially to their confidence. The little outpost at the head of the Mohawk was to effectively stop the third part of the stratagem on which Burgoyne so much depended. The most important function was entrusted to St. Leger with the most inadequate of means.

This army so necessary to the success of the campaign was under the command of Barry St. Leger, suggested for this important position by Burgoyne, and appointed by the King himself. From his deeds we may infer that he deserved the confidence placed in him. His preventive measures, his stratagem at Oriskany, and the manner in which he directed the siege until the panic, which resulted at the rumor that Arnold was coming, shows that he was the man for the place. St. Leger had become an ensign in the regular army of England in 1756. In the year 1757 he came to America, where he served in the French and Indian War. Thus he gained a knowledge of the habits and disposition of the American Indians, and what he might expect from them under any circumstance. His regular rank was Lieutenant-Colonel of the Thirty-fourth Regulars. He was skilled in military affairs and his writings prove him literary in taste.

Subordinate to St. Leger, in rank, but surpassing him in his talents and personal magnetism, was Joseph Brant, chief of the Mohawks. Brant had been instrumental in gaining the Six Nations as allies of George III, the Oneidas and Tuscaroras only remaining neutral. He was now thirty-five years of age, tall and spare, lithe and quick, the ideal Indian. His was all the genius of the tribe. He had been educated in Connecticut schools and trained in the private home of Sir Wm. Johnson. Among the Indians he was without a peer.

Early in the summer of 1777, four hundred regular British troops, with other white men, had gathered at Oswego under Sir John Johnson and Col. Dan Claus. At the same time six hundred Tories and Canadians, who had been assembling on Carelton Island, near the head of the St. Lawrence, advanced to Oswego. Brant was marching to Oswego with about three hundred Indians. Brant found, when he reached Oswego, a few hundred other Indians who, at a council some weeks before, had been advised that the King of England was all-powerful. Moreover, they were informed that there should never be a lack of food or clothing and that rum should be "as plentiful as water in Lake Ontario." All this would be so, if they sided with the Great King. The King advanced each warrior a suit of clothes, a brass kettle, a gun, a tomahawk, powder and money. He also offered a bounty on every white man's scalp they might take. This made the Indians eager for war. When St. Leger finally took command the entire body totalled 1700 men. The Indians, led by Brant, were assured that if they would accompany St. Leger to Fort Schuyler they might sit down and smoke their pipes while they watched the British "whip the rebels."

Authorities differ so widely concerning the number and composition of St. Leger's force that I am at a loss as to what statements to make. One writer refers to St. Leger's army as a "motely band." Another states that it was a picked force, composed of regulars, Hessian-chasseurs, Royal-greens, Canadians, axemen and non-combatants, who as well as the Indians proved an incumbrance and curse to the expedition.

The order of march showed the skill and finesse for which St. Leger was justly noted. A detachment under Lieut. Bird was in advance and the rest of the army was a day's march in the rear. Johnson's whole regiment was with him, together with Butler's Tory Rangers and at least one company of Canadians. The country from Schoharie westward had been searched thoroughly for Royalists to add to this body. The route which the army took was by way of Oneida Lake. St. Leger was already acquainted with Burgoyne's success in the north and in view of this fact he confidently believed that the fort at the head of the Mohawk would surrender.

As regards this "fort at the head of the Mohawk," I would say that it was formerly Fort Stanwix, which had been built in 1758 during the French and Indian War and was named after General Stanwix, a British officer. In 1776 General Schuyler, at Washington's suggestion, had repaired and strengthened it. Accordingly it had been renamed "Fort Schuyler," in his honor. At this period it was strongly garrisoned with a force of 750 men under Col. Peter Gansevoort, with Col. Marinus Willet as second in command. It had provisions sufficient for a siege of six weeks, but with a short supply of ammunition for cannon; though enough for the small arms. It mounted fourteen guns. In fact it could boast all that any fortress which was up to date in that period could require, with the exception that it had no flag. The Stars and Stripes had been formally adopted by Congress in June, 1777. That summer, in Philadelphia, Betsey Ross had made the first American flag. No flag had reached this far western fort, as yet. Accordingly a specimen was rudely fashioned, one tradition has it, from a red flannel shirt, the white from a cotton shirt and the blue from a petticoat owned by one of the soldier's wives. The flag was soon floating proudly above the rampart. This, it seems, is the first recorded instance in our history in which the Stars and Stripes were ever hoisted in battle.

St. Leger, to return to that worthy, reached Fort Schuyler on August 3rd. He at once sent in a flag of true offering protection to all who might submit. Since the offer was resolutely refused, he began the siege on the following day. Concealed completely by the surrounding forest, the Indians were enabled to entirely encompass the fort. The besieged put up a gallant defense. St. Leger, upon his arrival, had sent a messenger to Burgoyne, to announce it. Of course he was ignorant of the difficulties into which that general was hourly advancing. Burgoyne's supply of stores was wholly inadequate and more than one-third of his horses had been unable to follow him from Canada. The streams were blocked with trees, as were the Indian trails. The British Ministry little knew into what perils they were sending the gallant and poetic Burgoyne. His advance was completely blocked. So seeking, by some brilliant stroke, relief, he sent the ill-fated expedition which failed to make "Molly Stark a widow."

St. Leger's army was given as much consideration as any army which had, thus far, been sent against the colonists. The residents of Tryon county had learned in early summer, of the arrival of St. Leger at Oswego, through Thomas Spencer, the Cherry Valley orator, who brought the tidings from Canada.

The most influential man of that section was Nicholas Herkimer, then sixty-five years of age, the hero of Oriskany and of this narrative. He was a Palatine, as were most of the settlers there. His figure, features, and mannerisms bespoke the typical German. I have read that he was uneducated. I will admit that he was unschooled and unlettered as his epistles betray; but a man who can wrest a living from the wilderness, become a factor in the community and lead soldiers as he could, certainly was not uneducated. So this stern old Indian fighter and political demagogue took upon himself the task of raising an army to oppose St. Leger. He issued a proclamation, calling upon the frontiersmen to organize in defense of their homes. Men between sixteen and sixty years of age were urged to enter the service, while those above sixty were to defend the women and children. About 800 or 1000 men assembled at Herkimer's call; a part of whom had gone with him to Unadilla, to meet Brant.

The meeting place was now made German Flatts. Herkimer, as soon as he learned that the fort had been besieged, set out for its relief. He encamped, on August 5th, about eight miles east of the besieged fortress. Here the officers under Herkimer grew intolerant of his delay and urged immediate advance. They called him a coward. They accused him of disloyalty. This latter was more stinging because he had a brother in the service of the King. So he finally gave the command to proceed. He has often been censured for this act; but if he had not followed their wishes it is not at all improbable that he would have lost his control over his troops and the relief expedition would have ended in a dismal failure. The soldiers had resumed their march but this time no precautions were taken. At the beginning of the march, Herkimer had advanced slowly and sent out scouts and skirmishers. Now it seemed as if he flung all caution to the winds. He must have been very angry and disgusted to have acted thus.

Look! the band is now entering a ravine, semi-circular in form and marshy at the bottom. What an opportune place for an ambuscade. And an ambuscade it is with Col. Butler leading his Tory Rangers and Brant commanding the Indians. Suddenly without the slightest warning an Indian warhoop is sounded and a terrific fire is opened upon the little army. What a scene of carnage presents itself. They are entirely surrounded. The men are falling like leaves. See that poor fellow on the right there pierced through the breast by a musketball. He falls, and a horribly-painted savage springs forward to complete the destruction. This is happening in countless other parts of the encounter. But now the Americans are recovering from their surprise and are seeking cover. Notice the shrewd method of Indian attack; he waits until the soldier behind the tree or stone has discharged his musket and then he rushes in to scalp him. To remedy this the Americans place two men behind each tree; one of whom, after the other has fired, will protect him while he is reloading. Ah! Herkimer is wounded. He has fallen from his horse, with his leg shattered just below the knee. They lift him and bear him along on his saddle, placing him beneath an oe'r-shadowing tree. The brave hero still intends to direct the battle. Other officers have been killed, including Col. Cox and Captains Davis and Van Sluyck. The slaughter resulting at these leaders' deaths is terrible. Even with these distressing scenes about him, the brave old Herkimer directs the battle with as much composure as a drill officer would conduct a dress parade. After the action has lasted about forty-five minutes and the Provincials were forming themselves into circles, the black clouds above, which have been threatening, suddenly open and the combatants are drenched by a terrific downpour of rain. This curbs the ardor and cools the heated blood of the Indians, and there is a lull in the battle. After the slight storm, the battle was renewed with vigor and gradually became a death struggle. Tories, neighbors to Herkimer's Provincials, find acquaintances on whom they wish to vent their anger in revenge for ancient grudges and so the battle evolves into a hand-to-hand conflict. At length the Indians hearing firing in the direction of the fort, where Willet made his sortie, became panic-stricken and fled into the deep woods. They were soon followed by the equally alarmed Tories and Canadians.

The Patriots were left masters of the field. The remains of Herkimer's command retreated to old Fort Schuyler (now Utica) carrying their wounded but without burying their dead; and made no further attempt at relieving the fort. Except the rear-guard, the army fought bravely. So far as is known the rear took flight with the first volley. Herkimer was carried to his home below Little Falls, where he died from the effects of the excessive bleeding of his wound. His age (sixty-five) probably was a factor in causing his death.

The Americans claimed a victory in this field, because the survivors were allowed to retire unmolested. This they were able to do because the Indians had fled and the white troop had been recalled to the defense of their camp. Oriskany deserves rightly the name of the bloodiest battle of the war. St. Leger says in his different reports that not over two hundred (out of eight hundred or nine hundred) escaped. The smallest list gives one hundred and sixty killed and about two hundred wounded and prisoners. Here, again, historians differ.

In the meanwhile St. Leger was having the time of his life "whipping the rebels." When Herkimer sent word that he was coming to their relief, a detachment, drawn from Gansevoort's and Wesson's regiments, made a sortie on the camp of Johnson's Royal Greens. This was done so suddenly and unexpectedly that the Royal Greens fled. Johnson's papers and baggage with those of the other officers and the clothing, blankets, stores and camp accessories, sufficient to fill twenty wagons, were captured. Five British standards were trophies of the attack. It is nearly always regarded as a notable achievement or a magnificent feat of arms, this sortie of Willet's. That it was entirely destitute of peril, and throughout uninterrupted is shown by the thoroughness with which Willet ransacked the Royal Green and Indian camps and the complete leisure that was afforded for looting them with only a slight chance of retaliation by the absent enemy. St. Leger's total number of whites was said to be four hundred and ten. At first he sent out about eighty of these and perhaps later one hundred went to the assistance of Johnson. This would leave St. Leger at most 257 whites. Substracting the number of men required on detached duty and any fair-minded and just person will believe the British commander when he said he had only two hundred whites and no savages with him when Willet made the attack. The Indians who had accompanied St. Leger had all gone to Oriskany with Johnson and Brant. Willet made the sortie with two hundred and fifty whites while St. Leger had only two hundred to oppose him.

After Oriskany, St. Leger still continued the siege and the garrison bravely held out. Col. Willet himself undertook the perilous journey to Schuyler with Gansevoort's appeal for aid. Gen. Schuyler wisely saw the advantage which would be gained if St. Leger could be kept from joining Burgoyne. Accordingly, he called a council of his officers to consider the matter. The officers objected to this measure on the grounds that the army would then be too weak to successfully oppose Burgoyne. Angered at a slanderous remark which he had overheard, he announced that he would make his call for volunteers on the following day. He then asked for a leader. The adventure-loving Arnold stepped forward.

By noon of the following day (August 13th) eight hundred men had been enrolled. They were mostly members of the Massachusetts brigade of Gen. Larned. They advanced as far as German Flatts. Here Arnold found a half-idiotic Tory. He was a prisoner and had been tried and condemned to death. Pardon was promised, if he would go with a friendly Oneida Indian among the savages in St. Leger's camp, and tell them of the great number of the enemy advancing upon them. He agreed to this. Having shot several holes through his coat and quite out of breath, he appeared among the astonished savages. The evidence of a "terrible encounter" with the approaching Americans was sufficient to cause great excitement among the Indians, and when the Oneida came running from another direction, the Indians ignominiously fled. The whites soon followed them and the siege of Fort Schuyler was at an end. So ended this Invasion which, if it had turned out more successfully, would, in any event, have prevented the tragic fate of Burgoyne's army. The failure of St. Leger's Expedition was a severe blow to the aspirations of Burgoyne. He and his army were doomed to be captured. It was inevitable.

Oriskany has been compared to Thermopylae. The substance of the matter is that it was not the defense of Fort Schuyler but the patriotism and self-devotion of Herkimer and his militia that saved the Mohawk Valley and likens Oriskany to Thermopylae. Oriskany was the crisis and turning-point against the British of the Burgoyne campaign and the decisive conflict of America's long war for Independence. It prevented St. Leger from joining with Burgoyne. The retreat of St. Leger made possible the battle of Saratoga. Oriskany saved the Mohawk Valley from devastation and the horrors of Indian massacre. It showed that the Indians were not only a disadvantage but a positive danger to the body with whom they are connected. And it was apparent that men, though untrained militia, when fighting for their homes and all that is sacred and are in the right, can make a creditable showing against men trained in the art of warfare and paid to take the lives of their fellow-men.

ST. LEGER'S INVASION AND THE BATTLE OF ORISKANY

SECOND PRIZE ESSAY

Miss Pearl Thurber, Masten Park High School, Buffalo.

Who am I, good friend, you ask? Have no fear of me. I come to do no harm. I could no longer refrain from revisiting this beautiful valley of the Mohawk where one hundred and thirty-five years ago we were besieged by St. Leger in Fort Stanwix.

Oh! I see you are interested immediately upon hearing the name of that little fort that stood there at the edge of civilization so long, serving the French, the English and then, us of the Continental Army. Tell you more of it! Yes, if you do not fear to be in the company of the ghost of a departed mortal. For the time being you will have to leave your human form and join me in the spirit. Come, I must hasten in order to get back before break of day.

You know from the study of history that the plan of the English was that Burgoyne should come from the north by way of Lake Champlain to Albany where he was to be joined by Howe from New York, and St. Leger who was to go up the St. Lawrence river to Lake Ontario, to Oswego, take Fort Stanwix and gather all the loyalists, of whom there were many, on his way down the Mohawk to Albany. By this great move which they considered a masterstroke, they intended to separate the strongly patriotic New England states from the southern states.

When news of this reached us at the fort, Gansevoort, our commander, determined not to give in, and we strongly seconded him, if we could but finish rebuilding the fort and get more ammunition and men to help us withstand the attack. It so happened that we had scarcely managed to accomplish this before St. Leger and his band of about one thousand hooting Indians and six hundred Greens and rangers were before us and surrounded the fort, cutting us off from all communication with the outside world.

St. Leger sent two of his officers, Captain and Walter Butler, under a flag of truce, to demand that we surrender the fort, threatening that if we did not do so, the Indians would be let loose on settlements along the Mohawk to kill men, women and children. Colonel Gansevoort had us bring them, blindfolded, into a room, where the shades were drawn and candles burned on a table, set to receive visitors, and there he told Walter Butler, the spokesman, that he might look at the fort from the outside but not enter it as a result of our surrender. It was inspiring to hear our Colonel tell him in such emphatic terms just what were our intentions. He said that he would not consider a verbal demand of surrender, for common courtesy required a written demand. The next day, you may be assured, the written message was sent, to which Colonel Gansevoort replied:—

"In answer to your letter of this day's date, I have only to say that it is my determined resolution, with the forces under my command, to defend this fort at every hazard to the last extremity, in behalf of the United American States who have placed me here to defend it against all their enemies.

I have the honor to be sir,

Your most obedient and humble servant,

PETER GANSEVOORT."

Was that not quite a brief answer to the lengthy demand sent by St. Leger?

St. Leger, thereupon, opened fire on us, but to no effect, and finding this method useless, he sought to annoy us by throwing shells and burning the outside barracks, but that did not worry us very much. What did worry us was that our provisions, after a while, ran low and as a result a few cowards deserted.

About ten o'clock in the morning of the sixth of August we heard a distant firing and were very much puzzled as to what it should mean. About one o'clock when Adam Helmer and another messenger arrived, weary, footsore and hungry, they told us they had come to tell us that General Herkimer wanted us to make a furious sortie to cover his arrival with re-enforcements, 800 men in all.

About the time we were ready to make the sortie, a terrific thunderstorm broke forth and we had to wait until after the storm. The sortie was so unexpected that the English that were in camp left everything in their hasty flight. Sir John Johnson had not even time enough to put on his coat which he had removed because of the intense heat. We took twenty-one loads of booty to the fort. St. Leger attempted to interfere with our returning to the fort, but he was obliged to give up. Among other things were five British standards which we soon had floating beneath our flag which we had made the day of the investiture, by using a shirt for the white, part of a red petticoat which we found for the red, and my cloak that I had taken in a previous skirmish with the British for the blue field. This was the first American flag. Ah! you say that you know who I am, now that I mention that about the cloak. Well, let me see whether or not you can guess correctly. Yes, Captain Abraham Swartwout is the name I bore while on earth.

The next day, Jonathan Gore came to the fort and told us that the firing we had heard had come from Oriskany where General Nicholas Herkimer and his men had been caught in a veritable death trap in the marsh.

The General, who was the chairman of the Committee of Safety of Tryon County, received word from Thomas Spencer, a half breed Oneida, that a force of some seventeen hundred Indians and English were coming from Oswego, intending to take our fort and swee pdown the Mohawk, devastating as they went. Spencer urged the men of Tryon County to arouse themselves and fight for their homes and loved ones. He said that the Indians hostile to our cause had accepted the tomahawk as a sign of their having united with the English and that as soon as they discovered the Oneidas, Onondagas and Tuscaroras, the three weakest tribes, had not joined the league, they would proceed to wreak vengeance on them as well as the settlers and they would not be able to protect themselves unless the Americans wree willing to join forces. The General upon receipt of this news ordered all able-bodied men to join him to come to our aid, and threatened cowards.

General Herkimer had not wanted to march until he heard the firing from the sortie, but his subordinates were so impatient that they accused him of being a Tory and waiting for affairs to reach such a point that he might be able to turn and take up the cause of the hated "Britishers." These accusations stung him to the quick and he gave the order, "March on!" though he did it against his better judgment. The men were so delighted that within an hour they had broken camp and were marching in a very disorderly fashion—as they thought, to our aid, but for many of them to their deaths.

Gore said that as the advance guard, preceded by the baggage train, descended into the ravine where they were intending to follow the corduroy road to our assistance, they heard the most blood curdling yells and were soon hemmed in by the Indians and Butler's rangers, the rear-guard thereby being cut off from assisting them. A few of the Indians followed the rear guard and caused them to suffer greatly, very few escaping the tomahawk.

The General, who was on a white horse, an easy mark for the rangers, was struck by a ball which shattered his limb below the knee and killed his horse. He had some of the men put him on his saddle at the foot of a birch tree where he calmly proceeded to light his pipe with the aid of his tinder-box and from this position he gave his orders. When urged to retire from so prominent a position he said, "I will face the enemy!" and calmly turned his attention to the fight.

Gore said the struggle was awful to see, and I know it, for after the siege was raised we passed the field of battle and there we saw neighbors, and Indians and patriots dead in each other's clutches.

One cause of the terrible loss of life was the fact that, as the rifles we used in those days were not repeaters such as you use now, but had to be reloaded after each shot, the Indians took advantage of this and whenever they saw a man fire, rushed up and tomahawked the poor fellow before he had time to reload his gun.

After they had fought for a long time, the storm which I mentioned with reference to the sortie, interrupted the fight for the space of about three-quarters of an hour. This respite, many of us thought in after days, was decreed by our heavenly Father, so that the patriots might have time to rest and arrange a plan of battle, and that the Indians might have time to take an inventory of their losses, and compare the reality with what had been promised them.

Herkimer and his officers decided that to counteract the mode of fighting adopted by the Indians, two men should be ordered behind a tree, the one to shoot and the other to reserve his shot till the Indian came running to scalp the one who had fired the first shot. In addition to this they formed a circle which it was well nigh impossible to break.

Johnson's Greens came to re-enforce Butler and Thayendanegea or Joseph Brant, the leader of the Indians, but as they were Tories from the very locality from whence our patriot band had come, they feared the frenzied fighting of their neighbors and therefore attempted to deceive them by turning their coats inside out, but they paid dearly for the ruse. Cox, one of the most powerful men of physique as well as in influencing and inspiring the men under him detected the ruse almost instantly, but others, not as quick of perception, were taken prisoners before they realized that these were not friends, but enemies. Cox shouted to his men, "Look at their coats," and then ensued as you know, one of the fiercest battles in history, for there were brothers against brothers, neighbors against neighbors and fiendish savages against infuriated farmers. Everyone fought with a irght good will, for in many cases there were personal grudges to be repaid and differences to be settled.

The Indians, finding they were being worsted at their own game, gave the cry of retreat, "Oonah! Oonah!" and nothing that Butler could say or do could keep them from leaving the field, for had they not lost enough, nineteen of their favorite chiefs beside many of their warriors? In answer to all inducements Butler presented to them, Gore said a prisoner he took told him they replied "You told us we need do no fighting. We could take this fort as Ticonderoga had been. Instead, we are losing our best warriors. You wanted only to kill us off," and they left the English to fight the men of Tyron County who were left, saying they "did not care to fight Dutch Yankees any more." Many of them turned and fired on the English, giving new hope and strength to Herkimer's men, when they saw that their opponents were disagreeing.

Our men, as did the Greeks at Thermoplae, did "Strike for their altars and their fires, strike for the green graves of their sires, God and their native land," and woe betide those whom they struck.

The rain put the rifles out of commission, but the awful slaughter continued, for there were knives and hatchets left to carry it on.

The morning of the seventh we missed Colonel Marinus Willet and Lieutenant Stockwell and after a while we discovered that they had been sent out the night before on some unknown expedition.

After we had been surrounded by St. Leger and Johnson and Brant with their men for some time, Colonel Gansevoort, almost giving up hope of receiving help from outside, for he had not heard from Colonel Willet, who we found had been sent to arouse the militia to action, determined that if no other course presented itself, he would make an attempt to march by night, right through the enemy's ranks.

This was not necessary, for on the twenty-second we were surprised to see our besiegers breaking up camp in a great hurry and rushing away from us. This was soon explained by Hans Yost Schuyler, a Tory, who was held in awe by the Indians as are all half-witted people. He told us that he had been sent by

General Arnold, who was coming to re-enforce us, to appear in the camp of the Indians in St. Leger's band and frighten them by accounts of the large force that was coming to the assistance of the handful of men in the fort. When asked how many were coming he pointed to the leaves on the trees. That was the last straw for the Indians. They had lost heavily in the battle at Oriskany and here their allies were going to use them again as a shield against the attacks of the enemy. They were thoroughly frightened and would listen to none of St. Leger's pleadings, when three or four Oneidas appeared at different times from different directions and confirmed Han Yost's report, but ran for the woods, and the few English who were left had nothing to do but make their way to Oswego as fast as they could. The Indians to get revenge ran behind them calling, "They're coming" every time they lagged a bit and killed or scalped all who could not keep up in the race.

We learned later, that Han Yost's brother was held as hostage to insure his performance of this task, for he had been condemned to be hanged, but his mother pleaded so for him that Arnold promised him his liberty on condition that he do this. His clothes were shot full of holes before he left and he pointed to the bullet holes as a sign to the Indians of his narrow escape.

Was not this an instance of the foolish things of this world being done to confound the wise?

We have passed the places where all these exciting things happened, and here is the grave of General Nicholas Herkimer, beloved of all Tryon County, the hero of Oriskany, neglected and almost unknown.

You may think that he was indiscreet in giving the command to march before hearing the firing of the sortie, but I know, that had you been in his place, you would not have borne the taunts as long as he did.

He paid dearly for his having yielded, but he became the idol of all of us New Yorkers, because there he sat for nearly five hours after having been wounded so badly and directed the battle. We heard after the siege was raised that he died several days after as a result of the lack of proper care. An operation was performed, but those who were in attendance at his bedside could not resist the temptation to partake of liquor and when they awoke, he as well as the rest realized that his hours were numbered. He was a hero on the field and he was also a Christian hero. He calmly read the thirty-eight Psalm to those about him and a few hours later he died. How true were the words of that psalm, "My heart panteth, my strength faileth me," in his case.

It is this, that those who wish to call themselves loyal and patriotic Americans should not erect a monument to honor those who died in or as a result of this bloody battle, which has caused my spirit so much unrest.

I hoped that I might meet some mortal to talk to and arouse to his sense of duty to his forefathers who gave their all of this world and their lives that their posterity might be free.

In the October following the battle, the Continental Congress directed that a monument of the value of five hundred dollars be erected to "the memory of those who equally with them perilled life and fortune and sacred honor in the cause of their country." New York was made trustee of the fund.

What has happened to you people of the United States? Is the tariff issue of more importance than the patriotism of the heroes which made it possible that you might have a country and a government which can and may levy duties without the interference of another power ?

I say, Awake, O America, and slumber not! Be reminded, New York, of the trust placed in you when that sum was so sacredly and solemnly pledged! Bestir yourselves, you people of the United States (how much that should mean) and swell that sum to an amount large enough to erect a column whose head "the earliest beams of the morning shall gild and parting day linger and play upon its summit!"

Pardon, my friend, I could not restrain myself. I have kept this feeling pent up for over a century. Ah! there is the warning sent me by the sun that I must depart. Farewell! Farewell!

ST. LEGER'S INVASION AND THE BATTLE OF ORISKANY

THIRD PRIZE ESSAY·

Alvan LeRoy Barach, Townsend Harris Hall, High School Division of College of the City of New York.

The campaign of 1777 or, as it is more popularly called, Burgoyne's Invasion, was one of the most important plans conceived against the Revolution. In no other campaign could the consequences have been so great, if successful, or the results so far-reaching, as a failure. In the War for Independence it was the turning point upon which everything hung. The success of the plan would have meant the failure of the Revolution, and the failure of the plan determined the success of the Revolution. The campaign, as originated by Lord Germain, Secretary of War, had for its immediate object the thorough possession of New York state, its ultimate aim the separation of the colonies.

The plan was threefold. Howe, who had driven Washington from Long Island, thereby obtaining control of the base of the Hudson and New York and the islands in the vicinity, was to sail up the Hudson to Albany. Burgoyne was ordered to proceed down from Canada, capture the forts Ticonderoga and Crown Point, and push his way through the wilderness to join Howe. The completion of the plan required Lieutenant Colonel Barry St. Leger to advance from Montreal, by way of Lake Ontario, to Oswego, march east to Fort Stanwix, and, after reducing that fort and subjugating the Mohawk Valley, effect a junction with Howe and Burgoyne. The three commanders would then crush to pieces the American force between them, effectually stamp out the last vestige of resistance on the part of the New York patriots, and be complete and undisputed masters of that colony. This possession of New York state would "drive a wedge into the heart of the union," cut off New England from all hope of succor from the rest of the states, and give the British a "vantage ground for sweeping and decisive operations." Undoubtedly, it would have been a short time before the New England states, hemmed in between Canada and a strong hostile force in New York, would have been compelled to surrender. The rest of the colonies, weakened by the helplessness of New England, deprived of the support of France, who would have assuredly withheld any assistance had we been defeated, and beset by invading English armies, would have been able to resist the British for a short time only. The possession of the state of New York by England would thus have caused both the separation of the colonies and the dissolution of the union. The design was a great one, and admirably planned, but its execution was, for a large part, lax.

Burgoyne, having captured Ticonderoga and Crown Point, at length pushed his way, hindered and obstructed by Schuyler, to Fort Edward, twenty miles from Albany. Howe did not get his orders in time to be of any use, and so failed to co-operate with Burgoyne. The success of the campaign thus hung upon St. Leger. Should he be able to reduce the Mohawk Valley and reach Albany, Burgoyne thought, and very rightly, it would be a very easy matter to crush the American army between them.

St. Leger started from Montreal July, 1777, with a force of trained European soldiers and a regiment of Canadians. On arriving at Oswego his command was increased by Sir John Johnson and his regiment of Tories gathered from the surrounding country, the Butlers with their Rangers, and eight or nine hundred Indians under the noted Joseph Brant or Thayendanegea. This gave him a force of finely-equipped, excellently trained men with competent, experienced, and sagacious leaders. The army of St. Leger probably numbered all together sixteen or seventeen hundred men. The expedition reached Fort Stanwix or Fort Schuyler, on the second of August without losing a man, and the siege began at once.

Colonel Peter Gansevoort was in command of the garrison of the fort, which comprised seven hundred and fifty men. Although young in years, he possessed not only the bravery and fortitude of youth, but also the caution and sagaciousness of the aged and the experienced. Lieutenant-Colonel Marinus Willet, a hardy, daring and practiced soldier, was second in command. Both acted in a most worthy and commendable manner and both were rewarded by Congress for their zealous defense of the fort. When Col. Gansevoort learned of the expedition against him he issued a call for help to the Committee of Safety of Tryon County. The people of the county eagerly responded to his appeal, and soon eight hundred patriots had set out to the relief of the fort. The commander and gatherer of these men was General Herkimer, small, dark, and thin, cool, cautious and deliberate, and brave, honest, and sincere. When the force had come within a few miles of the fort Gen. Herkimer sent messengers to tell Col. Gansevoort to fire three guns as a signal that he should advance and, at the same time, to make a sortie from the fort. But the messengers were detained and the cannon-shots were not heard. The younger officers, impatient at delay, opposed the good counsel of Herkimer to wait for the signals, and hotly urged the brave but prudent general to proceed. When they found him quite determined to halt they reviled him with bitter taunts and even accused him of cowardice. At length, having endured their unjust insults as long as he could, he gave the order to advance.

In the meantime, St. Leger, who had heard of the approach of Herkimer, sent his Indian force under Brant, Sir Johnson with his regiment, and Col. Butler and his rangers to prepare an ambush for the patriots. With Indian cunning Brant picked out the position, which was a narrow, raised pass or road traversing a marshy ravine and almost entirely surrounded by trees and shrubberies. Johnson, who was in command, stationed marksmen around the road in a semicircle and ordered no one to fire until the American force was fully enclosed in the pass. The Americans, who were proceeding quickly and without caution, marched unsuspectingly into the trap and all but the rear guard had entered the road when the attack was begun by the too impatient Indians. The rear guard, cut off from the main body by the onslaught, was compelled to flee and suffered very heavily from the pursuing Indians. The rest of the army, stunned by the suddenness of the attack, surrounded on all sides, and thrown into confusion by the murderous fire of the enemy, seemed on the verge of annihilation. But the terrible destruction continued only for a short time when the Americans, forming circles and taking advantage of every possible cover, began to resist the attack more vigorously and more effectively. Gen. Herkimer, his leg having been shattered by a musket-ball and his horse having been shot from under him, was placed upon his saddle against a tree.

There, amidst the roar of battle and the shower of bullets and arrows, he cooly lit his pipe, and continued to direct the battle with the utmost calm. His fortitude greatly encouraged the patriots, who, back to back, were now returning shot for shot. At length, when the din and fire of the battle had just begun to subside, while the dead and wounded lay undistinguished on the bloody ground, a terrific rain storm burst upon the struggling combatants. But it served only as a respite, in which both commanders took new measures for conducting the fight. Hitherto, when an American fired a shot from behind a tree an Indian would rush out and tomahawk him before he had a chance to reload. To remedy this it was arranged that two men should station themselves behind a single tree, so that, when one man fired, the other would be ready with his shot for the Indian who would run out.

The rain finally stopped and the struggle was renewed. The new arrangement of the Americans worked admirably, and the Indians were made to suffer severely by the more co-operative patriots. A troop of Johnson's Greens, disguised as Americans, now arrived, apparently as a relief from the fort; but the ruse was detected in time and nearly all were shot down. This threw greater bitterness into the contest. Men who had been old neighbors before now met and vented their deadly hatred upon each other with shot, sword, and gunstock. The conflict was characterized by all the animosity of a civil war, and all the fortitude of a religious war. Many were the deeds of valor and daring which were performed that day; many were the feats of strength and hardihood. At length, the Indians, seeing that they were getting the worst of it, set up their retreating cry, "Oonah," and fled from the field. Thus abandoned, Johnson, who now heard firing from the direction of his camp, which was the sortie that Herkimer had arranged with Gansevoort, ordered a general retreat. Gen. Herkimer and the remnants of his force were now left in full possession of the field. Thus ended the Battle of Oriskany, a struggle of brave, determined men against almost overwhelming odds.

The casualties of the battle have been much disputed. St. Leger does not state his white loss, but mentions thirty Indians killed. The British estimate of the American loss puts it about four hundred killed and two hundred captured. This is doubt-less an exaggeration. The Americans admit about two hundred killed. Careful estimates of the British loss place the number of Indians killed, including some favorite chiefs, at least a hundred, and of white men about fifty. For the amount of men engaged it was by far the bloodiest battle of the Revolution. Gen. Herki-mer died ten days after from the wound he received.

The Battle of Oriskany has been taken by some as a victory for the British. Admitting that St. Leger's force retreated from the field, they base their claim first, upon the great loss the Amer-ican army suffered; secondly, upon the fact that the relief ex-pedition failed in its object of bringing aid to the fort, since it was practically broken up by the battle. These considerations, though they are of some weight, fade away into insignificance, when the ultimate results loom into sight. Directly and indirect-ly, we shall see the effects of the Battle of Oriskany spread itself over the campaign of 1777 and the War of the Revolution.

St. Leger's force was undoubtedly weakened by the engage-ment. Although he lost but a hundred and fifty men, yet it was no inconsiderable number for the amount of soldiers he had in his whole army. Realizing what an arduous task it would be to compel the garrison to surrender by force, he tried to frighten them into giving up the fort by misrepresentations. He reported the American force terribly routed at the Battle of Oriskany; he announced as a fact, what seemed quite probable at that time, that Burgoyne had defeated the Americans and was in posses-sion of Albany; and he furthermore declared that he would be unable to control his Indians if an engagement took place, and that they would probably massacre every one in the fort. He assured them that further resistance would cause only slaughter and certain defeat. But no manner of intimidations could daunt the hardy commander who had determined to hold out until the last.

St. Leger then energetically attempted to take the fort by force. His artillery was put into use, but it made no impression upon the sod breastworks of the enemy. He attempted to ap-proach the fort by sap, and was quite far advanced in that tedi-ous undertaking when some unexpected tidings were brought to his camp.

The Indians, because they had lost a hundred of their warriors and several favorite chiefs in the Battle of Oriskany, had become intractable and burdensome to St. Leger. When they now heard the exaggerated reports of Arnold's number they insisted that St. Leger retreat. They declared that they would not fight any more and that, were he not to go, they would abandon him and go away themselves. This attitude can be explained only as a direct result of the Battle of Oriskany, and it virtually forced St. Leger to raise the siege and retreat with the Indians, who afterward proved a positive trouble and danger to his whole army.

The campaign in the Mohawk Valley was now ended, and what was its effect upon that valley? The loyalists were effectually subdued, thus rendering impossible forever after any danger of a Tory uprising. On the other hand, the enthusiastic and exultant patriots rallied under Arnold and helped to win the first battle of Bemis Heights.

Upon the campaign of 1777, its effect was ruinous. The failure of St. Leger to co-operate, caused in great part by the results of the Battle of Oriskany, cut off the right wing of Burgoyne's army and was a most potent cause of his defeat at Saratoga. For had St. Leger's army been successful, had it marched victoriously through the Mohawk Valley and joined Burgoyne advancing from the North, Gates' army would have been caught between two fires and would probably have been entirely wiped out.

As it was, however, Burgoyne was defeated at Bemis Heights, and that practically decided the war in our favor. We thus establish a chain of events from the Battle of Oriskany to the establishment of our Independence, each link depending on the one proceeding. We may roughly say that the connected links in this chain are the following closely related events, the Battle of Oriskany, the failure of St. Leger's Invasion, Burgoyne's defeat at Saratoga, and the establishment of our Independence.

PRESENTATION TO ASSOCIATION OF COLONIAL WARS TABLET, AT FORT AMHERST

(Being part of the Final Dedicatory Ceremonies connected with
the Ter-Centenary Celebration of the Discovery of
Lake Champlain, July 5, 1912.)

James Austin Holden.
State Historian and Treasurer New York State Historical Association.

The tablet was formally accepted for the New York State Historical Association by State Historian James A. Holden of Glens Falls, who is ex-officio a member of the committee in charge of the Crown Point Reservation, as well as Treasurer of the New York State Historical Association. He spoke briefly as follows:

Your Excellency, Ter-Centenary Commissioners, Representatives of Vermont, of France, of Patriotic and Historical Societies, Ladies and Gentlemen:

It is with great pleasure that I accept on behalf of the New York State Historical Association, the official custodian of the Crown Point Reservation, this beautiful and distinctive tablet which has just been presented by the Society of Colonial Wars to the State of New York, through you, its Governor.

It is especially gratifying to the Association to receive it from your hands, for it is to you, and your broad and patriotic conception of the duties of the chief executive of the State, that our hearty thanks are due for the generous and welcome local appropriations which you lately have approved, making so largely for the preservation, the maintenance and popularity of the reservation.

On this torrid July day whose sun's rays reflected from these crumbling walls are full as deadly as any of the bullets which blazed forth at them in days of old, my words of acceptance must be brief indeed.

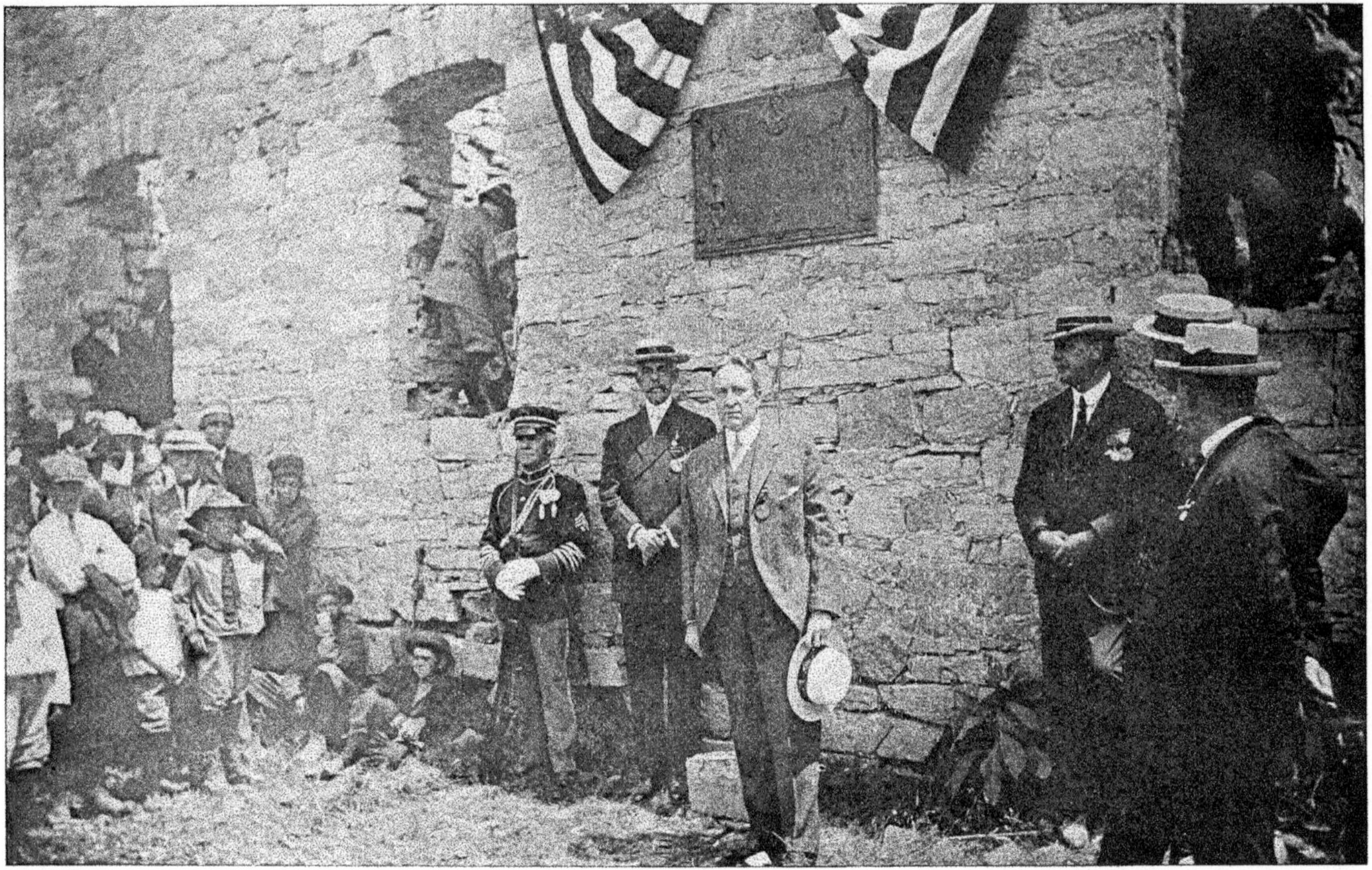

UNVEILING TABLET AT FORT AMHERST, JULY 5, 1912

This expressive addition then, to these historic walls, whose story is rife with actions of emprise and derring-do, around which still hover the historic spirits of the olden wars, connected with which are the inspiring deeds of the knightly souls of Montcalm and Amherst, of Warner and Burgoyne, yes, even of Arnold the patriot, not yet the traitor, full of the memories of the now shadowy hosts of white coated Bourbons, the red attired British, and the buff and blue covered Revolutionists, we accept and assure your Excellency that it shall be our earnest endeavor to prove worthy in every way of the confidence reposed in us in making this Association the State's representative for this reservation.

On behalf of the Association I now turn over to the Secretary of the Association the formal care of the tablet, thanking once more your Excellency and all who have been concerned in the presentation of this memorial, for giving to the Association this further opportunity to prove its historical usefulness, and to justify its being, and for providing this occasion to exemplify practically the purposes for which it was founded.

Frederick B. Richards, Secretary of the New York State Historical Association, at the unveiling of the Tablet on Fort Amherst at Crown Point, N. Y., July 5, 1912.

I supplement State Historian Holden because I feel that it will take at least two to make up for the absence of our esteemed President, Ex-Comptroller Roberts, who was to have represented the New York State Historical Association this morning.

We feel deeply honored that the State has designated our Association as custodians of this Reservation. We are still further honored by being entrusted with this beautiful tablet, erected by the Society of Colonial Wars, which, linking as it does the past with the present, adds to the interest of these old ruins.

I will not detain you longer this morning except to call your attention to one feature of the tablet in which I am particularly interested. You will notice that the list of the Regiments is supported on the left by a Highlander, a private of the Royal Highlanders as they were known in this campaign, otherwise called the 42nd, "Old Forty-Twa," or the Black Watch.

The Black Watch, the oldest Highland regiment in the British Army and one of the regiments under Amherst which helped to build this old fort, was selected for this place of honor because of its unparalleled gallantry in the assault on Fort Ticonderoga under General Abercrombie the year before, in which engagement it lost 646, killed and wounded, out of a total strength of a thousand men who went into action, or a mortality twice that of the Light Brigade at Balaklava, immortalized by Tennyson.

TABLET ERECTED BY THE SOCIETY OF COLONIAL WARS AT FORT
AMHERST, CROWN POINT

NECROLOGY

"Oh may I join the choir invisible
Of those immortal dead who live again
In minds made better by their presence; live
In pulses stirred to generosity,
In deeds of daring rectitude, in scorn
For miserable aims that end with self,
In thoughts sublime that pierce the night like stars,
And with their mild persistence urge man's search
To vaster issues. * * * May I reach
That purest heaven; be to other souls
The cup of strength in some great agony;
Be the sweet presence of a good diffused,
And in diffusion even more intense.
So shall I join the choir invisible
Whose music is the gladness of the world."

FRANCIS JOHN CHENEY.

This teacher of teachers was born at Warren, Pennsylvania, June 5th, 1848, and 'passed over to the great majority' at his home in Cortland, N. Y., on March 9th, 1912.

He was graduated with high honors from Syracuse University in 1872, his class being the first to graduate from that institution. From that time on until his death he gave his life to the work of education, only turning aside for a brief space,—1878 to 1880— to study law and to be admitted as a member of the bar of this State.

As professor of Mathematics in the Northern New York Conference Seminary at Antwerp, N. Y.; as principal of the Union School at Dryden, N. Y.; and later as principal of the Kingston Free Academy his time was fully employed until 1890. He then became inspector of academies under the Regents of the State of New York, which position he held until 1891. In the last named year he became principal of the Cortland (N. Y.) State Normal and Training School and continued in that position until the time of his death.

The opportunity which this position gave him for moulding the character of numbers of those who later became teachers in our public schools,—and elsewhere—was one of unusual importance and of corresponding responsibility.

It was the uniform testimony of those who came under the instruction of Doctor Cheney that his influence upon them was great and all for good. The results of the work of such a man, availing himself of such opportunities to shape, directly and indirectly, the lives and characters of multitudes, can never be computed. Thousands of men and women who never saw his face, or even heard his name, will have reason to 'rise up and call him blessed.'

Doctor Cheney—he received the degree of Ph. D. from Syracuse University and so became 'Doctor'—took an active part in the work of his church and in all movements for the social and political uplift of the community in which he lived.

His record is that of an active, cultured Christian gentleman whose influence was all for good and whose life was a benediction.

The State Historic Association has lost a most worthy member by his death.

WHITELAW REID.

Newspaper correspondent, editor, diplomat.

Born at Xenia, Ohio, October 27, 1837. Died at London, England, December 15, 1912.

Mr. Reid's ancestors were Scotch. His parents were in very moderate circumstances financially, so much so that the expense of the lad's education was borne by a relative.

He graduated at Miami University (Oxford, Ohio) in 1856. His interest in political affairs was already very great and he took an active part in the Freemont campaign of that year although he was only nineteen years old. Again, in 1860, in the Lincoln campaign he was very active, so much so as to seriously impair his health for a time. Meanwhile, in 1858, he bought the Xenia

News and as its editor, and as correspondent for it and later for the Cincinnati Gazette during the war, and afterwards, he was kept hard at work for a number of years. He was Librarian of the House of Representatives for two or three years, and tried his fortune as a cotton-planter in Louisiana in 1866 and 7. In 1866 he was invited by Horace Greeley to take a position on the Editorial Staff of the New York Tribune. This invitation he accepted and in 1869 he became Editor-in-Chief of that paper. Three years later he acquired the controlling interest in the Tribune and held the same while he lived. In 1877 and again in 1881 he declined the proffered appointment as Minister to Germany but accepted in 1889 the corresponding appointment to France. He was Special Ambassador to represent this country at the "Jubilee" of Queen Victoria and a Member of the Peace Commission which met at Paris in 1898. His appointment as 'Ambassador' of the United States at the Court of St. James' is of so recent date that it is remembered by all. This position he held at the time of his death and every honor was shown his memory both by England and the United States. If praise can 'soothe the dull cold ear of death' he must rest in peace.

This brief sketch does not cover or enumerate all the work of Mr. Reid's active life. He was the candidate of the Republican party for Vice-President in 1892.

In 1873 he was elected a member of the Board of Regents of the University of the State of New York, and later was chosen President of that body. In addition to all the foregoing he was the author of a number of books.

Mr. Reid's career shows the results of a combination of marked ability and great tact and adaptiveness with unusual good fortune. His marriage (1881) to Miss Mills, a daughter of D. Ogden Mills, placed at his disposal a princely fortune; and his own personal qualities enabled him to use it in the promotion of the high and worthy objects of his ambition. Sometimes in his later years when he recalled the circumstances of his early life he must have been reminded of those lines of Tennyson's

"Dost thou look back on what has been
As some divinely gifted man
Whose life in low estate began

And on a simple village green.''
*   *   *   *   *
"Who breaks his birth's invidious bar,
And grasps the skirts of happy chance,
And breasts the blows of circumstance
And grapples with his evil star.''

JOHN RUTGER PLANTEN.

The descendants of the "Knickerbockers" are proud of their ancestors and justly so. Holland sent to this country some of our early settlers who were, beyond all question, excellent citizens, and the progenitors of long lines of worthy descendants.

The subject of this sketch shows that the Motherland is still doing her part to supply America with a high type of citizen. He was born at Amsterdam, Holland, on November 10th, 1835. In 1836 his father, Hermanus Planten, established a wholesale drug business in the City of New York and in 1857, soon after the son— John Rutger Planten—attained his majority, he became a partner in his father's business. In this he continued until he retired in 1909. Under his hand the business grew and prospered so that Mr. Planten became a man of great influence in the commercial, circles of the city in which his life was spent. His high standing and ability as a business man were recognized both at home and abroad, and led to his appointment to several positions and offices of great honor and importance.

He was Vice-Consul of the Netherlands at the Port of New York in 1874; Consul in 1881 and Consul-General in 1884; and this important position he held until his death.

He was also Honorary Vice-President of the Netherlands Chamber of Commerce of New York; Honorary Vice-President of the Netherlands Benevolent Society of New York; Honorary President of the Netherlands Benevolent Society of Passaic, N. J., and Honorary Life Member of the Netherlands Society "Eendracht Maakt Macht" of New York.

The following decorations were conferred upon him : Knight of the Order of the Netherland Lion ; Commander of the Order of Orange Nassau of the Netherlands; Officer of the Order of the Oaken Crown of Luxemburg; Commander of the Order of Bolivar of Venezuela.

He was a member of various Historical Societies abroad and of a number of similar bodies in this country,—among others of The New York Geographical Society; The New York Genealogical Society; The New York Biographical Society; The New York Historical Society.

After a long, useful and successful life he passed to his rest on December 8th, 1912, "full of years and of honors."

MRS. ESTHER BAKER STEELE, Lit. D.

Educator, Authoress, Philanthropist.

Mrs. Esther Baker Steele, widow of Joel Dorman Steele, died at her home, "The Gables," in Elmira, N. Y., Nov. 23, 1911. She was a daughter of Rev. Gardner Baker and Esther Scott, his wife, and was born in Lysander, N. Y., in 1835. From both parents she inherited certain admirable and sterling traits, which in her own personality flowered into a splendid development.

Her father was a man of fine character, exemplary, energetic, and faithful to the claims of every duty. These traits were conspicuous in Mrs. Steele, and to her father she also owed the quick, keen sense of humor which served to light up the serious aspects of an eventful life.

The parsonage home life was tempered and refined by the guidance and oversight of an unusual mother. The love, the labors and sacrifices, the wholesome companionships of that home, together with its strict discipline of routine, left a lasting and fortunate impress on the mind of its gifted child.

For her education she was furnished the best advantages which the country afforded at that period. These opportunities she eagerly improved. And in addition to an aptitude for the usual academic branches she developed a fine taste for art and music.

It was as the newly appointed teacher of music in the Mexico, N. Y., Academy that she met in the fall of 1858 a young teacher of science—Joel Dorman Steele—also newly appointed. An immediate attachment resulted in marriage in July, 1859.

In the autumn of the above year he became principal of the academy. In 1861 he resigned to become Captain of a company that did noble service in the Civil War. The following year, because of wounds and impaired health, he was honorably discharged. He later became principal of the Newark, N. Y., Academy, from which position he responded to an urgent call to the Elmira Free Academy in 1866.

Into this new field of wider prossibilities and greater importance Mrs. Steele passed, aiding her husband, became equally equipped with him to share its opportunities for effort and growth. She, like her husband, soon made herself felt not only in the school, but also in church and society. To the limit of her strength by word and deed she responded to every demand and gained early recognition of her brilliant powers and high-minded aims.

Dr. Steele being possessed of literary ability as well as technical knowledge soon began to publish the results of his thought and research. Besides work on science, he also published short histories suitable for schools. Mrs. Steele colaborated with her husband in preparing what became widely known and used as Barnes' Brief Histories of the United States, France, Ancient Peoples, Greece, with selected readings, and Rome, with selected readings.

Dr. Steele's sudden death in 1886 was a sorrow from which Mrs. Steele never quite recovered, and her years of widowhood held always some labor of love by which she hoped to prolong the beneficent influence of his life. For example, with great generosity she renounced a life annuity and assumed two others derived from a legacy of $50,000 which was to go to Syracuse University at her death. Besides this she gave unstintedly to that University so long as she lived.

The magnificent Steele Memorial Library, a gift to Elmira and costing $65,000, is another monument to her generosity. In 1897 it was voted by the University auhorities of Syracuse to carve in stone over the door of its new and spacious science building the words "Esther Baker Steele Hall of Science." The University had already conferred upon her, out of respect for her attainments and achievements, the degree of Doctor of Literature. In 1907 she was made a member of the Phi Beta Kappa Society, an honorary fraternity confined to collegians of highest standing.

Mrs. Steele might have died a rich woman had she not given so lavishly of her means. But she anticipated in actual practice Andrew Carnegie's dictum that "it is a shame for anyone to die rich." Hers was a heart that kne wnot avarice, craft, nor bitterness. Its latest conscious beat was love and loyalty. Who shall

doubt that love and loyalty was its dominant note at the blest re-
union in the better country?

Her funeral was held at her home in Elmira. Chancellor Day
of Syracuse University conducted the services. She was laid to
rest by the side of her husband in beautiful Woodlawn cemetery.

ALBERT K. SMILEY.

Born at Vassalboro, Maine, March 17th, 1828: Died at Red-
lands, California, December 2nd, 1912. Between those two dates
lies the record of a long and useful life. Mr. Smiley would have
been surprised, probably, if anybody had suggested to him that he
was a man of genius. But that is what he was if genius consists,
as is believed, of the power to see things which other people do
not see and to do things which others cannot do. He saw the
charms of Lake Mohonk, and the uses to which it could be put,
when no one else had seen them; and he used the place in such
wise and to the accomplishment of such ends as no one else would
have deemed possible. He had what Henry Ward Beecher termed
the genius of "sanctified common sense."

To the general public he was merely the proprietor of the
"Lake Mohonk House" which was known far and wide as one
of the most beautifully located summer retreats in this part of
the world and altogether unique in its methods of conducting
business. It was not at all like the "hotel" where the visitor is
deemed a "patron" and may do about as he pleases as long as he
keeps within the rules of good social usage. Rather it was Mr.
Smiley's home where the inmates were his guests and were expected—and required—to observe the rules which he deemed essential to the welfare of his household. He was a profoundly religious man—a member of the denomination of "Friends"—
("Quakers".) He was opposed on principle to dancing, to card
playing and to the use of intoxicating liquors. These things were
prohibited at the Lake Mohonk House and the prohibition was
enforced against all alike, kindly and gently but very firmly.

No profanation of the Sabbath was permitted—and strangest of all—no automobile was allowed to enter within the gates of
Mr. Smiley's lordly domain. This last regulation was imposed
because he saw, with his usual good judgment, that the peaceful,
quiet beauty of his mountain retreat would be impaired and dese-

crated if its fifty miles of private driveways were thrown open to the rush and din of a swarm of automobiles. That all these unusual regulations were enforced gently and politely, but with unyielding firmness, shows the force of character and the tact which Mr. Smiley brought to the management of his business affairs.

His good judgment was demonstrated by the results he achieved. His business grew from year to year and resulted in yielding him an ample fortune.

Then came the real work of his life. He used his mountain home and the fortune it had brought him for the promotion and practical application of the principles which had been the underlying features of his character. He loved righteousness and peace and believed that they should be applied and cultivated in national, as well as individual, affairs. He felt that as a Nation we had treated our Indian tribes unjustly, unrighteously. He deemed war not only a curse but a sin. Hence he strove to procure fairer treatment for the Indians and endeavored to promote the cause of international peace. To this end he invited likeminded men and women to attend conferences at Lake Mohonk to consider these two important subjects. Each of these conferences drew together, ultimately, several hundred people, who all came by Mr. Smiley's personal invitation and were entertained by him as his guests during the three or four days the meeting lasted.

The influence exerted in this way is past all computation. That the attitude of the people of this country now towards the Indian question differs greatly from that of twenty-five years ago is unquestionable,—and much of this change can be traced directly to the "Lake Mohonk Conferences." The results of the peace conferences are not so obvious as yet but the seed has been sown in good soil and only He who "giveth the increase" knows to what it will grow. For a private individual, holding no official position, to exert such an influence on affairs of national and even international importance is a great achievement and justifies the statement made at the beginning of this article that Mr. Smiley used Lake Mohonk "in such wise and to the accomplishment of such ends as no one else would have deemed possible."

GEORGE R. SUTHERLAND.

(Banker.)

Born October 21, 1848, at Candor, Tioga County, New York; died November 20, 1912, at New York City.

He came of good Revolutionary stock on both sides. On his maternal side his grandfather, George Robertson, was a commissioned officer in the Continental Army.

His early life was spent in the section of the State where he was born and his educational advantages were such as the schools of the vicinity afforded.

While still a young man he removed to the Town of Campbell, in Steuben County, and there in the year 1877 he was instrumental in organizing the Bank of Campbell, of which he became President,—a position which he held to the end of his life. His success in the management of this institution was such that he was encouraged to embark in a similar business in a much larger field. In the year 1888 he accordingly opened a private banking house in the City of New York, which he conducted very successfully, until the time of his death. His home was in the City of New York during the later years of his life but he retained his interest in, and affection for, his old home at Campbell and made frequent visits there—and there he was buried.

In early life, Mr. Sutherland took a somewhat active part in political matters. Twice he was elected to the State Assembly— 1878 and 1879—and was an active and useful member of that body. He had been previously a member of the Board of Supervisors of his county and had served as chairman of the board. In politics he was a Republican.

He left surviving him his widow and one daughter, Mrs. Charles W. Coit, of Rochester, N. Y.

ANNUAL REPORT OF LIBRARIAN

The thanks of the Association are extended for the following gifts and contributions to the Library for the years 1911-1912.

J. A. HOLDEN, Librarian.

Address,
    27 Elm St.,
        Glens Falls, N. Y.

AMERICAN ANTIQUARIAN SOCIETY, Worcester, Mass.—Proceedings 1911-12.

AMERICAN HISTORICAL ASSOCIATION, Washington, D. C.—Proceedings of Seventh Annual Conference of Historical Societies.

T. ASTLEY ATKINS, Yonkers, N. Y.—Yonkers Historical Literary Association Bulletin, No. 1.

WILLIAM ABBATT, New York City.—Magazine of History, 1912.

WOODBURY BLAIR, Washington, D. C.—Woodbury Lowrey, Spanish Settlements in the United States.

MRS. G. H. BASSINGER, Glens Falls, N. Y.—Old almanacs from the Fifties to the Eighties of the Nineteenth century.

COLONIAL DAMES OF AMERICA, New York.—Year Book, Vol. 1.

CONNECTICUT HISTORICAL SOCIETY.—Annual Report, 1912.

CHICAGO HISTORICAL SOCIETY.—Proceedings, 1912.

MISS K. J. C. CARVILLE, New Rochelle.—Proceedings New Rochelle Huguenot Association, 1911.

S. M. DAVIDSON.—J. M. DeGarno's "History of Hicksite Quakers, N. Y." 1897; Rev. H. O. Ladd, "Founding of the Episcopal Church in Dutchess Co.," 1894; "The Old is Better," Sermon Trinity Church by Rev. Rob. B. VanKleeck, D. D., Fishkill, 1870.

ESSEX INSTITUTE.—Historical Collections for 1912.

ALVAH P. FRENCH.—Magazine of American History, Port Chester, N. Y., 1912.

HUGUENOT SOCIETY OF CHARLESTON, South Carolina.—Transactions for 1911.

HYDE PARK, Mass.—Historical Record for 1912.

JOHNS HOPKINS PRESS.—Studies for 1912.

HISTORICAL DEPARTMENT OF IOWA.—Annals of Iowa, and Index for 1911-1912.

INDIANA HISTORICAL SOCIETY.—Publications, vol. v.

JOURNAL OF AMERICAN HISTORY.—For 1912.

JOURNAL OF HISTORY, Lamoni, Iowa.—For 1912.

KANSAS STATE HISTORICAL SOCIETY.—Historical Collections 1911-12.

LOUISIANA STATE MUSEUM.—Seven Reports and Publications from 1904-1912, also Centennial medal.

MANCHESTER HISTORICAL ASSOCIATION, Manchester, N. H.—Collections, vols. i and iv, Proceedings N. H. Press Association, 5 volumes; Lamb's Battle of Chelsea Creek; Descendants of Robert Savory; Centennial Celebrations of Manchester.

STATE HISTORICAL SOCIETY OF MISSOURI.—Historical Review for 1912.

NEW ENGLAND SOCIETY IN NEW YORK.—Proceedings 1911-1912, fac-similes Bay Psalm Book and Puritan's Farewell.

NEW HAMPSHIRE HISTORICAL SOCIETY.—Dedication of New Building 1912.

NEW JERSEY HISTORICAL SOCIETY.—Proceedings for 1912.

NEW YORK HISTORICAL SOCIETY.—Collections 1906-09.

ONTARIO HISTORICAL SOCIETY, Toronto, Ont.—Annual Report for 1912.

HISTORICAL AND PHILOSOPHICAL SOCIETY OF OHIO.—Quarterly for 1912.

PENNSYLVANIA SOCIETY.—Year Book, 1912.

F. B. RICHARDS, Secretary.—21 miscellaneous pamphlets, catalogues, society proceedings and historical magazines.

SONS OF THE AMERICAN REVOLUTION, Empire State Society.—Monograph, Descendants Revolutionary Sires, Year Books for 1911-1912-1913.

GRAYSON N. SHELDON.—Romance of St. Sacrement.

SMITHSONIAN INSTITUTION.—Model of a Brahmin Temple.

SCHENECTADY COUNTY HISTORICAL SOCIETY.—Year Books 1908-12.

SOCIETY OF COLONIAL WARS, New York.—Year Book 1912.

A. K. SMALLEY LIBRARY, Redland, Cal.—Catalogue 1912.

STATE HISTORICAL SOCIETY OF IOWA.—Iowa Journal of History and Politics for 1912.

SOUTH CALIFORNIA HISTORICAL SOCIETY.—Annual Publication for 1911.

SUFFOLK COUNTY, New York Historical Society.—Year Book for 1912.

UNIVERSITY CHICAGO PRESS.—Catalogue of Publications for 1912-13.

UNIVERSITY OF NORTH CAROLINA.—James Sprunt Historical Publications and Monographs for 1912.

UNIVERSITY NORTH DAKOTA.—Quarterly for 1912.

WISCONSIN HISTORICAL SOCIETY.—Proceedings for 1911.

VERMONT HISTORICAL SOCIETY.—Proceedings for 1909-10, 1911-12.

VINELAND, N. J. HISTORICAL AND ANTIQUARIAN SOCIETY.—Annual Report, 1911.

NOTICE OF CHANGES IN RESOLUTIONS FOR 1914.

Notice is hereby given that at the Sixteenth Annual Meeting of the New York State Historical Association, to be held in the City of Utica, New York, October 5, 6, 7 and 8, 1914, the following Resolutions will be voted upon:

RESOLVED: That the following amendments be made to the Constitution of the New York State Historical Association:

1. That Subdivision Third of Article II be amended to read:

Third. To gather books, manuscripts, pictures and relics relating to the history of the State of New York, and to establish a museum therein for their preservation.

2. That Article V shall be amended so as to read as follows:

3. That Section 1 of Article VII be amended to read:

Section 1. The annual meeting of the Association shall be held at such time and place as shall be fixed by the Board of Trustees. A notice of said meeting shall be sent to each member at least ten days prior thereto.

4. That Section 4 of Article VII be stricken out.

ARTICLE V.

Officers.

Section 1. The officers of this Association shall be a President, three Vice Presidents, a Treasurer and a Secretary, all of whom shall be elected by the Board of Trustees from its own number at its first annual meeting after the annual meeting of the Association, and shall hold office for one year and until their successors shall be elected.

Section 2. The Board of Trustees shall appoint an Assistant Secretary at its mid-winter session from among the members of the Association residing near the place at which the ensuing annual meeting is to be held. The Assistant Secretary shall hold office for one year.

Section 3. The Board of Trustees may appoint such other officers, committees or agents, and delegate to them such powers as it sees fit, for the prosecution of its work.

Section 4. Vacancies in any office or committee may be filled by the Board of Trustees.

And be it further Resolved, That the following amendments be made to the By-Laws of the New York State Historical Association:

ARTICLE VI.

1. That Section 4 of Article II be amended to read:

Section 4. The Board of Trustees shall hold at least one meeting each year, beside the meetings held during the annual meeting of the Association.

2. That Section 5 of Article II be stricken out.

3. That Article VII of said By-Laws be designated as Article VIII.

4. That Article VIII of said By-Laws be designated as Article IX.

5. That Article IX of said By-Laws be designated as Article X.

6. That Article X of said By-Laws be designated as Article XI.

7. That a new Article be adopted which shall be designated as Article VII which shall read as follows:

ARTICLE VII.

The Assistant Secretary shall work in conjunction with, and under the direction of the Committee on Program.

Dated, Glens Falls, N. Y., November 10th, 1913.

FREDERICK B. RICHARDS,
Secretary.

NOTE.—The Articles of Incorporation, Constitution and By-Laws as amended would read as follows:—

ARTICLES OF INCORPORATION.

The names and residences of the directors of said corporation, to hold office until the first annual meeting, and who shall be known as the Board of Trustees, are:

James A. Roberts,	Buffalo.
Timothy L. Woodruff,	Brooklyn.
Daniel C. Farr,	Glens Falls.
Everett R. Sawyer,	Hudson Falls.
James A. Holden,	Glens Falls.
Robert O. Bascom,	Fort Edward.
Morris Patterson Ferris.	Dobbs Ferry.
Elwyn Seelye,	Lake George.
Grenville M. Ingalsbe,	Hudson Falls.
Frederick B. Richards,	Ticonderoga.
Anson Judd Upson,	Glens Falls.
Asahel R. Wing,	Fort Edward.
William O. Stearns,	Glens Falls.
Robert C. Alexander,	New York.
Elmer J. West,	Glens Falls.
Hugh Hastings,	Albany.
Pliny T. Sexton,	Palmyra.
William S. Ostrander,	Schuylerville.
Sherman Williams,	Glens Falls.
William L. Stone,	Mt. Vernon.
Henry E. Tremain,	New York.
William H. Tippetts,	Lake George.
John Boulton Simpson,	Bolton.
Harry W. Watrous,	Hague.
Abraham B. Valentine,	New York.

The name of such corporation is the "New York State Historical Association."

The principal objects for which said corporation is formed are:

First: To promote and encourage original historical research.

Second: To disseminate a greater knowledge of the early history of the State, by means of lectures, and the publication and distribution of literature on historical subjects.

Third: To gather books, manuscripts, pictures, and relics relating to the early history of the State of New York and to establish a museum therein for their preservation.

Fourth: To suitably mark places of historic interest.

Fifth: To acquire by purchase, gift, devise or otherwise, the title to, or custody and control of, historic spots and places.

The territory in which the operations of this corporation are to be principally conducted is the State of New York.

The principal office of said corporation is to be located at the City of Albany, New York.

The number of directors of said corporation, to be known as the Board of Trustees, is twenty-five.

CONSTITUTION.

ARTICLE I.

Name.

This Society shall be known as "New York State Historical Association.

ARTICLE II.

Objects.

Its objects shall be:

First. To promote and encourage original historical research.

Second. To disseminate a greater knowledge of the early history of the State, by means of lectures and the publication and distribution of literature on historical subjects.

Third. To gather books, manuscripts, pictures and relics relating to the history of the State of New York, and to establish a museum therein for their preservation.

Fourth. To suitably mark places of historic interest.

Fifth. To acquire by purchase, gift, devise, or otherwise, the title to, or custody and control of, historic spots and places.

ARTICLE III.

Members.

Section 1. Members shall be of four classes—Active, Associate, Corresponding and Honorary. Active and Associate members only shall have a voice in the management of the Society.

Section. 2. All persons interested in American history shall be eligible for Active membership.

Section 3. Persons residing outside the State of New York, interested in historical investigation, may be made Corresponding members.

Section 4. Persons who have attained distinguished eminence as historians may be made Honorary members.

Section 5. Persons who shall have given to the Association donations of money, time, labor, books, documents, MSS., collections of antiquities, art or archaeology of a value equivalent in the judgment of the trustees to a life membership may be made Associate members.

ARTICLE IV.
Management.

Section 1. The property of the Association shall be vested in, and the affairs of the Association conducted by the Board of Trustees to be elected by the Association. Vacancies in the Board of Trustees shall be filled by the remaining members of the Board, the appointee to hold office until the next annual meeting of the Association.

Section 2. The Board of Trustees shall have power to suspend or expel members of the Association for cause, and to restore them to membership after a suspension or expulsion. No member shall be suspended or expelled without first having been given ample opportunity to be heard in his or her own defense.

Section 3. The first Board of Trustees shall consist of those designated in the Articles of Incorporation, who shall meet as soon as may be after the adoption of this Constitution and divide themselves into three classes of, as nearly as may be, eight members each, such classes to serve respectively, one until the first annual meeting, another until the second annual meeting, and the third until the third annual meeting of the Association. At each annual meeting the Association shall elect eight or nine members (as the case may be) to serve as Trustees for the ensuing three years, to fill the places of the class whose terms then expire.

Section 4. The Board of Trustees shall have no power to bind the Association to any expenditure of money beyond the actual resources of the Association except by the consent of the Board of Trustees, expressed in writing and signed by every member thereof.

ARTICLE V.
Officers.

Section 1. The officers of this Association shall be a President, three Vice Presidents, a Treasurer and a Secretary, all of whom shall be elected by the Board of Trustees from its own number at its first annual meeting after the annual meeting of the Association, and shall hold office for one year and until their successors shall be elected.

Section 2. The Board of Trustees shall appoint an Assistant Secretary at its mid-winter session from among the members of the Association residing near the place at which the ensuing annual meeting is to be held. The Assistant Secretary shall hold office for one year.

Section 3. The Board of Trustees may appoint such other officers, committees, or agents, and delegate to them such powers as it sees fit, for the prosecution of its work.

Section 4. Vacancies in any office or committee may be filled by the Board of Trustees.

ARTICLE VI.

Fees and Dues.

Section 1. Each person on being elected to active membership between January and July of any year, shall pay into the Treasury of the Association the sum of two dollars, and thereafter on the first day of January in each year a like sum for his or her annual dues. Any person elected to membership subsequent to July 1st, and who shall pay into the treasury two dollars, shall be exempt from dues until January 1st of the year next succeeding his or her consummation of membership.

Section 2. Any member of the Association may commute his or her annual dues by the payment of twenty-five dollars at one time, and thereby become a life member exempt from further payments.

Section 3. Any member may secure membership which shall descend to a member of his or her family qualified under the Constitution and By-Laws of the Association for membership therein, in perpetuity, by the payment at one time of two hundred and fifty dollars. The person to hold the membership may be designated in writing by the creator of such membership, or by the subsequent holder thereof subject to the approval of the Board of Trustees.

Section 4. All receipts from life and perpetual memberships shall be set aside and vested as a special fund, the income only to be used for current expenses.

Section 5. Associate, Honorary and Corresponding Members and persons who hold Perpetual Membership shall be exempt from the payment of dues.

Section 6. The Board of Trustees shall have power to excuse the non-payment of dues, and to suspend or expel members for non-payment when their dues remain unpaid for more than six months.

Section 7. Historical societies, educational institutions of all kinds, libraries, learned societies, patriotic societies, or any incorporated or unincorporated association for the advancement of learning and intellectual welfare of mankind, shall be considered a "person" under Section 2 of this article.

ARTICLE VII.

Meetings.

Section 1. The annual meeting of the Association shall be held at such time and place as shall be fixed by the Board of Trustees. A notice of said meeting shall be sent to each member at least ten days prior thereto.

Section 2. Special meetings of the Association may be called at any time by the Board of Trustees and must be called upon the written request of ten members. The notice of such meeting shall specify the object thereof, and no business shall be transacted thereat excepting that designated in the notice.

Section 3. Ten members shall constitute a quorum at any meeting of the Association.

ARTICLE VIII.

Seal.

The seal of the Association shall be a group of statuary representing the Mohawk Chief, King Hendrick, in the act of proving to Gen. William Johnson the unwisdom of dividing his forces on the eve of the battle of Lake George. Around this a circular band bearing the legend, New York State Historical Association, 1899.

ARTICLE IX.

Amendments.

Amendments to the Constitution may be made at any annual meeting, or at a special meeting called for that purpose. Notice of a proposed amendment with a copy thereof must have been mailed to each member at least thirty days before the day upon which action is taken thereon.

The adoption of an amendment shall require the favorable vote of two-thirds of those present at a duly-constituted meeting of the Association.

BY-LAWS.

ARTICLE I.
Members.

Candidates for membership in the Association shall be proposed by one member and seconded by another, and shall be elected by the Board of Trustees. Three adverse votes shall defeat an election.

ARTICLE II.
Board of Trustees.

Section 1. The Board of Trustees may make such rules for its own government as it may deem wise, and which shall not be inconsistent with the Constitution and By-Laws of the Association. Five members of the Board shall constitute a quorum for the transaction of business.

Section 2. The Board of Trustees shall elect one of its own number to preside at the meeting of the Board in the absence of the President.

Section 3. The Board of Trustees shall at each annual meeting of the Association render a full report of its proceedings during the year last past.

Section 4. The Board of Trustees shall hold at least one meeting each year, beside the meetings held during the annual meeting of the Association.

ARTICLE III.
President.

The President shall preside at all meetings of the Association and of the Board of Trustees, and perform such other duties as may be delegated to him by the Association or the Board of Trustees. He shall be ex-officio a member of all committees.

ARTICLE IV.
Vice Presidents.

The Vice Presidents shall be denominated First, Second and Third Vice Presidents. In the absence of the President his duties shall devolve upon the senior Vice President.

ARTICLE V.
Treasurer.

Section 1. The Treasurer shall have charge of all the funds of the Association. He shall keep accurate books of account, which shall at all times be open to the inspection of the Board of Trustees. He shall present a full and comprehensive statement of the Association's financial condition, its receipts and expenditures, at each annual meeting, and shall present a brief statement to the Board of Trustees at each meeting. He shall pay out money only on the approval of the majority of the Executive Committee, or on the resolution of the Board of Trustees.

Section 2. Before assuming the duties of his office, the Treasurer-elect shall, with a surety to be approved by the Board, execute to the Association his bond in the sum of one thousand dollars, conditioned for the faithful performance of his duties as Treasurer.

Section 3. The President shall, thirty days prior to the annual meeting of the Association, appoint two members of the Association who shall examine the books and vouchers of the Treasurer and audit his accounts, and present their report to the Association at its annual meeting.

ARTICLE VI.
Secretary.

The Secretary shall preserve accurate minutes of the transactions of the Association and of the Board of Trustees, and shall conduct the correspondence of the Association. He shall notify the members of meetings, and perform such other duties as he may be directed to perform by the Association or by the Board of Trustees. He may delegate any portion of his duties to the Assistant Secretary.

ARTICLE VII.
Assistant Secretary.

The Assistant Secretary shall work in conjunction with, and under the direction of the Committee on Program.

ARTICLE VIII.
Executive Committee.

The officers of the Association shall constitute an Executive Committee. Such committee shall direct the business of the Association between meetings of the Board of Trustees, but shall have no power to establish or declare a policy for the Association, or to bind it in any way except in relation to routine work. The Committee shall have no power to direct a greater expenditure than fifty dollars without the authority of the Board of Trustees.

ARTICLE IX.
Procedure.

Section 1. The following, except when otherwise ordered by the Association, shall be the order of business at the annual meetings of the Association.

Call to order.

Reading of minutes of previous annual, and of any special meeting, and acting thereon.

Reports of Officers and Board of Trustees.

Reports of Standing Committees.

Reports of Special Committees.

Unfinished business.

Election.

New business.

Adjournment.

Section 2. The procedure at all meetings of the Association and of the Board of Trustees, where not provided for in this Constitution and By-Laws, shall be governed by Roberts' Rules of Order.

Section 3. The previous question shall not be put to vote at any meeting unless seconded by at least three members.

Section 4. All elections shall be by ballot, except where only one candidate is nominated for an office.

Section 5. All notices shall be sent personally or by mail to the address designated in writing by the member to the Secretary.

ARTICLE X.

Nominating Committee.

A committee of three shall be chosen by the Association at its annual meeting, to nominate Trustees to be voted for at the next annual meeting. Such Committee shall file its report with the Secretary of this Association at least thirty days prior to the next annual meeting. The Secretary shall mail a copy of such report to every member of the Association with the notice of the annual meeting at which the report is to be acted upon. The action of such committee shall, however, in no wise interfere with the power of the Association to make its own nominations, but all such independent nominations shall be sent to the Secretary at least twenty days prior to the annual meeting. A copy thereof shall be sent to each member by the Secretary with the notice of meeting, and shall be headed "Independent Nominations." If the Nominating Committee fails for any reason to make its report so that it may be sent out with the notice of the annual meeting, the Society may make its own nominations at such annual meeting.

ARTICLE XI.

Amendments.

These By-Laws may be amended at any duly-constituted meeting of the Association by a two-thirds vote of the members present. Notice of the proposed amendment with a copy thereof must have been mailed to each member at least twenty days before the day upon which action thereon is taken.

ARTICLES CHANGED ARE

Constitution.

ARTICLE V.

Section 1. The officers of the Association shall be a President, three Vice Presidents, a Treasurer, a Secretary, and an Assistant Secretary, all of whom shall be elected by the Board of Trustees from its own number, at its first meeting after the annual meeting of the Association, and shall hold office for one year, or until their successors are chosen. Temporary officers shall be chosen by the Incorporators to act until an election as aforesaid, by the Board of Trustees.

ARTICLE VII.

Section 4. The Board of Trustees shall arrange for the holding of a series of meetings at Lake George during the summer months, for the reading of original papers on history and kindred subjects, and for special intercourse between the members and their guests.

By-Laws.

ARTICLE II.

Section 4. The Board of Trustees shall hold at least four meetings in each year. At each of such meetings it shall consider and act upon the names of candidates proposed for membership.

Section 5. The Board of Trustees each year appoint committees to take charge of the annual gathering of the Association.

INSIGNIA OF THE ASSOCIATION

The Insignia of the Association consists of a badge, the pendant of which is circular in form, one and three-sixteenths inches in diameter and is suspended on scarlet and orange ribbon (scarlet for British, orange for Dutch), which are the colors of the Association.

Obverse: In the center is represented the discovery of the Hudson River; the "Half-Moon" is surrounded by Indian Canoes, and in the distance is shown the Palisades. At the top is the coat-of-arms of New Amsterdam and a tomahawk, arrow and Dutch sword. At the bottom is shown the seal of New York State. Upon a ribbon, surrounding the center medallion, is the legend: "New York State Historical Association," and the dates 1609 and 1899; the former being the date of the discovery of New York, and the latter the date of the founding of the Historical Association.

Reverse: The Seal of the Association.

The badges are made of 14k gold, sterling silver and bronze, and will be sold to members of the Association at the following prices:

14k Gold, complete with bar and ribbon..................$11.00
Silver Gilt, complete with bar and ribbon................ 5.50
Sterling Silver, complete with bar and ribbon 5.00
Bronze, complete with bar and ribbon.................... 4.00

Application for badges should be made to the Secretary of the Association, Frederick B. Richards, Glens Falls, N. Y., who will issue permit, authorizing the member to make the purchase from the official Jewelers, J. E. Caldwell & Co., 902 Chestnut Street, Philadelphia.

ROSETTE

Rosette adopted in 1913. Scarlet and orange silk. For sale by the Secretary at 25c each.

ROSETTE

INSIGNIA OF THE NEW YORK STATE HISTORICAL ASSOCIATION

MEMBERS NEW YORK STATE HISTORICAL ASSOCIATION

HONORARY MEMBERS.

Adams, Charles Francis, LL. D.   84 State St., Boston, Mass.

✔ Beauchamp, Rev. William Martin, S. T. D.   121 Mark Ave., Syracuse.

Belcher, Rev. Henry, M. A. LL. D.   Lewes, Sussex, England.

Hadley, Arthur Twining, LL. D.   Pres. Yale University, New Haven, Conn.

Hoes, Chaplain Roswell Randall, U. S. N.   1636 Rhode Island Ave., Washington, D. C.

Roosevelt, Col. Theodore, Ph. D., LL. D.   "The Outlook," 287 Fourth Ave., New York.

Wilson, Woodrow, Ph. D., Litt. D., LL. D.   Washington, D. C.

CORRESPONDING MEMBERS.

✗ McMaster, John Bach, A. M., Ph. D., Litt. D.   University of Pennsylvania, Philadelphia, Pa.

✗ Wheeler, Arthur Martin, M. A., LL. D.   Yale University, New Haven, Conn.

LIFE MEMBERS.

Barnhart, John Hendley, A. M., M. D.   N. Y. Botanical Garden, Bronx Park, New York.

Beckett, James A.   Hoosick Falls.

Bixby, W. K.   Bolton Landing.

Delafield, Lewis L.   20 Exchange Place, New York.

Field, Cortlandt de Peyster — Peekskill.

Fish, Stuyvesant — 52 Wall St., New York.

Fulton, Louis M. — 31 Nassau St., New York.

Hand, Hon. Richard L., LL. D. — Elizabethtown.

Hanna, Charles A. — 15 Rockledge Road, Montclair, N. J.

Hartley, Mrs. Frances G. — 232 Madison Ave., New York.

Hawes, Harry Hammond — 157 Hudson Ave., Peekskill.

Howland, Fred D. — Hudson Falls.

Jones, Mrs. Oliver Livingston — 116 W. 72nd St., New York.

Mingay, James — 100 Lake Ave., Saratoga Spa.

Mingay, Mrs. James — 100 Lake Ave., Saratoga Spa.

Pitcher, Mrs. Charlotte A. — 15 Faxton St., Utica.

Potts, Charles Edwin — 170 Rugby Road, Brooklyn.

Ralph, Mrs. George F. — 837 Genesee St., Utica.

See, Mrs. Horace — Care Mrs. Miner, 264 So. Franklin St., Wilkes Barre, Penn.

Stillman, Charles Chauncey — 9 E. 67th St., New York.

Straus, Hon. Oscar S., LL. D., — 5 W. 76th St., New York.

Tracy, Ira Otis, M. D. — Long Island Hospital, Flatbush, Brooklyn.

Webb, Dr. W. Seward — 51 E. 44th St., New York.

Wheeler, Edward J., Ph. D. — 79 Chapel St., Albany.

Witherbee, Hon. Frank S. — Port Henry.

MEMBERS.

Abbatt, William — West Chester.

Abercrombie, David T. — 197 Ballantine Parkway, Newark, N. J.

Abrams, Alfred W. — 429 Western Ave., Albany.

Acker, Milo M. — Hornell.

Ackerly, Orville B. — 210 Warburton Ave., Yonkers.

Adams, Henry Sherman — 152 Montague St., Brooklyn.

Adams, Rev. John Quincy — 82 North St., Auburn.

Adamson, W. H. — Glens Falls.

Adler, Elmer — 561 University Ave., Rochester.

Adler, Isaac, A. M., M. D. — 22 E. 62nd St., New York.

Ainsworth, Hon. Danforth E. — 93 State St., Albany.

Aldrich, Charles S·   7 Collins Ave·, Troy.
× Alexander, Hon. D. S., LL. D. 31 North St., Buffalo.
Allen, Charles C.   Schuylerville.
Allen, Freeman H., Ph. D.   Hamilton.
Andrews, Capt. James M.   Saratoga Spa.
×Anthony, Walter C.   Newburgh.
Arthur, Miss L. Louise   515 Lexington Ave., New York.
Atkins, Miss Kate   280 Broadway, New York.
Atkins, Dubois G.   43 John St., Kingston.
·₁Atkins, Hon. T· Astley   280 Broadway, New York.
Auringer, Rev. O. C.   Forestport.

Bacon, Carroll B., M. D.   Waterloo.
Bailey, Theodorus, M. D.   122 W. 78th St., New York.
Bailey, Horace W.   Rutland, Vt.
Baker, Rev. E. Folsom   East Aurora·
Baker, Frederick I.   Fort Ann.
Baldwin, Stephen C·   73 Remsen St., Brooklyn.
Ballard, W. J.   Waterford, R. F. D. Brookwood.
Banker, Dr. Silas J.   Fort Edward.
Banta, J. Edward   Care Seymour School, Syracuse.
Barber, Arthur William, LL. M. 32 Nassau St., New York.
Barber, Junius E.   4 Dix Ave., Glens Falls.
Barcus, James Q.   57 State St., Albany.
Bardeen, C. W.   315 E· Washington St., Syracuse.
Barhydt, T. Low   Schenectady.
Barker, Mrs. Daniel Folger   12 So. Catherine St., Plattsburg.
Barnes, Ezra A.   40 E. Bridge St., Oswego.
Barney, Edgar S., Sc. D.   c/o Hebrew Technical Institute,
                                365 Stuyvesant St., New York.

Bartholomew, Alanson Douglass   Whitehall.
Bartlett, Eugene M.   644 Ellicott Sq., Buffalo.
Barton, Philip P., Ph. B.   352 Buffalo Ave., Niagara Falls.
Bascom, Wyman S.   Fort Edward.
Bassette, Alfred S.   400 Garfield Ave., Syracuse.
Batcheller, Geo. Clinton   237 W. 72nd St., New York.
Bates, Norman L·   Oswego.
Beach, Edward Stevens   Singer Building, New York
Beadle, Miss Cynthia H.   33 W 6th St., Oswego.

Bean, Charles D., LL. D.	9 Masonic Temple, Geneva.
Beard, Curtis J.	41 W. 34th St., New York.
Beardslee, Roosevelt	East Creek, Herkimer Co.
Beardslee, Mrs. Roosevelt	East Creek, Herkimer Co.
Beekman, Hon. Dow	Middleburgh.
Beemer, James G.	Yonkers.
Beer, George Lewis	329 W. 71st St., New York.
Belford, Hon. James M.	Riverhead.
Bell, Clark, LL. D.	39 Broadway, New York.
Bennet, Hon. William S.	60 Wall St., New York.
Bensberg, F. W.	79 Oneida St., Utica.
Betts, Chas. H·	41 William St·, Lyons.
Betts, Hon. James A.	204 Pearl St., Kingston.
Bevier, Miss Margaret S.	Marbletown.
Bigelow, Rev. Dana W., D. D.	410 State St., Utica.
Black, Hon. Peter C.	Fernandinà, Fla.
Blackburn, John T. D.	Albany.
Bloodgood, Clarence E.	Catskill.
Boardman, Waldo E., D. M. D.	419 Boylston St., Boston, Mass.
Bosworth, Mrs. C. H.	90 Lake Ave., Saratoga Spa.
Botsford, Elmer F·, A. M.	Plattsburg.
Boxall, George H.	366 Plymouth Ave., Buffalo.
Brackett, Hon. Edgar T.	Saratoga.
Brandow, Rev. John H.	59 Manning Boulevard, Albany.
Brayton, M. Jesse	222 Genesee St., Utica.
Brink, Theo.	Lake Katrine, Ulster Co.
Bristol, George P.	5 Grove Place, Ithaca.
Broadhead, Miss Stella F.	130 So. Main St., Jamestown.
Brockport State Normal Library	Brockport.
Brockway, Miss Mary L·	417 Broadway, Saratoga Spa.
Brooklyn Public Library	26 Brevoort Place, Brooklyn.
Brooks, James Byron, D. C. L.	1013 E· Adams St., Syracuse.
Broughton, Charles H.	307 Turin Road, Rome.
Broughton, Mrs. Charles H.	307 Turin Road, Rome.
Broughton, Harry L.	Hudson Falls.
Brown, Edwin J.	37 Main St., Oneida.
Brown, Ernest C.	280 Broadway, New York.
Brown, Rev. Samuel E.	Pulaski.

Bullard, Charles E.	Glens Falls.
Bullard, Frederick H.	Glens Falls.
Burnham, John B.	Essex.
Burroughs, John H.	15 William St., New York.
Burt, George Noyes	Oswego.
Caldwell, Samuel Cushman, D. C. L.	P. O. Box 56, Pelham.
Callan, Peter A., M. D.	452 5th Ave., New York.
Callan, Mrs. Frank D.	Ilion.
Callanan, James H.	8 So. Church St., Schenectady.
Cameron, Edward M.	173 Western Ave., Albany.
Cameron, Frederick W.	34 Elk St., Albany.
Camp, Col. Walter B.	Sacketts Harbor.
Cannon, James G.	Scarsdale.
Carman, Nelson G.	166 Montague St., Brooklyn.
Carmody, Hon. Thomas	Albany.
Carpenter, Charles W.	526 West End Ave., New York.
Carpenter, Hon. Francis M.	Mount Kisco.
Carrington, Augustus B.	200 Broadway, New York.
Carroll, Fred Linus	Johnstown.
Carter, Robert C.	Glens Falls.
Carvalho, S. S.	238 William St., New York.
Carville, Miss Katharine J. C.	257 Webster Ave., New Rochelle.
Catlin, Maj. Gen. Isaac S.	Hotel St. George, Brooklyn.
Cayuga County Historical Society	Auburn.
Chalmers, Arthur A.	Amsterdam.
Chalmers, Mrs. Arthur A.	Amsterdam.
Champion, Charles S.	2 Rector St., New York.
Channing, J. Parke	61 Broadway, New York.
Chase, Hon. Emory A.	25 Prospect Ave., Catskill.
Chase, George	174 Fulton St., New York.
Chase, Rev. Platt N., Ph. D.	15 Green St., Kingston.
Cheney, Hon. O. H.	78 Madison Ave., New York.
Chesebrough, Robert A.	17 State St., New York.
Chester, Hon. Alden	County Building, Albany.
Chorley, Rev. E. Clowes	Garrison-on-Hudson.
Chormann, Frederick	315 Jefferson Ave., Niagara Falls.

Church, Irving P.   Ithaca.
Clapp, Morris B.   Cincinnatus.
Clark, James T.   100 W. 5th St., Oswego.
Clark, Miss Mary Hodges   Oswego.
Clark, Walter A.   755 Main St., Geneva.
Clarke, Frederick O.   Oswego.
Clarke, John M., LL. D. Ph. D.   State Hall, Albany.
Clearwater, Hon. Alphonso T.,
    LL. D.   316 Albany Ave., Kingston.
Cleaveland, Frank N.   Canton.
Clemans, Dr. Sylvester C.   20 Spring St., Gloversville·
Clews, Hon. Henry   15 Broad St., New York.
Clinch, Hon. Edward S.   133 W. 121st St., New York.
Close, Stuart, M. D.   248 Hancock St., Brooklyn.
Clute, Jesse H.   Room 601, 39 W. 34th St., New
    York.
Codding, G. H., M. D.   Amenia.
Coddington, Rev. Herbert G.,   1006 Harrison St·, Syracuse.
    D. D.
Coffin, Charles A.   30 Church St., New York.
Cogswell, William Brown   Syracuse.
Cole, Rev. Arthur S.   193 Clinton Ave., Kingston.
Cole, Charles K., M. D., A. M.   Chelsea-on-Hudson.
Cole, Harry E.   Rensselaer.
Cole, Peter B.   801 O. C. S. Bank Bldg·, Syra-
    cuse.
Coleman, Frank B.   2 Pleasant St., Fitchburg, Mass.
Coles, Mrs. Theodore   2 Broad St., Oneida.
Coley, Rev. Edward H., S. T. D.   31 Howard Ave., Utica.
Colgate University Library   Hamilton.
Collins, Hon. C. V.   Troy.
Colonial Dames of America   18 E. 8th St., New York.
Colton, Rt. Rev· Chas. H.   1025 Delaware Ave., Buffalo.
Columbia University Library   116th St·, New York.
Colvin, Andrew   280 Broadway, New York.
Comstock, Hon. Anthony   140 Nassau St., New York.
Conway, John B.   Argyle.
Cook, Mrs. Joseph   Ticonderoga.

Cook, Newton, M. D. — Sandy Creek.
Cook, Thos. J. — Ticonderoga.
Cooley, Dr. James S. — Mineola, Nassau Co.
Cooley, Dr. Leroy C. — 2 Reservoir Square, Poughkeepsie.

Coolidge, Thomas S. — Glens Falls.
Corbin, Harold H· — Saratoga Spa.
Corbin, Miss Sarah E. — Rome.
Corbusier, Lt. Col. Wm. H. — 612 Park Ave·, Plainfield, N. J.
Cornell, Douglas — Municipal Building, Buffalo.
Corse, F. Dudley — Sandy Creek.
Cortelyou, Hon. George B. — 4 Irving Place, New York.
Cortland State Normal and Training School — Cortland.
Cox, Rev. Henry M. — 58 W. 9th St., New York.
Cox, Mrs. Wilmot Townsend — Harrington Park, N. J.
Craig, Charles S., M. D. — Hamlin.
Crandall, Dr· Floyd M. — 113 W. 95th St., New York.
Crandall, William Henry — 8 So. Main St., Alfred.
Crandall Library — Glens Falls·
Crane, Frederick — 33 W. 67th St., New York.
Crane, Ralph Adams — 15 Beacon St., Boston, Mass.
Crimmins, Hon. John D. — 40 E. 68th St., New York.
Crisp, W· Benton — 161 W· 79th St., New York.
Crosby, Hon. Harley N. — Falconer.
Crosby, Col. John Schuyler — 206 W. 52nd St., New York.
Cross, Dr. Andrew Jay — 20 E. 23rd St., New York.
Crossett, Mayor Frederick M. — 55 Liberty St., New York.
Crothers, Miss Rachel — 550 Park Ave., New York.
Cruikshank, Frederick R. — 1 Liberty St., New York.
Cullen, Francis E. — 122 W. 8th St., Oswego.
Cullinan, Hon. Patrick W· — Oswego.
Culver, Chas. Mortimer, M. D. — 36 Eagle St., Albany.
Culver, Miss Mary Louise — 11 Clark Place, Utica.
Cummings, Dr. W. A. E. — Ticonderoga.
Cunningham, Col. J. L. — Glens Falls.
Curtis, Hon. George M. — 5 Beekman St., New York.
Curtis Memorial Library — Meriden, Conn.
Curtis, Miss May Belle — 4 Park Ave., Glens Falls.

Curtiss, Benjamin DeForest — 983 Park Ave., New York.
Cutler, Hon. James G. — Cutler Building, Rochester.

Danforth, Loomis L., M. D. — 49 W. 52nd St., New York.
Davidson, Silvanus Miller — 7 Stratford Ave., Fishkill-on-Hudson.
Davies, Julien Tappen — 32 Nassau St., New York.
Davies, Richard T. — 314 W. 77th St., New York.
Davis, Gen. Charles L., U. S. A. — 23 Front St., Schenectady.
Davis, Maj. William Church, U. S. A. — Fort Rosecrans, San Diego, Cal.
Day, Benjamin — 78 Fifth Ave., New York.
DeBoer, L. P., LL. B., M. A. — 223 W. 129th St., New York.
Decker, Hon. Martin S. — Public Service Commission, Albany.

DeGarmo, William Burton, M. D. — 616 Madison Ave., New York.
DeKoven, Mrs. Anna F. — 1025 Park Ave., New York.
de la Montanye, James — 220 Broadway, New York.
DeLano, Hon. Clayton H. — Ticonderoga.
de Laporte, Mrs. Theo. — Rhinebeck.
DeMott, John Jacques — Metuchen, N. J.
Denham, Edward — New Bedford, Mass.
Denman, Frederick H. — 170 Broadway, New York.
Denniston, Rear Admiral Henry Martyn — Washingtonville.
Denslow, Rev. Herbert M., D. D. — 2 Chelsea Sq., New York.
Denton, Mrs. Elizabeth B. — Hudson Falls.
Derby, Archibald S. — Hudson Falls.
Derby, Lt. Col. Geo. McClellan — 1015 Carrollton Ave., New Orleans, La.

Derby, Hon. John H. — Hudson Falls.
Diefendorf, Warren T. — 164 Montague St., Brooklyn.
Diehl, Hon. Clarence A. — 95 William St., New York.
Dillenback, Maj. John W., U. S. A. — 40 Washington St., Watertown.
Ditmas, Charles Andrew — 60 Amersfort Place, Brooklyn.
Dodds, Rev. R. C., DD. — 195 Tremper Ave., Kingston.
Doherty, Henry L. — 60 Wall St., New York.
Dolan, James C. — Gouveneur.

Don, John	676 N. Broadway, Saratoga.
Dorrance, Charles Pierson	35 Nassau St., New York.
Dorrlamm, George	679 Harmon St., Brooklyn.
Dougherty, Hon. J· Hampden	27 William St., New York.
Douglas, Edward W.	207 Pawling Ave., Troy.
Douglass, James, LL. D.	99 John St·, New York.
Dowling, Hon. Victor J., LL. D.	County Court House, New York.
Downey, Robert A.	Oswego.
Dows, Henry A.	25 Fort Washington Ave., New York.
Draper, Rev. Gideon Frank	Aoyama Gakuin No. 4. Aoyama Tokyo, Japan.
DuBois, Charles A.	3551 Broadway, New York.
Duffey, Edwin	Cortland.
Dunham, George E.	Utica.
Dunn, Gano	117 W. 58th St., New York.
Dunn, Henry E.	346 Broadway, New York.
Dunn, Hon. T. B.	296 East Ave., Rochester.
Dunnell, Rev. Wm· Nichols, D. D.	Rector Place, Red Bank, N. J.
Dunning, William B., D. D. S.	129 E. 76th St., New York.
Durkee, Charles D.	2 South St., New York.
Duryee, Charles C., M. D.	1352 Union St., Schenectady.
Dutton, E. P.	24 W. 51st St., New York.
Dwyer, Maj. John	Hudson Falls.
Eager, Miss Margaret MacLaren	Old Deerfield, Mass.
Earp, Wilbur F.	80 Wall St., New York·
Eastman, Henry M. W.	Roslyn, Nassau Co.
Easton, Robert T. B.	120 Broadway, New York.
Eaton, James W.	Babylon, Suffolk Co.
Edson, Walter H.	Falconer.
Ehrhorn, Oscar W.	15 William St., New York.
Eilers, Frederic Anton	751 St. Marks Ave., Brooklyn.
Ellis, George W.	149 Broadway, New York.
Ellis Willis C.	Shortsville.
Elsberg, Hon. Nathaniel A.	27 William St., New York.
Elting, Philip	278 Wall St., Kingston·

Emerick, F. A. — Oswego.

Emerson, George D. — 171 Whitney Place, Buffalo.

Empire State Society, S. A. R. — 220 Broadway, New York.

Englehardt, Francis Ernest, Ph. D. — 405 City Hall, Syracuse.

Enos, Alonson Trask. — 160 W. 16th St., New York.

Enyart, H. Shugart — 1147 Fulton Ave., New York.

Erganian, John K., D. D. S. — 175 Fifth Ave., New York.

Estes, Webster C. — 74 Warren St., New York.

Everest, Mrs. Lillian Pike — Plattsburg.

Everett, Major James Hervey — 105 Maiden Lane, Kingston.

Fahnestock, Rev. Alfred H. D. D. — 1411 Park St., Syracuse.

Fairbank, Alexander W., M. D. — Chazy.

Fairley, William — 195 Kingston Ave., Brooklyn.

Farnham, Mrs. George A. — 150 Warburton Ave., Yonkers.

Farrington, William H., M. D. — Astor House, New York.

Faust, Albert Bernhardt, Ph. D. — Cornell University, Ithaca.

Fay, Miss Amy — 68 W. 91st St., New York.

Fenton, George — 38 Watson Place, Utica.

Ferris, Morris P. — Garden City.

Ferris, Mortimer Yale — Ticonderoga.

Fielding, Dr. Fred G. — Glens Falls.

Fiero, Hon. James Newton — 100 State St., Albany.

Finegan, Thomas E., LL. D. — State Education Dept., Albany.

Finley, Hon. John H., LL. D. — State Education Dept., Albany.

Fitch, Hon. Charles Elliott — Skaneateles.

Flagler, John Haldane — 200 Broadway, New York.

Fletcher, Miss Louise — Norwood.

Flower, The Roswell P. Memorial Library — Watertown.

Foote, Miss Anna Elizabeth — The Franklin, Jamaica.

Foote, George C. — Port Henry.

Fordham, Herbert L. — 111 Broadway, New York.

Fortnightly, The Club — Oswego.

Foster, C. H. — 31 Belle Ave., Troy.

Foulds, Dr. Thos. H. — Glens Falls.

Fowler, Everett — Kingston.
Fowler, Hon. Joseph M. — 293 Wall St., Kingston.
Francis, Rev. Lewis, D. D. — 10 E. 73rd St., New York.
Francis, Lewis W. — 2 Rector St·, New York.
Fraser, Miss Margaret M. — Glens Falls.
Fredonia State Normal School — Fredonia.
Friederang, Maximilian Franz — 1236 Atlantic Ave., Brooklyn.
Frisbie, Hon. Miles R. — 514 State St., Schenectady.
Furness, Charles V. — Glens Falls.

Gallagher, James — Cleveland.
Gallup, F. A., A. M. — 117 So. Pine Ave., Albany.
Getten, Frederick J. — Glens Falls.
Gilbert, Charles N. — 787 Madison Ave., Albany.
Gilman, Hon· Theodore P., A. M. — 440 West End Ave., New York.
Gilpin, C. Monteith, A. B., LL. B. — 11 Wall St., New York.
Goodrich, Mrs. Alfred L. — 2 Broad St., Oneida.
Goodrich, Miss Susan — 508 State St., Utica.
Goodridge, Edwin Alonzo, M. D. — 632 N. Broadway, Saratoga Spa·
Gordon, Wellington E., Ph. D. — Patchogue.
Gordon, Rev. W. C. — Auburndale, Mass.
Goshen Library & Hist. Society — Goshen.
Granger, Miss A. P. — Canandaigua.
Granger, William A., D· D. — 70 No. Fulton Ave., Mt. Vernon.
Graul, John C. — 116 Union Ave., Saratoga Spa.
Gray, Niel, Jr. — Oswego.
Greenman, Mrs. J. C. — 262 Genesee St., Utica.
Griffis, William Elliot, A. M. D. D., L. H. D. — Ithaca.
Griswold, E. T. — Bennington, Vt.

Hadley, Howard D. — Plattsburgh.
Haight, Ilon. Albert — City Hall, Buffalo.
Haldane, Miss Mary H. — Cold Spring.
Hale, Charles A. — 3604 Broadway, New York.
Hall, Fred J. — Tarrytown.
Halsey, Francis W. — Century Club, 7 W. 43d St., New York.
Ham, Charles — 176 Lefferts Ave., Brooklyn.

Hanson, Willis T., Jr.   20 Union Ave., Schenectady.
Hart, Mrs. H. Gilbert   366 Genesee St., Utica.
Hart, W. O.   134 Carondelet St., New Orleans,
                                   La.
✓ Hasbrouck, Hon. Gilbert D· B.   Kingston.
HasBrouck, J. DePuy   238 Fair St., Kingston.
Hatfield, Miss Addie E.   28 Elm St., Oneonta.
Hausmann, Philip Wm.   39 Central Ave., Albany.
↵ Hawkins, George K., D. Sc.   Plattsburgh.
Hayden, Henry W.   16 Exchange Place, New York.
Hayes, Harold A.   1298 Main St., Buffalo.
Hays, Eugene D.   Premium Point, New Rochelle.
Healey, Hon. R. E.   Plattsburgh.
Healy, A. Augustus   90 Gold St., New York.
Heermance, Van Ness   97 Taylor St., Brooklyn.
Hempsted High School   Hempstead.
—Herkimer Co. Hist. Society   Herkimer.
Herrick, Mrs. Frank   Rhineback.
Hewitt, Fred W.   Granville.
Higgins, John D.   Oswego.
Higginson, Rear Admiral Fran-
    cis J., U. S. N.   Kingston.
Higley, Brodie G.   Hudson Falls.
Hill, Edward B.   49 Wall St., New York.
Hill, Hon. Henry Wayland   471 Linwood Ave., Buffalo.
Hill, Richmond C.   237 Green St., Schenectady.
Hogue ,Arthur S.   Plattsburg.
Holden, C. E.   Whitehall.
⨍ Holden, Hon. James A.   Glens Falls.
Hoopes, Maurice   Glens Falls.
Hopson, Rev. George B., D. D.   Annandale, Dutchess Co.
Horner, Harlan Hoyt   872 Lancaster St., Albany.
Horton, Dr. Claude A.   Glens Falls.
Horton, Dr. Ernest T.   Whitehall.
Horton, Mrs. John Miller   477 Delaware Ave., Buffalo.
Howard, Hon. Harry A.   Glens Falls.
Howland, Miss Emily   Sherwood.
Hull, Philip M.   Kenwood, Oneida Co.
Hunt, Miss M. Berna   Cobleskill

Hunt, William J., M. D.,	Glens Falls.
Huntington Historical Society	Huntington, L. I.
Hurd, Arthur W., M. D.	State Hospital, Buffalo.
Hyde, Louis Fiske	Glens Falls.
Hyland, John	Penn Yan.
Ingalls, George A.	Hudson Falls·
Ingalsbe, Hon. Grenville M.	Hudson Falls·
Ingalsbe, Mrs. Franc G.	Hudson Falls·
Ingraham, Charles A., M· D.	Cambridge.
Irish, Edward F.	216 Glen St., Glens Falls.
Jackson, Rev. T. G., D. D.	68 St. Paul Place, Brooklyn.
Jeffers, Henry Leavens	Glens Falls.
Jeffers, Willard G.	North Rose, Wayne Co.
Jewett, Hon. Edgar B.	148 Morris Ave., Buffalo.
Joerissen, Mrs. Joseph	7 Henry St., Utica.
Johnston, Allen W.	500 State St., Schenectady.
Johnston, Robert B.	108 Circular St., Saratoga Spa.
Johnstown Historical Society	Johnstown.
Judson, William Pierson	Broadalbin, Fulton Co.
Judson, Mrs. William Pierson	Broadalbin, Fulton Co.
Kellogg, Rev. Charles D., D. D.	Hudson Falls.
Kellogg, Hon. J. Augustus	Glens Falls.
Kelly, J· M.	Saratoga Spa·
Kemble, Gouverneur	Cold Spring.
Kennedy, Hugh	Buffalo.
Kennedy, John	Batavia.
Kennedy, Hon. John S.	380 Western Ave., Albany.
Kernan, Miss Elizabeth B.	62 Elizabeth St., Utica.
Kernan, Hon. John D.	62 Chancellor Square, Utica.
Kilbourn, Mrs. Judson G.	247 Genesee St., Utica.
King, Charles F.	Glens Falls.
King, Mrs. Joseph E.	Fort Edward.
Kings Co. Historical Society, Inc.	350 Fulton St., Brooklyn.
Kingsford, Thomas P.	Oswego.
Kingsley, Dr. H. F.	Schoharie.
Knapp, Hon. Clyde W.	Lyons.
Knapp, George O.	Shelving Rock.

Kneil, Thomas R., A. M.　　　Saratoga Spa.
Kretzmann, Rev. Karl　　　　585 E. 178th St., New York.

LaFontaine, Hon. Louis C.　　Champlain.
Lamb, Mrs. George E.　　　　Port Henry.
L'Amoreaux, Hon. J. S.　　　Ballston Spa.
Lange, Gustave, Jr.　　　　　257 Broadway, New York.
Lansing, Catherine Gansevoort　115 Washington Ave., Albany.
Lansing, Hugh H·　　　　　　Watervliet.
Lansing, J. Townsend　　　　Albany.
Lapham, Byron　　　　　　　Glens Falls.
Law, Robert R.　　　　　　　Cambridge.
Lawrence, Rev. Egbert Charles,
　Ph. D.　　　　　　　　　　36 University Place, Schenectady.
Leeper, Rev. J. L., D. D.　　Kingston. .
Le Fevre, Dr. Sherwood　·　Glens Falls.
Lent, Andrew Wright　　　　Newburgh.
Leonard, Edgar Cotrell　　　Albany.
Leonard, Gardner Cotrell　　Albany.
Lewis, Theodore G.　　　　605 Richmond Ave., Buffalo.
Liddle, Henry S., M. D.　　212 Union St·, Schenectady.
Lincoln, Hon. Charles Z.　　523 Ellicott Square, Buffalo.
Lincoln, A. M., Rev. Julius　116 Chandler St., Jamestown.
Lindsley, Mrs. Smith M.　　35 The Olbiston, Utica.
Little, Russell A.　　　　　Glens Falls.
Locke, F. T.　　　　　　　Ticonderoga.
Luckhurst, Mrs. Charlotte T.　446 Hulett St., Schenectady.
Ludlow, Henry S.　　　　　Saratoga Spa.
Lyttle, Dr. E. W.　　　　　Education Dept., Albany.

Mace, Prof. William H.　　　127 College Place, Syracuse.
Macfarlane, Carrington, M. D.　Oswego·
Maher, John L.　　　　　　15 Kemble St., Utica.
Mann, Col. William D.　　　Hague.
Manning, William H.　　　　Saratoga Spa.
Marsh, Homer P., M. D.　　708 James St., Syracuse.
Marshall, Charles A.　　　　Saratoga Spa.
Martin, Rev. Daniel Hoffman,
　D. D.　　　　　　　　　　650 W. 170th St., New York.
Mason, Miss Elizabeth　　　41 Greenbush St., Cortland.
McAneny, Hon. George　　　19 E. 47th St., New York.

McCabe, John J. — Glens Falls.
McCarrol, Hon. William — 758 St. Marks St., Brooklyn.
McClumpha, Charles F. — Amsterdam.
MacCracken, Rev. Henry M., D. D., LL. D. — University Heights, New York.
MacDonald, Benjamin J. — 44 Third St., Newburg.
McDonald, William A. — Gloversville.
McLellan, Hugh — 3 W. 29th St., New York.
McVickar, Mrs. Robert — 269 No. Fulton Ave., Mt. Vernon.
Mead, Leroy R. — Ticonderoga.
Menges, Fred — 472 Broadway, Saratoga Springs.
Menges, Mrs. Frederick — 136 Circular St., Saratoga Spa.
Meredith, Mrs. Louise Hardenburg — San Luis Obispo, Cal.
Merrell, A. J. — 106 Edgerton St., Rochester.
Merritt, Edward L. — 297 Washington Ave., Kingston.
Messer, L. Franklin — 403 Main St., Buffalo.
Michael, Edward — 241 Delaware Ave., Buffalo.
Michael, Myron J. — Kingston.
Michigan State Library — Lansing, Mich.
Milholland, Hon. John E. — 305 Mariner & Merchant Building, 3rd and Chestnut Sts., Philadelphia, Pa.

Miller, Miss Helen L. — 18 Oxford Road, New Hartford.
Miller, John P. — 94 W. 3rd St., Oswego.
Mills, Miss Phebe — Glens Falls.
Milton, J. E. — Brewerton.
Minisink Valley Historical Society — Port Jervis.
Mohawk Valley Chapter, D. A. R. — Ilion.
Moore, Edwin G. — Plattsburg.
Moore, William A., A. M. — 54 Laurel Place, New Rochelle.
Morehouse, Frank D. — Glens Falls.
Morton, Hon. Levi Parsons, LL. D. — 998 Fifth Ave., New York.
Mother M. Loretta — Ursuline Academy, Middletown.
Mott, Elliott B. — Oswego.
Mott, Hon. Luther W. — Oswego.
Mott, Hon. John T. — Oswego.

Moulthrop, Samuel P.   40 Phelps Ave., Rochester.
Mowris, John D.   440 Manhattan Ave., New York.
Moyer, Fayette E.   Johnstown.

Nelson, Ven. Dr. Geo. F.   416 LaFayette St., New York.
Newark High School   Newark.
Newburgh Bay and the Highlands. Historical Society of   Newburgh.
New Paltz State Normal School   New Paltz.
New York Public Library   New York.
Nichols, Edgar B.   76 Mohawk St., Cohoes.
Noble, Henry Harmon   Essex.
Noeth, George E.   2200 East Ave., Rochester.
North Tonawanda High School   No. Tonawanda.
Nottingham, William   701 Walnut Ave., Syracuse.

Olmstead, Rt. Rev. Chas. Tyler   159 Park Ave., Utica.
O'Neil, Mrs. Mary V.   122 St. James St., Kingston.
Oneonta Normal School   Oneonta.
Ontario Co. Hist. Society   Canandaigua.
Oppenheim, Samuel   811 Dawson St., Bronx, New York.
Osborne, Thomas Mott, A. B., L. H. D.   Auburn.
Oswego Dept. of Education   Oswego.
Owen, Mrs. William H.   70 Chancellor Square, Utica.

Page, Mrs. David B.   157 W. 3d St., Oswego.
Paine, Silas H.   Silver Bay.
Paltsits, Hon. Victor H.   1855 Morris Ave., New York.
Paradis, Adrian   Rockaway Park, L. I.
Parry, Mrs. John E.   Glens Falls.
Parsons, John S.   Oswego.
Patchogue Library   Patchogue.
Patterson, Mortimer Bliss   Nyack.
Peabody, George Foster, LL. D.   Saratoga Spa.
Peck, Gen. Theo. S.   Burlington, Vt.
Peckham, Stephen Farnum   150 Halsey St., Brooklyn.
Pell, Hon. Howland   7 Pine St., New York.
Pell, Stephen H. P.   43 Exchange Place, New York.

Pennsylvania, Historical Society of   1300 Locust St., Philadelphia Pa.
Pettis, Ilon. Clifford R.   916 Myrtle Ave., Albany.
Phoenix, Miss Lydia E., A. M.   142 W. Seneca St., Oswego.
Pierce, Miss Grace M.   The Columbia, 14th & Girard Sts., Washington, D. C.

Plattsburg Public Library   Plattsburg.
Porter, Ilon. Peter A.   North Tonawanda.
Potter, Rev. Clayton J.   107 Union St., Schenectady.
Powelson, Miss Louise   232 E. Main St., Middletown.
Powers, C. F.   Schuylerville.
Pratt Institute Free Library   Ryerson St., Brooklyn.
Preston, David C.   11 William St., Middletown.
Proctor, Thomas Redfield   Utica.
Pryer, Charles   New Rochelle.
Public Library High School   Saratoga Spa.
—Putnam Co. Historical Society   Cold Spring.
Pyrke, Berne A.   Port Henry.

Queen of the Rosary Academy Library   Amityville, L. I.

Ransom, Frank H.   137 Main St., Buffalo.
Reeves, George W.   Court House, Watertown.
Reist, Henry G.   110 Avon Road, Schenectady.
Reynolds, V. Rev. Fidelis   St. Bonaventure.
Reynolds, Cuyler   197 Western Ave., Albany.
Reynolds, Hon. Elba   Belmont.
Richards, Frederick B.   Glens Falls.
Richfield Springs Public Library   Richfield Springs.
Riggs, James G., Pd. D.   Oswego.
Riley, Hon. John B.   Plattsburgh.
Roberts, Mrs. Frances W.   14 Clinton Place, Utica.
✗ Roberts, Hon. James A., LL. D.   257 Broadway, New York.
Roberts, Mrs. Martha D.   257 Broadway, New York.
Roberts, Joseph Banks   141 Broadway, New York.
Roberts, Mrs. Joseph Banks   141 Broadway, New York.
Robertson, D. L.   Glens Falls.
Robison, Hanford   6 Front St., Schenectady.

Robison, Mrs. William — Massapequa, L. I.
Rochester Historical Society — Rochester.
Rockwood, Hon. Nash — Saratoga.
Roosevelt, Hon. Franklin D. — Hyde Park, Dutchess Co.
Rosa, Nelson W. — 320 Clinton St., Schenectady.
Rosch, Hon. Joseph — Liberty.
Rowe, Louis Cass — 40 E. Utica St., Oswego.
Rowe, Franklin A. — Glens Falls.
Royce, Mrs. Caroline H. — 476 Fifth Ave., New York.
Rudd, Hon. William P. — Tweedle Building, Albany.
Ryan, John J., LL. B. — Medina·

Samson, William H· — 454 Riverside Drive, New York.
Sanders, Charles P. — Scotia, Schenectady.
Saranac Chapter, D. A. R. — Plattsburgh.
Satterlee, Esther E. — 517 W. Gray St., Elmira.
Sawyer, Rev. Everett R., D. D. — Hudson Falls.
Sawyer, John E. — Hudson Falls.
Sawyer, Willoughby L. — Hudson Falls.
Sayre, Miss Amelia V. R. — 142 Park Ave., Utica.
Schenectady Co. Hist. Society — Schenectady.
Schenck, Miss Alice A. — 303 Worth St., Fulton.
Schmid, Dr. H. Ernest — White Plains.
Schuyler, Ackley C. — 333 West 36th St., New York.
Schuyler, Miss Fanny — New Rochelle.
Scully, Mrs. Wiliam T. — Schuylerville.
Searing, John W. — 37 Wall St., New York.
Sears, Mrs. Frank L. — 208 Worth St., Fulton.
Seay, James Miller — 13 Jefferson St., Glens Falls.
Seelye, Elwin — Lake George.
Selth, Walter R. — 106 Eleventh Ave., Mt. Vernon.
Severance, Hon· Frank H. — Buffalo.
Shaver, Mrs. C. C. — 30 The Olbiston, Utica.
Shepherd, F. B. — 98 W. 5th St., Oswego.
Sidway, Frank St. John — 37 Oakland Place, Buffalo.
Sidway, Mrs. Frank St. John — 37 Oakland Place, Buffalo.
Silas Towne Chapter D. A. R. — Mexico.
Sills, Rev. Chas. Morton, D. D. — Trinity Rectory, Geneva.
Sill, Rev. Frederick S., D. D. — Cohoes.

Sim, John R. — Amsterdam Ave., cor, 138th St., New York.
Simpson, John Boulton — Sagamore-on-Lake, George.
Sims, Clifford S. — c|o D. & H. Co., Albany.
Singleton, J. Edward — Glens Falls.
Sister M. Ignatia — Holy Angel's Academy, Buffalo.
Sister M. Margaret — Ladycliff Academy, Highland Falls.
Sister Mary Patricia — St. Patrick's Ac. School, Rouses Point.
Skinner, Avery W. — Mexico, Oswego Co.
Slade, John A. — 10 Citizens' Bk. Bldg., Saratoga Spa.
Slade, Mrs. Emma H. — 332 W. 87th St., New York.
Smith, Mrs. Abram D. — Fultonville.
Smith, James F. — S. Hartford.
Snitzler, Mrs. John H. — care of Snitzler Adv. Co., 256 Madison St., Chicago.
Sohmer, Hon. William — 1 Third Ave., New York.
Spalding, Chas. A. — Saugerties.
Spalding, Rev. George B., Jr. — Stonington, Conn.
Spencer, Charles Worthen, Ph. D. — 114 Fitz Randolph Road, Princeton, N. J.
Spencer, Miss Jane L. — 239 East First St., Oswego.
Spraker, Mrs. B. F. — Palatine Bridge.
Squires, Eben H. P. — White Plains.
Stackpole, George F. — Riverhead.
Stanton, Hon. Lucius M. — 596 Broadway, New York.
State Normal and Training School — Plattsburg.
Steers, Mrs. Katherine V. — 606 Liberty St., Schenectady.
Stephens, W. Hudson — Lowville, Lewis Co.
Stevens, Miss Harriet E. — 142 West Seneca St., Oswego.
Stevenson, Miss Helen G., Ph. B. — 118 Main St., Ossining.
✗ Stillman, William Olin, M. D. — 287 State St., Albany.
Stoddard, S. R. — Glens Falls.
Stover, Dr. Charles — Amsterdam.
Stowe, Rev. Wilbur Fiske — 167 Clinton Ave., Kingston.
Strong, Hon. Alonzo P. — 311 State St., Schenectady.

Stuart, Henry Clarence	450 Riverside Drive, New York.
Stump, Mrs. Herman	Bel-Air, Harford Co., Md.
Sullivan, Hermon E.	Whitehall.
Swartwout F. Robert	105 So. Division St., Peekskill.
Syracuse Public Library	Syracuse.
Tack, Theo. E.	52 Broadway, New York.
Tallmadge, Henry Overing	80 Wall St., New York.
Tate, Lewis A.	Gloversville.
Tawasentha Chapter, D. A. R.	Slingerland.
Tefft, Miss Frances A.	Hudson Falls.
Tefft, Richard C.	Hudson Falls.
Tewey, Miss Margaret M.	60 Main St., Irvington-on-Hudson.
Thompson, Alfred C.	Brockport·
Thompson, Charles Bothwell	Glens Falls.
Thornton, Mrs. C. H.	70 Ridge St., Glens Falls.
Tibbits, Miss Mary Edla	34 Brookside Place, New Rochelle.
Tillotson, B. H.	Olathe, Kansas.
Tinstman, B. E·	248 Glen St., Glens Falls.
Tipling, Chas. A., LL. B.	1 Bridge Plaza, Long Island City.
Todd, Hiram C.	Saratoga Spa.
Troy Public Library	Troy.
Turner, Mrs. W. H.	65 St. James St., Kingston.
Tuttle, George F.	Plattsburg.
Tuttle, Mrs. George F.	Plattsburg.
Tuxedo High School	Tuxedo Park.
Underwood, Henry C.	Penn Yan.
University of Michigan, General Library	Ann Arbor, Mich.
Utica Public Library	Utica
Van Alstyne, William B.	15A. W. 106 St., New York.
Van Buren, Miss Catharine G.	Spring Lake, N. J.
Van Buskirk, Miss Frances L.	65 River St., Saranac Lake.
Van Camp, Frederick W.	Fine View.
Van Campen, C. H.	328 Security Bank Bldg., Minneapolis, Minn.
Van Cortlandt, Miss Anne S.	Manor House, Croton-on-Hudson·
Van Cortlandt, James S.	Croton-on-Hudson.

VanderVeer, A., M. D. — 28 Eagle St., Albany.
VanEvery, Martin — 15 Horton Place, Buffalo.
Van Hee, Daniel L. — 236 Dartmouth St., Rochester.
Van Laer, Arnold J. F. — 433 Western Ave., Albany
Vann, Hon. Irving G. — Syracuse.
Van Rensselaer, Mrs. Schuyler — 9 W. 10th St., New York.
Van Santvoord, Seymour — Troy.
Van Vliet, George Stockwell — Staatsburgh.
Van Wormer, Rodney — Argyle.
Vermilyea, Miss Helen F. — 298 Saratoga St., Cohoes.
Viele, Miss Kathlyne K. — 357 Park Ave., Yonkers.
Vosburgh, Royden W. — 13 Lenox Place, New Brighton.
Vrooman, Col. John W. — Herkimer.
Vrooman, Mrs. John W. — Herkimer.

Waddell, Miss Helen — Hoosick Falls·
Wait, Mrs. J. W. — Hudson Falls.
Wait, John C. — 38 Park Row, New York.
Wait, William — 237 Smith St., Peekskill.
Wallander, A. H. — 168 Park Ave., Mount Vernon.
Wallin, Wm. J· — 16 Livingston Ave., Yonkers.
Walters, Mrs. Katharine P. — 68 Warren St., Glens Falls.
Walton, Charles — Kingston.
Ward, Hon. Geo. W. — Little Falls
Warner, Clarence Macdonald — Napanee, Ont., Canada.
Warner, J. B. Y. — Scottsville.
Warner, Walter A. — Whitehall.
Warren, Mrs. Edward Stevens — 20 Lincoln Parkway, Buffalo.
Warren, Oscar Leroy — White Plains.
Warren, E. Burgess — The Sagamore, Lake George.
Warren, Edward S. — 614 White Bldg., Buffalo.
Warren, Wm. Y. — 271 Porter Ave·, Buffalo.
Warwick Historical Society — Warwick.
Waterbury, W. H. — Saratoga Springs.
Waterloo Union School — Waterloo.
Watkins, DeLancey W. — 23 Washington Ave., Schenectady.
Watrous, Harry W. — 145 W. 58th St., New York.
Watrous, Mrs. Harry W. — Hague-on-Lake George.
Watson, Miss Lucy Carlile — 270 Genesee St., Utica.
Webster, W· B., M. D. — Schuylerville.

Weed, Hon. Geo. S.	Plattsburg.
Weed, Hon. Smith M.	Plattsburg.
Wells, Frederick H.	41 DeKalb Ave., White Plains.
Wemple, Hon. William W.	Schenectady.
West, Arthur F.	Lake George.
West, Charles F.	300 Glen St., Glens Falls.
West, Elmer J.	Glens Falls.
Weston, Albert T·, M. D.	204 West 86th St·, New York.
Westover, Myron U.	Schenectady.
Wetmore, Edmund, LL. D.	34 Pine St., New York.
Wheat, Benjamin P.	Saratoga Spa.
Wheeler, Hon. Charles B., LL. D.	Supreme Court Chambers, Buffalo.
Wheelock, Edward, M. D.	26 Gibbs St., Rochester.
White, Wm. Pierrepont	Utica.
Wickes, Frank B.	Ticonderoga.
Wilder, Frank J.	46 Cornhill, Boston, Mass.
Willard, James LeBaron	194 Clinton St., Brooklyn.
Willey, Rev. John H.	311 So. Graham, St., Pittsburg, Pa.
Williams College	Williamstown, Mass.
Williams, Hon. Clark	293 Madison Ave., New York.
Williams, David	69 W. 68th St., New York·
Williams, Mrs. Helen B.	"Athenaeum," Saratoga Spa.
⋏ Williams, Sherman, Pd. D.	Glens Falls.
Willis, Clarence	1 Liberty St., Bath.
Wilson, Mrs. Georgianna Richards	Glens Falls.
Wilson, Mrs· J. S.	118 East 30th St., New York.
Wing, Ashael R.	Fort Edward.
Winston, James O.	Kingston.
Witherbee, Hon. Walter C.	Port Henry.
Wood, Frank H.	Albany.
Wood, Mrs. Joseph S.	135 Second Ave., Mt. Vernon.
Woodward, Hon. John	Appellate Division, Buffalo.
Wooley, J. S.	Ballston Spa.
Worden, Edwin J.	Lake George.
Wright, Harold A.	R. R. 4, Fulton.
Wright, Miss Abbie A.	Hudson Falls.
Wright, Mrs. Jennie Esmond	Saratoga Spa, R. F. D. No· 1.

Wright, Tobias A.   150 Bleecker St., New York.
Wyckoff, Alice Brooks   Elmira.

Yonkers Historical and Library
   Association   Yonkers.
Young, Alonzo M.   Johnstown.

GEOGRAPHICAL DISTRIBUTION

Albany.

Abrams, Alfred W.
Ainsworth, Hon. Danforth E.
Barcus, James Q.
Blackburn, John T. D.
Brandow, Rev. John H·
Cameron, Edward M.
Cameron, Frederick W.
Carmody, Thomas
Chester, Hon. Alden
Clarke, John M., LL. D., Ph D.
Culver, Charles Mortimer, M. D
Decker, Hon. Martin S.
Fiero, Hon. James Newton
Finegan, Thomas E·
Finley, John H., LL. D.
Gallup, F. A., A. M.
Gilbert, Charles N.

Hausmann, Philip Wm.
Horner, Harlan Hoyt
Kennedy, Hon. John S.
Lansing, Catherine Gansevoort
Lansing, J. Townsend
Leonard, Edgar Cotrell
Leonard, Gardner Cotrell
Lyttle, Dr. E. W.
Pettis, Hon. Clifford R.
Reynolds, Cuyler
Rudd, Hon. William P.
Sims, Clifford S.
Stillman, William Olin, M. D.
Vander Veer, A., M. D.
Van Laer, Arnold J. F.
Wheeler, Edward J., Ph. D.
Wood, Frank H.

Alfred.

Crandall, William Henry

Amenia.

Codding, G. H., M. D.

Amsterdam.

Chalmers, Arthur A.
Chalmers, Mrs. Arthur A.

McClumpha, Charles F.
Stover, Dr. Charles

Anandale.

Hopson, Rev. George B., D. D.

Argyle.

Conway, John B.

Van Wormer, Rodney

Auburn.

Adams, Rev. John Quincy

Osborne, Thomas Mott, A. B.

Babylon.

Eaton, James W.

Ballston Spa.

L'Amoreaux, Hon. J. S.

Wooley, J. S.

Batavia.

Kennedy, John

Bath.

Willis, Clarence

Belmont.

Reynolds, Hon. Elba

Bolton Landing.

Bixby, W. K.

Brewerton.

Milton, J. E.

Broadalbin.

Judson, William Pierson

Judson, Mrs. William Pierson

Brockport.

Thompson, Alfred C.

Brooklyn.

Adams, Henry Sherman
Baldwin, Stephen C.
Carman, Nelson G.

Catlin, Maj. Gen. Isaac S.
Close, Stuart, M. D.
Diefendorf, Warren T.

Ditmas, Charles Andrew
Dorlamm, George
Eilers, Frederic Anton
Fairley, William
Friederang, Maximilian F.
Ham, Charles
Heermance, Van Ness

Jackson, Rev· T. G., D. D.
McCarroll, Hon. William
Peckham, Stephen Farnum
Potts, Charles Edwin
Tracy, Ira Otis, M. D.
Willard, James LeBaron

Buffalo.

Alexander, Hon. D. S. LL. D.
Bartlett, Eugene M.
Boxall, George H.
Colton, Rt. Rev. Chas. H.
Cornell, Douglas
Emerson, George D.
Haight, Hon. Albert
Hayes, Harold A·
Hill, Hon. Henry Wayland
Horton, Mrs. John Miller
Hurd, Arthur W. ,M. D.
Sister M. Ignatia.
Jewett, Hon. Edgar B.
Kennedy, Hugh

Lewis, Theodore G.
Lincoln, Hon. Charles Z.
Messer, L. Franklin
Michael, Edward
Ransom, Frank H.
Severance, Hon. Frank H.
Sidway, Frank St. John
Sidway, Mrs. Frank St. John
Van Every, Martin
Warren, Mrs. Edward S.
Warren, Edward Stevens
Warren, William Y.
Wheeler, Hon. Charles B.
Woodward, Hon. John

Cambridge.

Ingraham, Charles A., M. D·   Law, Robert R.

Canandaigua.

Granger, Miss A. P.

Canton.

Cleaveland, Frank N.

Catskill.

Bloodgood, Clarence E.   Chase, Hon. Emory A.

Champlain.

LaFountaine, Hon. Louis C.

Chazy.

Fairbank, Alexander W., M. D.

Chelsea-on-Hudson.

Cole, Charles K. M. D.

Cincinnatus.

Clapp, Morris B.

Cleveland.

Gallagher, James.

Cobleskill.

Hunt, Miss M. Berna

Cohoes.

Nichols, Edgar B.　　　　　Vermilyea, Miss Helen F.
Sill, Rev. Frederick S., D. D.

Cold Spring.

Haldane, Miss Mary H.　　　Kemble, Gouverneur

Cortland.

Duffey, Edwin　　　　　　　Mason, Miss Elizabeth

Croton-on-Hudson.

Van Cortlandt, Miss Anna S.　　Van Cortlandt, James S.

East Aurora.

Baker, Rev. E. Folsom.

East Creek.

Beardslee, Roosevelt　　　　Beardslee, Mrs. Roosevelt

Elizabethtown.

Hand, Hon. Richard L., LL. D.

Elmira.

Satterlee, Esther E.   Wyckoff, Alice Brooks

Essex.

Burnham, John B.   Noble, Henry Harmon

Falconer.

Crosby, Hon. Harley N.   Edson, Walter H.

Fine View.

Van Camp, Frederick W.

Fishkill-on-Hudson.

Davidson, Silvanus Miller

Forestport.

Auringer, Rev. O. C.

Fort Ann.

Baker, Frederick I.

Fort Edward.

Banker, Dr. Silas J.   King, Mrs. Joseph E.
Bascom, Wyman S.   Wing, Ashael R.

Fulton.

Schenck, Miss Alice A.   Wright, Harold A.
Sears, Mrs. Frank L.

Fultonville.

Smith, Mrs. Abram D.

Garden City.

Ferris, Morris P.

Garrison-on-Hudson.

Chorley, Rev. E. Clowes

Geneva.

Bean, Charles D., LL. D.
Clark, Walter A.

Sills, Rev. Charles Morton D. D.

Glens Falls.

Adamson, W. H.
Barber, Junius E.
Bullard, Charles E.
Bullard, Frederick H.
Carter, Robert C.
Coolidge, Thomas S.
Cunningham, Col. J. L.
Curtis, Miss May Belle
Fielding, Dr. Fred G.
Foulds, Dr· Thos. H.
Fraser, Miss Margaret M.
Furness, Charles V.
Getten, Frederick J.
Holden, Hon. James A.
Hoopes, Maurice
Horton, Dr. Claude A.
Howard, Hon. Harry A.
Hunt, William J., M. D.
Hyde, Louis Fiske
Irish, Edward F.
Jeffers, Henry L.
Kellogg, Hon. J. Augustus
King, Charles F.

Lapham, Byron
Le Fevre, Dr. Sherwood
Little, Russell A.
McCabe, John J.
Mills, Miss Phebe
Morehouse, Frank D.
Parry, Mrs. John E.
Richards, Frederick B.
Robertson, D. L.
Rowe, Franklin A.
Seay, James Miller
Singleton, J· Edward
Stoddard, S. R.
Thompson, Charles Bothwell
Thornton, Mrs. C. H.
Tinstman, B. E.
Walters, Mrs. Katherine P.
West, Charles F.
West, Elmer J.
Williams, Sherman, Pd: D.
Wilson, Mrs. Georgianna Richards.

Gloversville.

Clemans, Dr· Sylvester C.
McDonald, William A.

Tate, Lewis A.

Gouveneur.

Dolan, James C.

Granville.

Hewitt, Fred W.

Hague.

Mann, Col. William D.

Watrous, Mrs. Harry W.

Hamilton.

Allen, Freeman H., Ph. D.

Hamlin.

Craig, Charles S., M. D.

Herkimer.

Vrooman, Mrs. John W .

Vrooman, Col. John W.

Highland Falls.

Sister M. Margaret

Hoosick Falls.

Beckett, James A.

Waddell, Miss Helen

Hornell.

Acker, Milo. M.

Hudson Falls.

Broughton, Harry L.
Denton, Mrs. Elizabeth
Derby, Archibald S.
Derby, Hon. John H.
Dwyer, Major John
Higley, Brodie G.
Howland, Fred D.
Ingalls, George A.
Ingalsbe, Hon. Grenville M.

Ingalsbe, Mrs. Franc G.
Kellogg, Rev. Charles D., D. D.
Sawyer, Rev. Everett R., D. D.
Sawyer, John E.
Sawyer, Willoughby L.
Tefft, Miss Frances A.
Tefft, Richard C.
Wait, Mrs. J. W.
Wright, Miss Abbie A.

Hyde Park.

Roosevelt, Hon. Franklin D.

Ilion.

Callan, Mrs. Frank D.

Mohawk Valley Chapter, D. A. R.

Irvington-on-Hudson.

Tewey, Miss Margaret M.

Ithaca.

Bristol, George P.
Church, Irving P.

Faust, Albert Bernhardt, Ph. D.
Griffis, William Elliot, D. D.

Jamaica.

Foote, Miss Anna Elizabeth

Jamestown.

Broadhead, Miss Stella F.

Lincoln, A. M., Rev. Julius

Johnstown.

Carroll, Fred Linus
Moyer, Fayette E.

Young, Alonzo M.

Kenwood, Oneida Co.

Hull, Philip M.

Kingston.

Atkins, Du Bois G.
Betts, Hon. James A.
Chase, Rev. Platt N., Ph. D.
Clearwater, Hon. Alphonso T.
Cole, Rev. Arthur S.
Dodds, Rev. R. C., D. D.
Elting, Philip
Everett, Maj. James Hervey
Fowler, Everett
Fowler, Hon. Joseph M.
Hasbrouck, Hon. Gilbert D. B.

Hasbrouck, J. DePuy, LL. D.
Higginson, Rear Admiral Francis J.
Leeper, Rev. J. L., D. D.
Merritt, Edward L.
Michael, Myron J.
O'Neil, Mrs. Mary V.
Stowe, Rev. W. F.
Turner, Mrs. W. II.
Walton, Charles
Winston, James O.

Lake George.

Seelye, Elwin
Warreu, E. Burgess

West, Arthur F.
Worden, Edwin J.

Lake Katrine.

Brink, Theo.

Liberty.

Rosch, Hon. Joseph

Little Falls.

Hon. Geo. W. Ward

Long Island City.

Tipling, Chas. A.

Lowville.

Stephens, W. Hudson

Lyons.

Betts, Charles H.   Knapp, Hon. Clyde W.

Marbletown.

Bevier, Miss Margaret S.

Massapequa, L. I.

Robison, Mrs. William

Medina.

Ryan, John J., LL. D.

Mexico.

Skinner, Avery W.

Middleburgh.

Beekman, Hon. Dow

Middletown.

Mother M. Loretta   Preston, David C.
Powelson, Miss Louise

Mineola.

Cooley, Dr. James S.

Mount Kisco.

Carpenter, Hon. Francis M.

Mt. Vernon.

Granger, William A., D. D.
McVickar, Mrs. Robert
Selth, Walter R.

Wallander, A. H.
Wood, Mrs. Joseph S.

Newburgh.

Anthony, Walter C.
Lent, Andrew Wright

MacDonald, Benjamin J.

New Brighton.

Vosburgh, Royden W.

New Hartford.

Miller, Miss Helen L.

New Rochelle.

Carville, Miss Katherine J. C.
Hays, Eugene D.
Moore, William A., A. M.

Pryer, Charles
Schuyler, Miss Fanny
Tibbits, Miss Mary Edla

New York City.

Abbatt, William
Adler, Isaac, A. M., M. D.
Arthur, Miss L. Louise
Atkins, Miss Kate
Atkins, Hon. T. Astley
Bailey, Theodorus, M. D.
Barber, Arthur William, LL. M.
Barney, Edgar S., Sc. D.
Barnhart, John Hendley, A. M.,
    M. D.
Batcheller, George Clinton
Beach, Edward Stevens
Beard, Curtis J.
Beer, George Lewis
Bell, Clark, LL. D.
Bennet, Hon. William S.
Brown, Ernest C.

Burroughs, John H.
Callan, Peter A., M. D.
Carpenter, Charles W.
Carrington, Augustus B.
Carvalho, S. S.
Champion, Charles S.
Channing, J. Parke
Chase, George
Cheney, Hon. O. H.
Chesebrough, Robert A.
Clews, Hon. Henry
Clinch, Hon. Edward S.
Clute, Jesse H.
Coffin, Charles A.
Colvin, Andrew
Comstock, Hon. Anthony
Cortelyou, Hon. George B.

Cox, Mrs. Wilmot Townsend
Crandall, Dr. Floyd M.
Crane, Frederick
Crimmins, Hon. John D.
Crisp, W. Benton
Crosby, Col. John Schuyler
Cross, Dr. Andrew Jay
Crossett, Mayor Frederick M.
Crothers, Miss Rachel
Cruikshank, Frederick R.
Curtis, Hon. George M.
Curtiss, Benjamin DeForest
Danforth, Loomis, L., M. D.
Davies, Julien Tappen
Davies, Richard T.
Day, Benjamin
DeBoer, L. P.
DeGarmo, William Burton, M. D.
DeKoven, Mrs. Anna F.
Delafield, Lewis L.
de la Montanye, James
Denman, Frederick H.
Denslow, Herbert M., D. D.
Diehl, Hon. Clarence A.
Doherty, Henry L.
Dorrance, Charles Pierson
Dougherty, Hon. J. Hampden
Douglass, James, LL. D.
Dowling, Hon. Victor J., LL. D.
Dows, Henry A.
DuBois, Charles A.
Dunn, Gano
Dunn, Henry E.
Dunning, William B., D. D. S.
Durkee, Charles D.
Dutton, E. P.
Earp, Wilbur F.
Easton, Robert T. B.
Ehrhorn, Oscar W.

Ellis, George W.
Elsberg, Hon. Nathaniel A.
Enos, Alonson Trask
Enyart, H. Shugart
Erganian, John K., D. D. S.
Estes, Webster C.
Farrington, William H.
Fay, Miss Amy
Fish, Stuyvesant
Flagler, John Haldane
Fordham, Herbert L.
Francis, Lewis W.
Francis, Rev. Lewis, D. D.
Fulton, Louis M.
Gilman, Hon. Theodore P.
Gilpin, C. Monteith, A. B., LL. B.
Hale, Charles A.
Halsey, Francis W.
Hartley, Mrs. Frances G.
Hayden, Henry W.
Healy, A. Augustus
Hill, Edward B.
Jones, Mrs. Oliver Livingston
Kretzmann, Rev. Karl
Lange, Gustave, Jr.
Martin, Rev. Daniel H., D. D.
McAneny, Hon. George
MacCracken, Rev. Henry M., D. D., LL. D.
McLellan, Hugh
Morton, Hon. Levi Parsons, LL. D.
Mowris, John D.
Nelson, Ven. Dr. George F.
Oppenheim, Samuel
Paltsits, Hon. Victor H.
Pell, Hon. Howland
Pell, Stephen H. P.
Roberts, Hon. James A., LL. D.
Roberts, Mrs. Martha D.

Roberts, Joseph Banks
Roberts, Mrs. Joseph Banks
Roosevelt, Col. Theodore, LL. D.
Royce, Mrs. Caroline H.
Samson, William H.
Schuyler, Ackley C.
Searing, John W.
Sim, John R.
Slade, Mrs. Emma H.
Sohmer, Hon. William
Stanton, Hon. Lucius M.
Straus, Hon. Oscar S., LL. D.
Stuart, Henry Clarence
Stillman, Charles Chauncey

Tack, Theo. E.
Tallmadge, Henry Overing
Van Alstyne, William B.
Van Rensselaer, Mrs. Schuyler
Wait, John C.
Watrous, Harry W.
Webb, Dr. W. Seward
Weston, Albert T., M. D.
Wetmore, Edmund, LL. D.
Williams, Hon. Clark
Williams, David
Wilson, Mrs. J. S.
Wright, Tobias A.

Niagara Falls.

Barton, Philip P.
Chormann, Frederick

Porter, Hon. Peter A.

North Rose.

Jeffers, Willard G.

Norwood.

Fletcher, Miss Louise

Nyack.

Patterson, Mortimer Bliss

Oneida.

Brown, Edwin J.
Coles, Mrs. Theodore

Goodrich, Mrs. Alfred

Oneonta.

Hatfield, Miss Addie E.

Ossining-on-the-Hudson.

Stevenson, Miss Helen G., Ph. B.

Oswego.

Barnes, Ezra A.
Bates, Norman L.

Beadle, Miss Cynthia H.
Burt, George Noyes

Clark, James T.
Clark, Miss Mary Hodges
Clarke, Frederick O.
Cullen, Francis E.
Cullinan, Hon. Patrick W.
Downey, Robert A.
Emerick, F. A.
Gray, Niel, Jr.
Higgins, John D.
Kingsford, Thomas P.
Macfarlane, Carrington, M. D.
Miller, John P.

Mott, Elliott B.
Mott, Hon. Luther W.
Mott, Hon. John T.
Page, Mrs. David B.
Parsons, John S.
Phoenix, Miss Lydia E., A. M.
Riggs, James G.
Rowe, Lewis Cass
Shepherd, F. B.
Spencer, Miss Jane L.
Stevens, Miss Harriet E.

Palatine Bridge.

Spraker, Mrs. B. F.

Patchogue.

Gordon, Wellington E., Ph. D.

Peekskill.

Hawes, Harry Hammond
Swartwout, F. Robert

Field, Cortlandt de Peyster
Wait, William

Pelham.

Caldwell, Samuel Cushman, D. C. L.

Penn Yan.

Hyland, John

Underwood, Henry C.

Plattsburg.

Barker, Mrs. Daniel Folger
Botsford, Elmer F.
Everest, Mrs. Lillian P.
Hadley, Howard D.
Hawkins, George K., D. Sc.
Healey, Hon. R. E.
Hogue, Arthur S.

Moore, Edwin G.
Riley, Hon. John B.
Tuttle, George F.
Tuttle, Mrs. George F.
Weed, Hon. George S.
Weed, Hon. Smith M.

Port Henry.

Foote, George C.
Lamb, Mrs. George E.
Pyrke, Berne A.

Witherbee, Hon. Frank S.
Witherbee, Hon. Walter C.

Poughkeepsie.

Cooley, Dr. Leroy C.

Pulaski.

Brown, Rev. Samuel E.

Rensselaer.

Cole, Harry E.

Rhinebeck.

de Laporte, Mrs. Theo.

Herrick, Mrs. Frank

Riverhead.

Belford, Hon. James

Stackpole. George F.

Rochester.

Adler, Elmer
Cutler, Hon. James G.
Dunn, Hon. T. B.
Merrell, A. J.
Moulthrop, Samuel P.

Noeth, George E.
Rider, Wheelock, M. D.
Van Hee, Daniel L.
Wheelock, Edward, M. D.

Rockaway Park, L. I.

Paradis, Adrian

Rome.

Broughton, Charles H.
Broughton, Mrs. Charles H.

Corbin, Miss Sarah E.

Roslyn.

Eastman, Henry M. W.

Rouses Point.

Sister Mary Patricia.

Sacketts Harbor.

Camp, Col. Walter B.

Sagamore-on-Lake George.

Simpson, John Boulton

Sandy Creek.

Cook, Newton, M. D.   Corse, F. Dudley

Saranac Lake.

Van Buskirk, Miss Francis L.

Saratoga Springs.

Andrews, Capt. James M.
Bosworth, Mrs. C. H.
Brackett, Hon. Edgar T.
Brockway, Miss Mary L.
Corbin, Harold H.
Don, John
Goodridge, Edwin Alonzo
Graul, John C.
Johnston, Robert B.
Kelly, J. M.
Kneil, Thomas R.
Ludlow, Henry S.
Marshall, Charles A.

Manning, Wm. H.
Menges, Fred
Menges, Mrs. Frederick
Mingay, James
Mingay, Mrs. James
Peabody, George Foster
Rockwood, Hon. Nash
Slade, John A.
Todd, Hiram C.
Waterbury, W. H.
Wheat, Benjamin P.
Williams, Mrs. Helen
Wright, Mrs. Jennie Esmond

Saugerties.

Spalding, Charles A.

Scarsdale.

Cannon, James G.

Schenectady.

Barhydt, T. Low
Callanan, James H.
Davis, Gen. Charles L., U. S. A.
Duryee, Charles C., M. D.
Frisbie, Hon. Miles R.

Hanson, Willis T., Jr.
Hill, Richmond C.
Johnston, Allen W.
Lawrence, Rev. Egbert Charles,
    Ph. D.

Liddle, Henry S., M. D.
Luckhurst, Mrs. Charlotte T.
Potter, Rev. Clayton J.
Reist, Henry G.
Robison, Hanford
Rosa, Nelson W.

Sanders, Charles P.
Steers, Mrs. Katherine V.
Strong, Hon. Alonzo P.
Watkins, DeLancey W.
Westover, Myron N.
Wemple, Hon. William W.

Schoharie.

Kingsley, Dr. H. F.

Schuylerville.

Allen, Charles C.
Powers, C. F.

Scully, Mrs. Wm. T.
Webster, W. B., M. D.

Scottsville.

Warner, J. B. Y.

Shelving Rock.

Knapp, George O.

Sherwood.

Howland, Miss Emily

Shortsville.

Ellis, Willis C.

Silver Bay.

Paine, Silas H.

Skaneateles.

Fitch, Hon. Charles Elliott

South Hartford.

Smith, James F.

Staatsburg.

Van Vliet, George Stockwell

St. Bonaventure.

Reynolds, V. Rev. Fidelis

Syracuse.

Beauchamp, Rev. Wm. Martin, S. T. D.

Banta, J. Edward

Bardeen, C. W.

Bassette, Alfred S.

Brooks, James Byron, D. C. L.

Coddington, Rev. Herbert G.

Cogswell, William Brown

Cole, Peter B.

Englehardt, Francis Ernest, Ph. D.

Fahnestock, Rev. Alfred H., D. D.

Mace, Prof. William H.

Marsh, Homer P., M. D.

Nottingham, William

Vann, Hon. Irving G.

Tarrytown.

Hall, Fred J.

Ticonderoga.

Cook, Mrs. Joseph

Cook, Thomas J.

Cummings, Dr. W. A. E.

DeLano, Hon. Clayton H.

Ferris, Mortimer Yale

Locke, F. T.

Mead, Leroy R.

Wickes, Frank B.

Troy.

Aldrich, Charles S.

Collins, Hon. C. V.

Douglas, Edward W.

Foster, C. H.

Van Santvoord, Seymour

Utica.

Bensberg, F. W.

Bigelow, Rev. Dana W., D. D.

Brayton, M. Jesse

Coley, Rev. Edward H., S. T. D.

Culver, Miss Mary L.

Dunham, George E.

Fenton, George

Goodrich, Miss Susan

Greenman, Mrs. J. C.

Hart, Mrs. H. Gilbert

Joerissen, Mrs. Joseph

Kernan, Miss Elizabeth B.

Kernan, Hon. John D.

Kilbourn, Mrs. Judson G.

Lindsley, Mrs. Smith M.

Maher, John L.

Olmstead, Rt. Rev. Chas. Tyler

Owen, Mrs. William H.

Pitcher, Mrs. Charlotte A.

Proctor, Thomas Redfield

Ralph, Mrs. G. F.

Roberts, Mrs. Frances W.

Sayre, Miss Amelia V. R.

Shaver ,Mrs. C. C.

Utica Public Library

Watson, Miss Lucy C.

White, Wm. Pierrepont

Washingtonville.

Denniston, Rear Admiral Henry Martyn

Waterford, R. F. D. Brookwood.

Ballard, W. J.

Waterloo.

Bacon, Carroll B., M. D.

Watertown.

Reeves, George W.   Dillenback, Maj. John W., U. S. A.

Watervliet.

Lansing, Hugh H.

Whitehall.

Bartholomew, Alanson Douglass   Sullivan, H. E.
Holden, C. E.   Warner, Walter A.
Horton, Dr. Ernest T.

White Plains.

Schmid, Dr. H. Ernest   Warren, Oscar LeRoy
Squires, Eben H. P.   Wells, Frederick H.

Yonkers.

Ackerly, Orville B.   Viele, Miss Kathlyne K.
Beemer, James G.   Wallin, William J.
Farnham, Mrs. George A.

San Diego, Cal.

Davis, Major Wm. Church, U. S. A.

San Luis Obispo, Cal.

Meredith, Mrs. Louise Hardenburg

New Haven, Conn.

Hadley, Arthur Twining, LL. D.   Wheeler, Arthur Martin, LL. D.

Stonington, Conn.

Spalding, Rev. George B., Jr.

Washington, D. C.

Wilson, Woodrow, LL. D., Ph. D.   Pierce, Miss Grace M.
Hoes, Chaplain, R. R., U. S. N.

Fernandina, Fla.

Black, Hon. Peter C.

Chicago, Ill.

Snitzler, Mrs. John H.

Olathe, Kansas.

Tillotson, B. H.

New Orleans, La.

Derby, Lt. Col. Geo. McClellan.   Hart, W. O.

Bel-Air, Md.

Stump, Mrs. Herman

Auburndale, Mass.

Gordon, Rev. W. C.

Boston, Mass.

Adams, Charles Francis, LL. D.   Crane, Ralph Adams
Boardman, Waldo E., M. D.   Wilder, Frank J.

Fitchburg, Mass.

Coleman, Frank B.

New Bedford, Mass.

Denham, Edward

Old Deerfield, Mass.

Eager, Miss Margaret MacLaren

Minneapolis, Minn.

Van Campen, C. H.

Harrington Park, N. J.

Cox, Rev. Henry M.

Metuchen, N. J.

DeMott, John Jacques

Montclair. N. J.

Hanna, Charles A.

Newark, N. J.

Abercrombie, David T.

Plainfield, N. J.

Corbusier, Lt. Col. Wm. H.

Princeton, N. J.

Spencer, Charles W., Ph. D.

Red Bank, N. J.

Dunnell, Rev. Wm. N., D. D.

Spring Lake, N. J.

Van Buren, Miss Catherine G.

Philadelphia, Pa.

Milholland, Hon. John E.   McMaster, John Bach, A. M.

Pittsburgh, Pa.

Willey, Rev. John H.

Wilkes Barre, Pa.

See, Mrs. Horace

Bennington, Vt.

Griswold, E. T.

Burlington, Vt.

Peck, Gen. Theo. S.

Rutland, Vt.

Bailey, Horace W.

Napanee, Ontario, Canada.

Warner, Clarence Macdonald

England.

Belcher, Rev. Henry, LL. D., Lewes Sussex.

Japan.

Draper, Rev. Gideon F., Aoyama, Tokyo.

Schools, Colleges, Libraries, Historical and Patriotic Societies.

Brockport State Normal Library, Brockport.
Brooklyn Public Library, 26 Brevoort Place, Brooklyn.
Cayuga Co. Hist. Society, Auburn.
Colgate University Library, Hamilton.
Colonial Dames of America, 18 E. 8th St., New York.
Columbia University Library, 116th St., New York.
Cortland State Normal and Training School, Cortland.
Crandall Library, Glens Falls.
Curtis Memorial Library, Meriden, Conn.
Empire State Society, S. A. R., 220 Broadway, New York.
Flower, The Roswell P. Memorial Library, Watertown.
The Fortnightly Club, Oswego.
Fredonia State Normal School, Fredonia.
Goshen Library & Historical Society, Goshen.
Hempstead High School, Hempstead.
Herkimer Co. Hist. Society, Herkimer.
Historical Society of Newburgh Bay and the Highlands, Newburgh
Holy Angels' Academy, Buffalo.
Huntington Historical Society, Huntington, L. I.
Johnstown Historical Society, Johnstown.
Kings County Historical Society, Inc., 350 Fulton St., Brooklyn.
Ladycliff Academy, Highland Falls.
Michigan State Library, Lansing, Mich.
Minisink Valley Historical Society, Port Jervis.
Mohawk Valley Chapter, D. A. R., Ilion.

New Paltz State Normal School, New Paltz.

Newark High School, Newark.

New York Public Library, New York.

North Tonawanda High School, North Tonawanda.

Oneonta Normal School, Oneonta.

, Ontario County Historical Society, Canandaigua.

Oswego Dept. of Education, Oswego.

Patchogue Library, Patchogue.

Pennsylvania Historical Society of, Philadelphia, Pa.

Plattsburgh Public Library, Plattsburgh.

Plattsburgh State Normal and Training School, Plattsburgh.

Pratt Institute Free Library; Ryerson St., Brooklyn.

Putnam County Historical Society, Cold Spring.

Queen of the Rosary Academy Library, Amityville.

Richfield Springs Public Library, Richfield Springs.

Rochester Historical Society, Rochester.

Saranac Chapter, D. A. R., Plattsburgh.

Saratoga High School Library, Saratoga Spa.

Schenectady Co. Historical Society, Schenectady.

Silas Towne Chapter, D. A. R., Mexico.

St. Patrick's Academy, Rouses Point.

Syracuse Public Library, Syracuse.

Tawasentha Chapter D. A. R., Slingerlands.

Troy Public Library, Troy.

Tuxedo High School, Tuxedo Park.

University of Michigan General Library, Ann Arbor, Mich.

Ursuline Academy, Middletown.

Utica Public Library, Utica.

Warwick, The Historical Society of, Warwick.

Waterloo Union School, Waterloo.

Williams College, Williamstown, Mass.

Yonkers Historical and Library Association, Yonkers.

Lightning Source UK Ltd.
Milton Keynes UK
UKHW021241080119
335202UK00013B/738/P